The Practical Skeptic

The Practical Skeptic
Readings in Sociology

Lisa J. McIntyre
Washington State University

Mayfield Publishing Company
Mountain View, California
London • Toronto

Library of Congress Cataloging-in-Publication Data

McIntyre, Lisa J.
    The practical skeptic : readings in sociology / Lisa J. McIntyre.
       p.   cm.
    ISBN 0-7674-0685-0
    1. Sociology.   2. Social problems.   3. United States — Social
conditions.   I. McIntyre, Lisa J.
    HM51.P68   1998
    301 — dc21   98–22180
                                         CIP

Manufactured in the United States of America
10   9   8   7   6   5   4   3

Mayfield Publishing Company
1280 Villa Street
Mountain View, CA 94041

Sponsoring editor, Serina Beauparlant; *production editor,* Julianna Scott Fein; *manuscript editor,* Thomas L. Briggs; *design manager,* Susan Breitbard; *text designer,* Joan Greenfield; *cover designer,* Laurie Anderson; *art manager,* Robin Mouat; *illustrator,* Ann Eldredge; *manufacturing manager,* Randy Hurst. The text was set in 10/12 Book Antiqua by ColorType and printed on acid-free 50# Finch Opaque by Malloy Lithographing, Inc.

Acknowledgments and copyrights continue at the back of the book on pages 311–313, which constitute an extension of the copyright page.

Preface

There are dozens of anthologies available for introductory-level sociology classes, but I think that this one is different. It's different because as I compiled and edited these articles, I kept the needs of introductory students in mind. That's important. When sociologists write for their professional colleagues, they take for granted (as they should) that their readers are equipped with a great deal of knowledge. Student readers, by contrast, generally lack this sort of preparation; consequently, many students find that reading the works of sociologists is not so much a challenge as an onerous chore. I suspect that beginning students assigned to read sociology feel much like the theatergoer who stumbles into a foreign film that lacks subtitles. No matter how dramatic or comedic the action, unless one can follow the dialog, the movie is boring.

In this volume, I have tried to bridge the gap between the sociologists who wrote these articles and the students who will read them. Each article begins with a brief introduction to help orient students to the author's aims and point of view, includes footnotes containing explanations of concepts that are likely to be unfamiliar to novice sociologists, and concludes with some questions that will help students sort through and make sense of what they have read. My goal is to replace boredom with intellectual challenge, to make sociology not "easy," but accessible.

Both classic and contemporary articles were selected because they help to illustrate the importance of understanding the social contexts through which people move and to highlight some of the core concepts that sociologists and other social observers use to make sense of the social world. The classic articles especially were selected to illustrate the foundational concepts that most contemporary writers take for granted. But while these fundamentals might seem old hat to professional sociologists, they still contain important revelations for beginners.

Accompanying Test Bank

For the benefit of instructors, I have written a test bank to accompany the reader. The test bank includes multiple-choice, true-false, and short answer/essay questions as well as suggested short paper assignments.

The Practical Skeptic: Core Concepts in Sociology

Created to serve as a companion to the reader, *The Practical Skeptic: Readings in Sociology,* this text focuses on core concepts as the central building blocks for understanding sociology. Written in a lively, conversational style, this text includes numerous pedagogical features to help students grasp key sociological concepts.

Acknowledgments

The following colleagues reviewed the manuscript and choice of articles and made many helpful suggestions: Sheila Cordray, Oregon State University; Rebecca Erickson, University of Akron; Allen Scarboro, Augusta State University; and Martha L. Shockey, St. Ambrose University.

Contents

In the 1980s, several social researchers concluded that college fraternities are dangerous places for women visitors. In this more even-handed account of the impact of fraternity culture on individual behavior, the authors explain that not all fraternities are alike.

Marc Lépine killed fourteen women he didn't even know — not because of anything they had done, but merely because of who they were. In this chilling account of the massacre, Morgan concludes that most people never really wanted to understand how this could have happened.

What is the relationship between economic conditions and impersonal violence against people who belong to particular groups? What role does the scapegoat play in society?

Part Seven   *INEQUALITY*

Sociologists' obsession with social inequality surprises many laypeople (and most students). Why is that? Historian Loewen claims it's because most students leave high school as "terrible sociologists."

In this classic discussion of stratification, Tumin shows the illogic of traditional theories of social inequality in society.

How is poverty useful to society? Professor Gans provides a seriously tongue-in-cheek answer.

In their account of the problems faced by workers in the inner cities, Newman and Lennon provide an important warning for anyone who thinks that there are easy answers to unemployment.

Everybody liked him, so what possessed this mild-mannered college professor to transform himself into a scary person? Why would he want to strike terror into the hearts of others? Why was this transformation so easy?

Members of some groups are subjected to discrimination because they are deemed to be "inferior"; members of other groups are subjected to discrimination because they are deemed to be superior. Leung's account of the status of Asian Americans helps us to unravel the paradox.

" 'Why are women's brains smaller than men's?' asked a surgeon of a group of male students in the doctors' lounge . . . 'Because they're missing logic!' " It wasn't the sort of lesson Dr. Berman had expected to learn in medical school, but it was one they tried to teach her over and over again.

·1·

The Promise

C. Wright Mills

"The Promise," published in 1959 by C. Wright Mills, is probably the most famous essay ever written by a modern sociologist. In this article, Mills captures the essential lesson of sociology: To truly understand people's behavior, we must look beyond those individuals to the larger social contexts in which they live. Individuals make choices, to be sure, but their choices are constrained by social, historical, cultural, political, and economic factors. Most importantly, people frequently do not even realize the extent to which their lives are affected by things that are external to them and outside of their control. Mills's point is that if we are to understand people's behavior, we must take into account these nonindividual factors. (This is not an especially easy article to read, but it is fundamental. You might find it helpful to read the section on Mills in *The Practical Skeptic: Core Concepts in Sociology*, chapter 3, before you tackle this reading.)

Nowadays men often feel that their private lives are a series of traps. They sense that within their everyday worlds, they cannot overcome their troubles, and in this feeling, they are often quite correct: What ordinary men are directly aware of and what they try to do are bounded by the private orbits in which they live; their visions and their powers are limited to the close-up scenes of job, family, neighborhood; in other milieux[1] they move vicariously and remain spectators. And the more aware they become, however vaguely, of ambitions and of threats which transcend their immediate locales, the more trapped they seem to feel.

Underlying this sense of being trapped are seemingly impersonal changes in the very structure of continent-wide societies. The facts of contemporary history are also facts about the success and the failure of individual men and women. When a society is industrialized, a peasant becomes a worker; a feudal lord is liquidated or becomes a businessman. When classes rise or fall, a man is employed or unemployed; when the rate of investment goes up or down, a man takes new heart or goes broke. When wars happen, an insurance salesman becomes a rocket launcher; a store clerk, a radar man; a wife lives alone; a child grows up without a father. Neither the life of an individual nor the history of a society can be understood without understanding both.

Yet men do not usually define the troubles they endure in terms of historical change and institutional contradiction.[2] The well-being they

---

[1] *Milieux* is French; it means "social environments." (*Milieux* is plural; *milieu* is singular.) — Ed.

[2] Mills is using the term *institution* in its sociological sense— which is a bit different from the way this term is used in everyday or conventional speech. To the sociologist, institution refers to *a set of social arrangements, an accepted way of resolving important social problems.* Thus, the institution of the family is our society's way of resolving the important social problem of raising children. The institution of the economy is how we resolve the problem of distributing goods and services (for example, in the case of the United States, capitalism). The concept of institutional contradiction refers to situations in which the demands of one institution are not compatible with the

enjoy, they do not usually impute to the big ups and downs of the societies in which they live. Seldom aware of the intricate connection between the patterns of their own lives and the course of world history, ordinary men do not usually know what this connection means for the kinds of men they are becoming and for the kinds of history-making in which they might take part. They do not possess the quality of mind essential to grasp the interplay of man and society, of biography and history, of self and world. They cannot cope with their personal troubles in such ways as to control the structural transformations that usually lie behind them.

Surely it is no wonder. In what period have so many men been so totally exposed at so fast a pace to such earthquakes of change? That Americans have not known such catastrophic changes as have the men and women of other societies is due to historical facts that are now quickly becoming "merely history." The history that now affects every man is world history. Within this scene and this period, in the course of a single generation, one sixth of mankind is transformed from all that is feudal and backward into all that is modern, advanced, and fearful. Political colonies are freed; new and less visible forms of imperialism installed. Revolutions occur; men feel the intimate grip of new kinds of authority. Totalitarian societies rise, and are smashed to bits—or succeed fabulously. After two centuries of ascendancy, capitalism is shown up as only one way to make society into an industrial apparatus. After two centuries of hope, even formal

democracy is restricted to a quite small portion of mankind. Everywhere in the underdeveloped world, ancient ways of life are broken up and vague expectations become urgent demands. Everywhere in the overdeveloped world, the means of authority and of violence become total in scope and bureaucratic in form. Humanity itself now lies before us, the super-nation at either pole concentrating its most co-ordinated and massive efforts upon the preparation of World War Three.

The very shaping of history now outpaces the ability of men to orient themselves in accordance with cherished values. And which values? Even when they do not panic, men often sense that older ways of feeling and thinking have collapsed and that newer beginnings are ambiguous to the point of moral stasis. Is it any wonder that ordinary men feel they cannot cope with the larger worlds with which they are so suddenly confronted? That they cannot understand the meaning of their epoch for their own lives? That—in defense of selfhood—they become morally insensible, trying to remain altogether private men? Is it any wonder that they come to be possessed by a sense of the trap?

It is not only information that they need—in this Age of Fact, information often dominates their attention and overwhelms their capacities to assimilate it. It is not only the skills of reason that they need—although their struggles to acquire these often exhaust their limited moral energy.

What they need, and what they feel they need, is a quality of mind that will help them to use information and to develop reason in order to achieve lucid summations of what is going on in the world and of what may be happening within themselves. It is this quality, I am going to contend, that journalists and scholars, artists and publics, scientists and editors are coming to expect of what may be called the sociological imagination.

demands of another institution. For example, there is institutional contradiction when the institution of the family is based on the norm that dad goes to work and mom stays home with the kids but the institution of the economy is such that it takes two employed adults to support a family. You will find more examples of institutional contradictions in reading 3 by Stephanie Coontz. You can read more about the nature of institutions in *The Practical Skeptic*, chapter 8, "Culture" and chapter 9, "Social Structure." —Ed.

1

The sociological imagination enables its possessor to understand the larger historical scene in terms of its meaning for the inner life and the external career of a variety of individuals. It enables him to take into account how individuals, in the welter of their daily experience, often become falsely conscious of their social positions. Within that welter, the framework of modern society is sought, and within that framework the psychologies of a variety of men and women are formulated. By such means the personal uneasiness of individuals is focused upon explicit troubles and the indifference of publics is transformed into involvement with public issues.

The first fruit of this imagination — and the first lesson of the social science that embodies it — is the idea that the individual can understand his own experience and gauge his own fate only by locating himself within his period, that he can know his own chances in life only by becoming aware of those of all individuals in his circumstances. In many ways it is a terrible lesson; in many ways a magnificent one. We do not know the limits of man's capacities for supreme effort or willing degradation, for agony or glee, for pleasurable brutality or the sweetness of reason. But in our time we have come to know that the limits of "human nature" are frighteningly broad. We have come to know that every individual lives, from one generation to the next, in some society; that he lives out a biography, and that he lives it out within some historical sequence. By the fact of his living he contributes, however minutely, to the shaping of this society and to the course of its history, even as he is made by society and by its historical push and shove.

The sociological imagination enables us to grasp history and biography and the relations between the two within society. That is its task and its promise. . . . And it is the signal of what is best in contemporary studies of man and society.

No social study that does not come back to the problems of biography, of history and of their intersections within a society has completed its intellectual journey. Whatever the specific problems of the classic social analysts, however limited or however broad the features of social reality they have examined, those who have been imaginatively aware of the promise of their work have consistently asked three sorts of questions:

1. What is the structure of this particular society as a whole? What are its essential components, and how are they related to one another? How does it differ from other varieties of social order? Within it, what is the meaning of any particular feature for its continuance and for its change?

2. Where does this society stand in human history? What are the mechanics by which it is changing? What is its place within and its meaning for the development of humanity as a whole? How does any particular feature we are examining affect, and how is it affected by, the historical period in which it moves? And this period — what are its essential features? How does it differ from other periods? What are its characteristic ways of history-making?

3. What varieties of men and women now prevail in this society and in this period? And what varieties are coming to prevail? In what ways are they selected and formed, liberated and repressed, made sensitive and blunted? What kinds of "human nature" are revealed in the conduct and character we observe in this society in this period? And what is the meaning for "human nature" of each and every feature of the society we are examining?

Whether the point of interest is a great power state or a minor literary mood, a family, a prison, a creed — these are the kinds of questions the best social analysts have asked. They are the intellectual pivots of classic studies of man in society — and they are the questions inevitably raised by any mind possessing the sociological imagination. For that imagination is the capacity to shift from one perspective to another — from the political to the psychological; from examination of a single family to comparative assessment of the national budgets of the world; from the theological school to the military establishment; from considerations of an oil industry to studies of contemporary poetry. It is the capacity to range from the most impersonal and remote transformations to the most intimate features of the human self — and to see the relations between the two. Back of its use there is always the urge to know the social and historical meaning of the individual in the society and in the period in which he has his quality and his being.

That, in brief, is why it is by means of the sociological imagination that men now hope to grasp what is going on in the world, and to understand what is happening in themselves as minute points of the intersections of biography and history within society. In large part, contemporary man's self-conscious view of himself as at least an outsider, if not a permanent stranger, rests upon an absorbed realization of social relativity and of the transformative power of history. The sociological imagination is the most fruitful form of this self-consciousness. By its use men whose mentalities have swept only a series of limited orbits often come to feel as if suddenly awakened in a house with which they had only supposed themselves to be familiar. Correctly, or incorrectly, they often come to feel that they can now provide themselves with adequate summations, cohesive assessments, comprehensive orientations. Older decisions that once appeared sound now seem to them products of a mind unaccountably dense. Their capacity for astonishment is made lively again. They acquire a new way of thinking, they experience a transvaluation of values; in a word, by their reflection and by their sensibility, they realize the cultural meaning of the social sciences.

2

Perhaps the most fruitful distinction with which the sociological imagination works is between "the personal troubles of milieu" and "the public issues of social structure." This distinction is an essential tool of the sociological imagination and a feature of all classic work in social science.

Troubles occur within the character of the individual and within the range of his immediate relations with others; they have to do with his self and with those limited areas of social life of which he is directly and personally aware. Accordingly, the statement and the resolution of troubles properly lie within the individual as a biological entity and within the scope of his immediate milieu — the social setting that is directly open to his personal experience and to some extent his willful activity. A trouble is a private matter: values cherished by an individual are felt by him to be threatened.

Issues have to do with matters that transcend these local environments of the individual and the range of his inner life. They have to do with the organization of many such milieux into the institutions of an historical society as a whole, with the ways in which various milieux overlap and interpenetrate to form the larger structure of social and historical life. An issue is a public matter: some value cherished by publics is felt to be threatened. Often there is a debate about what that value really is and about what it is that really threatens it. This debate is often without focus if only because it is the very nature of an issue, unlike even widespread trouble, that it cannot very well be defined in terms of the immediate and everyday environments of ordinary men. An issue, in fact, often involves a crisis in institutional arrangements, and often too it involves what Marxists call "contradictions" or "antagonisms."

In these terms, consider unemployment. When, in a city of 100,000, only one man is unemployed, that is his personal trouble, and for its relief we properly look to the character of the man, his skills, and his immediate opportunities. But when in a nation of 50 million employees, 15 million men are unemployed, that is an issue, and we may not hope to find its solution within the range of opportunities open to any one individual. The very structure of opportunities has collapsed. Both the correct statement of the problem and the range of possible solutions require us to consider the economic and political institutions of the society, and not merely the personal situation and character of a scatter of individuals.

Consider war. The personal problem of war, when it occurs, may be how to survive it or how to die in it with honor; how to make money out of it; how to climb into the higher safety of the military apparatus; or how to contribute to the war's termination. In short, according to one's values, to find a set of milieux and within it to survive the war or make one's death in it meaningful. But the structural issues of war have to do with its causes; with what types of men it throws up into command; with its effects upon economic and political, family and religious institutions, with the unorganized irresponsibility of a world of nation-states.

Consider marriage. Inside a marriage a man and a woman may experience personal troubles, but when the divorce rate during the first four years of marriage is 250 out of every 1,000 attempts, this is an indication of a structural issue having to do with the institutions of marriage and the family and other institutions that bear upon them.

Or consider the metropolis—the horrible, beautiful, ugly, magnificent sprawl of the great city. For many upper-class people, the personal solution to "the problem of the city" is to have an apartment with private garage under it in the heart of the city, and forty miles out, a house by Henry Hill, garden by Garrett Eckbo, on a hundred acres of private land. In these two controlled environments—with a small staff at each end and a private helicopter connection—most people could solve many of the problems of personal milieux caused by the facts of the city. But all this, however splendid, does not solve the public issues that the structural fact of the city poses. What should be done with this wonderful monstrosity? Break it all up into scattered units, combining residence and work? Refurbish it as it stands? Or, after evacuation, dynamite it and build new cities according to new plans in new places? What should those plans be? And who is to decide and to accomplish whatever choice is made? These are structural issues; to confront them and to solve them requires us to consider political and economic issues that affect innumerable milieux.

In so far as an economy is so arranged that slumps occur, the problem of unemployment becomes incapable of personal solution. In so far as war is inherent in the nation-state system and in the uneven industrialization of the world, the ordinary individual in his restricted milieu will be powerless—with or without psychiatric aid—to solve the troubles this system or lack of system imposes upon him. In so far as the family as an institution turns women into darling little slaves and men into their chief providers and unweaned dependents, the problem of a satisfactory marriage remains incapable of purely private solution. In so far as the overdeveloped megalopolis and the overdeveloped automobile are built-in features of the overdeveloped society, the issues of urban living will not be solved by personal ingenuity and private wealth.

What we experience in various and specific milieux, I have noted, is often caused by structural changes. Accordingly, to understand the changes of many personal milieux we are required to look beyond them. And the number and variety of such structural changes increase as the institutions within which we live become more embracing and more intricately connected with one another. To be aware of the idea of social structure and to use it with sensibility is to be capable of tracing such linkages among a great variety of milieux. To be able to do that is to possess the sociological imagination. . . .

Questions

1. What is the sociological imagination? (You might begin with quoting Mills's definition, but try to describe this phenomenon in your own words as well.)

2. In brief, what kinds of questions are asked by those who possess a sociological imagination?

3. What are "personal troubles of milieu"? What are "public issues of social structure"? Why does Mills say that the distinction between troubles and issues is "an essential tool of the sociological imagination"?

·2·

Social Causes of Psychological Distress

John Mirowsky and Catherine Ross

Nothing sounds more personal and individual than the state of one's mind, and so it is that the psychological well-being of individuals hardly sounds like a topic that would be of interest to sociologists. And yet, as sociologists John Mirowsky and Catherine Ross remark in their book, *psychological "misery is an inherently meaningful yardstick in social research"* (emphasis added). Mirowsky and Ross find that a great deal of what appears to be psychological distress is explainable by social factors. In particular, an individual's income, education, employment, occupation, and marital status are all strong predictors of well-being.

Community Mental Health Surveys

Before the 1960's little was known about social patterns of emotional well-being and distress.[1] Mental health studies looked at people in psychiatric treatment or in institutions such as the Army or mental hospitals. Ideas about social stress were based on clinical interviews with small numbers of patients or on records of groups in unusual circumstances. The first representative community surveys uncovered several unexpected findings.

All the findings we discuss are based on community surveys of mental health. Large, representative samples of people in the community are interviewed either in person or by telephone. This avoids the biases of basing conclusions on people who have sought help; people with the time, money, or inclination to do so. Everyone has an equal chance of being interviewed: those who sought help and those who did not, the middle class and the poor, men and women, those for whom visiting a psychiatrist is shameful and those for whom it is acceptable, those with access to care and those without it. . . .

Four basic social patterns of distress were revealed in early community surveys done in the 1960's and in many surveys conducted since: (1) women are more distressed than men; (2) married persons are less distressed than unmarried persons; (3) the greater the number of *undesirable* changes in a person's life the greater his or her level of distress; (4) the higher a person's socioeconomic status (defined by education, job, and income) the lower that person's level of distress. These findings are now well established and thus may seem obvious, but they were not common knowledge thirty years ago.

Before community surveys, many theorists believed that responsibility, commitment to work, and upward mobility were stressful, whereas dependency, protection, and freedom from responsibility were not. Three decades ago

---

[1]In this article, the concepts of "psychological distress" and "well-being" are seen as opposite ends of a continuum. Earlier in their book, Mirowsky and Ross define distress as "an unpleasant subjective state." It may take one of two major forms—depression ("feeling sad, demoralized, lonely, hopeless, worthless, wishing one were dead, having trouble sleeping, crying, feeling everything is an effort, and being unable to get going") or anxiety ("being tense, restless, worried, irritable, and afraid"). Everyone may experience these symptoms periodically, but being in distress generally suggests that an individual is in a constant state of depression or anxiety, or (more typically) both. —Ed.

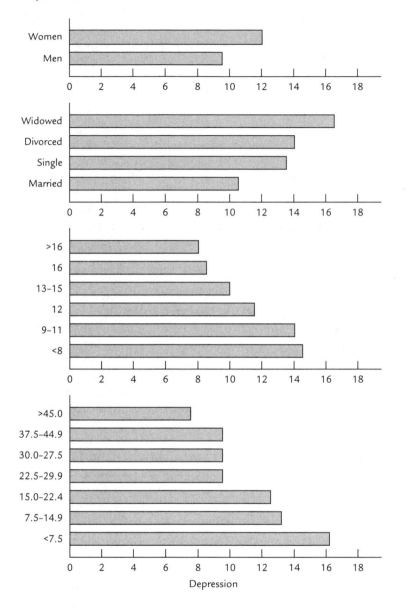

Mean depression levels in different categories of sex, marital status, education, and family income, based on 2000 adults in the United States.

women had little economic responsibility. Men had to go out and beat the world or be beaten by it, daily braving the rigors of commuter traffic and workplace tension. Women could stay home contentedly (so it was assumed) ministering to the needs of the family, kept safe by protecting males. Many were surprised to learn that women have higher levels of depression, anxiety, and malaise than men. Some people thought that married people, especially married men, faced burdensome responsibilities whereas singles led a free and happy life. In fact, married people have lower levels of distress than singles, especially married men. Similarly, many assumed that executives and others at the top of the status hierarchy were made tense and anxious by heavy responsibilities (a view reinforced by the heart disease literature on "type A personality"), while those at the bottom were relatively carefree and content. Harried executives, rushing to the next meeting, might envy laborers with few responsibilities; but in fact, power, responsibility, and control have been found to reduce distress.

These findings at first stood as fascinating new discoveries, then as core facts in the growing body of research. After it became clear that these are robust and replicable findings, the focus of research switched from *demonstrating* the facts to *explaining* them. Just as astronomers were once driven by the desire to explain the recorded motions of the sun, moon, and planets, research on psychological distress is currently based on the desire to explain the recorded association with gender, marriage, events, and status. . . .

First we need to clarify the nature of the facts. To begin with, they are probabilistic. When we say that women are more distressed than men we do not mean that all women are more distressed than all men. We mean that, on average, women are more distressed than men, and that a randomly chosen woman is more likely to be distressed than a randomly chosen man. Second, social facts are hard facts, but not eternal ones. The facts about distress can change as society changes. In particular, the difference in distress between men and women could disappear if certain trends continue. The reasons social differences in distress exist are also reasons the differences might disappear.

The Four Basic Patterns

GENDER

Gove and his colleagues were among the first sociologists to examine why women are more distressed than men. While biologists might think to scrutinize hormones or patterns of sex-typed behavior among primates, sociologists have a different perspective. For heuristic purposes they think of people as essentially interchangeable at birth. It is clear that by adulthood there are many important differences in the things people prefer, value, believe, and do. Many of these differences are shaped by individual situations and personal histories; perhaps the same is true of differences in emotions. Perhaps women are more distressed than men because of differences in the lives that men and women live. Fifteen years ago the majority of adult women were exclusively housewives and men were the breadwinners and job holders. Gove reasoned that if women are more distressed than men because of something different in their lives, then women who are employed will be less distressed than women who are exclusively housewives. This is exactly what he found in his sample of 2248 respondents (chosen by stratified random sampling) throughout the United States. A number of follow-up studies replicated the finding (Gove and Geerken 1977; Gove and Tudor 1973; Kessler and McRae, 1982; Richman 1979; Rosenfield 1980; Ross, Mirowsky, and Ulbrich 1983). It was an important discovery. Freud argued that women are born to be housewives and mothers and cannot be happy in the competitive world outside the home. Parsons (1949), an influential social theorist of the 1950's and 1960's, argued that society and the people in it function most smoothly when women specialize in the loving, nurturing family realm and men specialize in the competitive, acquisitive job-holding realm. The discovery that women with jobs are less distressed than women without them overturned a century of armchair theorizing.

Gove's research shook certain preconceptions about women, but did not explain everything. Although employed women are less distressed than housewives, employed women are *more* distressed than employed men. Having a job is not the whole story. What explains the difference in distress between employed men and women? A clue turned up in a study by Kessler and McRae (1982), using data from 2440 randomly sampled American adults interviewed in 1976. They found that employment is associated with less distress among women whose husbands help with housework and child care, but that there is little advantage to employment among women whose husbands do not help. Surprisingly, they also found that the housework and child care contributed by husbands of employed women does not increase the husband's distress. Researchers had been comparing different types of women; perhaps it was time to compare different types of couples.

American marriages are changing, from arrangements in which the husband has a job and the wife stays home caring for the children and doing housework to arrangements in which the husband and wife both have jobs and share the housework and child care (Oppenheimer 1982). Although many today may believe this a positive change, not many would have thought so in 1900. The change did not happen because of preferences and values, but because the logic of social arrangements in 1900 undermined itself as the economy grew and changed from one based on manufacturing to one based on services.

At the beginning of the century, women only took jobs in the period between graduating school and getting married. A married woman worked outside the home only if her husband could not support the family. Women could be paid much less than men with equivalent education and skills because the women's jobs were temporary or supplemental. Many jobs quickly became "women's work," particularly services such as waiting on tables, operating telephone switchboards, elementary schoolteaching, nursing, and secretarial work. The economic incentive for employers to hire women, combined with economic growth and the shift from manufacturing to services, in-

creased the demand for female employees. Eventually there were not enough unmarried or childless women to fill the demand, and employers began reducing the barriers to employment for married women and encouraging those whose children were grown to return to work. Still the demand for labor in female occupations continued to grow faster than the supply of women in accepted social categories, and by the 1950's growth in female employment reached the *sanctum sanctorum*[2] — married women with young children (Oppenheimer 1973). Throughout the century individual women were drawn into the labor force by contingencies: economic need, the availability of work, and the freedom to work (Waite 1976). Despite the low pay and limited opportunities, many women came to prefer working and earning money, and many husbands began to realize the benefits of two paychecks instead of one. But who was taking care of the house and children? This brings us back to the question of why employed women are more distressed than employed men.

In 1978, Huber surveyed a national probability sample of 680 married couples (Huber and Spitze 1983). Respondents, chosen by random digit dialing, were interviewed by telephone. If the respondent was married, his or her spouse was also interviewed, making it one of the first surveys of a large, representative sample of married persons throughout the United States to interview both the husband and wife in each couple. With Huber, we compared the husband's and wife's distress in four types of marriages (Ross, Mirowsky, and Huber 1983). Distress was measured by a modified form of the Center for Epidemiological Studies' depression scale. . . .

In the first type of marriage the wife does not have a job, she and her husband believe her place is in the home, and she does all the

---

[2]*Sanctum sanctorum* is Latin for a "place of great privacy," or "off-limits." — Ed.

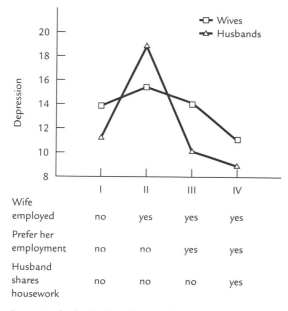

Depression levels of wife and husband in four types of marriages. Data are from 680 couples. Marriage types are based on the wife's employment status, preferences for her employment, and the household division of labor. The results are shown adjusting for income, education, age, religion, and race.

housework and child care. This is the traditional marriage and in 1978 accounted for roughly 44% of all couples. Because this type of marriage is internally consistent — preferences match behavior — it may be psychologically beneficial, but more so for the husband. He is head of the household and has the power and prestige associated with economic resources. The wife, on the other hand, is typically dependent and subordinate. We found that the wife in this type of marriage has a higher level of depression than her husband.

In the second type of marriage the wife has a job but neither she nor her husband want her to, and she does all the housework and child care. This accounted for roughly 19% of the couples. Both of them believe that he should provide for the family while she cares for the home and children, but she has taken a job because they need the money. Psychologically,

this is the worst type of marriage for both partners, and their distress is greater than in any other marriage type. The wife may feel that it is not right that she has to work, that her choice of husband was a poor one, that she cannot do all the things a "good" mother should; and she carries a double burden of paid and unpaid work. To the extent that the husband has internalized the role of breadwinner, he may feel that his wife's employment reflects unfavorably on him, indicating that he is not able to support his family. He may feel guilty and ashamed that she has a job, worry about his loss of authority, and suffer self-doubt and low self-esteem. This is the only type of marriage in which the husband is more distressed than his wife.

Although adjustment may come slowly, people do not long sustain tension between the way they live and the way they think they should live. As economic, demographic, and historical changes nudge lives into new patterns, husbands and wives come to view her employment more positively, particularly as more of their friends and neighbors become two paycheck families. Thus, in the third type of marriage the wife has a job and she and her husband favor her employment, but she remains responsible for the home. About 27% of all couples fell into this category. The husband is better off than ever before. He has adjusted psychologically, his standard of living is higher, and the flow of family income is more secure. He has even lower distress than men in the first type of marriage. However, things are not quite as good for his wife. She is better off than in the second type of marriage, but still carries a double burden. In a system in which the wife stays home and the husband goes out to work it makes sense for her to do the most time-consuming household chores. When she also works outside the home, and particularly when she stops thinking of her job as temporary, it becomes clear to her that the traditional division of the chores is no longer sensible or fair.

Typically she assigns tasks to the children, mechanizes tasks like dishwashing, uses frozen foods and eats out more often, cuts down on optional events like dinner parties, and does not clean as often. Even so, the demands on her time are likely to be much greater than those on her husband's (Robinson 1980). The wife's level of distress in this type of marriage is about the same as in the first type, and the gap between her distress and her husband's is greater than in any other type of marriage.

Once the wife accepts the permanence of her new role as employed worker, she may begin pressing for greater equality in the division of household labor. Although the husband may initially resist, once he has grown accustomed to the economic benefits of two paychecks he is likely to be open to negotiation. If his wife presses the issue, he often makes concessions rather than lose her earnings. In the fourth type of marriage the wife has a job, she and her husband approve of her employment, and they share housework and child care *equally*. This accounted for about 11% of the couples. Both the husband and the wife are less distressed in this type of marriage than in any other, and the gap between them is smaller than in any other type of marriage.

The gap that remains is probably due to two things: First, the large majority of wives in type IV marriages still earn less than their husbands. Second, the category contains a small minority of wives who are very distressed because they are employed mothers of young children and have difficulty arranging child care.

In adapting to the wife's employment, the central problem for husbands seems to be one of self-esteem—of overcoming any embarrassment, guilt, or apprehension associated with the wife's employment. For wives the central problem is getting the husband to share the housework.

We began with the unexpected discovery that women are more distressed than men, and housewives are more distressed than women with jobs. We conclude that couples who share both the economic responsibilities and the household responsibilities also share much the same level of psychological well-being, and are less distressed than other couples. The difference in distress between men and women does not appear to be innate. The difference is there because men and women lead different lives, and as their lives converge the difference begins to disappear. . . .

MARRIAGE

We now come to the second major social pattern of psychological distress: Married people are less distressed than unmarried ones. Most of us are not surprised that widowed, divorced, and separated people are more distressed than married people, but it is surprising to find that adults who are single are almost as distressed as those who are divorced or separated.

What is it about marriage that improves emotional well-being? At first researchers thought it might be simply the presence of another adult in the household. A person who lives alone may be isolated from an important network of social and economic ties: the privileges and obligations centered on the home and family. These ties help create a stabilizing sense of security, belonging, and direction. Without them a person may feel lonely, adrift, and unprotected. Since unmarried people often live alone but married people almost always live together (often with children), this might explain why unmarried people are more distressed. Hughes and Gove subdivided three types of unmarried persons (never married, divorced or separated, widowed) according to whether they lived alone (1981). Contrary to what they expected, Hughes and Gove found that unmarried people are not more distressed if they live alone. The big difference is between married people and others, not between people who live alone and others.

One fact about marriages is that some are better than others. Is it better to be in a bad marriage than to be unmarried? Gove and his colleagues surveyed married people about happiness with marriage (Gove, Hughes, and Style 1983). The 62% who report being very happy with their marriage are less distressed than unmarrieds, but the 34% who only say they are pretty happy with their marriage are no less distressed than the unmarrieds, and the 4% who say they are not too happy or not at all happy with their marriage are *more* distressed than unmarrieds of all types.

A good marriage provides something very important: the sense of being cared for, loved, esteemed, and valued as a person. Pearlin interviewed a representative sample of 2300 Chicago-area adults in 1972, and interviewed the same people again in 1976. He asked them if they could talk to their wives (or husbands) about things they felt were important to them, and count on their spouses for understanding and advice. Those who said "yes" were much less distressed by job disruptions such as being laid off, fired, or sick than those who said "no" (Pearlin et al. 1981). A close, confiding relationship actually protected the men and women against these stressful events. On the other hand, in situations when a spouse expects more than he or she is willing to give back, acts like the only important person in the family, and cannot be counted on for esteem and advice, men and women feel demoralized, tense, worried, neglected, unhappy, and frustrated (Pearlin 1975a,b). Thus, it is not enough merely to have someone around. It is better to live alone than in a marriage characterized by a lack of consideration, caring, and equity.

It is easy to imagine that the victim of an unfair marriage is distressed by the situation, but what about the exploiter? Does a person gain or lose psychologically by taking unfair advantage of a spouse? The cynical view is that spouses are less depressed the more they get things their own way. Because one part-ner's dominance depends upon the other's submission, it follows that one partner's well-being results in the other's depression. The optimistic view is that exploiters, as well as victims, are more distressed than they would be in an equitable relationship. According to equity theory,[3] exploiters face the disapproval of others, worry about retaliation and punishment, feel guilty, and must live with the obstruction and hostility of the victim (Mirowsky 1985). In their hearts the husband and wife both know what is fair; if they do what is right they will both lead happier and more productive lives (Walster, Walster, and Berscheid 1978).

Using the data on 680 married couples described earlier, we found some truth in both the cynical and the optimistic views (Mirowsky 1985). The respondents were asked who decides what house or apartment to live in, where to go on vacation, whether the wife should have a job, and whether to move if the husband gets a job offer in another city. The responses ranged from the wife deciding to sharing the decisions equally to the husband deciding. Mapping the average levels of depression across this range revealed U-shaped patterns for wives and for husbands. Each spouse is least depressed if, to some extent, decisions are shared. However, the balance of influence associated with the lowest average depression is different for husbands and wives: each is least depressed having somewhat more influence than the other. The actual influence in these major decisions is typically closer to the balance that would minimize the husband's depression than it is to the balance that would minimize his wife's depression. This is one reason wives tend to be more depressed

---

[3]Equity theory is a social psychological theory which suggests that people are most happy when they and their partners participate equally in the relationship. Equity theorists argue that people experience a sense of unease when they receive more than their share of benefit from a relationship. — Ed.

than their husbands. In one out of ten marriages, the wives are so far from their ideal balance of influence they are about 50% more depressed than would otherwise be the case.

We know why some marriages are worse than others or worse than no marriage at all, but the question of why unmarried persons are more distressed than marrieds is still not completely answered. The hypothesis is that unmarried persons are less likely to have a close, confiding relationship—someone they talk to about personal things and count on for understanding, help, and advice. If this explanation is correct, future research should find that unmarried persons with high levels of social support have levels of psychological well-being comparable to those of married persons.

UNDESIRABLE LIFE EVENTS

So far we have been discussing the amount of distress people feel in different ongoing situations, such as being married, divorced, or widowed. Distress may also be associated with *changing* from one situation to another. The third major fact revealed in community surveys is that undesirable changes are distressing. At first, researchers believed that all major changes, good and bad, are distressing. As research progressed it became clear that only undesirable life events produce distress.

In the 1960's medical researchers noticed that major changes in a person's life seemed to increase susceptibility to disease. How could changes have this effect? Reasoning from laboratory experiments on regulatory mechanisms, the researchers concluded that every person's behavior tends to settle into an optimal pattern that minimizes the energy and resources expended to meet daily needs. Habits are easy, efficient solutions to everyday problems. Big changes in a person's life (such as getting married or taking a new job) disrupt habits and force the person to use mental and physical energy to adapt—that is, to develop a new set of habits that are optimal in the new situation.

To study the impact of change, Holmes and Rahe asked a group of people to judge the amount of change produced by each of a number of events (1967). Each event was assigned a value, called a life-change unit. The researchers then asked another group to name the changes that had happened in their lives in the past year, counted up the life-change units for each person, and found that people with more units of change suffered more illness and psychological distress. This finding initiated a wave of research that spilled across scientific and national boundaries. Researchers around the world began counting life-change units and correlating them with all kinds of physical and mental problems. Wherever they looked they seemed to find a devastating effect of change.

Although it was never the intent of the researchers involved, an image of the healthy, happy life emerged: a placid existence of undisturbed routines. Should we each withdraw to an asylum of our own making? The studies correlating change with sickness and distress seemed to say we should. In fact, the change theory of distress was so well-accepted that for years researchers never examined the impact of negative and positive events separately. When they did the evidence was clear: study after study found that undesirable events—not desirable ones—cause distress (Gersten et al. 1974; Mueller, Edwards, and Yarvis 1977; Myers, Lindenthal, and Pepper 1971; Ross and Mirowsky 1979; Vinokur and Selzer 1975; Williams, Ware, and Donald 1981).

We analyzed data from the New Haven Study headed by J. K. Myers (Ross and Mirowsky 1979). The project collected information on life events and distress of 720 randomly chosen adults in New Haven, Connecticut, interviewed in 1967 and again in 1969 (Myers, Lindenthal, and Pepper 1971, 1974). We found that the more negative events people experienced the greater their distress. Positive events did *not* increase distress—change per se is not distressing. Subsequent research further refined this conclusion. Undesirable events over which a person has no control are most detrimental to psychological well-being (McFarlane et al. 1983). Controllable events—those in which the person has played some part and shared some responsibility—are less distressing. Some people had speculated that uncontrollable negative events are less distressing than controllable ones because fate, rather than oneself, can be blamed. Events outside the person's control suggest less personal inadequacy and thus protect self-esteem. This argument, while plausible, is not supported by research. Negative events over which a person has no control are more distressing than ones in which the person has played a part. Uncontrollable negative events increase feelings of helplessness and powerlessness. They leave people with the demoralizing sense that they are at the mercy of the environment; that no action will be effective in preventing bad things from happening in the future; and that they are not in control of their lives.

There is a postscript to this research. Not only is positive change not distressing, but people who view change as a challenge, who are instrumental, who set new goals and struggle to achieve them, have *low* levels of psychological distress (Kobasa, Maddi, and Courington 1981). Change is not a useful explanation for the social patterns of distress while feelings of instrumentalism and control (as opposed to powerlessness and lack of control) are.

SOCIOECONOMIC STATUS

Events are brief periods that mark a transition. If undesirable events take their toll, ongoing situations are worse. If you lose your job, the event itself is distressing. Being unemployed for a prolonged period of time is more distressing. The problems that are always there can wear at the nerves and demoralize the spirit.

Some people have more problems and fewer resources with which to solve them. They are the poor and uneducated, working at menial jobs or living on welfare in rundown neighborhoods where crime is a constant threat. Others have fewer problems and more resources to help them cope. They are the well-to-do and educated, working at challenging and fulfilling jobs, and living in pleasant neighborhoods. The difference between these two groups is remarkable. It dwarfs the difference between men and women or between the married and unmarried, bringing us to the fourth fact: High socioeconomic status improves psychological well-being and low status increases psychological distress.

Although the impact of social status and achievement on distress seems obvious, there is a cultural myth of the successful person as driven by a sense of inadequacy, loneliness, or neurotic anxiety. This myth is not accurate. In fact, the typical successful person is active, inquisitive, open, and self-assured. If ever there was a formula for psychological well-being, this is it. How do some people get there, and others find themselves so far away?

The reasons for the vast difference in distress between the upper and lower ranks of society are intimately linked to the reasons those ranks exist. It is a self-amplifying process. Some people begin with fewer advantages, resources, and opportunities; this makes them less able to achieve and more likely to fail. Failure in the face of effort increases cognitive and motivational deficits, which, in turn, produce more failure and distress. These forces have been examined by Kohn and his colleagues (Kohn 1972; Kohn and Schooler 1982), Pearlin and his colleagues (Pearlin and Schooler 1978; Pearlin et al. 1981), Wheaton (1980, 1983), and by us (Mirowsky and Ross 1983, 1984).

There are two things that combine to produce psychological distress: one is a problem, the other is the inability to cope with the problem. A person who can solve his or her problems is, in the long run, happier than a person with no problems at all. There are two crucial characteristics of people who cope with problems successfully. The first is *instrumentalism*, which is the belief that you control your own life, that outcomes depend on your own choices and actions, and that you are not at the mercy of powerful people, luck, fate, or chance. When a problem arises, the instrumental person takes action. He or she does not ignore the problem or passively wait for it to go away. Furthermore, he or she takes action before problems occur, shaping the environment to his or her advantage. A second crucial characteristic is cognitive *flexibility*. The flexible person can imagine complex and/or multiple solutions to a problem and sees many sides to an issue. He or she does not cling to habit and tradition. When necessary, the flexible person can negotiate and innovate. Instrumentalism and flexibility together eliminate the impact of undesirable events and of chronic stressful situations on distress (Wheaton 1983).

These characteristics are needed most where they are found least. Instrumentalism is learned through a long history of success in solving increasingly difficult problems, and flexibility is learned in solving complex problems. Instrumentalism and flexibility are mostly learned in college and on the job, but only jobs that are complex, unsupervised, and not routine have the desired effect (Kohn and Schooler 1982). Kohn and his colleagues interviewed a representative sample of 3101 employed men in the United States in 1964 and again in 1974. They found that jobs that are simple, closely supervised, and routine reduce cognitive flexibility.

The people at the bottom of society are the most burdened with chronic hardship, barriers to achievement, inequity, victimization, and exploitation. Their instrumentalism is reduced by demoralizing personal histories. Their cognitive flexibility is reduced by limited horizons and constraining jobs in which they are told what to do rather than allowed to make their own decisions. Wheaton noted the important distinction between coping ability and coping effort: Low flexibility reduces the *ability* to cope with problems (1980). Low instrumentalism reduces the *motivation* to use whatever energy and resources are available. Without the will or ability to cope with the overwhelming stressors present at the bottom of the social hierarchy, the unsolved problems of the poor and poorly educated accumulate. This combination of more problems and fewer resources to cope with them increases the psychological distress of the disadvantaged.

A NOTE ON RACE

In the United States, blacks are disproportionately disadvantaged. On average, blacks have lower levels of education and income than whites, in large part due to a long history of discrimination. Thus, blacks have higher levels of psychological distress than whites because they tend to have low socioeconomic status (Mirowsky and Ross 1980). Even at the same income level, blacks may be worse off than whites: recent evidence indicates that poor blacks have higher levels of distress than poor whites (Kessler and Neighbors 1986). This may be because discrimination and blocked opportunity interfere with the upward mobility of this group. Perceptions of blocked goals are especially likely to make a person feel helpless, powerless, and unable to control life.

Discussion

Patterns of psychological distress tell us about the quality of life in various social positions. Misery is an inherently meaningful yardstick in social research, serving much the same function as mortality in medical research. Although community surveys of the social patterns of distress only began in the 1960's, they have already corrected some erroneous preconceptions. In particular, the observed patterns of distress challenge the idea that emotional well-being results from a placid life of dependency, protection, and freedom from responsibility. Instead, the surveys show that responsibility, commitment, achievement, and a sense of control in one's own life, and reciprocity, consideration, and equity in personal relationships, are the sources of well-being.

The United States is in the middle of far-reaching historical changes. As forms of production become outmoded, the skills associated with them become obsolete. As families get smaller and more women are employed, traditional household arrangements also become obsolete. In the aggregate, people make these changes. As individuals, people are made over by them. They adapt in one of two ways. Individuals can be overwhelmed, demoralized, discouraged, and distressed or they can be creative, curious, openminded, active, and distressed.

References

Gersten, Joanne C., Thomas S. Langner, Jeanne G. Eisenberg, and Lida Orzek. 1974. "Child Behavior and Life Events: Undesirable Change or Change Per Se?" Pp. 159–170 in Barbara S. Dohrenwend and Bruce P. Dohrenwend (eds.), *Stressful Life Events*. New York: Wiley.

Gove, Walter R., and Michael R. Geerken. 1977. "The Effect of Children and Employment on the Mental Health of Married Men and Women." *Social Forces* 56: 66–76.

Gove, Walter R., and Jeannette F. Tudor. 1973. "Adult Sex Roles and Mental Illness." *American Journal of Sociology* 78: 812–835.

Gove, Walter R., Michael M. Hughes, and Carolyn B. Style. 1983. "Does Marriage Have Positive Effects on the Psychological Well-Being of the Indi-

vidual?" *Journal of Health and Social Behavior* 24: 122–131.

Holmes, Thomas H., and Richard H. Rahe. 1967. "The Social Readjustment Rating Scale." *Journal of Psychosomatic Research* 11: 213–218.

Huber, Joan, and Glenna Spitze. 1983. *Sex Stratification: Children, Housework, and Jobs*. New York: Academic Press.

Hughes, Michael M., and Walter R. Gove. 1981. "Living Alone, Social Integration, and Mental Health." *American Journal of Sociology* 87: 48–74.

Kessler, Ronald C., and James A. McRae. 1982. "The Effect of Wives' Employment on the Mental Health of Married Men and Women." *American Sociological Review* 47: 216–227.

Kessler, Ronald C., and Harold W. Neighbors. 1986. "A New Perspective on the Relationships Among Race, Social Class, and Psychological Distress." *Journal of Health and Social Behavior* 27: 107–115.

Kobasa, Suzanne C., Salvatore R. Maddi, and Sheila Courington. 1981. "Personality and Constitution as Mediators in the Stress–Illness Relationship." *Journal of Health and Social Behavior* 22: 368–378.

Kohn, Melvin. 1972. "Class, Family and Schizophrenia." *Social Forces* 50: 295–302.

Kohn, Melvin, and Carmi Schooler. 1982. "Job Conditions and Personality: A Longitudinal Assessment of Their Reciprocal Effects." *American Journal of Sociology* 87: 1257–1286.

McFarlane, Allan H., Geoffrey R. Norman, David L. Streiner, and Ranjan G. Roy. 1983. "The Process of Social Stress: Stable, Reciprocal, and Mediating Relationships." *Journal of Health and Social Behavior* 24: 160–173.

Mirowsky, John. 1985. "Depression and Marital Power: An Equity Model." *American Journal of Sociology* 91: 557–592.

Mirowsky, John, and Catherine E. Ross. 1980. "Minority Status, Ethnic Culture, and Distress: A Comparison of Blacks, Whites, Mexicans, and Mexican-Americans." *American Journal of Sociology* 86: 479–495.

———. 1983. "Paranoia and the Structure of Powerlessness." *American Sociological Review* 48: 228–239.

———. 1984. "Mexican Culture and Its Emotional Contradictions." *Journal of Health and Social Behavior* 25: 2–13.

Mueller, D. D., W. Edwards, and R. M. Yarvis. 1977. "Stressful Life Events and Psychiatric Symptomatology: Change or Undesirability?" *Journal of Health and Social Behavior* 18: 307–316.

Myers, Jerome K., Jacob J. Lindenthal, and Max P. Pepper. 1971. "Life Events and Psychiatric Impairment." *Journal of Nervous and Mental Disease* 152: 149–157.

———. 1974. "Social Class, Life Events, and Psychiatric Symptoms: A Longitudinal Study." Pp. 191–205 in Bruce P. Dohrenwend and Barbara S. Dohrenwend (eds.), *Stressful Life Events*. New York: Wiley.

Oppenheimer, Valerie Kincade. 1973. "Demographic Influence on Female Employment and the Status of Women." Pp. 184–199 in Joan Huber (ed.), *Changing Women in a Changing Society*. Chicago: University of Chicago Press.

———. 1982. *Work and Family: A Study in Social Demography*. New York: Academic Press.

Parsons, Talcott. 1949. "The Social Structure of the Family." Pp. 173–201 in Ruth Anshen (ed.), *The Family: Its Function and Destiny*. New York: Harper.

Pearlin, Leonard I. 1975a. "Sex Roles and Depression." Pp. 191–208 in Nancy Datan and Leon H. Ginsberg (eds.), *Life Span Developmental Psychology: Normative Life Crisis*. New York: Academic Press.

———. 1975b. "Status Inequality and Stress in Marriage." *American Sociological Review* 40: 344–357.

Pearlin, Leonard I., and Carmi Schooler. 1978. "The Structure of Coping." *Journal of Health and Social Behavior* 19: 2–21.

Pearlin, Leonard I., Morton A. Lieberman, Elizabeth G. Menaghan, and Joseph T. Mullan. 1981. "The Stress Process." *Journal of Health and Social Behavior* 22: 337–356.

Richman, Judith. 1979. "Women's Changing Work Roles and Psychological-Psychophysiological Distress." Presented at the American Sociological Association annual meeting, Boston.

Robinson, John P. 1980. "Housework Technology and Household Work." Pp. 53–67 in Sarah Fenstermaker Berk (ed.), *Women and Household Labor*. Beverly Hills, CA: Sage.

Rosenfield, Sarah. 1980. "Sex Differences in Depression: Do Women Always Have Higher Rates?" *Journal of Health and Social Behavior* 21: 33–42.

Ross, Catherine E., and John Mirowsky. 1979. "A Comparison of Life Event Weighting Schemes: Change, Undesirability, and Effect-Proportional Indices." *Journal of Health and Social Behavior* 20: 166–177.

Ross, Catherine E., John Mirowsky, and Joan Huber. 1983. "Dividing Work, Sharing Work, and In-Between: Marriage Patterns and Depression." *American Sociological Review* 48: 809–823.

Ross, Catherine E., John Mirowsky, and Patricia Ulbrich. 1983. "Distress and the Traditional Female Role: A Comparison of Mexicans and Anglos." *American Journal of Sociology* 89: 670–682.

Vinokur, A., and M. Selzer. 1975. "Desirable Versus Undesirable Life Events: Their Relationship to Stress and Mental Distress." *Journal of Personality and Social Psychology* 32: 329–337.

Waite, Linda J. 1976. "Working Wives: 1940–1960." *American Sociological Review* 41: 65–80.

Walster, Elaine, G. William Walster and Ellen Berscheid. 1978. *Equity: Theory and Research*. Boston: Allyn & Bacon.

Wheaton, Blair. 1980. "The Sociogenesis of Psychological Disorder: An Attributional Theory." *Journal of Health and Social Behavior* 21: 100–124.

———. 1982. "Uses and Abuses of the Langner Index: A Reexamination of Findings on Psychological and Psychophysiological Distress." Pp. 25–53 in David Mechanic (ed.), *Psychosocial Epidemiology: Symptoms, Illness Behavior and Help-Seeking*. New Brunswick, NJ: Rutgers University Press.

———. 1983. "Stress, Personal Coping Resources, and Psychiatric Symptoms: An Investigation of Interactive Models." *Journal of Health and Social Behavior* 24: 208–229.

Williams, Ann W., John E. Ware, and Cathy A. Donald. 1981. "A Model of Mental Health, Life Events, and Social Supports Applicable to General Populations." *Journal of Health and Social Behavior* 22: 324–336.

Questions

1. Would Mills conclude that Mirowsky and Ross have a sociological imagination? Why or why not?

2. Mirowsky and Ross conclude that "the difference in distress between men and women does not appear to be innate [that is, biological or genetic in origin]." Why do they conclude this?

3. What is the relationship between "change" and people's levels of distress?

4. What do Mirowsky and Ross mean when they say that "the vast difference in distress between the upper and lower ranks of society" is part of a "self-amplifying process"?

5. Mirowsky and Ross assert that "a person who can solve his or her own problems is, in the long run, happier than the person with no problems at all." Do you agree or disagree with their assessment? Why?

6. Given what you've learned from this article, what kinds of life choices could you make in order to decrease your chances of experiencing psychological distress?

· 3 ·

How History and Sociology Can Help Today's Families

Stephanie Coontz

In this article (the introductory chapter to her book *The Way We Really Are*), Stephanie Coontz demonstrates the sociological imagination as she discusses the nature of relations between men and women and between parents and kids. Again, these issues *seem* personal; but Coontz demonstrates how taking the larger — sociological and historical — view is very important if we want to find practical answers to such crucial questions as "What's wrong with male–female relationships in modern society?" and "What's happening to today's youth?"

When lecture audiences first urged me to talk about how family history and sociology were relevant to contemporary life, I wasn't sure I wanted to abandon the safety of my historical observation post. But my experiences in recent years have convinced me that people are eager to learn whether historians and social scientists can help them improve their grasp of family issues. And I've come to believe that it's our responsibility to try.

I don't want to make false promises about what history and sociology offer. I can't give you five tips to make your relationship last. I don't have a list of ten things you can say to get your kids to do what *you* want and make them think it's what *they* want. Nor can I give kids many useful pointers on how to raise their parents.

But a historical perspective can help us place our personal relationships into a larger social context, so we can distinguish individual idiosyncrasies or problems from broader dilemmas posed by the times in which we live. Understanding the historical background and the current socioeconomic setting of family

changes helps turn down the heat on discussion of many family issues. It can alleviate some of the anxieties of modern parents and temper the recriminations that go back and forth between men and women. Seeing the larger picture won't make family dilemmas go away, but it can reduce the insecurity, personal bitterness, or sense of betrayal that all of us, at one time or another, bring to these issues. Sometimes it helps to know that the tension originates in the situation, not the psyche.

Putting Teen – Parent Conflicts in Perspective

Consider the question of what's happening to American youth. It's extremely difficult for parents today to look at a specific problem they may have with their teenager, whether that is sneaking out at night or experimenting with alcohol and drugs, without seeing it as a sign of the crisis we are told grips modern youth. Parents tell me they are terrified by headlines about the "epidemic" of teen suicide and by chilling television stories about kids too young to drive a car but old enough to carry an AK-47.

Concerns over adolescent behavior are not entirely new. "Let's Face It," a *Newsweek* cover story of September 6, 1954, declared: "Our Teenagers Are Out of Control." The 1955 film, *Blackboard Jungle,* claimed that teens were "savage" animals because "gang leaders have taken the place of parents." Still, there *are* new structural and historical changes in American life that have recently complicated the transition from early adolescence to young adulthood, making youth–adult relations seem more adversarial.

It doesn't help us understand these changes, however, when people exaggerate the problems of today's teens or turn their normal ups and downs into pathologies. Most teens do not get involved in violence, either as criminals or victims. While teen suicide rates have indeed been increasing, any growth from a low starting point can sound dramatic if presented as a percentage. For example, a 1995 report from the Centers for Disease Control stated that suicides among 10- to 14-year-old youths had "soared" between 1980 and 1992. What this meant in real figures, points out researcher Mike Males, was that 1 in 60,000 youths in this age group killed themselves in 1992, compared to 1 in 125,000 in 1980. The actual death rate among teens from firearms and poisoning has scarcely changed since the 1950s, but the proportion attributed to suicide has risen dramatically, while the proportion attributed to accident has declined (Holinger 1994; Males 1996).

Furthermore, many "teen" suicide figures are overstated because they come from a database that includes people aged 15 to 24. Suicide rates for actual teenagers, aged 13 to 19, are among the lowest of any age group. In fact, notes Kirk Astroth, "teens as a whole are *less likely* to commit suicide than any other age group *except* preteens. . . . Occupational sur-

veys consistently show that parents and teachers are *twice* as likely, counselors and psychologists are *four* times as likely, and school administrators are *six* times as likely to commit suicide as are high school students" (Astroth, 1993, 413). (When I read this statistic to a teenage acquaintance of mine, he told me dourly, "Yeah, but they'll just say we drove them to it.")

It's not that we have more bad parents or more bad kids today than we used to. It's not that families have lost interest in their kids. And there is no evidence that the majority of today's teenagers are more destructive or irresponsible than in the past. However, relations between adults and teens are especially strained today, not because youths have lost their childhood, as is usually suggested, but because they are not being adequately prepared for the new requirements of adulthood. In some ways, childhood has actually been prolonged, if it is measured by dependence on parents and segregation from adult activities. What many young people have lost are clear paths for gaining experience doing responsible, socially necessary work, either in or out of the home, and for moving away from parental supervision without losing contact with adults.

The most common dilemma facing adolescents, and the one that probably causes the most conflicts with adults, is their "rolelessness" in modern society. A rare piece of hard data in all the speculation about what makes adolescents tick is that young people do better on almost every level when they have meaningful involvement in useful and necessary tasks. This effect exists independently of their relationships with parents and friends. Teens also benefit from taking responsibility for younger or less-fortunate children. As one author observes, teens "need some experience of being older, bigger, stronger, or wiser" (Hamburg 1992, 201; Maton 1990, 297).

But today's adolescents have very few opportunities to do socially necessary work. The issue of rolelessness has been building for eighty years, ever since the abolition of child labor, the extension of schooling, and the decline in farm work that used to occupy many youths in the summer. The problem has accelerated recently, as many of the paths that once led teenagers toward mastery of productive and social roles have turned into dead ends. Instead of having a variety of routes to adulthood, as was true for most of American history, most youngsters are now expected to stay in high school until age 17 or 18.

High schools were originally designed for the most privileged sector of the population. Even now they tend to serve well only that half of the high school population that goes on to college. Non-college-bound students often tell me they feel like second-class citizens, not really of interest to the school. And in recent decades a high school degree has lost considerable value as a ticket to a stable job. Even partial college work confers fewer advantages than in the past. Because of these and other trends, researcher Laurence Steinberg claims, adolescence "has become a social and economic holding period" (1992, 30).

Parents are expected to do the holding. In 1968, two researchers commented that most teen–parent conflicts stemmed from the fact that "readiness for adulthood comes about two years *later* than the adolescent claims and about two years *before* the parent will admit" (Stone and Church 1968, 447; emphasis added). There is some evidence that the level of miscalculation has widened for *both* parents and kids.

From the point of view of parents, it is more necessary than ever for kids to stay in school rather than seek full-time work, and to delay marriage or pregnancy. After all, the age at which youths can support themselves, let alone a *family*, has reached a new high in the past two decades. From the kids' point of view, though, this waiting period seems almost unbearable. They not only know a lot more than their folks about modern technology but they feel that they also know more about the facts of life than yesterday's teens. Understandably, they strain at the leash.

The strain is accentuated by the fact that while the age of economic maturation has been rising, the age of physical maturation has been falling. The average age of puberty for girls, for instance, was 16 in 1820, 14 in 1900, and 13 in 1940. Today it is 12, and may still be dropping. For boys, the pace and timing of pubertal development is the most important factor in determining the age at which they first have sex; the influence of parents, friends, income, and race is secondary. Although parents and friends continue to exert considerable influence on the age at which girls begin to have sex, there are obvious limits to how long parents can hold their teenagers back (Nightingale and Wolverton 1988, 1994).

And even as the job market offers fewer and fewer ways for teens to assert their independence and show that they are more grown up than younger kids, consumer markets and the media offer more and more. Steinberg points out that while teens "have less autonomy to pursue societally-valued *adult* activities" than in the past, they "have more autonomy than did their counterparts previously in matters of leisure, discretionary consumption, and grooming." As a result, adolescents "find it easier to purchase illicit drugs than to obtain legitimate employment" (Steinberg 1992, 30).

Another problem for parent–child relations is society's expectation that teens abide by rules and habits that grown-ups have abandoned, and that parents ought to be able to *make* them do so. In preindustrial societies most kids were integrated into almost all adult activities, and right up until the twentieth century there were few separate standards or different laws for teens and adults. For centuries, youth and adults played the same games by the same rules, both literally and figuratively.

From "blind man's bluff" to "follow the leader," games we now leave to children were once played by adults as well. There were few special rules or restrictions that applied solely to teens. *All* premarital sex was supposedly out of line in the nineteenth century; teen sex was not singled out as a special problem. In fact, as late as 1886, the "age of consent" for girls was only 10 in more than half the states in the union (Luker 1996). However, girls or women who *did* consent to premarital sex were ostracized, regardless of their age.

Today's adults have moved on to new amusements and freedoms, but we want teens to play the old games by the old rules. There may be some good reasons for this, but any segregated group soon develops its own institutions, rules, and value systems, and young people are no exception.

Sports is virtually the only adult-approved and peer-admired realm where teens can demonstrate successive gains in competency, test their limits, and show themselves bigger, stronger, and better than younger children. But for teens who aren't good at sports, or those who reject it as busywork designed to keep them out of trouble, what's left? Music, clothes, drugs, alcohol—the choices differ. Many kids experiment and move on. Others get caught in the quagmire of seeking their identity through consumption. What we often call the youth culture is actually adult marketers seeking to commercially exploit youthful energy and rebellion. But sometimes consumerism seems the only way teens can show that they are growing up and experimenting with new social identities while adults try to keep them suspended in the children's world of school or summer camp.

Of course, many teens get a lot out of school and summer camp. But the dilemmas of rolelessness often put adolescents and their parents on a collision course. Young people feel that adults are plying them with make-work or asking them to put their lives on hold as

they mature. They're pretty sure we didn't put *our* lives on hold at comparable levels of maturity, so they suspect us of hypocrisy. Often, they have a point.

On the other hand, while many parents recognize that risk taking among teenagers hasn't changed much since their own youth, they feel that there are more serious consequences for those behaviors than there used to be, given the presence of AIDS (acquired immune deficiency syndrome), high-tech weapons, and new potent drugs. So adults are not necessarily being hypocritical when they hold kids to higher standards than they met themselves. Many of us fear that the second chances and lucky breaks we got may not be available to the next generation.

Balancing the legitimate fears of adults against the legitimate aspirations of teens is not easy. But it helps for both teens and adults to realize that many of their conflicts are triggered by changes in social and economic arrangements, not just family ones. The best way I've found to personally confirm the sociological studies of rolelessness is to ask older men to talk about their life histories. Some of the most interesting discussions I've had over the past few years have been with men over age 60, whose memories extend beyond the transitional period of the 1960s and 1970s to what teen life was like in the 1930s, 1940s, or early 1950s.

The conversations usually start with comments on irresponsible behavior by today's teenage males. "I'd have had my hide tanned if I'd been caught doing that," someone always says, which generally leads to examples of how they got "whomped" or "taught a lesson." Soon, though, the subject switches to the things these upstanding men *didn't* get caught doing in their youth. And most of the time, it turns out the first lesson they learned by getting whomped was how not to get caught.

When they talk about what *really* set them on the right path, almost every older man I've talked with recalls his first job. "I was supporting myself when I was 17" (16, 18, 19, even 15), or "I was in the army with a job to do," the stories go: "What's the matter with today's kids?" And soon they provide their own answers. The typical job a teenager can get today provides neither the self-pride of economic independence nor the socializing benefits of working alongside adult mentors. Teens work in segregated jobs where the only adult who ever comes around is the boss, almost always in an adversarial role. Few jobs for youth allow them to start at the bottom and move up; the middle rungs of the job ladder have been sawed off. Marking time in dead-end jobs that teach no useful skills for the future, teens remain dependent on their parents for the basic necessities of life, simultaneously resenting that dependence and trying to manipulate it.

The stories older men tell about their first jobs are quite different from those told by today's teens. Even men who later became businessmen or highly educated professionals say that their first jobs were in construction, factory work, or some menial setting where they worked beside older men who were more skilled or highly paid. The senior men teased the youngsters, sending them out for a left-handed hammer or making them the butt of sometimes painful practical jokes, but they also showed kids the ropes and helped protect them from the foreman or boss. And they explained why "putting up with the crap" was worth it. After older men talk for a while about what these work experiences meant to them, they are almost always surprised to find themselves agreeing that the loss of nonparental male mentoring may be a bigger problem for boys today than the rise of single-mother homes.

Even allowing for nostalgia, such work relations seem to have been critical experiences for the socialization of many young men in the past. Such jobs integrated youths into adult society, teaching skills they would continue to use as they aged, instead of segregating them

in a separate peer culture. As late as 1940, about 60 percent of employed adolescents aged 16–17 worked in traditional workplaces, such as farms, factories, or construction sites. The jobs they did there, or at least the skills they used, might last well into their adult lives. By 1980, only 14 percent worked in such settings (Greenberger and Steinberg 1986).

Girls, who were excluded from many such jobs, have lost less in this arena of life. Up through the 1960s an adolescent girl typically had more responsibilities at home, from washing dishes to taking care of siblings, than she does today. While such tasks may have prepared girls for adult roles as wives and mothers, they also held girls back from further education or preparation for future work outside the home. The change in work patterns for girls has thus made it *easier* for them to see that they have paths toward adult independence. On the other hand, it raises a different set of tensions between girls and their parents. The decline of the sexual double standard, without an equal decline in economic and social discrimination against women, leads parents to worry that their daughters may have too much opportunity, too early, to engage in sexual risk taking for which girls still pay a far higher price than boys.

Another issue facing teens of both sexes is their increasing exclusion from public space. People talk about how kids today are unsupervised, and they often are; but in one sense teens are under *more* surveillance than in the past. Almost anyone about the age of 40 can remember places where young people could establish real physical, as opposed to psychic, distance from adults. In the suburbs it was undeveloped or abandoned lots and overgrown woods, hidden from adult view, often with old buildings that you could deface without anyone caring. In the cities it was downtown areas where kids could hang out. Many of these places are now gone, and only some kids feel comfortable in the malls that have replaced them.

Much has been written about the gentrification of public space in America, the displacement of the poor or socially marginal from their older niches, followed by fear and indignation from respectable people suddenly forced to actually see the homeless doing what they always used to do. Over the years we have also seen what I think of as an "adultification" of public space. Kids are usually allowed there, as long as they're young enough to be in their parents' charge. But where in your town are teenagers welcome on their own?

Teens today have fewer opportunities than in the past for gradual initiation into productive activities, both at home and in public, and fewer places to demonstrate their autonomy in socially approved ways. At the same time, though, they have more access to certain so-called adult forms of consumption than ever before. This makes it hard for adults to avoid the extremes of overly controlling, lock-'em up positions on the one hand and frequent breakdowns of supervision on the other. Some parents clearly underprotect their kids. We've all seen parents who are too stressed to monitor their kids effectively or who have had their limits overrun so many times that they have given up. Other parents, however, overprotect their kids, trying to personally compensate for the loss of wider adult contacts and of safe retreats. Both extremes drive kids away. But, in most cases, both are reactions to structural dilemmas facing parents and teens rather than abdications of parental responsibility.

What Social Science Tells Us About Male–Female Conflicts

The same kind of perspective can be useful in sorting through conflicts between modern couples. I vividly remember the first people who forced me to bring my historical and social analysis down to individual cases. Following one of my talks, a couple stood up and described a conflict they were having in their marriage. She complained about how unappreciative he was of the effort she took in making gourmet dinners and keeping the house clean. He said: "Hang on a minute. I never asked her to do any of those things. I can't help it if she has higher standards than I do. I don't *care* what we have for dinner. I don't *care* if the floor gets mopped twice a week." They wanted me to comment on their situation.

This is not fair, I thought, as I tried to wriggle out of doing so. I've just summed up the history of family diversity and changing gender roles since colonial times and they want me to settle a marital argument — over housework, of all things? I'm not a counselor; I don't know anything about mediating these issues. I tried to change the subject, but they wouldn't let up, and the audience was clearly on their side. You think family history is relevant, they seemed to be saying. Prove it.

Trapped, but unwilling to pretend I had therapeutic expertise, I cast about for something in my own research or training that might by any stretch of the imagination be helpful. The only thing that came to mind was a concept I had read about in an academic journal. "So," I said, feeling a bit silly, "perhaps the problem we have here lies in what social scientists would call your 'situated social power'" (Wartenberg 1988).

It sounded very academic, even downright pompous, but the more we talked about it, the more I realized this *was* a useful concept for them. In plain English it means that various groups in society have unequal access to economic resources, political power, and social status, and these social differences limit how fair or equal a personal relationship between two individuals from different groups can really be. Such social imbalances affect personal behavior regardless of sincere intentions of both parties to "not let it make a difference."

Teachers, for example, have social power over students. I tell my students that I want them to speak their minds and express their disagreements with me. And I mean it. But often I don't even notice that they continue to defer until someone finally gets angry at me for "dominating the discussion." Even after all these years, my initial reaction is usually indignation. "I told you to speak up," I want to say; "it's not my fault if you hold back." Then I remind myself that in any situation of unequal power, it's the party with the most power who always assumes that other people can act totally free of outside constraints.

When a person with power pretends not to have it, people with less power feel doubly vulnerable. Although they continue to be unequal, they are now asked to put aside the psychological defenses they have constructed against that inequality, including a certain amount of self-protective guardedness. So they clam up or get sore, which leaves the more powerful person feeling that his or her big-hearted gestures are being rebuffed. This tension arises between people of different races and classes, between employees and supervisors, and between men and women, as well as between my students and me.

With this awareness, I try to remember that my students are never going to feel as free criticizing my work as I'm going to feel criticizing theirs. I have to adjust the structure of my class to facilitate discussion. I need to institute protected spaces for criticism, such as providing anonymous evaluation forms for assessing my performance. But I also have to recognize that our power imbalance will always create tensions between us. I should neither blame my students for that nor feel that I've failed to communicate my "authentic self" to them. None of us exists independently of the social relations in which we operate.

Remembering how helpful this concept is to me in depersonalizing conflicts with students, I reminded the couple that men and women have different options in our society, outside and independent of their personal relation-

ships. Research shows that men are happiest in a relationship when they don't have to do much housework and yet meals get made, clothes get ironed, and the house looks good. This doesn't mean they are chauvinist pigs. Who *wouldn't* be happier under those conditions?

But the wives of such men tend to be depressed. A wife may feel, especially if she jeopardized her earning power by taking time off to raise children, that she can't give up the domestic services she performs, because if her husband *does* get dissatisfied, she has fewer options than he does in the work world, and will be far worse off after a divorce.

Consciously or not, the wife in this particular marriage seemed to be assessing the risk of not keeping a nice house or putting delicious meals on the table, and finding it too high to just relax and let the housework go. But she was also resenting her husband's unwillingness to help out. This very common pattern of seemingly voluntary sacrifice by the woman, followed by resentment for the man's failure to reciprocate, originates outside the individual relationship. The man was probably completely sincere about not caring if the work got done, but he was missing the point. His wife had looked around, seen what happened to wives who failed to please their husbands, and tried extra hard to make her husband happy. He could not understand her compulsion, and resented being asked to participate in what he saw as unnecessary work. Counseling and better communication might help, but would probably not totally remove the little kernel of fear in the wife's heart that stems from her perfectly reasonable assessment of the unequal social and economic options for men and women.

Similarly, two people trying to raise a child while they both work full-time are going to get stressed or angry. Part of the problem may be that the man isn't doing enough at home (on average, research shows, having a man in the house *adds* hours to a woman's workday)

(Brace, Lloyd, and Leonard 1995; Hartmann 1981). Part of the problem may be that the woman is sabotaging her own stated desire to have the man do more—treating him as an unskilled assistant, refusing to relinquish her control over child-raising decisions, and keeping her domestic standards too high for him to meet. But another part of the problem will remain even if they are the most enlightened individuals in the world.

There's no nonstressful way to divide three full-time jobs between two individuals. Better communication can make the sacrifices more fair, or help clear away the side issues that get entangled with the stress, but the strains are a social problem existing outside the relationship. The solution does not lie in Martians learning to talk Venusian or Venusians being tolerant of the cultural oddities of Martians, as one pop psychologist describes the differences between men and women, but in changing the job structures and social support networks for family life. Until businesses and schools adjust their hours and policies to the realities of two-earner families, even the best-intentioned couples are going to have difficult times.

Improving communication or using the shortcuts offered by self-help books can alleviate some of the conflicts between men and women in this period of rapidly changing roles and expectations. But addressing communication problems alone ignores the differing social options and the patterned experiences of inequality that continually *re-create* such problems between men and women. So people move from one self-help book to another; they try out new encounter groups and memorize new techniques; they slip back and must start all over again. They are medicating the symptoms without solving the problem.

For example, the Venusian–Martian reference comes from best-selling author John Gray, who has found a strikingly effective analogy for getting men and women to realize that they bring different assumptions and experiences

to relationships: Men and women, he says, come from different planets. They need to learn each other's culture and language. Gray tells women why men's periodic withdrawals from communication do not mean lack of interest in a relationship. Martians, he says, like to retreat to caves in times of stress, while Venusians tend to crowd around, offering each other support and empathy. He explains to men that women are often just asking for reassurance, not trying to control men's lives, when they pursue subjects past the male comfort zone (Gray, 1992).

But Gray doesn't urge either sex to make any big changes, merely to take "tiny steps toward understanding the other." He offers women hints on how to ask their partners for help without antagonizing them or making them feel manipulated, but he doesn't demand that men share housework or that women accept the responsibilities that go with egalitarian relationships. For Gray, a healthy relationship exists "when both partners have permission to ask for what they want and need, and they both have permission to say no if they choose." This is certainly better than no one feeling free to ask, but it leaves a rather large set of issues unresolved (Gray 1992, 265; Peterson 1994).

The problem is that many advice books refuse to ask hard questions about the division of household work and decision-making power. In a section called "scoring points with the opposite sex," for example, Gray's advice to women revolves around issues such as not criticizing men for their driving or choice of restaurants. Men, by contrast, are advised: "offer to make dinner," "occasionally offer to wash the dishes," "compliment her on how she looks," "give her four hugs a day," and "don't flick the remote control to different channels when she is watching TV with you" (Gray 1992; Sen 1983).

Now, most women will say that the book would be worth its weight in gold if their husbands would just follow that last tip, but the fact remains that the unequal bargaining power and social support systems for men and women are not addressed, *or even acknowledged,* in this kind of advice. In the long run, failure to address the roots of gender differences perpetuates the problem of communication, or merely replaces one set of misunderstandings with another. As therapist Betty Carter writes, communicating about feelings rather than addressing issues of power and daily behavior can lead to manipulation that eventually degenerates into mutual blame and psychological name-calling (Carter 1996).[1] If we're going to think of men and women as being from different planets, they need more than guidebooks and language translations; we must make sure that the social, economic, and political treaties they operate under are fair to both parties.

It's not only women's dissatisfactions that are addressed by a historical and sociological perspective. Men often complain that feminists ignore male insecurities and burdens, and they have a point. Men *do* feel injured and alienated, despite their economic and political advantages over women of the same social group. But history and sociology can identify the sources of men's pain a lot more accurately than myths about the loss of some heroic age of male bonding when Australian aborigines, Chinese sun kings, and Greek warriors marched to their own drumbeat. Going "back to the woods" makes a nice weekend retreat, but it doesn't help men restructure their long-term relationships or identify the social, economic, and political changes they need to improve their family lives (Bly 1990).[2]

Male pain is the other side of male power. Not all men, contrary to the rhetoric of masculinity, can be at the top of the pyramid. The contrast between rhetoric and reality is very painful for men whose race, class, health, or even height does not allow them to wield power, exercise authority, or just cut a figure imposing enough to qualify as a "real man." Even successful men pay a high price for their control and authority. The competitive, hierarchical environments men are encouraged to operate in cut them off from intimacy and penalize them for letting down their guard. The myth that male power is all individually achieved, not socially structured, means masculinity can be lost if it is not constantly proven in daily behavior (Brines 1994; Lehne 1989).

Structural analysis helps us get beyond the question of "who hurts more" to explore the different rewards and penalties that traditional gender roles impose on today's men and women. For girls, societal pressures descend heavily at about age 11 or 12, penalizing them for excelling and creating a sharp drop in their self-esteem. There is overwhelming evidence, for example, that girls are treated in ways that hinder their academic and intellectual development. But sometimes this discrimination takes the form of too easy praise and too little pressure to complete a task, leading boys to feel that "girls get off easy." And almost any parent can testify that boys are subject to a much earlier, more abrupt campaign to extinguish the compassion, empathy, and expression of feelings that young boys initially display as openly as girls. The list of derogatory words for boys who don't act masculine is miles longer than the list of disparaging words for girls who don't act feminine. Boys who don't get the message quickly enough are treated brutally. Those who do get the message

---

[1] As Andrew Greeley points out (1989), women's morale has declined far more significantly than men's. Unless their frustrations with the marriage bargain are addressed more directly, not just placated, men and women *could* end up on different planets.

[2] For a critique of Bly's point of view, see Connell 1992.

find that the very success of their effort to "be a man" earns mistrust and fear as well as admiration. In an article that my male students invariably love, Eugene August points out that people always talk about "innocent women and children" in describing victims of war or terrorism. Is there no such thing as an innocent man? (August 1992; Gilligan and Brown 1992; Gilligan, Lyons, and Hammer 1990; Kann 1986; Ornstein 1994; Sadker and Sadker 1994).

It's good to get past caricatures of female victims and male villains, but it is too simplistic to say that we just have to accept our differences. A man's fear of failure and discomfort with intimacy, for example, come from his socially structured need to constantly have others affirm his competence, self-reliance, or superiority. This is the downside of what he must do to exercise power and privilege. For women, lack of power often leads to fear of *success*. The downside of women's comfort with intimacy is discomfort with asserting authority.

As three researchers in the psychology of gender summarize the tradeoffs, boys "get encouraged to be independent and powerful, possibly at the cost of distancing themselves from intimacy." The result is that boys "tend to be overrepresented in the psychopathologies involving aggression." Girls, by contrast, "get rewarded for being compliant and for establishing intimate relations, possibly at the cost of achieving autonomy and control over their choices." This may be why girls are "overrepresented in the psychopathologies involving depression" (Cowan, Cowan, and Kerig 1993, 190).

The solution suggested by historical and social analysis is not for men and women to feel each other's pain but to equalize their power and access to resources. That is the only way they can relate with fairness and integrity, so that unequal and therefore inherently dishonest relations do not deform their identities.

Men must be willing to give up their advantages over women if they hope to build healthy relationships with either sex. Women must be willing to accept tough criticism and give up superficial "privileges" such as being able to cry their way out of a speeding ticket if they hope to develop the inner resources to be high achievers. . . .

References

Astroth, Kirk. 1993. "Beyond Ephebiphobia: Problem Adults or Problem Youths?" *Phi Delta Kappan,* January.

August, Eugene. 1992. "Real Men Don't: Anti-Male Bias in English." Pp. 131–141 in Melita Schaum and Connie Flanagan (eds.), *Gender Images: Reading for Composition.* Boston: Houghton Mifflin.

Bly, Robert. 1990. *Iron John: A Book About Men.* Reading, MA: Addison-Wesley.

Brace, Judith, Cynthia Lloyd, and Ann Leonard, with Patrice Engle and Niev Duffy. 1995. *Families in Focus: New Perspectives on Mothers, Fathers, and Children.* New York: The Population Council.

Brines, Julie. 1994. "Economic Dependency, Gender, and the Division of Labor at Home." *American Journal of Sociology* 100.

Carter, Betty. 1996. *Love, Honor, and Negotiate: Making Your Marriage Work.* New York: Pocket Books.

Connell, R. W. 1992. "Drumming Up the Wrong Tree." *Tikkun* 7.

Cowan, Philip A., Carolyn Pape Cowan, and Patricia K. Kerig. 1993. "Mothers, Fathers, Sons and Daughters: Gender Differences in Family Formation and Parenting Styles" in Philip Cowan et al., (eds.), *Family, Self, and Society: Toward a New Agenda for Family Research.* Hillsdale, NJ: Erlbaum.

Gilligan, Carol, and Lynn Mickel Brown. 1992. *Meeting at the Crossroads: Women's Psychology and Girl's Development.* Cambridge, MA: Harvard University Press.

Gilligan, Carol, Nona Lyons, and Trudy Hammer. 1990. *Making Connections: The Relational World of Adolescent Girls at Emma Willard School.* Cambridge, MA: Harvard University Press.

Gray, John. 1992. *Men Are from Mars, Women Are from Venus.* New York: HarperCollins.

Greeley, Andrew. 1989. "The Declining Morale of Women." *Sociology and Social Research* 73.

Greenberger, Ellen, and Laurence Steinberg. 1986. *When Teenagers Work: The Psychological and Social Costs of Adolescent Employment.* New York: Basic Books.

Hamburg, David. 1992. *Today's Children: Creating a Future for a Generation in Crisis.* New York: Times Books.

Hartmann, Heidi. 1981. "The Family as the Locus of Gender, Class and Political Struggle: The Example of Housework." *Signs* 6.

Holinger, Paul. 1994. *Suicide and Homicide Among Adolescents.* New York: Guilford.

Kann, Mark. 1986. "The Costs of Being on Top." *Journal of the National Association for Women Deans* 49.

Lehne, Gregory. 1989. "Homophobia Among Men: Supporting and Defining the Male Role." Pp. 416–429 in Michael Kimmel and Michael Messner (eds.), *Men's Lives.* New York: Macmillan.

Luker, Kristin. 1996. *Dubious Conceptions: The Politics of Teenage Pregnancy.* Cambridge, MA: Harvard University Press.

Maddrick, Jeffrey. 1995. *The End of Affluence: The Causes and Consequences of America's Economic Dilemma.* New York: Random House.

Males, Mike. 1996. *The Scapegoat Generation: America's War on Adolescents.* Monroe, ME: Common Courage Press.

Maton, Kenneth. 1990. "Meaningful Involvement in Instrumental Activity and Well-Being: Studies of Older Adolescents and At Risk Urban Teen-Agers." *American Journal of Community Psychology* 18.

Nightingale, Elena, and Lisa Wolverton. 1988. "Adolescent Rolelessness in Modern Society." Working paper, Carnegie Council on Adolescent Development, September.

———. 1994. "Sex and America's Teenagers." New York: Alan Guttmacher Institute.

Orenstein, Peggy. 1994. *School Girls: Young Women, Self-Esteem, and the Confidence Gap.* New York: Doubleday.

Peterson, Karen. 1994. "A Global Ambassador Between the Sexes." *USA Today*, March 28.

Sadker, Myra, and David Sadker. 1994. *Failing at Fairness: How American Schools Cheat Girls.* New York: Scribner.

———. 1992. *How Schools Shortchange Girls: The AAUW Report: A Study of Major Findings on Girls and Education.* Washington, DC: AAUW Educational Foundation.

Sen, Amartya. 1983. "Economics and the Family." *Asian Development Review* 1.

Steinberg, Laurence. 1992. "The Logic of Adolescence." In Peter Edelman and Joyce Ladner (eds.), *Adolescence and Poverty: Challenge for the 1990s.* Washington, DC: Center for National Policy Press.

Stone, L. J., and J. Church. 1968. *Childhood and Adolescence: A Psychology of the Growing Person.* New York: Random House.

Wartenberg, Thomas. 1988. "The Situated Concept of Social Power." *Social Theory and Practice* 14.

Questions

1. Would Mills conclude that Coontz has a sociological imagination? Why or why not?

2. What is "rolelessness"? As a teenager, did you experience (or are you now experiencing) this phenomenon? Explain.

3. What is "situated social power"? Describe an example of situated social power that you have experienced or witnessed personally.

4. Consider the concept of "adultification." To what extent did it exist in the place(s) where you grew up? Explain. How might this problem be resolved?

· 4 ·

Hernando Washington

Lisa J. McIntyre

One of the things that sets sociologists apart from ordinary people is their concern for the social. In their professional lives, sociologists tend to ignore individual cases and focus on aggregates or groups. For example, Émile Durkheim studied suicide in order to discover what factors contributed to fluctuations in the overall rates of suicide; he had no interest in what might lead particular individuals to take their lives.

Professional sociologists study *social* facts simply because these are interesting (at least to us). But to the layperson trying to live life in society, social facts may seem irrelevant. Why a society's crime rate goes up and down seems much less intriguing than why *my* house was robbed, or why *I* was mugged on the street. Likewise, the social forces that propel the unemployment rate are not nearly as interesting as the matter of why I am having a difficult time finding a job.

As C. Wright Mills pointed out, however, having a sociological imagination allows us to make connections between individuals and the societies in which they live. And, for the student of sociology, the acquisition of this imagination brings with it an enhanced ability to make sense of the behavior of individuals. Recall what Mills stressed as the "first fruit" of the sociological imagination: "the idea that the individual can understand his own experience and gauge his own fate only by locating himself within his period." It was in this sense that Stephanie Coontz (in the previous reading) brought to bear the sociological concept of "situated social power" to help her understand her own relationships with her teaching assistants, as well as the personal troubles of the woman whose husband did not appreciate her heroic housework.

From the viewpoint of the professional sociologist, the following reading may seem out of place in a sociology reader, because its focus is on an individual and how he responded to his immediate social milieu. But I have included it for the benefit of nonsociologists; it provides an example of how having an understanding of the impact of the social milieu can help us to understand the all-too-frequently unintelligible behaviors of individuals in our environment.

To get a Ph.D., one has to write something called a dissertation. It's essentially a research paper, and sometimes a very long research paper. Mine, for example, ended up being two hundred plus pages. I wrote my dissertation on public defenders—those attorneys who are paid by the state to defend people who are accused of crimes but can't afford to hire their own lawyer. The basic question was this: How can these attorneys defend individuals they know are guilty of crimes, especially if they are terrible crimes? Ultimately, I arrived at my answer by looking not just at the private consciences of the public defenders but also at what Mills would have called their social milieux or surroundings.

I met a number of murders in the course of my research, but Hernando was my first one; and in part because he was my first, he left a large impression on me. But this crime also made a big impression on me because it seemed so bizarre. It never should have happened the way it did. But you can judge for yourself. I will tell you the story as I learned it.

Warning: The first time I heard this story, I remember being shocked. I remember, in fact, feeling nauseous. It's not because anyone showed me terrible pictures of the crime scene; it's just because the whole thing seemed so awful. And it *seemed* so awful because it *was* awful. That led me to wonder, Should I share this story with college students? Possibly, no one is (or should be) worldly enough to hear about this sort of thing.

The Case

This story takes place in Chicago. The major player in the story is a man named Hernando Washington. At various times, his nicknames included the Reverend and the Deacon, because he was president of the youth choir. His other nickname was Prince, because he was so charming and good-looking.

Before I get to the story, let me tell you a bit about the neighborhood in which Hernando lived, or as Mills would put it, his *social milieu*. It was on the South Side of Chicago. In a song from the 1970s, Jim Croce called the South Side of Chicago "the baddest part of town." That was an astute observation. It is the baddest part of town; chances are, if you lived on the South Side, you'd never be able to get a cab driver to take you home at night; some cabs won't even venture there in the daytime.

The police refer to a murder that involves a man and woman on the South Side as a "South Side divorce." A great deal of its reputation involves the fact that the South Side of Chicago is heavily populated by people who are poor — mostly African Americans. Perhaps that's why the police tend to disrespect the people who live there. The police often call murders that involve African American killers and victims as "63rd Street misdemeanors." Police also take much longer to respond to calls on the South Side. The clear message to the people who live there is that they really aren't a part of the community that the Chicago police are pledged to "serve and to protect." This, I think, is an important fact.

On April 1, 1978, Hernando "Prince" Washington was arrested and charged with robbery, aggravated kidnapping, rape, and murder. His victim, 29-year-old Sara Gould, was the wife of a physician and the mother of a small child. Sarah Gould had the great misfortune to be one of the 787 people in Chicago and one of the 20,432 people in the United States who were murdered that year.

When I say that Sarah had the "great misfortune" to be murdered, I mean that. Statistically, she should not have been a murder victim. Nationally, the murder rate for white women in 1978 was 2.8 per 100,000 population. For white men, it was 9.0; for black women, 12.8; and for black men, 58.1. Not only was Sarah white, but she was killed by a stranger. And in 1978, most murder victims were killed by people they knew — friends, lovers, family members, acquaintances, or neighbors. Of all the recorded acts of criminal violence — batteries, assaults, murders — in 1978, less than a third were committed by strangers. This was especially true for women: When the violent act was committed by a stranger, the victim was typically male.

Finally, Sarah Gould was white while Hernando was black. This was one of the more unusual aspects of the case. Most violence, and certainly most murders, involve persons of the same race.

So, the odds were really against Sarah Gould being murdered—however you want to look at it.

That year, April 1, April Fool's Day, fell on a Saturday. The story actually begins two days earlier. That Thursday afternoon, Hernando went out to do his sister Leah a favor. She had just bought a car, a used two-year-old Oldsmobile Cutlass, and the dealer had called the day before to tell her it was ready to be picked up. Hernando offered to do this for her, partly because he wanted to drive the car. His sister, who is ten years older than Hernando, said that would be fine as long as Hernando came to pick her up when she was done with work. Leah worked at the post office and got off work ten minutes before midnight.

Hernando picked up the car, but of course he didn't drive it straight home. Instead, he cruised around his South Side neighborhood for a while. However, he didn't see any of his friends, so he decided to cruise up to the north part of the city.

For Sarah Gould, that was a fatal decision.

Hernando later said he didn't have any particular plan, but eventually he admitted that just maybe, in the back of his mind, he thought he might rob someone. But it was nothing definite. He would simply drive around and see what happened.

Once up north, he drove to Northwestern University's hospital parking lot. He got out of his car and sat on the steps of a nearby building.

ROBBERY AND ABDUCTION

Around 7:30 P.M., Hernando saw a woman getting out of a reddish-orange VW Rabbit. He approached her, gun in hand, and demanded her money. Sarah gave him $25 dollars, explaining that it was all the money she had, but he grabbed her by the arm, dragged her back to his car, and shoved her inside.

Later, when asked why he did that, he told his lawyers that he'd noticed a bunch of people walking toward them and he didn't want them to know that he had just robbed this woman. He said he was afraid that she'd scream or run or something.

Once Hernando got Sarah into the car, he was still afraid that she'd somehow make trouble, so he ordered her to take off her slacks and underpants. He threw her clothing underneath her car and then drove off.

In his confession to the police, Hernando had this to say:

> She was real excited, you know, asking me not to hurt her and I was constantly telling her I wouldn't hurt her, that all I want is money. She was sitting in the front seat alongside of me. We drove off, and she asked me, "What are you going to do to me?" and I told her that I would take her away from the area, so I would have a chance, you know, to get away without being caught.

He kept assuring her that he would not hurt her.

THE PHONE CALL

After Hernando drove around for several hours, Sarah said that he should let her go because her husband and son would be getting worried about her. He considered this for a while and then asked her if she'd like to call home. He stopped at a gas station that was closed for the evening but that had a phone booth.

Sarah's husband, who was indeed worried about her, later told police that she had said something to the effect that she was okay. He asked her, "When are you coming home?" There was a pause, and then he could hear Sarah asking someone when she'd be home. In the background, he heard a male voice saying "an hour." He then asked, "Where are you?" She asked, "Where are we?" Her husband heard the answer: "You'll be home in an hour, bitch, come on."

After the phone call, Hernando told police,

> I turned from the phone, going around the car and at this time, when I, you know, walked around to my car, she broke and ran. I was running after her. I asked her, I said, "Why are you acting like that? I have not hurt you, I told you I will let you go, I just want to make it as safe for me as you want it safe for yourself."

Then, as it was approaching midnight, Hernando pulled the car into a dark alley. He explained to Sarah that he had to go pick someone up and that she couldn't stay in the front seat of the car while he did this. Perhaps for a moment Sarah thought he was going to let her go, but instead, he forced her into the trunk telling her that if she was quiet, everything would be okay.

At exactly 11:50 P.M., Hernando was where he was supposed to be—in the car in front of the main post office. His sister Leah came out and got into the front seat with him. As he drove her home, they talked about the sorts of things that you would expect a brother and sister to talk about—mostly about the new car.

When they got home, Hernando waited in the car until Leah was inside the house. He had always been very concerned about her safety.

A few years earlier, Leah had been raped on her way home from work. Two men grabbed her, dragged her into an alley, stripped off her clothes, and raped her repeatedly. Afterwards, she crawled out of the alley and was relieved to see a police car there. The two officers looked at her, a black woman with her face bleeding and her clothes torn up, and said "Get home by yourself, bitch." Maybe they didn't want her to mess up the back of their patrol car.

Usually, Hernando met his sister after work —but that night he'd had a bike accident and was running late.

Indeed, Hernando's family had not had a great deal of luck when it came to dealing with the police. A few years earlier, Hernando's brother James had been at a party when he was shot by one of the neighborhood guys. Some of James's friends took him to the emergency room, but they were afraid to stay with him because gunshot wounds tend to attract attention. They left him in the emergency room, where he bled to death before the medical staff got to him. "Everyone knew" who had shot Hernando's brother, but for some reason the police didn't take him into custody. It was at that point that Hernando bought his first gun.

Then Hernando drove a few blocks away, stopped, and let Sarah out of the trunk. She reminded him of his promise to let her go, but he said they'd have to go back and get her clothes, because he didn't want to let her go until she was fully dressed again. He drove back to the hospital parking lot, but her clothes were gone; by now, the police had them.

When Sarah had driven into that parking lot earlier in the evening, she was on her way to a Lamaze class she was supposed to teach that night. Eventually, her students became worried about her, called her husband, and found out that she wasn't home. And, of course, he thought she was in class. Next, the class notified hospital security, which investigated and found Sarah's car in the parking lot. When they saw her keys in the ignition and her pants and underpants under the car, the security officers were naturally concerned. They called her husband, who immediately called the police to file a missing person's report.

Finding the clothes missing from under the car scared Hernando. Sarah told him that it didn't matter, that she could go home without them—she was covered enough, she said, by her long raincoat. But he was adamant that he wasn't going to let her go until he'd found her something to wear or, as he put it, until she was "decent" again. He said, "I've got to think of somewhere to get you some clothes."

THE RAPE

By now, it was well past midnight. Hernando thought it was much too late to go to a friend's house and borrow some clothes, so instead, he drove them back down to the South Side. On the way, he stopped and bought a pint of rum, leaving Sarah alone in the car for a moment. Then, he drove to a motel, got out of the car (again leaving Sarah in the front seat alone), registered for a room—in his name. He later told police, "I let her wash up. First she was kind of skeptical. I guess she was frightened. I kept reassuring her that I would not do anything to her. After a while, she went into the bathroom and washed up." Then, he told police, they both went to sleep.

But that was a lie. What really happened next, as Hernando admitted to his attorneys, was that he raped Sarah.

The next morning, Hernando left Sarah alone in the room while he checked out. After they left the motel, he stopped the car and put her back into the trunk. Then he drove to his parents' house to get a change of clothing for himself.

A few blocks later, Hernando let Sarah out of the trunk. Then he drove to a northwestern suburb where he had an appointment. On the way, he again stopped in an alley and forced her into the trunk while he "took care of some business."

What was this urgent appointment? Hernando's "appointment" was in one of the felony trial courtrooms in Cook County, Illinois. At the time all this was going on, Hernando was out on bail. A year earlier, Hernando had been arrested on charges of rape and aggravated kidnapping. His parents had taken out a loan, paid his bail, and hired him a private lawyer, who told Hernando that he would probably beat the rap and not to worry.

In any case, that Friday, March 31, was the scheduled trial date for the year-old rape case.

When the case was called, however, the prosecutor requested a continuance, which the judge granted. Feeling good, Hernando walked out of the courtroom a relatively free man; he even offered his lawyer's assistant a ride back downtown.

When Hernando got back to his car, he saw a couple of people standing near it, seemingly talking to his trunk. Hernando told them to get lost and sped away. But one of the people got Hernando's license plate number and called it in to the police. The dispatcher who took the call about a "woman in the trunk" relayed the message to the detective division; someone placed it on a detective's desk.

Unfortunately, that particular detective had taken off—unannounced—for the weekend, and so no one found the message until the next morning. By then, it was too late. Sarah was dead.

Hernando let Sarah out of the trunk and told her he was disappointed that she'd tried to get help. After all, hadn't he told her that he wasn't going to hurt her and that he would let her go as soon as she got some clothes?

Hernando drove around for a while, and then, as he later told his lawyers, he noticed how dirty her raincoat was. Once again, he told Sarah that he just had to find some decent clothes for her. And once again, she protested that it really wasn't necessary, that she could get home without being fully dressed. Instead, Hernando went to the home of an old girlfriend to borrow some clothes. But he ended up not getting any clothes, claiming that he just didn't quite know how to ask and that her boyfriend was home and he didn't want the boyfriend to hear.

So he released Sarah from the trunk and drove around some more.

As evening approached, Hernando put Sarah back into the trunk of the car and went to meet some friends at a bar. Actually, they ended up going to several bars. He was, he said, getting pretty tired, but he liked being with his friends. And he was "reluctant" to go back to his car because he knew he'd have to deal with this problem. Finally, well after midnight, he returned to the car.

At this point, as they were listening to Hernando tell his story, one of his attorneys asked him, "If you were beginning to be uncomfortable about your situation, why didn't you just let her go, then and there?" Hernando said, "Because the neighborhood I was in wasn't a safe neighborhood for a white woman to be alone in."

Instead of letting her go, he took Sarah to another motel and again raped her. Details about the rape are sketchy because Hernando was a "little shy," as he put it, when it came to talking about "sex." And that's how he referred to the rapes—as sex.

THE MURDER

Early the next morning, Hernando checked out of the motel, drove around for about an hour, and then came to a decision: Clothing or no clothing, it was time to let Sarah go. He parked the car on a residential street, gave her some change, and told her to get on the bus. He said he told her, "All you got to do is walk straight down the street there and get on the bus. Go straight home."

And Sarah, as Hernando always emphasized when he got to this part of the story, Sarah Gould *promised* him that she would get on the bus and go straight home. And, of course, she *promised* not to tell the police.

Hernando let Sarah out of the car, and as he drove away, she was walking toward the bus stop. But, as soon as he was out of sight, she changed her course, walked up to a house, and rang the doorbell.

The house belonged to a Chicago firefighter, who was getting ready for work. He opened the door and saw Sarah—messy, dirty, bruised, and distraught. She told him that she needed help; he told her that he would call the police and that she should stay right there on the porch. Then he closed the door and went to phone the police.

Meanwhile, Hernando had begun to wonder whether Sarah had kept her promise and gotten on the bus. So he doubled back to where he had left her. He saw Sarah standing on the porch of that house; he saw the firefighter talking to her; he saw the firefighter close the door.

As Hernando recounted it, he felt betrayed—she had broken her promise to him. He parked and got out of the car. He said that he called out to her. In Hernando's words, here's what happened next:

> I called to her and she came down. I took her by the arm and around the corner to the alley.
> I said, "What are you doing? All you had to do was get on the bus. You promised that you would get on the bus."
> She protested that I was hurting her, that I was going to kill her.
> I said, "No. All you had to do was get on the bus!"
> She screamed "You are going to kill me!"
> I said, "No, you said you was going to get on the bus. All you had to do was to get on the bus. Stop screaming. I'm not going to hurt you."
> She said "You are going to kill me."
> I said, "I am not going to kill you, shut up, stop screaming."
> She said "You are going to kill me. You are going to kill me."
> I said, "I am not going to kill you."
> She said, "You are going to kill me. I know you are going to kill me."
> So I shot her. Then I shot her again. She fell. I looked at her, then I broke and ran to my car.

The Chicago firefighter kept his promise and called the police, but they were too late to save Sarah. Around one of her wrists was a cloth stamped with Hernando's father's name. When the police asked the firefighter why he didn't let Sarah into his home, he said that when he saw how beat up she was and saw a black man out on the street calling to her, he assumed it was a domestic dispute and didn't want to get in the middle of it.

Shortly thereafter, the police found Hernando at his parents' home, washing the trunk of his car. At first, he denied everything. Then, when police confronted him with the fact that witnesses had said he had a woman in the trunk of his car, he said it was a prostitute. He varied his story every time the police introduced more information. The police were gentle with him; they read him his Miranda rights, they offered him food and drink. But they confused him with their questions, and it didn't take too long for Hernando to confess to have robbed, kidnapped, and murdered Sarah.

But when police asked Hernando to sign the confession, he refused, saying that it might make his attorney mad. It didn't matter. That attorney didn't really want to have anything to do with Hernando the murderer, and besides, his parents had no money left to pay him.

Before his trial, his new attorneys—public defenders—persuaded him that his only chance to beat the death penalty was to plead guilty. This was one of those cases that defense attorneys in Chicago, not without a certain amount of irony, call a "dead bang loser case"—one in which, "the state has everything but a videotape of the crime." At first, Hernando didn't want to plead guilty; he didn't want his parents to know that he was guilty. But ultimately, in hopes of saving his own life, he did plead guilty.

It didn't work. In January 1980, Hernando was sentenced to death. Finally, on March 25, 1995, after his appeals were exhausted, Hernando was executed by lethal injection.

Hernando's lawyers spend a lot of time trying to find some explanation for what happened. Maybe if they could understand what had been going on in his mind, it would help to save his life. But Hernando couldn't really say. What he kept saying, in essence, was, "What is the big deal? Why is everyone so upset with me?" It was not that, in his mind, Hernando did not understand that robbery, kidnapping, rape, and murder are against the law. The fact that he at first denied doing them helped to prove that. So, Hernando was not legally insane—in the sense that he didn't know right from wrong. It was simply that he could not understand why everyone was so worked up about what he had done.

This is difficult for most of us to understand. Why would someone be surprised at getting into really serious trouble for robbing, kidnapping, raping, and murdering another human being? At first, I could not make any sense of Hernando's confusion on this point. But eventually, as my horror receded, I was able to bring a more sociological perspective to bear on the whole subject. In other words, I had to call upon my sociological imagination—I had to look for the general in the particular.

Let me begin my explanation with an analogy. Last semester, in my introductory class, two students decided to turn in the same paper. They weren't in the same section, so I guess they thought they could get away with it. Unfortunately for them, in my department the professors discuss the papers because we want to be sure that we are all grading consistently. We noticed that the two students had submitted the same paper, so we called them in and said, "Hey, you cheated. And, as it says in the syllabus, if you cheat, you flunk."

At first, in each case, the students denied the accusation. However, when confronted with positive proof (copies of the papers with their names on them), they admitted what they had done. But, they said, our reaction was way out of line. Yes, they had read in the syllabus that getting caught cheating meant flunking the course. But flunking was simply *too much* punishment. In one case, flunking meant more than getting an F; it meant losing scholarship and loan money.

Hernando's reaction was much the same: "Okay, I did this, but you shouldn't punish me; certainly you shouldn't punish me this much."

You may be thinking that my analogy isn't really appropriate, that there is no way to compare students who cheat with people who murder. And, of course, I would not compare the behaviors. What I am comparing is how the individuals thought about their acts, and especially their reactions to the punishment.

Both the murder and the cheating were done in hopes of not getting caught; and in neither case did the perpetrators plan on getting caught. Furthermore, when they were caught, each thought the punishment was way out of proportion to the crime. In the case of the students, they argued that the consequences were much too severe, that cheating on a paper wasn't that bad and that losing a scholarship is unfair. In part, too, I think the students were shocked to find that we actually were going to flunk them. I suspect that to the degree they thought about it in advance, they expected to be given another chance, or to receive some lesser punishment. It's possible that they knew of other students who had been caught but not punished for cheating. In any case, their view was that punishment was unfair.

Hernando's reaction was much the same. He acted as if he thought that people were simply too worked up over his deeds. Being sentenced to death was just not acceptable to him. Like our students, he showed no real remorse for what he had done. He was only sorry that he had been caught and had to deal with the consequences.

Again, I suspect that some of you won't like my analogy. Perhaps you can understand why

the students might feel that the punishment for cheating was too harsh. But you might wonder how Hernando could think that he should not be given the more serious punishment for what he'd done wrong.

This is where having a sociological imagination becomes helpful. The students felt abused because they did not see cheating as such a horrendous crime. After all, cheating happened all the time, and in any case, it was only a class paper.

The same kind of logic can be used to explain Hernando's reaction. Recall that Hernando had grown up on Chicago's South Side, where, when a husband killed his wife, it was jokingly referred to by police as a "South Side divorce." That sort of attitude from officials teaches people that life is not very valuable. And, as I mentioned previously, Hernando had learned some more personal, and painful, lessons about the low value placed on life. When his sister was raped, the police would not help her; they would not even give her a ride home. Also, when his brother was murdered, no one moved to identify the killer, much less to arrest him.

What I did not stress was the degree to which Hernando himself had committed violent acts against others. I did mention that he was out on bail on a rape and kidnapping charge, but in addition to that, he had raped at least three other women. No charges were brought in any of those cases—perhaps because they were not reported, for his victims knew there would be little point. *Those* victims also lived on the South Side.

What about the one charge he did have against him? Hernando's parents had mortgaged their home to get him a private lawyer, who told him he would beat the rape charge. Again, Hernando got the same message: His acts had no consequences. As a result of his life experiences, Hernando had learned that human life doesn't count for too much and that it's okay to take what you want. That's why he was so surprised that he was in so much trouble.

Let's look at what two psychiatrists had to say about Hernando.

> He appeared to mask any signs of strong emotions and states that "this is typical for me." He give an example of—if he were upset about something and it pertained mostly to himself, he wouldn't reveal it to anyone. He would give the impression that he didn't have any feelings, and that he does not reveal his real emotions. . . . He shows a recall of dates and times not in synchrony with reality—this, together with his difficulty with complex problem solving and concept formation—shows impairment, possibly indicative of minimal brain dysfunction. . . .
>
> The evaluation of this man indicates that he is suffering from a borderline personality disorder with episodic deterioration in reality testing and thought processes with episodic psychotic thinking. There is the impression of someone who may be seen as withdrawn or aloof, with a superficial intellectual achievement in the use of language which masks a lowered intellectual achievement. There is also the indication of a minimal brain damage, which combined with his psychological profile, would indicate that at times of stress (as existed prior to the commission of the alleged offense) he lacks the ability to plan and to comprehend to the consequences of action.

> He has at best a fragile purchase on reality. He feels overwhelmed by external stimulation and must constantly narrow his perceptual field in order to manage it. These overwhelmed feelings include those of inferiority and paranoia. While he generally stays close to the normal bounds of reality, he does occasionally lapse into abnormal perception and thinking. His capacity to recover from such lapses is the major reason for forgoing a diagnosis of schizophrenia. In general, his thinking and perception are idiosyncratic. He often does not see what others see. The mode of this distortion is to experience and understand the world in ways that are egocentric and sociopathic. . . . [The results of projective tests] present a picture of a highly impoverished internal world where fantasy and imagination are often enacted according to the most basic laws of "kill or be killed," or "eat or be eaten."

Note that this second psychiatrist stressed his expert opinion that *Hernando did not have much of a grasp of reality.* The psychiatrist made that judgment because Hernando persisted in seeing the world as a jungle in which the rule is to kill or be killed.

If this psychiatrist had possessed a sociological imagination, he might have realized that Hernando actually had an uncannily accurate grasp of reality. The understanding of his world as one in which the most basic law was kill or be killed was no delusion or misunderstanding; that was the way things worked on the South Side of Chicago. The very structure of social life in that part of the city meant that people were vulnerable—without help from the police, they had only themselves to fall back on.

But Hernando, too, lacked a sociological imagination—the ability to see beyond his own immediate social milieu, to understand that there are different rules for different people in places like Chicago. On the South Side, where the population is mostly poor and mostly African American, people don't have much power to call on "the establishment" to help them, so life is like a jungle. But on the North Side, things are different. When Hernando drove his sister's car to the North Side of Chicago, he made a fatal error because he drove into a part of the world where life does have value.

On the face of it, we seemingly can never understand what Hernando did. However, it is easier to understand if we use our sociological imagination (as Mills told us to do) and look past Hernando to his social milieu or environment. Then, things begin to make sense.

Don't get me wrong! I'm not saying that we should excuse Hernando for what he did because of the harsh environment in which he grew up. That's not the point. And certainly,

Mini-Glossary

borderline personality disorder   a personality disorder characterized by a long-standing pattern of instability in mood, interpersonal relationships, and self-image. Frequently severe enough to cause extreme distress or interfere with social and occupational functioning.

egocentric   centered around and focused on the self.

idiosyncratic   a personal reaction (not shared by other people).

minimal brain dysfunction   a relatively mild impairment of brain function which has subtle effects on perception, behavior, and academic ability.

psychotic   a form of thinking in which the individual has inaccurate perceptions. Specific symptoms of psychosis include delusions, hallucinations, markedly incoherent speech, disorientation, and confusion. Psychotic individuals generally do not know that they are confusing reality and fantasy.

sociopathic   like "psychopathic," a term for what is now usually called "antisocial personality disorder." This disorder is characterized by chronic and continuous antisocial behavior (and is not due to severe mental retardation, schizophrenia, or manic episodes). This behavior pattern, which is more common in males than in females, generally begins before the age of 15 with such infractions as lying, stealing, fighting, truancy, vandalism, theft, drunkenness, and substance abuse. It then continues after age 18 with at least four of the following manifestations: inability to work consistently, inability to function as a responsible parent, repeated violations of the law, inability to maintain an enduring sexual relationship, frequent fights and beatings inside and outside the home, failure to repay debts and provide child support, travel from place to place without planning, repeated lying and conning, and extreme recklessness in driving and other activities.

that's not the *sociological* point. The goal of sociology is to understand and make predictable people's behavior, to explain what can lead people to act as they do.

What's the benefit of this sort of sociological thinking? What if it were your job to help prevent such crimes? Wouldn't you want to understand how the social environment affects people so that you could, if possible, make changes in that environment? Wouldn't you want to have a sociological imagination?

Questions

1. After I tell them about Hernando, students frequently ask me: "Why didn't Sarah Gould escape? She seemed to have so many chances, why didn't she take advantage of them?" Because I never had an opportunity to speak with Sarah, I will never know the answers for sure, but like my students, I can't help but wonder about it.

    The sociologist Max Weber introduced sociologists to the concept of *verstehen* — that's a German term meaning "emphatic understanding." According to Weber, one way to better our understanding of people's behavior is to use empathy to put ourselves in their places to determine what they were thinking and feeling about their situations. With this concept in mind, why do you think Sarah didn't try to escape from Hernando?

2. Assume that you are a sociologist who is presented with the opportunity to act as an investigator for Hernando's defense team. In that role, you have the opportunity to ask questions of everyone involved in the case—Hernando himself; his attorneys, family, friends, and psychiatrists; and Sarah Gould's family and friends. Who would you want to interview? What questions would you ask?

3. Suppose you are the mayor of Chicago and you've just read all the facts of Hernando's murder of Sarah Gould. In a memo to your chief of police, what suggestions might you make to improve the structure of the city's law enforcement to help prevent this sort of crime happening again?

·5·

Men as Success Objects and Women as Sex Objects

A Study of Personal Advertisements

Simon Davis

As the following article recounts, Simon Davis used what social scientists refer to as an "unobtrusive method" to conduct his research. Unlike obtrusive methods—surveys, experiments, participant observation—in which the researcher's presence may have an effect on the people being studied, unobtrusive measures do not. Specifically Davis studied the personal ads that people place in newspapers. The research is unobtrusive because it is done after the fact, and none of the people being studied is aware of what's going on.

To give himself (and the readers) confidence in his findings, Davis used a basic statistical test known as "chi-square" (χ^2). This test enables the researcher to determine whether it's valid to say that a relationship exists between the variables being studied. How does that work?

Suppose you are gambling with a coin. We would expect, simply by chance, that the coin would come up heads about 50 percent of the time. But what if you got heads two times in a row? Would you conclude that something was fishy? No, two heads in a row is not that different from what you would expect from chance. But what if you got heads fifty times in a row? In this case, you would rightly be suspicious that something was wrong with the coin, that something other than random chance was operating.

If two heads is okay but fifty heads makes you suspicious, what about three heads? Four heads? Ten heads? At what point do you begin to suspect that the outcome is not owing to random chance? To determine where to draw the line, we would use something like a chi-square test. Doing a chi-square test allows us to determine if what we actually get is significantly different statistically from what we would expect to get by chance.

The bottom line is this: When researchers report that their findings are "significant" or "statistically significant," they are saying that there is most likely a real relationship between the variables, that their findings are not owing merely to random chance.

Previous research has indicated that, to a large extent, selection of opposite-sex partners is dictated by traditional sex stereotypes (Urberg 1979). More specifically, it has been found that men tend to emphasize sexuality and physical attractiveness in a mate to a greater extent than women (e.g., Deaux and Hanna 1984; Harrison and Saeed 1977; Nevid 1984); this distinction has been found across cultures, as in the study by Stiles and colleagues (1987) of American and Icelandic adolescents.

The relatively greater preoccupation with casual sexual encounters demonstrated by men (Hite 1987, 184) may be accounted for by the greater emotional investment that women place in sex; Basow (1986, 80) suggests that the "gender differences in this area (different meaning attached to sex) may turn out to be the strongest of all gender differences."

Women, conversely, may tend to emphasize psychological and personality characteristics (Curry and Hock 1981; Deaux and Hanna 1984), and to seek longevity and commitment in a relationship to a greater extent (Basow 1986, 213).

Women may also seek financial security more so than men (Harrison and Saeed 1977). Regarding this last point, Farrell (1986, 25) suggests that the tendency to treat men as success objects is reflected in the media, particularly in advertisements in women's magazines. On the other hand, men themselves may reinforce this stereotype in that a number of men still apparently prefer the traditional marriage with working husband and unemployed wife (Basow 1986, 210).

Men have traditionally been more dominant in intellectual matters, and this may be reinforced in the courting process: Braito (1981) found in his study that female coeds feigned intellectual inferiority with their dates on a number of occasions. In the same vein, Hite, in her 1981 survey, found that men were less likely to seek intellectual prowess in their mate (108).

The mate selection process has been characterized in at least two ways. Harrison and Saeed (1977) found evidence for a matching process, where individuals seeking particular characteristics in a partner were more likely to offer those characteristics in themselves.

This is consistent with the observation that "like attracts like" and that husbands and wives tend to resemble one another in various ways (Thiessen and Gregg 1980). Additionally, an exchange process may be in operation, wherein a trade-off is made with women offering "domestic work and sex for financial support" (Basow 1986, 213).

With respect to sex stereotypes and mate selection, the trend has been for "both sexes to believe that the other sex expects them to live up to the gender stereotype" (Basow 1986, 209).

Theoretical explanations of sex stereotypes in mate selection range from the sociobiological (Symons 1987) to radical political views (Smith, 1973). Of interest in recent years has been demographic influences, that is, the lesser availability of men because of population shifts and marital patterns (Shaevitz 1987, 40). Age may differentially affect women, particularly when children are desired; this, combined with women's generally lower economic status [particularly when unmarried (Halas 1981, 124)], may mean that the need to "settle down" into a secure, committed relationship becomes relatively more crucial for women.

The present study looks at differential mate selection by men and women as reflected in newspaper companion ads. Using such a forum for the exploration of sex stereotypes is not new; for instance, in the study by Harrison and Saeed (1977) cited earlier, the authors found that in such ads women were more likely to seek financial security and men to seek attractiveness; a later study by Deaux and Hanna (1984) had similar results, along with the finding that women were more likely to seek psychological characteristics, specific personality traits, and to emphasize the quality and longevity of the relationship. The present study may be seen as a follow-up of this earlier research, although on this occasion using a Canadian setting. Of particular interest was the following: Were traditional stereotypes still in operation, that is, women being viewed as sex objects and men as success objects (the latter defined as financial and intellectual accomplishments)?

Method

Personal advertisements were taken from the *Vancouver Sun*, which is the major daily newspaper serving Vancouver, British Columbia. The *Sun* is generally perceived as a conservative, respectable journal—hence it was assumed that people advertising in it represented the "mainstream." It should be noted that people placing the ads must do so in person. For the sake of this study, gay ads were not included. A typical ad would run about 50 words, and included a brief description of the person placing it and a list of the attributes desired by the other party. Only the parts pertaining to the attributes desired in the partner were included for analysis. Attributes that pertained to hobbies or recreations were not included for the purpose of this study.

The ads were sampled as follows: Only Saturday ads were used, since in the *Sun* the convention was for Saturday to be the main day for personal ads, with 40–60 ads per edition—compared to only 2–4 ads per edition on weekdays. Within any one edition *all* the ads were included for analysis. Six editions were randomly sampled, covering the period of September 30, 1988, to September 30, 1989. The attempt to sample through the calendar year was made in an effort to avoid an unspecified seasonal effect. The size of the sample (six editions) was large enough to meet goodness-of-fit requirements for statistical tests.

The attributes listed in the ads were coded as follows:

1. *Attractive:* specified that a partner should be, for example, "pretty" or "handsome."

2. *Physique:* similar to 1; however, this focused not on the face but rather on whether the partner was "fit and trim," "muscular," or had "a good figure." If it was not clear if body or face was being emphasized, this fell into variable (1) by default.

3. *Sex:* specified that the partner should have, for instance, "high sex drive," or should be "sensuous" or "erotic," or if there was a clear message that this was an arrangement for sexual purposes ("lunchtime liaisons—discretion required").

4. *Picture:* specified that the partner should include a photo in his/her reply.

5. *Profession:* specified that the partner should be a professional.

6. *Employed:* specified that the partner should be employed, e.g., "must hold steady job" or "must have steady income."

7. *Financial:* specified that the partner should be, for instance, "financially secure" or "financially independent."

8. *Education:* specified that the partner should be, for instance, "well educated" or "well read," or should be a "college grad."

9. *Intelligence:* specified that the partner should be "intelligent," intellectual," or "bright."

10. *Honest:* specified, for instance, that the partner should be "honest" or have "integrity."

11. *Humor:* specified "sense of humor" or "cheerfulness."

12. *Commitment:* specified that the relationship was to be "long term" or "lead to marriage," or some other indication of stability and longevity.

13. *Emotion:* specified that the partner should be "warm," "romantic," "emotionally supportive," "emotionally expressive," "sensitive," "loving," "responsive," or similar terms indicating an opposition to being cold and aloof.

In addition to the 13 attribute variables, two other pieces of information were collected: The length of the ad (in lines) and the age of the person placing the ad. Only if age was exactly specified was it included; if age was vague (e.g., "late 40s") this was not counted.

Variables were measured in the following way: Any ad requesting one of the 13 attributes was scored once for that attribute. If not explicitly mentioned, it was not scored. The scoring was thus "all or nothing," e.g., no matter how many times a person in a particular ad stressed that looks were important it was only counted as a single score in the "attractive" column; thus, each single score represented one person. Conceivably, an individual ad could mention all, some, or none of the variables. Comparisons were then made between the sexes on the basis of the variables, using percentages and chi-squares. Chi-square values were derived by cross-tabulating gender (male/female) with attribute (asked for/not asked for). Degrees of freedom in all cases equaled one. Finally, several of the individual variables were collapsed to get an overall sense of the relative importance of (a) physical factors, (b) employment factors, and (c) intellectual factors.

Results

A total of 329 personal ads were contained in the six newspapers editions studied. One ad was discarded in that it specified a gay relationship, leaving a total sample of 328. Of this number, 215 of the ads were placed by men (65.5%) and 113 by women (34.5%).

The mean age of people placing ads was 40.4. One hundred and twenty seven cases (38.7%) counted as missing data in that the age was not specified or was vague. The mean age for the two sexes was similar: 39.4 for women (with 50.4% of cases missing) and 40.7% for men (with 32.6% of cases missing).

Sex differences in desired companion attributes are summarized in Table 1. It will be seen that for 10 of the 13 variables a statistically significant difference was detected. The three largest differences were found for attractiveness, professional and financial status. To summarize the table: in the case of attractiveness, physique, sex, and picture (physical attributes) the men were more likely than the women to seek these. In the case of professional status, employment status, financial status, intelligence, commitment, and emotion (nonphysical attributes) the women were more likely to seek these. The women were also more likely to specify education, honesty and humor, however not at a statistically significant level.

The data were explored further by collapsing several of the categories: the first 4 variables were collapsed into a "physical" category, Variables 5–7 were collapsed into an "employment" category, and Variables 8 and 9 were collapsed into an "intellectual" category. The assumption was that the collapsed categories were sufficiently similar (within the three new categories) to make the new larger categories conceptually meaningful; conversely, it was felt the remaining variables (10–13) could not be meaningfully collapsed any further.

Sex differences for the three collapsed categories are summarized in Table 2. Note that the Table 2 figures were not derived simply by adding the numbers in the Table 1 categories: recall that for Variables 1–4 a subject could specify all, one, or none; hence simply adding the Table 1 figures would be biased by those individuals who were more effusive in specifying various physical traits. Instead, the Table 2 categories are (like Table 1) all or nothing: whether a subject specified one or all four of the physical attributes it would only count once. Thus, each score represented one person.

In brief, Table 2 gives similar, although more exaggerated results to Table 1. (The exaggeration is the result of only one item of

Table I Gender Comparison for Attributes Desired in Partner

	Gender		
Variable	Desired by Men (*n* = 215)	Desired by Women (*n* = 113)	Chi-square
1. Attractive	76 (35.3%)	20 (17.7%)	11.13[a]
2. Physique	81 (37.7%)	27 (23.9%)	6.37[a]
3. Sex	25 (11.6%)	4 (3.5%)	6.03[a]
4. Picture	74 (34.4%)	24 (21.2%)	6.18[a]
5. Profession	6 (2.8%)	19 (16.8%)	20.74[a]
6. Employed	8 (3.7%)	12 (10.6%)	6.12[a]
7. Financial	7 (3.2%)	22 (19.5%)	24.26[a]
8. Education	8 (3.7%)	8 (7.1%)	1.79 (ns)
9. Intelligence	22 (10.2%)	24 (21.2%)	7.46[a]
10. Honest	20 (9.3%)	17 (15.0%)	2.44 (ns)
11. Humor	36 (16.7%)	26 (23.0%)	1.89 (ns)
12. Commitment	38 (17.6%)	31 (27.4%)	4.25[a]
13. Emotion	44 (20.5%)	35 (31.0%)	4.36[a]

[a]Significant at the .05 level.

several being needed to score within a collapsed category.) The men were more likely than the women to specify some physical attribute. The women were considerably more likely to specify that the companion be employed, or have a profession, or be in good financial shape. And the women were more likely to emphasize the intellectual abilities of their mate. . . .

Discussion

SEX DIFFERENCES

This study found that the attitudes of the subjects, in terms of desired companion attributes, were consistent with traditional sex role stereotypes. The men were more likely to emphasize stereotypically desirable feminine traits (appearance) and deemphasize the nonfeminine traits (financial, employment, and intellectual status). One inconsistency was that emotional expressiveness is a feminine trait but was emphasized relatively less by the men. Women, on the other hand, were more likely to emphasize masculine traits such as financial, employment, and intellectual status, and valued commitment in a relationship more highly. One inconsistency detected for the women concerned the fact that although emotional expressiveness is not a masculine trait, the women in this sample asked for it, relatively more than the men, anyway. Regarding this last point, it may be relevant to refer to Basow's (1986, 210) conclusion that "women prefer relatively androgynous men, but men, especially traditional ones, prefer relatively sex-typed women."

These findings are similar to results from earlier studies, e.g., Deaux and Hanna (1984), and indicate that at this point in time and in this setting sex role stereotyping is still in operation. . . .

METHODOLOGICAL ISSUES

Content analysis of newspaper ads has its strengths and weaknesses. By virtue of being

Table 2 Gender Comparison for Physical, Employment, and Intellectual Attributes Desired in Partner

	Gender		
	Desired by Men (*n* = 215)	Desired by Women (*n* = 113)	Chi-square
Variable			
Physical	143	50	15.13[a]
(collapsing variables 1–4)	(66.5%)	(44.2%)	
Employment	17	47	51.36[a]
(collapsing variables 5–7)	(7.9%)	(41.6%)	
Intellectual	29	31	9.65[a]
(collapsing 8 and 9)	13.5%)	(27.4%)	

[a]Significant at the .05 level.

an unobtrusive study of variables with face validity, it was felt some reliable measure of gender-related attitudes was being achieved. That the mean age of the men and women placing the ads was similar was taken as support for the assumption that the two sexes in this sample were demographically similar. Further, sex differences in desired companion attributes could not be attributed to differential verbal ability in that it was found that length of ad was similar for both sexes.

On the other hand, there were some limitations. It could be argued that people placing personal ads are not representative of the public in general. For instance, with respect to this study, it was found that the subjects were a somewhat older group—mean age of 40— than might be found in other courting situations. This raises the possibility of age being a confounding variable. Older singles may emphasize certain aspects of a relationship, regardless of sex. On the other hand, there is the possibility that age differentially affects women in the mate selection process, particularly when children are desired. The strategy of controlling for age in the analysis was felt problematic in that the numbers for analysis were fairly small, especially given the missing data, and further, that one cannot assume the

missing cases were not systematically different (i.e., older) from those present.

References

Basow, S. 1986. *Gender stereotypes: Traditions and Alternatives*. Pacific Grove, CA: Brooks/Cole.

Curry, T., and R. Hock. 1981. "Sex Differences in Sex Role Ideals in Early Adolescence." *Adolescence* 16: 779–789.

Deaux, K., and R. Hanna. 1984. "Courtship in the Personals Column: The Influence of Gender and Sexual Orientation." *Sex Roles* 11: 363–375.

Farrell, W. 1986. *Why Men Are the Way They Are*. New York: Berkeley Books.

Halas, C. 1981. *Why Can't a Woman Be More Like a Man?* New York: Macmillan.

Harrison, A., and L. Saeed. 1977. "Let's Make a Deal: An Analysis of Revelations and Stipulations in Lonely Hearts Advertisements." *Journal of Personality and Social Psychology*, 35: 257–264.

Hite, S. 1981. *The Hite Report on Male Sexuality*. New York: Knopf.

———. 1987. *Women and Love: A Cultural Revolution in Progress*. New York: Knopf.

Nevid, J. 1984. "Sex Differences in Factors of Romantic Attraction." *Sex Roles* 11: 401–411.

Shaevitz, M. 1987. *Sexual Static*. Boston: Little, Brown.

Stiles, D., J. Gibbon, S. Hardardottir, and J. Schnellmann. 1987. "The Ideal Man or Women as Described by Young Adolescents in Iceland and the United States." *Sex Roles* 17: 313–320.

Symons, D. 1987. "An Evolutionary Approach." In J. Geer and W. O'Donohue (eds.), *Theories of Human Sexuality*. New York: Plenum Press.

Thiessen, D. and B. Gregg. 1980. "Human Assortive Mating and Genetic Equilibrium: An Evolution-ary Perspective." *Ethology and Sociobiology* 1: 111–140.

Urberg, K. 1979. "Sex Role Conceptualization in Adolescents and Adults." *Developmental Psychology* 15: 90–92.

Questions

1. What does Davis mean by "sex objects" and "success objects"?

2. According to Davis's findings, what are the major differences between the personal ads placed by men and those placed by women?

3. In the research reported here, Davis wants to investigate whether mate selection continues to be influenced by traditional sex stereotypes. Sociologists are always concerned about whether their results can be used to make generalizations about the larger population. This really only works to the degree that there are no important differences between the general population and those who place ads. Think about it—why might we hesitate before saying that the findings from this study of personal ads can inform us about the influence of sex-role stereotypes in mate selection more generally?

4. Since Davis conducted his research, have gender relations changed much? If you replicated this study today, do you think your results would be similar or different? Why?

·6·

Hate in the Suburbs

The Rise of the Skinhead Counterculture

Randy Blazak

In his study of skinheads and hate crimes, Randy Blazak relied upon a variety of sources. Watch for these as you read his analysis of why young men might choose to join such countercultures.

In 1988, skinheads seemed to be everywhere — on *Geraldo* and *The Morton Downey, Jr. Show,* as the mindless thugs on episodes of *The Equalizer,* and as real-life thugs on the news after the murder of Mulugeta Serraw in Portland, Oregon.[1] Skinheads were the new bad guys. Monitoring organizations like the Southern Poverty Law Center and the Anti-Defamation Leagues of B'nai B'rith[2] released dire reports on the rise of hate crimes in America. Some were saying that the waning days of the Reagan era were strikingly similar to the waning days of Germany's Weimar Republic,[3] opening the doors to a substantial fascist movement.[4]

As a young activist and sociologist, I wanted to understand this trend. It seemed too easy to demonize skinheads as devils. Many hung out in the same punk rock clubs I did. They seemed fairly human and vulnerable to me. Some were racist and some were not. Some were criminal and others were not. I needed to find out what drew so many of my peers into such a dramatic counterculture, one characterized by an almost religious attachment to violence and intolerance.

Growing Up with the Klan

The first step to understanding the skinheads was to drop the good/evil dichotomy and see myself in their eyes. I grew up in Stone Mountain, Georgia, a suburb of Atlanta. In racist circles, Stone Mountain is well known as the birthplace of the modern Ku Klux Klan in 1915. The annual Labor Day Klan rally was always a source of wonder to us as kids. When I was 12, my friend Kenny and I sat on our bikes and watched the Klansmen march through town in their robes to their annual cross lighting at the foot of the mountain. It was frightening and empowering at the same time. Even though I was taught that racism was not "polite," I knew that the Klan was there for me, to defend me. I had heard my father worry aloud about black families moving into our suburban

---

[1]Mulugeta Serraw, an Ethiopian, was murdered by three skinheads. A civil court later ruled that a branch of the Aryan movement was ultimately responsible for the murder; the court award nearly bankrupted the Aryans. — Ed.

[2]The B'nai B'rith is an American Jewish organization established in 1843. In 1913, in response to an upsurge of prejudice and discrimination against Jews, the B'nai B'rith created the Anti-Defamation League to combat anti-Semitism. — Ed.

[3]The Weimar Republic was established in Germany in 1919 when the National Constituent Assembly met at Weimar to draw up a constitution. In 1933, two months after becoming chancellor of Germany, Adolf Hitler suspended the constitution. — Ed.

[4]Fascism is an undemocratic political philosophy that places the well-being of the nation over that of individuals. — Ed.

Atlanta neighborhood and driving property values down. Maybe the Klan could help.

A few years later, I slipped a bit further into the defensive mode. I wrote an editorial in an eleventh-grade journalism class about the hypocrisy of celebrating Black History Month and not having a White History Month (nobody bothered to point out that every month is white history month). I saw black kids busing into my white high school and white kids moving out. I saw the ban on displaying the Confederate flag and singing "Dixie" at pep rallies. Nobody was explaining what was happening to my community. There was no new crime. No gangs or riots. Just change. Well, the Klan had an explanation. They began handing out literature to my classmates and me after school, which revealed the dark plot to unseat whites from their "natural" position of dominance. I was fascinated.

Fortunately, I made it into the shrinking federal college loan program and escaped to a liberal arts college where I learned a few things. I learned how groups like the Klan twist facts to fit their philosophy. I learned how appealing conspiracy theories are to young people and how we can trick ourselves into believing our stereotypes. I was lucky. My friend Kenny, who never went to college, became an Exalted Cyclops in the Southern White Knights of the Ku Klux Klan.

Deciding to Study Skinheads

My first encounter with skinheads came in 1982. I was 18 and on a study-abroad program in London. One day I hopped onto a train at Victoria Station with three toughs with shaven heads and heavy dockworker boots. At the time, I claimed membership in a punkish subculture called "Mod," and my first thought upon seeing the three was, "Here we are, four alienated youths full of rebelling." But this was no opportunity for male bonding. It soon became clear that I was an enemy. They took out markers and began graffiti-ing swastikas and "Kill a Mod Today" inside the train car. Then they came after me. I jumped out at the next stop. So much for youth unity.

Back home in Atlanta, where I was in graduate school, skinheads began popping up around 1985. They still didn't like Mods (proved to me when a group of skinheads stole my Vespa scooter and set it on fire), but clearly they had other, more serious targets: blacks, Asians, feminists, gays, communists, the homeless, and so on. Things became very political quickly. At any demonstration against Reagan's policies (the arms race, the secret wars in Central America, apartheid in South Africa, CIA recruiting) the skinheads would be there to break things up. They raised images of 1933 and the Nazi brownshirts.[5] As a 21-year-old graduate student, I had my research question: What impels suburban middle-class kids to become violent skinheads?

It was a question that would take me ten years to answer. I often wished I had picked an easier question. Qualitative fieldwork takes a lot of time and patience. My plan was to use my "white maleness" to get inside this counterculture and to try to see the world through their eyes. I spent years traveling around the country drinking beer with skinheads and attending Klan rallies and "white family picnics." I slam danced, fought, attended secret meetings, and even sang in a skinhead band. As the 1980s became the 1990s, and the Berlin Wall came down, I headed off to Eastern Europe to talk to skinheads there as well as back in London. Needless to say, I drank a lot of beer.

My method was participant observation. Others, like Rapheal S. Ezekial in his pioneer-

[5]Nazi brownshirts were the *Sturmabteilung,* or Storm Troops; members of this private army of Nazi's wore brown uniforms. —Ed.

ing work *The Racist Mind* (1995), had gained access to hate groups by asking permission. Ezekial was an older Jew. But I was a young WASP and I wanted them to trust me, so I played the role of a potential recruit. Drawing upon my Stone Mountain upbringing, I could talk the talk of the white man who feared change. It was relatively easy to gain acceptance into the group. Then, at a certain point, I would ask to interview individual members for a local newspaper or school project. I told them they should have their story heard by others. I ended up doing more than seventy interviews with young skinheads.

There were a few frightening moments. In Orlando, Florida, a skinhead recruiter threatened to torture me unless I gave him my Social Security number. In Berlin, I found myself suddenly surrounded by Nazi skinheads who thought I was a Jew. In Atlanta, I got caught up in the middle of a brawl between racist and antiracist skinheads in which one of the combatants had his ear bit off. These frightening encounters notwithstanding, I generally found the skinheads to be warm and engaging with me. They wanted to be understood. They needed to explain the plight of white males in the rapidly changing culture of America in the 1980s and 1990s.

Finding a Theory in Bill Cosby

Ethnographers usually work inductively. That is, instead of entering the field with a hypothesis to test, they use what they observe to help them generate a theory. I had several ideas about what was going on with the skinheads, but it took me a while to put together the pieces into some sort of theory. At the beginning of my study, I spent thirteen months with a group of skinheads in Orlando, Florida. Away from the tourist attractions, Orlando had a large underground youth scene that in-

cluded dozens of skinheads. Much of our time together was spent in parking lots outside music clubs. And a recurring topic was *The Cosby Show,* which, in 1988, was the most popular TV show in America.

Cosby was almost an obsession with these boys. The show was about a very well-off black family—doctor father, lawyer mother, and private school kids. The consensus of the Orlando skinheads was that the show was a sign of the end of white hegemony. Otto, 18, asked me: "What kind of a country is it where the Cosbys have everything and I have nothing? It isn't right!" While they would not have known the sociological term for it, the notion of ascribed status was very powerful to these boys: *They* had a birth right to the good things in life. The Cosbys *did not.*

Such comments about *The Cosby Show* helped lead me to a theoretical understanding of skinheads. These youths clearly were experiencing "status frustration" with respect to their positions as white males. In other words, they felt that they were not getting the status rewards to which they felt entitled. The more time I spent with them, the more I saw this frustration as economically based. In the postindustrial eighties, these boys were seeing an evaporation of their hopes of attaining the American Dream. As their parents were being laid off, downsized, and forced into low-wage service jobs, they were beginning to experience anomie. Building on Robert Merton's anomie theory,[6] criminologist Albert Cohen wrote in his book *Delinquent Boys* (1955) that economically frustrated boys will look to subcultures for "solutions" to their problems.

---

[6]Blazak draws here on Robert Merton's conception of anomie (discussed in chapter 11 of *The Practical Skeptic: Core Concepts in Sociology*). In brief, Merton suggested people share certain goals (especially success) in American society. When people find that the legitimate means to achieve these goals are blocked, they experience frustration, or what Merton called *anomie.* —Ed.

What Happened in the 1980s to Explain the Rise of Skinheads?

The Reagan-Bush years (1980–1992) were a time of great change in America. Along with the structural changes that attended "trickle down" economics,[7] there was a racial dynamic. In the wake of the changes fueled by civil rights legislation (including affirmative action), there was perceived to be a great movement of blacks into the middle class. In a kind of backlash, the leftist organizations of the 1960s and 1970s lost ground to rabid right-wing, anti-communist groups that adopted the extremes of Ronald Reagan's philosophy.

As the civil rights movement faded, a new taboo emerged — race talk. Now that the race issue had been "solved," it was deemed impolite to raise the issue in public. This meant that the generation of parents who had come of age in the civil rights era neglected to teach their Gen X children about the dynamics of racism. This neglect was relevant, but not sufficient to drive kids into countercultural movements. More important were following things: (1) the downward mobility of the increasingly downsized white middle class, (2) the frustration of straight males with the increasing gains of women and homosexuals in the public arena, and (3) the integration of the suburbs as millions of African Americans moved out of both urban and rural areas.

DOWNWARD MOBILITY IN THE AMERICAN MIDDLE CLASS

The 1992 presidential campaign promoted the theory that "this will be the first generation of Americans to be worse off than their parents." The notion of a contracting American middle class had first gained strength in the mid-1980s, and by the early 1990s, the reality of the economic threat came to be accepted by the wider social audience. The 6.8 percent unemployment rate of the 1992 election year included a great number of lower-middle-class/blue-collar workers who had lost jobs in the manufacturing, retail sales, and construction sections (Rose 1992).

The shrinking proportion of the middle class relative to other classes, and particularly the economic impact on the lower ranks of the middle class, has altered our conception of what the middle class actually is. Based on Department of Labor definitions, the middle-income group (families with incomes of $19,000 to $47,000 in 1986) has been shrinking: from 52.3 percent in 1978 to 44.3 percent in 1986. Using standardized family incomes, the middle class represented 46.7 percent of the population in 1979, but only 41.5 percent in 1989 (Rose 1992). The 1990 census revealed that the trend has continued: There was a significant decrease in the size of the middle class. Most importantly, most of those who had moved out of the middle class had moved downward. In 1979, the poverty rate was 11 percent. By the end of the 1980s, it hovered around 13 percent (U.S. Statistical Abstract 1990).

The recession of the early 1980s played a large role in changing people's perceptions.[8] Defining middle income as having a family income of between $20,000 and $49,000, Bradbury (1986) found that, after deflating incomes back to 1973 levels, the middle class had shrunk from 53 percent to 48 percent of all families in 1984. Again, the majority of those

---

[7]The trickle-down theory is based on the simplistic assumption that whatever benefits the wealthiest members of society will ultimately benefit the entire society. For example, the trickle-down theory would justify reducing the amount of income taxes paid by wealthy people by saying that wealthy people will use the savings to create businesses that will, in turn, create jobs for poor people. — Ed.

[8]Technically, the health of the economy is generally defined in terms of general business activity (as measured by the total market value of the goods and services brought into use; that is, the Gross National Product). If a decline in the GNP persists for six to nine months, a *recession* exists. A serious recession is called a depression. — Ed.

who left the middle class experienced downward social mobility. A primary factor in this movement was the displacement of workers. In 1986, the U.S. Department of Labor reported that about 10.8 million workers (age 20 and above) had lost their jobs owing to plant closings or employment cutbacks between 1981 and 1986 (Hovrath 1987). Of these, 5.1 million had been on the job for three years or more. Fewer than a third (3.4 million) of those displaced workers later found work; and only 2.7 million of them found full-time wage or salary jobs. Of the fully re-employed, 44 percent took jobs that paid less than their previous jobs. This represented a significant level of downward mobility within the lower middle class.

> A frequently mentioned example of displaced workers is the steel or automobile worker, who had been employed at a relatively high paying production job and who, upon losing that job, finds little prospect of replacing the earnings to which he and his family had become accustomed. (Hovrath 1984, 4)

In 1988, new studies mostly confirmed earlier Department of Labor findings. The level of re-employment was up from 66.7 percent to 71 percent, but still, 44 percent of those took lower-paying jobs and 30.4 percent were making at least 20 percent less than they had been earning in their previous jobs (Herz 1990). In addition, the types of jobs that were being created were much lower-paying service sector jobs that did not offer many benefits (health insurance, paid leave and vacations, and the like).

The replacement of good jobs with lower-paying ones was a new phenomenon. The growth of white-collar positions after World War II had brought people up from blue-collar and agricultural jobs into the swelling middle class (Macionis 1991). The bulk of jobs created in the 1960s and 1970s were in the high-income ($30,000 or more a year in 1988 dollars) or middle-income ($15,000 to $30,000) range. During the first half of the 1980s, the proportion of

these jobs decreased dramatically, while the proportion of low-income jobs (under $15,000) increased to 40 percent of new jobs (Thurow 1987).

The shrinking middle class also adversely affected the working class. First, it reduced the opportunities for upward mobility as the number of those positions contracted. Second, it increased competition within the working class by adding the often overqualified downwardly mobile to the labor market. And third, the forces that were behind the economic contraction, primarily deindustrialization and the rise of the service economy, hit the working class hardest. Before the downturn, a young unionized laborer with little education could find a secure position on the factory line. But when the factories moved abroad, the only jobs available were low-paying service sector jobs or jobs that generally require some educational training. So both the middle and working classes lost, even if it was only the potential for upward mobility.

Despite the brief economic upswing in the mid-1980s, the 1990s economy remained stagnant in terms of job opportunities for the lower middle class. The jobs that were created were largely in the service sector. Adding to real economic woes was the general perception of a slackening employment market. Nightly news stories featured factory closings, merger-fueled layoffs and downsizing, and thousands of applicants standing in line in the snow for a few hundred jobs. Even people who have not experienced real downward mobility may hold the perception that "it's happening and could happen to me." Rose wrote that

> we all seem to want to "keep up with the Joneses" (what economists call consuming potential goods) and measure our self-worth by how successful we are in meeting this challenge. In a society bombarded with advertisements on television, billboards, newspapers — virtually everywhere, everyone has a chance to covet what is available to those with money. So as the incomes of the rich have moved farther

away from those in the middle, this decline in relative standing has made people feel worse irrespective of the fact that their absolute standard of living may be a tad better. (1992, 16)

The widespread perception that "the American Dream is going down the tubes" arguably affects some groups more than others. Among the most effected seem to be young white males. Despite the traditional emphasis on social equality, the United States has long had, and still has, an informal status system based on ascribed characteristics. But now "white" no longer seems to carry the same benefits it once did, and "male" no longer provides the same guarantee of economic security. Skinheads and political conservatives alike often play up the image of the "straight white male" as a victim of a liberal society. In an uncertain economic environment, the loss of status once guaranteed to this group has created an environment of blame. Selective perception focuses on the haves of the previously disenfranchised — The Cosby Show family, for example — and the have-nots of the white working class.

PATRIARCHAL REACTION

The structure of gender power relations has changed as well. This is most evident in the work force. In 1950, 33 percent of adult women were in the paid work force. By 1990, that figure had risen to 58 percent and included an increase in the number of women in typically male-dominated professions. Add to this the fact that corresponding to the women's rights movement in the 1970s was the gay rights movement that followed the Stonewall riots in 1969.[9] Via the popular media (Madonna, Melrose Place, Ellen DeGeneres) the number of ho-

mosexuals "coming out" in the 1980s and 1990s snowballed, and nearly one million gays and lesbians attended a rally in Washington, DC, in 1993 (Houston 1993). "Gay bashing" hate crimes also increased during this period.[10] In her book The Chalice and the Blade (1988), Riane Eisler presents an interesting theory about why patriarchal systems endure. Based on her extensive examination of history, Eisler suggests that ruling systems have followed a pattern: Societies that give an elevated status to women and approach some level of sex-role partnership ("gylanic" societies) are short-lived. They are ultimately defeated by an active patriarchal system in which males dominate ("androcratic" society). The pattern, then, is one in which, when male domination is lost, it is soon reestablished. Thus, the patriarchal tone of the New Testament was a response to the elevated position of women in the original Christian cults. The Victorian era prohibitions were a response to the artistic, more gylanic activities of the Elizabethan era. Likewise, the macho arms race and the men's movements of the Reagan years can be seen as responses to the hippie and women's movements of the 1960s and 1970s. This is the "backlash" against feminism about which Susan Faludi warned:

> Unlike classic conservatives, these "pseudoconservatives" — as Theodore Adorno dubbed the constituents of such modern right-wing movements — perceive themselves as social outcasts rather than guardians of the status quo. They are not so much defending the prevailing order as resurrecting an out-moded or imagined one. (1991, 231)

Following this argument, the skinhead movement can be seen as a reassertion of the andro-

---

[9] On June 28, 1969, the New York police raided a gay bar called the Stonewall Inn in Greenwich Village. Frequently violent, such raids were almost a tradition in New York City and other places where it was illegal to associate with known homosexuals in an establishment that served alcohol. Until the Stonewall

raid, closeted lesbians and gays took their judicial and nonjudicial lumps quietly, fearing that any protest would bring them media exposure. The Stonewall rebellion marked a turning point, leading to the gay rights movement. — Ed.

[10] Hate crimes are discussed in the introduction to reading 28, "A Massacre in Montreal." — Ed.

Table 1 Suburban Racial Shifts Between 1980 and 1990 in Two Georgia Counties

Cobb County					
1980			**1990**		
White	281,625	(94.6%)	White	391,949	(87.5%)
Black	13,055	(4.4%)	Black	44,154	(9.9%)
Other	3,038	(1.0%)	Other	11,632	(2.6%)
Dekalb County					
1980			**1990**		
White	344,254	(71.3%)	White	292,310	(53.6%)
Black	130,980	(27.0%)	Black	230,425	(42.2%)
Other	7,790	(1.6%)	Other	23,102	(4.2%

Source: 1990 U.S. Census Abstracts.

cratic system. American skinheads in the 1980s followed the Reagan model. Skinheads in the 1990s can be seen as reacting against the gylanic tendencies of the political correctness movement associated with much of youth culture and with the Clinton administration, which has made the rights of women and gays and lesbians something of a priority. This negative view of women and homosexuals is shared by racist and antiracist skinheads. For example, skinheads of every stripe tend to see women as totally subordinate—to the point at which, in many Nazi groups, women's role is simply to produce "healthy white babies for the master race." Homophobia is similarly institutionalized in these countercultures.[11] Gay bashing and harassment are accepted forms of skinhead behavior.

THE CHANGING FACE OF THE SUBURBS

Add to economic and gender threats the changing face of suburban neighborhoods. Formerly

[11]The term *homophobia* was coined by G. K. Lehne in 1976 to refer to the widespread irrational fear and intolerance of homosexuals. See Lehne "Homophobia Among Men," in D. S. David and R. Brannon (eds.), *The Forty-Nine Percent Majority* (Reading, MA: Addison-Wesley, 1976), pp. 66–88. —Ed.

all-white enclaves where members of the dominant group could escape from the problems of urban life—including interaction with members of minority groups—the suburbs now are seeing an influx of urban dwellers. In the 1980s, the proportion of black residents in the city of Atlanta dropped by 7 percent (Hiskey 1993), as those with the money to do so joined the growing number of blacks in middle-class suburbs. William J. Wilson (1991) argues that the eroding job base in urban centers led to an out-migration of African Americans to formerly all-white suburban areas. Two suburban Atlanta counties from my research (see table 1) reflect this shift. Between 1980 and 1990, 150,027 minorities moved into Cobb County, an increase of 7.1 percent. Dekalb County saw an even larger shift: Minority residents increased by 17.8 percent while the number of whites decreased by 17.7 percent. Woodridge Elementary School in Dekalb County, from which I graduated with a nearly all-white class in 1976, lost 57 percent of its white students between 1991 and 1993 (White 1993).

Along with this racial shift came a noticeable increase in the number of racist skinheads in these areas. A 1990 article in the *Atlanta Constitution* entitled "More Skinheads Cropping up in Suburbs: Recruitment Reported in Middle, High Schools" discussed the rise in skinhead violence in metropolitan suburbs:

> Racist skinheads — once rarely seen in Georgia outside Atlanta's inner city — are cropping up in predominantly middle-class and affluent North Georgia suburbs. And they are apparently taking their message to the schools. In a national report completed last June, the Anti-Defamation League of B'nai B'rith said Lassiter and Sprayberry high schools in Cobb County have a noticeable skinhead presence, and "about 28 neo-Nazi skinheads are reliably reported active at Sprayberry." (Burson 1990, D1)

The new suburban skinheads may have been in more affluent areas, but these were still regions with a significant blue-collar and middle-class work force. Now the typical 16-year-old male was also competing with African, Asian, and Mexican Americans for the same service sector jobs.

Skinheads as Problem Solvers

To explain the relatively sudden appearance of skinheads on the American scene, it is important to look at macrolevel economic and social trends as well as microlevel subcultural trends. In the 1980s and 1990s, many people, particularly white males, have had to come to terms with their actual class position. Not only have there been threats to the status of white males on the economic front, but other social dynamics have shifted as well. The 1980s also saw the ascribed position of heterosexual males threatened by the gains made by gays and women. Some white males, then, saw their positions as being attacked on several fronts: economic, racial, gender, and sexual.

Many of the stories I heard were heartbreaking. A whole neighborhood plunged into poverty when the Ford Taurus plant laid off half its workers. White kids who were picked on as they became minorities in their own right. A bright 16-year-old with college plans

forced to work construction after his father was downsized in a merger. There was real anger and real frustration. The influence of right-wing groups led many of those effected to regard these changes as the "fault" of minorities who had been given unfair advantages through Affirmative Action programs, or of Jews who controlled the suburban real estate market, or of gay rights advocates who were seeking to destroy traditional gender roles. In this way, the very real frustration about the loss of status felt by these boys was channeled into the problem-solving mode of the skinhead counterculture. The good news is that most of the boys left the counterculture after they realized that, ultimately, it didn't solve their problems. The bad news is that as the ascribed status of the straight white suburban male continues to lose value for its incumbents, it is likely that racist groups will continue to recruit alienated youths who seek simplistic solutions.

References

Adorno, T. 1950. *The Authoritarian Personality*. New York: Harper and Brothers.

Appelbaum, Richard, and William J. Chamblis. 1995. *Sociology*. New York: HarperCollins.

Blazak, Randy. 1991. "Status Frustration and Racism: A Case Study of Orlando Skinheads." Masters thesis, Emory University.

Burson, Pat. 1990. "More Skinheads Cropping Up in Suburbs." *Atlanta Journal Constitution*, May 20, 1990, p. D1.

Cloward, Richard A., and Lloyd E. Ohlin. 1960. *Delinquency and Opportunity*. Glencoe, IL: Free Press.

Cohen, Albert. 1955. *Delinquent Boys*. New York: Free Press.

Eisler, Riane. 1987. *The Chalice and the Blade*. San Francisco: HarperCollins.

Ezekial, Raphael S. 1995. *The Racist Mind: Portraits of American Neo-Nazis and Klansmen*. New York: Anchor.

Faludi, Susan. 1991. *Backlash*. New York: Anchor.

Heiz, Diane. 1990. "Worker Displacement in a Period of Rapid Job Expansion: 1983-1987." *Monthly Labor Review*, Vol. 13, No. 5: 21–31.

Hiskey, Michelle. 1993. "The Atlanta Paradox," *Atlanta Journal Constitution*, Sept. 19, 1993, p. G1.

Horrigan, M., and S. Hayen. 1988. "The Declining Middle-Class Thesis: A Sensitivity Analysis," *Monthly Labor Review*, Vol. 10, No. 6:3–6.

Macionis, John J. 1991. *Sociology*. New Jersey: Prentice Hall.

Merton, Robert. 1938. "Social Structure and Anomie," *American Sociological Review*, 3:672–682.

Newman, Katherine. 1988. *Falling from Grace: The Experience of Downward Mobility in the American Middle Class*. New York: Free Press.

Phelps, Christopher. 1989. "Skinheads: The New Nazism." *Against the Current*, Sept./Oct. 1989, pp. 17–23.

Robertson, Ian. 1981. *Sociology*. New York: Worth.

Rose, Stephen J. 1993. *The Bunker Mentality of the Middle Class: The Real and Imagined Problems Facing America Today*. New York: New Press.

Statistical Abstract of the United States. 1991. U.S. Dept. of Commerce: Washington, D.C.

Thurow, Lester C. 1987. "A Surge of Inequality." *Scientific American* 246:5, May 1987, pp. 30–37.

White, Betsy. 1993. "Dekalb's Changing Schools," *Atlanta Journal Constitution*, March 29, 1993, p. A1.

Wilson, William Julius. 1991. "Studying Inner-City Dislocations: The Challange of Public Agenda Research." *American Sociological Review*, 56, February 1991, pp. 1–14.

Questions

1. Blazak says that his major research method was participant observation. Based on what you read in chapter 6 in *The Practical Skeptic: Core Ideas in Sociology*, explain what participant observation is. Why did Blazak rely so heavily on this method? Besides skinheads themselves, what sources of information did Blazak rely on in his research.

2. Why do you think Blazak chose a qualitative approach to this research as opposed to a quantitative approach?

3. Blazak conducted most of this research while a graduate student at Emory University. Assume that you are a member of the "Institutional Review Board" at Emory and that Blazak has submitted his research proposal. As a member of the board, it's your job to determine whether the research is ethical. Based on your reading of chapter 7 in *The Practical Skeptic*, what ethical issues would have to be discussed before Blazak's research is approved?

·7·

If Hitler Asked You to Electrocute a Stranger, Would You? Probably.

Philip Meyer

When he reflected back on the tales of Nazi horror that surfaced after World War II, Stanley Milgram wanted to know how ordinary people could be led to participate in such brutality. Like many others, Milgram had persuaded himself that it was something about the German character or culture that allowed the Holocaust to happen; such a horrible thing could never take place, for example, in the United States. Milgram's original plan was to go to Germany to test his hypothesis. Before he could do that, however, he needed a point of comparison. So, he tried out his experiment in New Haven and Bridgeport, Connecticut. As Philip Meyer explains, Milgram never got to Germany.

In the beginning, Stanley Milgram was worried about the Nazi problem. He doesn't worry much about the Nazis anymore. He worries about you and me, and perhaps, himself a little bit too.

Stanley Milgram is a social psychologist, and when he began his career at Yale University in 1960 he had a plan to prove, scientifically, that Germans are different. The Germans-are-different hypothesis has been used by historians, such as William L. Shirer,[1] to explain the systematic destruction of the Jews by the Third Reich. One madman could decide to destroy the Jews and even create a master plan for getting it done. But to implement it on the scale that Hitler did meant that thousands of other people had to go along with the scheme and

help to do the work. The Shirer thesis, which Milgram set out to test, is that Germans have a basic character flaw which explains the whole thing, and this flaw is a readiness to obey authority without question, no matter what outrageous acts the authority commands.

The appealing thing about this theory is that it makes those of us who are not Germans feel better about the whole business. Obviously, you and I are not Hitler, and it seems equally obvious that we would never do Hitler's dirty work for him. But now, because of Stanley Milgram, we are compelled to wonder. Milgram developed a laboratory experiment which provided a systematic way to measure obedience. His plan was to try it out in New Haven on Americans and then go to Germany and try it out on Germans. He was strongly motivated by scientific curiosity, but there was also some moral content in his decision to pursue this line of research, which was, in turn, colored by his own Jewish background. If he could show that Germans are more obedient than Americans, he could then

[1]William Lawrence Shirer began his career as a journalist. Shirer went to work for CBS in 1937, broadcasting the events of the war from both Europe and the United States. In 1940, Shirer took a job with the New York *Herald Tribune,* for which he wrote a column for a couple of years. In 1960, his book *The Rise and Fall of the Third Reich* won the National Book Award. —Ed.

vary the conditions of the experiment and try to find out just what it is that makes some people more obedient than others. With this understanding, the world might, conceivably, be just a little bit better.

But he never took his experiment to Germany. He never took it any farther than Bridgeport. The first finding, also the most unexpected and disturbing finding, was that we Americans are an obedient people: not blindly obedient, and not blissfully obedient, just obedient. "I found so much obedience," says Milgram softly, a little sadly, "I hardly saw the need for taking the experiment to Germany."

There is something of the theatre director in Milgram, and his technique, which he learned from one of the old masters in experimental psychology, Solomon Asch, is to stage a play with every line rehearsed, every prop carefully selected, and everybody an actor except one person. That one person is the subject of the experiment. The subject, of course, does not know he is in a play. He thinks he is in real life. The value of this technique is that the experimenter, as though he were God, can change a prop here, vary a line there, and see how the subject responds. Milgram eventually had to change a lot of the script just to get people to stop obeying. They were obeying so much, the experiment wasn't working—it was like trying to measure oven temperature with a freezer thermometer.

The experiment worked like this: If you were an innocent subject in Milgram's melodrama, you read an ad in the newspaper or received one in the mail asking for volunteers for an educational experiment. The job would take about an hour and pay $4.50. So you make an appointment and go to an old Romanesque stone structure on High Street with the imposing name of The Yale Interaction Laboratory. It looks something like a broadcasting studio. Inside, you meet a young, crew-cut man in a laboratory coat, who says he is Jack Williams, the experimenter. There is

another citizen, fiftyish, Irish face, an accountant, a little overweight, and very mild and harmless-looking. This other citizen seems nervous and plays with his hat while the two of you sit in chairs side by side and are told that the $4.50 checks are yours no matter what happens. Then you listen to Jack Williams explain the experiment.

It is about learning, says Jack Williams in a quiet, knowledgeable way. Science does not know much about the conditions under which people learn and this experiment is to find out about negative reinforcement. Negative reinforcement is getting punished when you do something wrong, as opposed to positive reinforcement which is getting rewarded when you do something right. The negative reinforcement in this case is electric shock. You notice a book on the table, titled *The Teaching-Learning Process,* and you assume that this has something to do with the experiment.

Then Jack Williams takes two pieces of paper, puts them in a hat, and shakes them up. One piece of paper is supposed to say, "Teacher" and the other, "Learner." Draw one and you will see which you will be. The mild-looking accountant draws one, holds it close to his vest like a poker player, looks at it, and says, "Learner." You look at yours. It says, "Teacher." You do not know that the drawing is rigged, and both slips say "Teacher." The experimenter beckons to the mild-mannered "learner."

"Want to step right in here and have a seat, please?" he says. "You can leave your coat on the back of that chair . . . roll up your right sleeve, please. Now what I want to do is strap down your arms to avoid excessive movement on your part during the experiment. This electrode is connected to the shock generator in the next room.

"And this electrode paste," he says, squeezing some stuff out of a plastic bottle and putting it on the man's arm, "is to provide a good contact and to avoid a blister or burn.

Are there any questions now before we go into the next room?"

You don't have any, but the strapped-in "learner" does.

"I do think I should say this," says the learner. "About two years ago I was at the veterans' hospital . . . they detected a heart condition. Nothing serious, but as long as I'm having these shocks, how strong are they — how dangerous are they?"

Williams, the experimenter, shakes his head casually. "Oh, no," he says. "Although they may be painful, they're not dangerous. Anything else?"

Nothing else. And so you play the game. The game is for you to read a series of word pairs: for example, blue-girl, nice-day, fat-neck. When you finish the list, you read just the first word in each pair and then a multiple-choice list of four other words, including the second word of the pair. The learner, from his remote, strapped-in position, pushes one of four switches to indicate which of the four answers he thinks is the right one. If he gets it right, nothing happens and you go on to the next one. If he gets it wrong, you push a switch that buzzes and gives him an electric shock. And then you go to the next word. You start with 15 volts and increase the number of volts by 15 for each wrong answer. The control board goes from 15 volts on one end to 450 volts on the other. So that you know what you are doing, you get a test shock yourself, at 45 volts. It hurts. To further keep you aware of what you are doing to that man in there, the board has verbal descriptions of the shock levels, ranging from "Slight Shock" at the left-hand side, through "Intense Shock" in the middle, to "Danger: Severe Shock" toward the far right. Finally, at the very end, under 435- and 450-volt switches, there are three ambiguous X's. If, at any point, you hesitate, Mr. Williams calmly tells you to go on. If you still hesitate, he tells you again.

Except for some terrifying details, which will be explained in a moment, this is the experiment. The object is to find the shock level at which you disobey the experimenter and refuse to pull the switch.

When Stanley Milgram first wrote this script, he took it to fourteen Yale psychology majors and asked them what they thought would happen. He put it this way: Out of one hundred persons in the teacher's predicament, how would their break-off points be distributed along the 15-to-450-volt scale? They thought a few would break off very early, most would quit someplace in the middle and a few would go all the way to the end. The highest estimate of the number out of one hundred who would go all the way to the end was three. Milgram then informally polled some of his fellow scholars in the psychology department. They agreed that very few would go to the end. Milgram thought so too.

"I'll tell you quite frankly," he says, "before I began this experiment, before any shock generator was built, I thought that most people would break off at 'Strong Shock' or 'Very Strong Shock.' You would get only a very, very small proportion of people getting out to the end of the shock generator, and they would constitute a pathological fringe."

In his pilot experiments, Milgram used Yale students as subjects. Each of them pushed the shock switches, one by one, all the way to the end of the board.

So he rewrote the script to include some protests from the learner. At first, they were mild, gentlemanly, Yalie protests, but, "it didn't seem to have as much effect as I thought it would or should," Milgram recalls. "So we had more violent protestation on the part of the person getting the shock. All of the time, of course, what we were trying to do was not to create a macabre situation, but simply to generate disobedience. And that was one of the first findings. This was not only a technical deficiency of the experiment, that we didn't get disobedience. It really was the first finding: that obedience would be much greater than we had assumed it would be and disobedience would be much more difficult than we had assumed."

As it turned out, the situation did become rather macabre. The only meaningful way to generate disobedience was to have the victim protest with great anguish, noise, and vehemence. The protests were tape-recorded so that all the teachers ordinarily would hear the same sounds and nuances, and they started with a grunt at 75 volts, proceeded through a "Hey, that really hurts," at 125 volts, got desperate with, "I can't stand the pain, don't do that," at 180 volts, reached complaints of heart trouble at 195, an agonized scream at 285, a refusal to answer at 315, and only heart-rending, ominous silence after that.

Still, sixty-five percent of the subjects, twenty- to fifty-year-old American males, everyday, ordinary people like you and me, obediently kept pushing those levers in the belief that they were shocking the mild-mannered learner, whose name was Mr. Wallace, and who was chosen for the role because of his innocent appearance, all the way up to 450 volts.

Milgram was now getting enough disobedience so that he had something he could measure. The next step was to vary the circumstances to see what would encourage or discourage obedience. There seemed very little left in the way of discouragement. The victim was already screaming at the top of his lungs and feigning a heart attack. So whatever new impediment to obedience reached the brain of the subject had to travel by some route other than the ear. Milgram thought of one.

He put the learner in the same room with the teacher. He stopped strapping the learner's hand down. He rewrote the script so that at 150 volts the learner took his hand off the shock plate and declared that he wanted out of the experiment. He rewrote the script some more so that the experimenter then told the teacher to grasp the learner's hand and physically force it down on the plate to give Mr. Wallace his unwanted electric shock.

"I had the feeling that very few people would go on at that point, if any," Milgram says. "I thought that would be the limit of obedience that you would find in the laboratory."

It wasn't.

Although seven years have now gone by, Milgram still remembers the first person to walk into the laboratory in the newly rewritten script. He was a construction worker, a very short man. "He was so small," says Milgram, "that when he sat on the chair in front of the shock generator, his feet didn't reach the floor. When the experimenter told him to push the victim's hand down and give the shock, he turned to the experimenter, and he turned to the victim, his elbow went up, he fell down on the hand of the victim, his feet kind of tugged to one side, and he said, 'Like this, boss?' ZZUMPH!"

The experiment was played out to its bitter end. Milgram tried it with forty different subjects. And thirty percent of them obeyed the experimenter and kept on obeying.

"The protests of the victim were strong and vehement, he was screaming his guts out, he refused to participate, and you had to physically struggle with him in order to get his hand down on the shock generator," Milgram remembers. But twelve out of forty did it.

Milgram took his experiment out of New Haven. Not to Germany, just twenty miles down the road to Bridgeport. Maybe, he reasoned, the people obeyed because of the prestigious setting of Yale University. If they couldn't trust a center of learning that had been there for two centuries, whom could they trust? So he moved the experiment to an untrustworthy setting.

The new setting was a suite of three rooms in a run-down office building in Bridgeport.

The only identification was a sign with a fictitious name: "Research Associates of Bridgeport." Questions about professional connections got only vague answers about "research for industry."

Obedience was less in Bridgeport. Forty-eight percent of the subjects stayed for the maximum shock, compared to sixty-five percent at Yale. But this was enough to prove that far more than Yale's prestige was behind the obedient behavior.

For more than seven years now, Stanley Milgram has been trying to figure out what makes ordinary American citizens so obedient. The most obvious answer—that people are mean, nasty, brutish and sadistic—won't do. The subjects who gave the shocks to Mr. Wallace to the end of the board did not enjoy it. They groaned, protested, fidgeted, argued, and in some cases, were seized by fits of nervous, agitated giggling.

"They even try to get out of it," says Milgram, "but they are somehow engaged in something from which they cannot liberate themselves. They are locked into a structure, and they do not have the skills or inner resources to disengage themselves."

Milgram, because he mistakenly had assumed that he would have trouble getting people to obey the orders to shock Mr. Wallace, went to a lot of trouble to create a realistic situation.

There was crew-cut Jack Williams and his grey laboratory coat. Not white, which might denote a medical technician, but ambiguously authoritative grey. Then there was the book on the table, and the other appurtenances of the laboratory which emitted the silent message that things were being performed here in the name of science, and were therefore great and good.

But the nicest touch of all was the shock generator. When Milgram started out, he had only a $300 grant from the Higgins Fund of Yale University. Later he got more ample support from the National Science Foundation, but in the beginning he had to create this authentic-looking machine with very scarce resources except for his own imagination. So he went to New York and roamed around the electronic shops until he found some little black switches at Lafayette Radio for a dollar apiece. He bought thirty of them. The generator was a metal box, about the size of a small footlocker, and he drilled the thirty holes for the thirty switches himself in a Yale machine shop. But the fine detail was left to professional industrial engravers. So he ended up with a splendid-looking control panel dominated by the row of switches, each labeled with its voltage, and each having its own red light that flashed on when the switch was pulled. Other things happened when a switch was pushed. Besides the ZZUMPHing noise, a blue light labeled "voltage energizer" went on, and a needle on a dial labeled "voltage" flicked from left to right. Relays inside the box clicked. Finally, in the upper left-hand corner of the control panel was this inscription, engraved in precise block letters:

SHOCK GENERATOR TYPE ZLB
DYSON INSTRUMENT COMPANY
WALTHAM, MASS.
OUTPUT: 15 VOLTS—450 VOLTS

One day a man from the Lehigh Valley Electronics Company of Pennsylvania was passing through the laboratory, and he stopped to admire the shock generator.

"This is a very fine shock generator," he said. "But who is this Dyson Instrument Company?" Milgram felt proud at that, since Dyson Instrument Company existed only in the recesses of his imagination.

When you consider the seeming authenticity of the situation, you can appreciate the agony some of the subjects went through. It was pure conflict. As Milgram explains to his students, "When a parent says, 'Don't strike old ladies,' you are learning two things: the content and, also, to obey authority. This experiment creates conflicts between the two elements."

Here is a partial transcription from one of the experiments. The naïve "teacher" is a heavyset, worried-looking man with prematurely grey hair. He is wearing a polo short. He is very polite. He has just pushed the 180-volt lever. A hidden camera is recording the performance.

LEARNER (*who, from the teacher's point of view is heard but not seen, an offstage voice*): Ow, I can't stand the pain. Don't do that. . . .

TEACHER (*pivoting around in his chair and shaking his head*): I can't stand it. I'm not going to kill that man in there. You hear him hollering?

EXPERIMENTER: As I told you before, the shocks may be painful, but—

TEACHER: But he's hollering. He can't stand it. What's going to happen to him?

EXPERIMENTER (*His voice is patient, matter-of-fact.*): The experiment requires that you continue, Teacher.

TEACHER: Aaah, but, unh, I'm not going to get that man sick in there . . . know what I mean?

EXPERIMENTER: Whether the learner likes it or not, we must go on, through all the word pairs.

TEACHER: I refuse to take the responsibility. He's in there hollering!

EXPERIMENTER: It's absolutely essential that you continue, Teacher.

TEACHER (*indicating the unused questions*): There's too many left here, I mean, Geez, if he gets them wrong, there's too many of them left. I mean who's going to take the responsibility if anything happens to that gentleman?

EXPERIMENTER: I'm responsible for anything that happens to him. Continue please.

TEACHER: All right. (*Consults list of words.*) The next one's "Slow—walk, truck, dance, music." Answer, please. (*A buzzing sound indicates the learner has signaled his answer.*)

Wrong. A hundred and ninety-five volts. "Dance." (*Zzumph!*)

LEARNER: Let me out of here. My heart's bothering me! (*Teacher looks at experimenter.*)

EXPERIMENTER: Continue, please.

LEARNER (*screaming*): Let me out of here, you have no right to keep me here. Let me out of here, let me out, my heart's bothering me, let me out! (*Teacher shakes head, pats the table nervously.*)

TEACHER: You see, he's hollering. Hear that? Gee, I don't know.

EXPERIMENTER: The experiment requires. . . .

TEACHER (*interrupting*): I know it does, sir, but I mean—hunh! He don't know what he's getting in for. He's up to 195 volts! (*Experiment continues, through 210 volts, 225 volts, 240 volts, 255 volts, 270 volts, delivered to the man in the electric chair, at which point the teacher, with evident relief, runs out of word-pair questions.*)

EXPERIMENTER: You'll have to go back to the beginning of that page and go through them again until he's learned them all correctly.

TEACHER: Aw, no. I'm not going to kill that man. You mean I've got to keep going up with the scale. No sir. He's hollering in there. I'm not going to give him 450 volts.

EXPERIMENTER: The experiment requires that you go on.

TEACHER: I know it does, but that man is hollering in there, sir.

EXPERIMENTER (*same matter-of-fact tone*): As I said before, although the shocks may be painful . . .

TEACHER (*interrupting*): Awwww. He—he—he's yelling in there.

EXPERIMENTER: Start with "Blue," please, at the top of the page. Continue, please, Teacher. Just go ahead.

TEACHER (*concentrating intently on list of words in front of him, as if to shut everything else out*): "Blue—boy, girl, grass, hat." (*Buzz indicates answer.*) Correct. "Night—day, sky, job, chair." (*Buzz*) Wrong. The answer is "day." Two hundred and eighty-five volts. (*Zzumph!*)

LEARNER: *Ohhhuhhoohhh!*

EXPERIMENTER: Continue, please.

TEACHER: "Fat—man, lady, tub, neck." Answer, please. (*Buzz*) Wrong. The answer is "neck." Three hundred volts. (*Zzumph!*)

LEARNER: Ohhh. I absolutely refuse to answer any more. (*Shouting urgently, now*) Let me out of here. You can't hold me here. Get me out. Get—me—out—of—here.

EXPERIMENTER: Continue. The next word is "Green," please.

TEACHER: "Green—grass, hat, ink, apple." (*Nothing happens. No answering buzz. Just gloomy silence.*)

TEACHER: I don't think he is going to answer.

EXPERIMENTER: If the learner doesn't answer in a reasonable time, about four or five seconds, consider the answer wrong. And follow the same procedures you have been doing for wrong answers. Say "Wrong," tell him the number of volts, give him the punishment, read him the correct answer. Continue, please.

TEACHER: "Green—grass, hat, ink, apple." Answer, please. (*More silence. Teacher just sits there.*)

EXPERIMENTER: Go on with the procedure, please, Teacher.

TEACHER: Three hundred and fifteen volts. The answer is "ink." (*Zzumph!*)

LEARNER: Ohh, Ooohh.

TEACHER (*relieved to hear response*): Next one . . .

LEARNER: I absolutely refuse to answer.

TEACHER: You got to. You get a shock if you don't answer. (*Experiment continues with learner refusing to answer, and finally failing even to grunt or groan. At 375 volts, the teacher stands up. Has he had enough? Will he break off the experiment? Will he disobey?*)

TEACHER: I think something's happened to that fellow in there. I don't get no answer. He was hollering at less voltage. Can't you check in and see if he's all right, please?

EXPERIMENTER (*same detached calm*): Not once we've started. Please continue, Teacher.

TEACHER (*sits down, sighs deeply*): "Cool—day, shade, water, paint." Answer, please. Are you all right in there? Are you all right?

EXPERIMENTER: Please continue, Teacher. Continue, please. (*Teacher pushes lever. Zzumph!*)

TEACHER (*swiveling around in his chair*): Something's happened to that man in there. (*Swiveling back*) Next one. "Low—dollar, necklace, moon, paint." (*Turning around again*) Something's happened to that man in there. You better check in on him, sir. He won't answer or nothing.

EXPERIMENTER: Continue. Go on, please.

TEACHER: You accept all responsibility.

EXPERIMENTER: The responsibility is mine. Correct. Please go on. (*Teacher returns to his list, starts running through words as rapidly as he can read them, works through to 450 volts.*)

TEACHER: That's that.

EXPERIMENTER: Continue using the last switch on the board, please. The four-fifty switch for each wrong answer. Continue, please.

TEACHER: But I don't get no anything!

EXPERIMENTER: Please continue. The next word is "White."

TEACHER: Don't you think you should look in on him, please.

EXPERIMENTER: Not once we've started the experiment.

TEACHER: But what if something has happened to the man?

EXPERIMENTER: The experiment requires that you continue. Go on, please.

TEACHER: Don't the man's health mean anything?

EXPERIMENTER: Whether the learner likes it or not . . .

TEACHER: What if he's dead in there? (*Gestures toward the room with the electric chair*) I mean, he told me he can't stand the shock, sir. I don't mean to be rude, but I think you should look in on him. All you have to do is look in the door. I don't get no answer, no noise. Something might have happened to the gentleman in there, sir.

EXPERIMENTER: We must continue. Go on, please.

TEACHER: You mean keep giving him what? Four hundred fifty volts, what he's got now?

EXPERIMENTER: That's correct. Continue. The next word is "White."

TEACHER (*now at a furious pace*): "White—cloud, horse, rock, house." Answer, please. The answer is "horse." Four hundred and fifty volts. (*Zzumph!*) Next word. "Bag—paint, music, clown, girl." The answer is "paint." Four hundred and fifty volts. (*Zzumph!*) Next word is "Short—sentence, movie . . ."

EXPERIMENTER: Excuse me, Teacher. We'll have to discontinue the experiment.

(*Enter Milgram from camera's left. He has been watching from behind one-way glass.*)

MILGRAM: I'd like to ask you a few questions. (*Slowly, patiently, he dehoaxes the teacher, telling him that the shocks and screams were not real.*)

TEACHER: You mean he wasn't getting nothing? Well, I'm glad to hear that. I was getting upset there. I was getting ready to walk out.

(*Finally, to make sure there are no hard feelings, friendly, harmless Mr. Wallace comes out in coat and tie. Gives jovial greeting. Friendly reconciliation takes place. Experiment ends.*)

Subjects in the experiment were not asked to give the 450-volt shock more than three times. By that time, it seemed evident that they would go on indefinitely. "No one," says Milgram, "who got within five shocks of the end ever broke off. By that point, he had resolved the conflict."

Why do so many people resolve the conflict in favor of obedience?

Milgram's theory assumes that people behave in two different operating modes as different as ice and water. He does not rely on Freud or sex or toilet-training hang-ups for this theory. All he says is that ordinarily we operate in a state of autonomy, which means we pretty much have and assert control over what we do. But in certain circumstances, we operate under what Milgram calls a state of agency (after agent, n . . . one who acts for or in the place of another by authority from him; a substitute; a deputy. —*Webster's Collegiate Dictionary*). A state of agency, to Milgram, is nothing more than a frame of mind.

"There's nothing bad about it, there's nothing good about it," he says. "It's a natural circumstance of living with other people. . . . I think of a state of agency as a real transformation of a person: if a person has different properties when he's in that state, just as water can turn to ice under certain conditions of temperature, a person can move to the state of mind that I call agency . . . the critical thing is that you see yourself as the instrument of the execution of another person's wishes. You do not see yourself as acting on your own. And there's a real transformation, a real change of properties of the person."

To achieve this change, you have to be in a situation where there seems to be a ruling authority whose commands are relevant to some legitimate purpose; the authority's power is not unlimited.

But situations can be and have been structured to make people do unusual things, and not just in Milgram's laboratory. The reason, says Milgram, is that no action, in and of itself, contains meaning.

"The meaning always depends on your definition of the situation. Take an action like killing another person. It sounds bad.

"But then we say the other person was about to destroy a hundred children, and the only way to stop him was to kill him. Well, that sounds good.

"Or, you take destroying your own life. It sounds very bad. Yet, in the Second World War, thousands of persons thought it was a good thing to destroy your own life. It was set in the proper context. You sipped some saki from a whistling cup, recited a few haiku. You said 'May my death be as clean and as quick as the shattering of crystal.' And it almost seemed like a good, noble thing to do, to crash your kamikaze plane into an aircraft carrier. But the main thing was, the definition of what a kamikaze pilot was doing had been determined by the relevant authority. Now, once you are in a state of agency, you allow the authority to determine, to define what the situation is. The meaning of your action is altered."

So, for most subjects in Milgram's laboratory experiments, the act of giving Mr. Wallace his painful shock was necessary, even though unpleasant, and besides they were doing it on behalf of somebody else and it was for science. There was still strain and conflict, of course. Most people resolved it by grimly sticking to their task and obeying. But some broke out. Milgram tried varying the conditions of the experiment to see what would help break people out of their state of agency.

"The results, as seen and felt in the laboratory," he has written, "are disturbing. They raise the possibility that human nature, or more specifically the kind of character produced in American democratic society, cannot be counted on to insulate its citizens from brutality and inhumane treatment at the direction of malevolent authority. A substantial proportion of people do what they are told to do, irrespective of the content of the act and without limitations of conscience, so long as they perceive that the command comes from a legitimate authority. If, in this study, an anonymous experimenter can successfully command adults to subdue a fifty-year-old man and force on him painful electric shocks against his protest, one can only wonder what government, with its vastly greater authority and prestige, can command of its subjects."

This is a nice statement, but it falls short of summing up the full meaning of Mil-gram's work. It leaves some questions still unanswered.

The first question is this: Should we really be surprised and alarmed that people obey? Wouldn't it be even more alarming if they all refused to obey? Without obedience to a relevant ruling authority there could not be a civil society. And without a civil society, as Thomas Hobbs pointed out in the seventeenth century, we would live in a condition of war, "of every man against every other man," and life would be "solitary, poor, nasty, brutish and short."

In the middle of one of Stanley Milgram's lectures at C.U.N.Y. recently, some mini-skirted undergraduates started whispering and giggling in the back of the room. He told them to cut it out. Since he was the relevant authority in that time and that place, they obeyed, and most people in the room were glad that they obeyed.

This was not, of course, a conflict situation. Nothing in the coeds' social upbringing made it a matter of conscience for them to whisper and giggle. But a case can be made that in a conflict situation it is all the more important to obey. Take the case of war, for example. Would we really want a situation in which every participant in a war, direct or indirect—from front-line soldiers to the people who sell coffee and cigarettes to employees at the Concertina barbed-wire factory in Kansas—stops and consults his conscience before each action. It is asking for an awful lot of mental strain and anguish from an awful lot of people. The value of having civil order is that one can do his duty, or whatever interests him, or whatever seems to benefit him at the moment, and leave the agonizing to others. When Francis Gary Powers was being tried by a Soviet military tribunal after his U-2 spy plane was shot down, the presiding judge asked if he had thought about the possibility that his flight might have provoked a war. Powers replied with Hobbesian clarity: "The people who sent me should think of these things. My job was to carry out orders.

I do not think it was my responsibility to make such decisions."

It was not his responsibility. And it is quite possible that if everyone felt responsible for each of the ultimate consequences of his own tiny contributions to complex chains of events, then society simply would not work. Milgram, fully conscious of the moral and social implications of his research, believes that people should feel responsible for their actions. If someone else had invented the experiment, and if he had been the naïve subject, he feels certain that he would have been among the disobedient minority.

"There is no very good solution to this," he admits, thoughtfully. "To simply and categorically say that you won't obey authority may resolve your personal conflict, but it creates more problems for society which may be more serious in the long run. But I have no doubt that to disobey is the proper thing to do in this [the laboratory] situation. It is the only reasonable value judgment to make."

The conflict between the need to obey the relevant ruling authority and the need to follow your conscience becomes sharpest if you insist on living by an ethical system based on a rigid code—a code that seeks to answer all questions in advance of their being raised. Code ethics cannot solve the obedience problem. Stanley Milgram seems to be a situation ethicist, and situation ethics does offer a way out: When you feel conflict, you examine the situation and then make a choice among the competing evils. You may act with a presumption in favor of obedience, but reserve the possibility that you will disobey whenever obedience demands a flagrant and outrageous affront to conscience. This, by the way, is the philosophical position of many who resist the draft. In World War II, they would have fought. Vietnam is a different, an outrageously different, situation.

Life can be difficult for the situation ethicist, because he does not see the world in straight lines, while the social system too often assumes such a God-given, squared-off structure. If your moral code includes an injunction against all war, you may be deferred as a conscientious objector. If you merely oppose this particular war, you may not be deferred.

Stanley Milgram has his problems, too. He believes that in the laboratory situation, he would not have shocked Mr. Wallace. His professional critics reply that in his real-life situation he has done the equivalent. He has placed innocent and naïve subjects under great emotional strain and pressure in selfish obedience to his quest for knowledge. When you raise this issue with Milgram, he has an answer ready. There is, he explains patiently, a critical difference between his naïve subjects and the man in the electric chair. The man in the electric chair (in the mind of the naïve subject) is helpless, strapped in. But the naïve subject is free to go at any time.

Immediately after he offers this distinction, Milgram anticipates the objection.

"It's quite true," he says, "that this is almost a philosophic position, because we have learned that some people are psychologically incapable of disengaging themselves. But that doesn't relieve them of the moral responsibility."

The parallel is exquisite. "The tension problem was unexpected," says Milgram in his defense. But he went on anyway. The naïve subjects didn't expect the screaming protests from the strapped-in learner. But they went on.

"I had to make a judgment," says Milgram. "I had to ask myself, was this harming the person or not? My judgment is that it was not. Even in the extreme cases, I wouldn't say that permanent damage results."

Sound familiar? "The shocks may be painful," the experimenter kept saying, "but they're not dangerous."

After the series of experiments was completed, Milgram sent a report of the results to his subjects and a questionnaire, asking whether they were glad or sorry to have been in the experiment. Eighty-three and seven-tenths percent said they were glad and only 1.3 percent were sorry; 15 percent were neither sorry nor glad. However, Milgram could not be sure at the time of the experiment that only 1.3 percent would be sorry.

Kurt Vonnegut Jr. put one paragraph in the preface to *Mother Night*, in 1966, which pretty much says it for the people with their fingers on the shock-generator switches, for you and me, and maybe even for Milgram. "If I'd been born in Germany," Vonnegut said, "I suppose I would have *been* a Nazi, bopping Jews and gypsies and Poles around, leaving boots stick-ing out of snowbanks, warming myself with my sweetly virtuous insides. So it goes."

Just so. One thing that happened to Milgram back in New Haven during the days of the experiment was that he kept running into people he'd watched from behind the one-way glass. It gave him a funny feeling, seeing those people going about their everyday business in New Haven and knowing what they would do to Mr. Wallace if ordered to. Now that his research results are in and you've thought about it, you can get this funny feeling too. You don't need one-way glass. A glance in your own mirror may serve just as well.

Questions

1. Ultimately, Milgram conducted this experiment with thousands of individuals from all walks of life. One series of experiments involved the use of women in the teacher role. Milgram notes that their performance was "virtually identical to the performance of men," although women experienced a higher level of conflict than men did. One variation that Milgram did not attempt was using women as "learners." What effect might this have had on, say, male teachers' performance?

2. In your judgment, if the technician ("Jack Williams") had been female, would this have changed the outcome of the experiment? Why or why not?

3. Milgram has been criticized for being unethical in conducting this research. Why? How did he respond to these criticisms? Are you more persuaded by Milgram or by his critics? Why?

4. Meyer implies that Milgram's motives were something other than purely scientific—that his decision was in part a "moral one," "colored by his own Jewish background." Did Milgram's moral convictions lead him to invalid findings? Why or why not?

5. Elsewhere, Milgram wrote this:

   The problem of obedience, therefore, is not wholly psychological. The form and shape of society and the way it is developed have much to do with it. There was a time, perhaps, when men were able to give a fully human response to any situation because they were fully absorbed in it as human beings. But as soon as there was a division of labor among men, things changed. Beyond a certain point, the breaking up of society into people carrying out narrow and very special jobs takes away from the human quality of work and life. A person does not get to see the whole situation but only a small part of it, and is thus unable to act without some kind of over-all direction. He yields to authority but in so doing is alienated [separated] from his own actions. (Milgram, *Obedience to Authority* [New York: Harper & Row, 1975], p. 11)

   Do you agree or disagree with Milgram? Why?

·8·

Queer Customs

Clyde Kluckhohn

Clyde K. M. Kluckhohn (1905–1960) was born in Iowa, and studied anthropology at Princeton, Wisconsin, Vienna, and Oxford universities. In 1935, Kluckhohn accepted a position at Harvard University, where he stayed for the remainder of his career. Kluckhohn's particular area of expertise was the Navajo. The following essay is excerpted from his book *Mirror for Man*, which Kluckhohn wrote in order to explain cultural theory to the lay public.

Why do the Chinese dislike milk and milk products? Why would the Japanese die willingly in a Banzai[1] charge that seemed senseless to Americans? Why do some nations trace descent through the father, others through the mother, still others through both parents? Not because different peoples have different instincts, not because they were destined by God or Fate to different habits, not because the weather is different in China and Japan and the United States. Sometimes shrewd common sense has an answer that is close to that of the anthropologist: "because they were brought up that way." By "culture" anthropology means the total life way of a people, the social legacy the individual acquires from his group. Or culture can be regarded as that part of the environment that is the creation of man.

This technical term has a wider meaning than the "culture" of history and literature. A humble cooking pot is as much a cultural product as is a Beethoven sonata. In ordinary speech a man of culture is a man who can speak languages other than his own, who is familiar with history, literature, philosophy, or the fine arts. In some cliques that definition is still narrower. The cultured person is one who can talk about James Joyce, Scarlatti, and Picasso.[2] To the anthropologist, however, to be human is to be cultured. There is culture in general, and then there are the specific cultures such as Russian, American, British, Hottentot,[3] Inca. The general abstract notion serves to remind us that we cannot explain acts solely in terms of the biological properties of the people concerned, their individual past experience, and the immediate situation. The past experience of other men in the form of culture enters into almost every event. Each specific culture constitutes a kind of blueprint for all of life's activities.

One of the interesting things about human beings is that they try to understand themselves and their own behavior. While this has

---

[1] Banzai is a Japanese war cry. — Ed.

[2] So, are you a cultured person by this definition? James Joyce (1882–1941) was an Irish author. His best-known book *Ulysses,* was a novel about a day in Dublin (June 4, 1904). It was published in Paris in 1922 but was banned in the United States until 1937. Alessandro Scarlatti (1660–1725) was a Sicilian composer noted mostly for his operas. Pablo Picasso (1881–1973) was a prolific artist. Born in Spain (in Málaga), he spent much of his life in France. During his lifetime, he created more than 50,000 works — drawings, paintings, sculptures, and even ceramics and lithographs. — Ed.

[3] More properly called the *Khoikhoi* — a people mostly of Namibia, Africa. Nomadic and pastoral, their numbers were decimated by Dutch colonists in the seventeenth and eighteenth centuries — Ed.

been particularly true of Europeans in recent times, there is no group which has not developed a scheme or schemes to explain man's actions. To the insistent human query "why?" the most exciting illumination anthropology has to offer is that of the concept of culture. Its explanatory importance is comparable to categories such as evolution in biology, gravity in physics, disease in medicine. A good deal of human behavior can be understood, and indeed predicted, if we know a people's design for living. Many acts are neither accidental nor due to personal peculiarities nor caused by supernatural forces nor simply mysterious. Even those of us who pride ourselves on our individualism follow most of the time a pattern not of our own making. We brush our teeth on arising. We put on pants—not a loincloth or a grass skirt. We eat three meals a day—not four or five or two. We sleep in a bed—not in a hammock or on a sheep pelt. I do not have to know the individual and his life history to be able to predict these and countless other regularities, including many in the thinking process, of all Americans who are not incarcerated in jails or hospitals for the insane.

To the American woman a system of plural wives seems "instinctively" abhorrent. She cannot understand how any woman can fail to be jealous and uncomfortable if she must share her husband with other women. She feels it "unnatural" to accept such a situation. On the other hand, a Koryak woman of Siberia, for example, would find it hard to understand how a woman could be so selfish and so undesirous of feminine companionship in the home as to wish to restrict her husband to one mate.

Some years ago I met in New York City a young man who did not speak a word of English and was obviously bewildered by American ways. By "blood" he was as American as you or I, for his parents had gone from Indiana to China as missionaries. Orphaned in infancy, he was reared by a Chinese family in a remote village. All who met him found him more Chi-

nese than American. The facts of his blue eyes and light hair were less impressive than a Chinese style of gait, Chinese arm and hand movements, Chinese facial expression, and Chinese modes of thought. The biological heritage was American, but the cultural training had been Chinese. He returned to China.

Another example of another kind: I once knew a trader's wife in Arizona who took a somewhat devilish interest in producing a cultural reaction. Guests who came her way were often served delicious sandwiches filled with a meat that seemed to be neither chicken nor tuna fish yet was reminiscent of both. To queries she gave no reply until each had eaten his fill. She then explained that what they had eaten was not chicken, not tuna fish, but the rich, white flesh of freshly killed rattlesnakes. The response was instantaneous—vomiting, often violent vomiting. A biological process is caught in a cultural web.

A highly intelligent teacher with long and successful experience in the public schools of Chicago was finishing her first year in an Indian school. When asked how her Navaho pupils compared in intelligence with Chicago youngsters, she replied, "Well, I just don't know. Sometimes the Indians seem just as bright. At other times they just act like dumb animals. The other night we had a dance in the high school. I saw a boy who is one of the best students in my English class standing off by himself. So I took him over to a pretty girl and told them to dance. But they just stood there with their heads down. They wouldn't even say anything." I inquired if she knew whether or not they were members of the same clan. "What difference would that make?"

"How would you feel about getting into bed with your brother?" The teacher walked off in a huff, but, actually, the two cases were quite comparable in principle. To the Indian the type of bodily contact involved in our social dancing has a directly sexual connotation. The incest taboos between members of the

same clan are as severe as between true brothers and sisters. The shame of the Indians at
the suggestion that a clan brother and sister
should dance and the indignation of the white
teacher at the idea that she should share a
bed with an adult brother represent equally
nonrational responses, culturally standardized
unreason. . . .

Culture and Society

Since culture is an abstraction, it is important
not to confuse culture with society. A "society"
refers to a group of people who interact more
with each other than they do with other individuals — who cooperate with each other for
the attainment of certain ends. You can see and
indeed count the individuals who make up a
society. A "culture" refers to the distinctive
ways of life of such a group of people. Not all
social events are culturally patterned. New
types of circumstances arise for which no cultural solutions have as yet been devised.

A culture constitutes a storehouse of the
pooled learning of the group. A rabbit starts
life with some innate responses. He can learn
from his own experience and perhaps from observing other rabbits. A human infant is born
with fewer instincts and greater plasticity. His
main task is to learn the answers that persons
he will never see, persons long dead, have
worked out. Once he has learned the formulas
supplied by the culture of his group, most of
his behavior becomes almost as automatic and
unthinking as if it were instinctive. There is a
tremendous amount of intelligence behind the
making of a radio, but not much is required to
learn to turn it on.

The members of all human societies face
some of the same unavoidable dilemmas,
posed by biology and other facts of the human
situation. This is why the basic categories of all
cultures are so similar. Human culture without
language is unthinkable. No culture fails to

provide for aesthetic expression and aesthetic
delight. Every culture supplies standardized
orientations toward the deeper problems, such
as death. Every culture is designed to perpetuate the group and its solidarity, to meet the demands of individuals for an orderly way of life
and for satisfaction of biological needs.

However, the variations on these basic
themes are numberless. Some languages are
built up out of twenty basic sounds, others out
of forty. Nose plugs were considered beautiful
by the predynastic Egyptians but are not by the
modern French. Puberty is a biological fact. But
one culture ignores it, another prescribes informal instructions about sex but no ceremony, a
third has impressive rites for girls only, a fourth
for boys and girls. In this culture, the first men-
struation is welcomed as a happy, natural
event; in that culture the atmosphere is full of
dread and supernatural threat. Each culture
dissects nature according to its own system of
categories. The Navaho Indians apply the same
word to the color of a robin's egg and to that of
grass. A psychologist once assumed that this
meant a difference in the sense organs, that
Navahos didn't have the physiological equipment to distinguish "green" from "blue." However, when he showed them objects of the two
colors and asked them if they were exactly the
same colors, they looked at him with astonishment. His dream of discovering a new type of
color blindness was shattered.

Every culture must deal with the sexual instinct. Some, however, seek to deny all sexual
expression before marriage, whereas a Polyne-
sian adolescent who was not promiscuous
would be distinctly abnormal. Some cultures
enforce lifelong monogamy, others, like our
own, tolerate serial monogamy; in still other
cultures, two or more women may be joined to
one man or several men to a single woman.
Homosexuality has been a permitted pattern
in the Greco-Roman world, in parts of Islam,
and in various primitive tribes. Large portions
of the population of Tibet, and of Christendom

at some places and periods, have practiced completely celibacy. To us marriage is first and foremost an arrangement between two individuals. In many more societies marriage is merely one facet of a complicated set of reciprocities, economic and otherwise, between two families or two clans.

The essence of the cultural process is selectivity. The selection is only exceptionally conscious and rational. Cultures are like Topsy. They just grew.[4] Once, however, a way of handling a situation becomes institutionalized, there is ordinarily great resistance to change or deviation. When we speak of "our sacred beliefs," we mean of course that they are beyond criticism and that the person who suggests modification or abandonment must be punished. No person is emotionally indifferent to his culture. Certain cultural premises may become totally out of accord with a new factual situation. Leaders may recognize this and reject the old ways in theory. Yet their emotional loyalty continues in the face of reason because of the intimate conditionings of early childhood.

A culture is learned by individuals as the result of belonging to some particular group, and it constitutes that part of learned behavior which is shared with others. It is our social legacy, as contrasted with our organic heredity. It is one of the important factors which permits us to live together in an organized society, giving us ready-made solutions to our problems, helping us to predict the behavior of others, and permitting others to know what to expect of us.

Culture regulates our lives at every turn. From the moment we are born until we die there is, whether we are conscious of it or not, constant pressure upon us to follow certain types of behavior that other men have created for us. Some paths we follow willingly, others we follow because we know no other way, still others we deviate from or go back to most unwillingly. Mothers of small children know how unnaturally most of this comes to us—how little regard we have, until we are "culturalized," for the "proper" place, time, and manner for certain acts such as eating, excreting, sleeping, getting dirty, and making loud noises. But by more or less adhering to a system of related designs for carrying out all the acts of living, a group of men and women feel themselves linked together by a powerful chain of sentiments. Ruth Benedict gave an almost complete definition of the concept when she said, "Culture is that which binds men together." . . .

No participant in any culture knows all the details of the cultural map. The statement frequently heard that St. Thomas Aquinas was the last man to master all the knowledge of his society is intrinsically absurd. St. Thomas would have been hard put to make a pane of cathedral glass or to act as a mid-wife. In every culture there are what Ralph Linton has called "universals, alternatives, and specialties." Every Christian in the thirteenth century knew that it was necessary to attend mass, to go to confession, to ask the Mother of God to intercede with her Son. There were many other universals in the Christian culture of Western Europe. However, there were also alternative cultural patterns even in the realm of religion. Each individual had his own patron saint, and different towns developed the cults of different saints. The thirteenth-century anthropologist could have discovered the rudi-

---

[4]To grow like Topsy means to flourish without being purposefully tended. The roots of this odd-sounding expression are to be found in *Uncle Tom's Cabin,* by Harriet Beecher Stowe. In 1850, the Congress enacted a Fugitive Slave Act which required the return of runaway slaves who fled to states where slavery had been abolished. Beecher Stowe's novel was written in a protest against this law and slavery in general. The character Topsy was a young slave girl of about eight or nine years old. Purchased from an abusive family, Topsy is brought to New England to be raised by the pious Ophelia St. Clare. Asked by Miss Ophelia how old she is, Topsy says she has no idea: Another slave explains to Miss Ophelia that it is common practice in the South for speculators to purchase black infants and raise them for the slave market. When queried about her parents, Topsy says, "I spect I growed. Don't think nobody never made me."

ments of Christian practice by questioning and observing whomever he happened to meet in Germany, France, Italy, or England. But to find out the details of the ceremonials honoring St. Hubert or St. Bridget he would have had to seek out certain individuals or special localities where these alternative patterns were practiced. Similarly, he could not learn about weaving from a professional soldier or about canon law from a farmer. Such cultural knowledge belongs in the realm of the specialties, voluntarily chosen by the individual or ascribed to him by birth. Thus, part of a culture must be learned by everyone, part may be selected from alternative patterns, part applies only to those who perform the roles in the society for which these patterns are designed.

Many aspects of a culture are explicit. The explicit culture consists in those regularities in word and deed that may be generalized straight from the evidence of the ear and the eye. The recognition of these is like the recognition of style in the art of a particular place and epoch. If we have examined twenty specimens of the wooden saints' images made in the Taos valley of New Mexico in the late eighteenth century, we can predict that any new images from the same locality and period will in most respects exhibit the same techniques of carving, about the same use of colors and choice of woods, a similar quality of artistic conception. Similarly, if, in a society of 2,000 members, we record 100 marriages at random and find that in 30 cases a man has married the sister of his brother's wife, we can anticipate that an additional sample of 100 marriages will show roughly the same number of cases of this pattern.

The above is an instance of what anthropologists call a behavioral pattern, the practices as opposed to the rules of the culture. There are also, however, regularities in what people say they do or should do. They do tend in fact to prefer to marry into a family already connected with their own by marriage, but this is not necessarily part of the official code of conduct. No disapproval whatsoever is attached to those who make another sort of marriage. On the other hand, it is explicitly forbidden to marry a member of one's own clan even though no biological relationship is traceable. This is a regulatory pattern—a Thou Shalt or a Thou Shalt Not. Such patterns may be violated often, but their existence is nevertheless important. A people's standards for conduct and belief define the socially approved aims and the acceptable means of attaining them. When the discrepancy between the theory and the practice of a culture is exceptionally great, this indicates that the culture is undergoing rapid change. It does not prove that ideals are unimportant, for ideals are but one of a number of factors determining action.

Cultures do not manifest themselves solely in observable customs and artifacts. No amount of questioning of any save the most articulate in the most self-conscious cultures will bring out some of the basic attitudes common to the members of the group. This is because these basic assumptions are taken so for granted that they normally do not enter into consciousness. This part of the cultural map must be inferred by the observer on the basis of consistencies in thought and action. Missionaries in various societies are often disturbed or puzzled because the natives do not regard "morals" and "sex code" as almost synonymous. The natives seem to feel that morals are concerned with sex just about as much as with eating—no less and no more. No society fails to have some restrictions on sexual behavior, but sex activity outside of marriage need not necessarily be furtive or attended with guilt. The Christian tradition has tended to assume that sex is inherently nasty as well as dangerous. Other cultures assume that sex in itself is not only natural but one of the good things of life, even though sex acts with certain persons under certain circumstances are forbidden.

This is implicit culture, for the natives do not announce their premises. The missionaries would get further if they said, in effect, "Look, our morality starts from different assumptions. Let's talk about those assumptions," rather than ranting about "immorality." . . .

In our highly self-conscious Western civilization that has recently made a business of studying itself, the number of assumptions that are literally implicit, in the sense of never having been stated or discussed by anyone, may be negligible. Yet only a trifling number of Americans could state even those implicit premises of our culture that have been brought to light by anthropologists. If one could bring to the American scene a Bushman who had been socialized in his own culture and then trained in anthropology, he would perceive all sorts of patterned regularities of which our anthropologists are completely unaware. In the case of the less sophisticated and less self-conscious societies, the unconscious assumptions characteristically made by individuals brought up under approximately the same social controls bulk even larger. But in any society, as Edward Sapir said, "Forms and significances which seem obvious to an outsider will be denied outright by those who carry out the patterns; outlines and implications that are perfectly clear to these may be absent to the eye of the onlooker." . . .

Questions

1. According to Kluckhohn, what is the difference between culture and society? (Many people improperly use these terms interchangeably, but now that you know the difference you can avoid that error.)

2. What does Kluckhohn mean by the phrase "culturally standardized unreason"? Can you think of any examples of this sort of unreason from your own culture?

3. What does Kluckhohn mean by the concept of "behavioral pattern"? What is a "regulatory pattern"? Give a couple of examples from your own culture of instances in which behavioral and regulatory patterns are consistent. Then, give examples from your own culture in which behavioral and regulatory patterns are inconsistent. (Which was harder to do — to find examples of consistency or of inconsistency between behavioral patterns and regulatory patterns? Why do you think this is?)

·9·

Hidden Culture

Edward T. Hall

Edward T. Hall is an anthropologist best known for his work on intercultural communication. Hall maintains that humanity's survival depends, in large part, on people's ability to communicate across cultures. Standing in the way of successful communication, he suggests, is a lack of understanding of how our culture conditions us.

... I can think of few countries Americans are likely to visit and work in in significant numbers where it is more difficult to control one's inputs and where life is more filled with surprises than Japan. Clearly, the above observation does not apply to short visits and the like, because all over the world suitable environments have been created for tourists that shield them from the reality of the life of the people. Tourists seldom stick around for long, and they are happier insulated from the full impact of the foreign culture. Businessmen, educators, government officials, and Foreign Service personnel are something else again. It is to this group that my thoughts are directed, because they stand to gain the most from understanding cultural processes in living contexts. Understanding the reality of covert culture and accepting it on a gut level comes neither quickly nor easily, and it must be lived rather than read or reasoned. However, there are times when examples of what is experienced most intimately can illustrate certain basic patterns that are widely shared. The events described below are taken from my own experiences in Japan and with the Japanese in other countries, and are designed not only to illustrate differences between cultures but to provide a natural history of insights into the contexting process. For no matter how well prepared one is intellectually for immersion in another culture, there is the inevitability of surprises.

A few years ago, I became involved in a sequence of events in Japan that completely mystified me, and only later did I learn how an overt act seen from the vantage point of one's own culture can have an entirely different meaning when looked at in the context of the foreign culture. I had been staying at a hotel in downtown Tokyo that had European as well as Japanese-type rooms. The clientele included a few Europeans but was predominantly Japanese. I had been a guest for about ten days and was returning to my room in the middle of an afternoon. Asking for my key at the desk, I took the elevator to my floor. Entering the room, I immediately sensed that something was wrong. Out of place. Different. I was in the wrong room! Someone else's things were distributed around the head of the bed and the table. Somebody else's toilet articles (those of a Japanese male) were in the bathroom. My first thoughts were, "What if I am discovered here? How do I explain my presence to a Japanese who may not even speak English?"

I was close to panic as I realized how incredibly territorial we in the West are. I checked my key again. Yes, it really was mine. Clearly they had moved somebody else into my room. But where was my room now? And where were my belongings? Baffled and mystified, I took the elevator to the lobby. Why hadn't they told me at the desk, instead of letting me risk embarrassment and loss of face by being caught in somebody else's room? Why had they moved me in the first place? It was a nice room and, being sensitive to spaces and how they work, I was loath to give it up. After all, I had told them I would be in the hotel for almost a month. Why this business of moving me around like someone who has been squeezed in without a reservation? Nothing made sense.

At the desk I was told by the clerk, as he sucked in his breath in deference (and embarrassment?) that indeed they had moved me. My particular room had been reserved in advance by somebody else. I was given the key to my new room and discovered that all my personal effects were distributed around the new room almost as though I had done it myself. This produced a fleeting and strange feeling that maybe I wasn't myself. How could somebody else do all those hundred and one little things just the way I did?

Three days later, I was moved again, but this time I was prepared. There was no shock, just the simple realization that I had been moved and that it would now be doubly difficult for friends who had my old room number to reach me. *Tant pis,*[1] I was in Japan. One thing did puzzle me. Earlier, when I had stayed at Frank Lloyd Wright's Imperial Hotel for several weeks, nothing like this had ever happened. What was different? What had changed? Eventually I got used to being moved and would even ask on my return each day whether I was still in the same room. . . .

[Later] we visited Kyoto, site of many famous temples and palaces, and the ancient capital of Japan. There we were fortunate enough to stay in a wonderful little country inn on the side of a hill overlooking the town. Kyoto is much more traditional and less indus-

trialized than Tokyo. After we had been there about a week and had thoroughly settled into our new Japanese surroundings, we returned one night to be met at the door by an apologetic manager who was stammering something. I knew immediately that we had been moved, so I said, "You had to move us. Please don't let this bother you, because we understand. Just show us to our new rooms and it will be all right." Our interpreter explained as we started to go through the door that we weren't in that hotel any longer but had been moved to *another* hotel. What a blow! Again, without warning. We wondered what the new hotel would be like, and with our descent into the town our hearts sank further. Finally, when we could descend no more, the taxi took off into a part of the city we hadn't seen before. No Europeans here! The streets got narrower and narrower until we turned into a side street that could barely accommodate the tiny Japanese taxi into which we were squeezed. Clearly this was a hotel of another class. I found that, by then, I was getting a little paranoid, which is easy enough to do in a foreign land, and said to myself, "They must think we are very low-status people indeed to treat us this way."

As it turned out, the neighborhood, in fact the whole district, showed us an entirely different side of life from what we had seen before, much more interesting and authentic. True, we did have some communication problems, because no one was used to dealing with foreigners, but few of them were serious.

Yet, the whole matter of being moved like a piece of derelict luggage puzzled me. In the United States, the person who gets moved is often the lowest-ranking individual. This principle applies to all organizations, including the Army. Whether you can be moved or not is a function of your status, your performance, and your value to the organization. To move someone without telling him is almost worse than an insult, because it means he is below the point at which feelings matter. In these circumstances,

---

[1] *Tant pis* is a French expression meaning "so much the worse." —Ed.

moves can be unsettling and damaging to the ego. In addition, moves themselves are often accompanied by great anxiety, whether an entire organization or a small part of an organization moves. What makes people anxious is that the move usually presages organizational changes that have been co-ordinated with the move. Naturally, everyone wants to see how he comes out vis-à-vis everyone else. I have seen important men refuse to move into an office that was six inches smaller than someone else's of the same rank. While I have heard some American executives say they wouldn't employ such a person, the fact is that in actual practice, unless there is some compensating feature, the significance of space as a communication is so powerful that no employee in his right mind would allow his boss to give him a spatial demotion — unless of course he had already reached his crest and was on the way down.

These spatial messages are not simply conventions in the United States — unless you consider the size of your salary check a mere convention, or where your name appears on the masthead of a journal. Ranking is seldom a matter that people take lightly, particularly in a highly mobile society like that in the United States. Each culture and each country has its own language of space, which is just as unique as the spoken language, frequently more so. In England, for example, there are no offices for the members of Parliament. In the United States, our congressmen and senators proliferate their offices and their office buildings and simply would not tolerate a no-office situation. Constituents, associates, colleagues, and lobbyists would not respond properly. In England, status is internalized; it has its manifestations and markers — the upper-class English accent, for example. We in the United States, a relatively new country, externalize status. The American in England has some trouble placing people in the social system, while the English can place each other quite accurately by reading ranking cues, but in general tend to look down on the importance that Americans attach to space. It is very easy and very natural to look at things from one's own point of view and to read an event as though it were the same all over the world.

I knew that my emotions on being moved out of my room in Tokyo were of the gut type and quite strong. There was nothing intellectual about my initial response. Although I am a professional observer of cultural patterns, I had no notion of the meaning attached to being moved from hotel to hotel in Kyoto. I was well aware of the strong significance of moving in my own culture, going back to the time when the new baby displaces older children, right up to the world of business, where a complex dance is performed every time the organization moves to new quarters.

. . . In Japan as I rode up and down in the elevators with various keys gripped in my hand, . . . I did have to put up a strong fight with myself to keep from interpreting what was going on as though the Japanese were the same as I. This is the conventional and most common response and one that is often found even among anthropologists. Any time you hear someone say, "Why, *they* are no different than the folks back home — they are just like I am," even though you may understand the reasons behind these remarks you also know that the speaker is living in a single-context world (his own) and is incapable of describing either his world or the foreign one.

The "they are just like the folks back home" syndrome is one of the most persistent and widely held misconceptions of the Western world, if not the whole world. There is very little any outsider can do about this, because it expresses views that are very close to the core of the personality. Simply talking about "cultural differences" and how we must respect them is a hollow cliché. And in fact, intellectualizing isn't much more helpful either, at least at first. The logic of the man who won't move into an office that is six inches smaller than his rival's is *cultural* logic; it works at a lower, more basic level in the brain, a part of the brain that synthesizes but does not verbalize. The response is a total response that is difficult to explain to someone who doesn't already understand, because it is so dependent on context for a correct interpretation. To do so, one must explain the entire system; otherwise, the man's behavior makes little sense. He may even appear to be acting childishly—which he most definitely is not.

It was my preoccupation with my own cultural mold that explained why I was puzzled for years about the significance of being moved around in Japanese hotels. The answer finally came after further experiences in Japan and many discussions with Japanese friends. In Japan, one has to "belong" or he has no identity. When a man joins a company, he does just that—joins himself to the corporate body —and there is even a ceremony marking the occasion. Normally, he is hired for life, and the company plays a much more paternalistic role than in the United States. There are company songs, and the whole company meets frequently (usually at least once a week) for purposes of maintaining corporate identity and morale. . . .

. . . The answer to my puzzle was revealed when a Japanese friend explained what it means to be a guest in a hotel. As soon as you register at the desk, you are no longer an outsider; instead, for the duration of your stay you are a member of a large, mobile family. *You belong.* The fact that I was moved was tangible evidence that I was being treated as a family member—a relationship in which one can afford to be "relaxed and informal and not stand on ceremony." This is a very highly prized state in Japan, which offsets the official properness that is so common in public. Instead of putting me down, they were treating me as a member of the family. Needless to say, the large, luxury hotels that cater to Americans, like Wright's Imperial Hotel, have discovered that Ameri-

cans do tenaciously stand on ceremony and want to be treated as they are at home in the States. Americans don't like to be moved around; it makes them anxious. Therefore, the Japanese in these establishments have learned not to treat them as family members.

While there are a few rare individuals who move along in the current of life looking around with innocent wonder regardless of what happens to them, most of mankind are not that relaxed. The majority are like men on a raft tossed about in a turbulent sea, who get only an occasional orienting glimpse of surrounding landmarks.

In the United States, the concern of the large middle class is to move ahead in the system, whichever part of it we happen to be in. With perhaps the exception of the younger generation just now entering the job market, we are very tied to our jobs. In fact, the more successful a man or a woman is, the more likely his or her life will revolve around a job to which home and personal relations assume secondary importance. We are only peripherally tied to the lives of others. It takes a long, long time for us to become deeply involved with others, and for some this never happens.

In Japan, life is a very different story, one that is puzzling in the extreme to Americans who interact regularly with the Japanese. Their culture seems to be full of paradoxes. When they communicate, particularly about important things, it is often in a roundabout way (indirection is a word that one hears often in the foreign colony). All of this points to a very high-context approach to life; yet, on the other hand, there are times when they swing in the opposite direction and move to the lower end of the context scale, where nothing can be taken for granted—"Be sure to put *brown* polish on the shoes." This was discovered by American GI's during the occupation. Years later, I had occasion to send some film to Japan for processing and was told to be *sure* to tell them everything I wanted done, because if

I left anything out it would be my fault. Weeks later, after having provided what I thought was a set of instructions that could be followed by a computer, I got the film back. Everything was as I had requested — exquisite work — except that I had forgotten one thing. I didn't tell them to roll the film up and put it in a little can or to protect it in some way. In the process of mailing, the negatives had been folded and scratched, in fact were useless for any further work. I had run afoul of the low-context side of Japanese life.

[Imagine the diplomat] who refused to practice the Foreign Service language drill and wouldn't learn the honorifics[2] — they were undemocratic! Well, the honorifics perform important functions that go far beyond telling the other person that you acknowledge and respect his position. In many offices, the honorifics are used at the beginning of the day and if things are going well they are gradually dropped, so that at the end of the day one is on a more intimate basis with others. Failure to drop the honorifics is a cue that something is wrong. This, along with a lot of other information, enables us to sketch out some dynamics of Japanese life.

The Japanese are pulled in two directions. The first is a very high-context, deeply involved, enveloping intimacy that begins at home in childhood but is extended far beyond the home. There is a deep need to be close, and it is only when they are close that they are comfortable. The other pole is as far away as one can get. In public and during ceremonial occasions (and there are ceremonies of a sort every day, even when people meet), there is great emphasis on self-control, distance, and hiding inner feelings. Like most of Japanese behavior, attitudes toward showing emotion are deeply rooted in a long past. At the time of the samurai knights and nobles, there was

_____
[2]Honorifics are titles — for example, madam president, Professor Jones, and Ms. Smith. — Ed.

survival value in being able to control one's demeanor, because a samurai could legally execute anyone who displeased him or who wasn't properly respectful. This standing on ceremony extended to all levels; not only was the servant expected to be respectful, but the samurai's wife was to show no emotion when she received the news that her husband or son had been killed in battle. Until very recently, there was no public showing of intimacy or touching in Japan.

Still, on the formal, ceremonial side it is very important for the Japanese to be able to place people in a social system. In fact, it is impossible to interact with someone else if this placing has not occurred, hence the requirement that you state who you are on your calling card — first, the organization you work for, second, your position in that organization, your degrees, honors you have received, followed by the family name, the given name, and address, in that order. . . .

. . . I was eventually able to discern the common thread that connected everything, which began to put Japanese behavior in context. The pattern is one that it is important to understand: In Japan there are the two sides to everyone — his warm, close, friendly, involved, high-context side that does not stand on ceremony, and the public, official, status-conscious, ceremonial side, which is what most foreigners see. From what I understand of Japanese culture, most Japanese feel quite uncomfortable (deep down inside) about the ceremonial, low-context, institutionalized side of life. Their principal drive is to move from the "stand on ceremony" side toward the homey, comfortable, warm, intimate, friendly side. One sees this even at the office and the laboratory, where the honorifics are dropped as the day progresses. By this, I do not mean to imply that the Japanese are not tough businessmen or that they aren't well organized, etc. Anyone who has had anything to do with them can only admire their capacity to get things done. The point is that their drive to be close and get to know other people is very strong — in some cases, more than the detached European is either used to or can stand. The record is very clear on this. Consider their practice of men and women sleeping side by side crowded together on the floor in a single room, and the camaraderie of communal bathing.

The American provides a real contrast. He is inclined to be more oriented toward achieving set goals and less toward developing close human relations. It is difficult for him to understand and act on the basis that once a customer in Japan "has been sold," that is just the beginning. He must be "massaged" regularly; otherwise he goes somewhere else. There are of course many other sides to the Japanese, such as their great dependence on tradition — as well as their group, rather than individual, orientation.

The message [here] is simple on the surface but does depend somewhat on the reader's being already contexted in cross-cultural communication. Two things get in the way of understanding: the linearity of language and the deep biases and built-in blinders that every culture provides. Transcending either is a formidable task. . . .

Questions

1. Why does Hall argue that it is naive (and possibly even dangerous) to believe that "people are just the same all over the world"?

2. Hall contrasts the processes of externalizing and internalizing status. How do the two processes differ? Can you think of any situations in which people in the United States show signs of having internalized status?

3. In the introduction to his book, Hall calls for a massive cultural literacy movement. "We can all benefit from a deeper knowledge of what an incredible organism we are. We can grow, swell with pride, and breathe better for having so many remarkable talents. To do so, however, we must accept that there are many roads to truth and no culture has a corner on the path or is better equipped than others to search for it. Furthermore, no man can tell another how to conduct that search." Do you agree with Hall? Why or why not?

·10·

Body Ritual Among the Nacirema

Horace Miner

The American anthropologist Horace Miner was one of the first to make public the results of anthropological research on the Nacirema. Although in the decades that followed the publication of Miner's work many more studies have been published, none more dramatically reveals the role of myth, magic, and ritual in the lives of this rather exotic group of people.

The anthropologist has become so familiar with the diversity of ways in which different peoples behave in similar situations that he is not apt to be surprised by even the most exotic customs. In fact, if all of the logically possible combinations of behavior have not been found somewhere in the world, he is apt to suspect that they must be present in some as yet undescribed tribe. This point has, in fact, been expressed with respect to clan organization by Murdock (1949, 71). In this light, the magical beliefs and practices of the Nacirema present such unusual aspects that it seems desirable to describe them as an example of the extremes to which human behavior can go.

Professor Linton first brought the ritual of the Nacirema to the attention of anthropologists [sixty] years ago (1936, 326), but the culture of this people is still very poorly understood. They are a North American group living in the territory between the Canadian Cree, the Yaqui and Tarahumare of Mexico, and the Carib and Arawak of the Antilles. Little is known of their origin, although tradition states that they came from the east. According to Nacirema mythology, their nation was originated by a culture hero, Notgnihsaw, who is otherwise known for two great feats of strength—the throwing of a piece of wampum across the river Pa-To-Mac and the chopping down of a cherry tree in which the Spirit of Truth resided.

Nacirema culture is characterized by a highly developed market economy which has evolved in a rich natural habitat. While much of the people's time is devoted to economic pursuits, a large part of the fruits of these labors and a considerable portion of the day are spent in ritual activity. The focus of this activity is the human body, the appearance and health of which loom as a dominant concern in the ethos of the people. While such a concern is certainly not unusual, its ceremonial aspects and associated philosophy are unique.

The fundamental belief underlying the whole system appears to be that the human body is ugly and that its natural tendency is to debility and disease. Incarcerated in such a body, man's only hope is to avert these characteristics through the use of the powerful influences of ritual and ceremony. Every household has one or more shrines devoted to this purpose. The more powerful individuals in the society have several shrines in their houses and, in fact, the opulence of a house is often referred to in terms of the number of such ritual centers it possesses. Most houses are of wattle and daub construction, but the shrine rooms of the more wealthy are walled with stone.

Poorer families imitate the rich by applying pottery plaques to their shrine walls.

While each family has at least one such shrine, the rituals associated with it are not family ceremonies but are private and secret. The rites are normally only discussed with children, and then only during the period when they are being initiated into these mysteries. I was able, however, to establish sufficient rapport with the natives to examine these shrines and to have the rituals described to me.

The focal point of the shrine is a box or chest which is built into the wall. In this chest are kept the many charms and magical potions without which no native believes he could live. These preparations are secured from a variety of specialized practitioners. The most powerful of these are the medicine men, whose assistance must be rewarded with substantial gifts. However, the medicine men do not provide the curative potions for their clients, but decide what the ingredients should be and they write them down in an ancient and secret language. This writing is understood only by the medicine men and by the herbalists who, for another gift, provide the required charm.

The charm is not disposed of after it has served its purpose, but is placed in the charm-box of the household shrine. As these magical materials are specific for certain ills, and the real or imagined maladies of the people are many, the charm-box is usually full to overflowing. The magical packets are so numerous that people forget what their purposes were and fear to use them again. While the natives are very vague on this point, we can only assume that the idea in retaining all the old magical materials is that their presence in the charm-box, before which the body rituals are conducted, will in some way protect the worshipper.

Beneath the charm-box is a small font. Each day every member of the family, in succession, enters the shrine room, bows his head before the charm-box, mingles different sorts of holy water in the font, and proceeds with a brief rite of ablution. The holy waters are secured from the Water Temple of the community, where the priests conduct elaborate ceremonies to make the liquid ritually pure.

In the hierarchy of magical practitioners, and below the medicine men in prestige, are specialists whose designation is best translated "holy-mouth-men." The Nacirema have an almost pathological horror of and fascination with the mouth, the condition of which is believed to have a supernatural influence on all social relationships. Were it not for the rituals of the mouth, they believe that their teeth would fall out, their gums bleed, their jaws shrink, their friends desert them, and their lovers reject them. They also believe that a strong relationship exists between oral and moral characteristics. For example, there is a ritual ablution of the mouth for children which is supposed to improve their moral fiber.

The daily body ritual performed by everyone includes a mouth-rite. Despite the fact that these people are so punctilious about care of the mouth, this rite involves a practice which strikes the uninitiated stranger as revolting. It was reported to me that the ritual consists of inserting a small bundle of hog hairs into the mouth, along with certain magical powders, and then moving the bundle in a highly formalized series of gestures.

In addition to the private mouth-rite, the people seek out a holy-mouth-man once or twice a year. These practitioners have an impressive set of paraphernalia, consisting of a variety of augers, awls, probes, and prods. The use of these objects in the exorcism of the evils of the mouth involves almost unbelievable ritual torture of the client. The holy-mouth-man opens the client's mouth and, using the above mentioned tools, enlarges any holes which decay may have created in the teeth. Magical materials are put into these holes. If there are no naturally occurring holes in the teeth, large sections of one or more teeth are gouged out so that the supernatural substance can be applied. In the client's view, the purpose of these ministrations is to arrest decay and to draw friends. The extremely sacred and traditional character of the rite is evident in the fact that the natives return to the holy-mouth-men year after year, despite the fact that their teeth continue to decay.

It is to be hoped that, when a thorough study of the Nacirema is made, there will be careful inquiry into the personality structure of these people. One has but to watch the gleam in the eye of a holy-mouth-man, as he jabs an awl into an exposed nerve, to suspect that a certain amount of sadism is involved. If this can be established, a very interesting pattern emerges, for most of the population shows definite masochistic tendencies. It was to these that Professor Linton referred in discussing a distinctive part of the daily body ritual which is performed only by men. This part of the rite involves scraping and lacerating the surface of the face with a sharp instrument. Special women's rites are performed only four times during each lunar month, but what they lack in frequency is made up in barbarity. As part of this ceremony, women bake their heads in small ovens for about an hour. The theoretically interesting point is that what seems to be a preponderantly masochistic people have developed sadistic specialists.

The medicine men have an imposing temple, or *latipso,* in every community of any size. The more elaborate ceremonies required to treat very sick patients can only be performed at this temple. These ceremonies involve not only the thaumaturge but a permanent group of vestal maidens who move sedately about the temple chambers in distinctive costume and headdress.

The *latipso* ceremonies are so harsh that it is phenomenal that a fair proportion of the really sick natives who enter the temple ever recover. Small children whose indoctrination is still incomplete have been known to resist attempts to take them to the temple because "that is where you go to die." Despite this fact, sick adults are not only willing but eager to undergo the protracted ritual purification, if they can afford to do so. No matter how ill the supplicant or how grave the emergency, the guardians of many temples will not admit a client if he cannot give a rich gift to the custodian. Even after one has gained admission and survived the ceremonies, the guardians will not permit the neophyte to leave until he makes still another gift.

The supplicant entering the temple is first stripped of all his or her clothes. In every-day life the Nacirema avoids exposure of his body and its natural functions. Bathing and excretory acts are performed only in the secrecy of the household shrine, where they are ritualized as part of the body-rites. Psychological shock results from the fact that body secrecy is suddenly lost upon entry into the *latipso.* A man, whose own wife has never seen him in an excretory act, suddenly finds himself naked and assisted by a vestal maiden while he performs his natural functions into a sacred vessel. This sort of ceremonial treatment is necessitated by the fact that the excreta are used by a diviner to ascertain the course and nature of the client's sickness. Female clients, on the other hand, find their naked bodies are subjected to the scrutiny, manipulation and prodding of the medicine men.

Few supplicants in the temple are well enough to do anything but lie on their hard beds. The daily ceremonies, like the rites of the holy-mouth-men, involve discomfort and torture. With ritual precision, the vestals awaken their miserable charges each dawn and roll them about on their beds of pain while performing ablutions, in the formal movements of which the maidens are highly trained. At other times they insert magic wands in the supplicant's mouth or force him to eat substances which are supposed to be healing. From time to time the medicine men come to their clients and jab magically treated needles into their flesh. The fact that these temple ceremonies may not cure, and may even kill the neophyte, in no way decreases the people's faith in the medicine men.

There remains one other kind of practitioner, known as a "listener." This witch-doctor has the power to exorcise the devils that lodge in the heads of people who have been bewitched. The Nacirema believe that parents bewitch their own children. Mothers are particularly suspected of putting a curse on children while teaching them the secret body rituals. The counter-magic of the witch-doctor is unusual in its lack of ritual. The patient simply tells the "listener" all his troubles and fears, beginning with the earliest difficulties he can remember. The memory displayed by the Nacirema in these exorcism sessions is truly remarkable. It is not uncommon for the patient to bemoan the rejection he felt upon being weaned as a babe, and a few individuals even see their troubles going back to the traumatic effects of their own birth.

In conclusion, mention must be made of certain practices which have their base in native esthetics but which depend upon the pervasive aversion to the natural body and its functions. There are ritual fasts to make fat people thin and ceremonial feasts to make thin people fat. Still other rites are used to make women's breasts larger if they are small, and smaller if they are large. General dissatisfaction with breast shape is symbolized in the fact that the ideal form is virtually outside the range of human variation. A few women afflicted with almost inhuman hypermammary

development are so idolized that they make a handsome living by simply going from village to village and permitting the natives to stare at them for a fee.

Reference has already been made to the fact that excretory functions are ritualized, routinized, and relegated to secrecy. Natural reproductive functions are similarly distorted. Intercourse is taboo as a topic and scheduled as an act. Efforts are made to avoid pregnancy by the use of magical materials or by limiting intercourse to certain phases of the moon. Conception is actually very infrequent. When pregnant, women dress so as to hide their condition. Parturition takes place in secret, without friends or relatives to assist, and the majority of women do not nurse their infants.

Our review of the ritual life of the Nacirema has certainly shown them to be a magic-ridden people. It is hard to understand how they have managed to exist so long under the burdens which they have imposed upon themselves. But even such exotic customs as these take on real meaning when they are viewed with the insight provided by Malinowski when he wrote (1948, 70):

> Looking from far and above, from our high places of safety in the developed civilization, it is easy to see all the crudity and irrelevance of magic. But without its power and guidance early man could not have mastered his practical difficulties as he has done, nor could man have advanced to the higher stages of civilization.

References

Linton, Ralph. 1936. *The Study of Man*. New York: Appleton-Century.

Malinowski, Bronislaw. 1948. *Magic, Science, and Religion*. Glencoe, IL: Free Press.

Murdock, George P. 1949. *Social Structure*. New York: Macmillan.

Questions

1. What is a thaumaturge?

2. Why would it be ethnocentric to think of the Nacirema as weird—or even silly—for their beliefs?

3. Can you see any signs that Miner experienced "culture shock" as he investigated the Nacirema? Explain.

4. Do you think you would enjoy taking a vacation in the land of Nacirema? Why or why not?

5. What is Nacirema spelled backwards?

·11·

Rule Enforcement Without Visible Means

Christmas Gift Giving in Middletown

Theodore Caplow

A closer look at everyday and routine events can be revealing. Here, Theodore Caplow analyzes the "rules" that underlie gift giving in Christian homes during Christmas in "Middletown." As Caplow makes clear, although these rules are not anywhere published, most people seem to know to follow them scrupulously.

The Middletown III study is a systematic replication of the well-known study of a midwestern industrial city conducted by Robert and Helen Lynd in the 1920s (Lynd and Lynd 1929/1959) and partially replicated by them in the 1930s (Lynd and Lynd 1937/1963). The fieldwork for Middletown III was conducted in 1976–79; its results have been reported in *Middletown Families* (Caplow et al. 1982) and in 38 published papers by various authors; additional volumes and papers are in preparation. Nearly all this material is an assessment of the social changes that occurred between the 1920s and the 1970s in this one community, which is, so far, the only place in the United States that provides such long-term comprehensive sociological data. The Middletown III research focused on those aspects of social structure described by the Lynds in order to utilize the opportunities for longitudinal comparison their data afforded, but there was one important exception. The Lynds had given little attention to the annual cycle of religious-civic family festivals (there were only two inconsequential references to Christmas in *Middletown* and none at all to Thanksgiving or Easter), but

we found this cycle too important to ignore. The celebration of Christmas, the high point of the cycle, mobilizes almost the entire population for several weeks, accounts for about 4% of its total annual expenditures, and takes precedence over ordinary forms of work and leisure. In order to include this large phenomenon, we interviewed a random sample of 110 Middletown adults early in 1979 to discover how they and their families had celebrated Christmas in 1978. The survey included an inventory of all Christmas gifts given and received by these respondents. Although the sample included a few very isolated individuals, all of these had participated in Christmas giving in the previous year. The total number of gifts inventoried was 4,347, a mean of 39.5 per respondent. The distribution of this sample of gifts by type and value, by the age and sex of givers and receivers, and by gift-giving configurations has been reported elsewhere (Caplow 1982). . . .

In this paper, I discuss a quite different problem: How are the rules that appear to govern Christmas gift giving in Middletown communicated and enforced? There are no enforcement agents and little indignation against violators. Nevertheless, the level of participation is very high.

Here are some typical gift-giving rules that are enforced effectively in Middletown without visible means of enforcement and indeed without any widespread awareness of their existence:

The Tree Rule

> Married couples with children of any age should put up Christmas trees in their homes. Unmarried persons with no living children should not put up Christmas trees. Unmarried parents (widowed, divorced, or adoptive) may put up trees but are not required to do so.

Conformity with the Tree Rule in our survey sample may be fairly described as spectacular....

Nobody in Middletown seems to be consciously aware of the norm that requires married couples with children of any age to put up a Christmas tree, yet the obligation is so compelling that, of the 77 respondents in this category who were at home for Christmas 1978, only one—the Venezuelan woman—failed to do so. Few of the written laws that agents of the state attempt to enforce with endless paperwork and threats of violence are so well obeyed as this unwritten rule that is promulgated by no identifiable authority and backed by no evident threat. Indeed, the existence of the rule goes unnoticed. People in Middletown think that putting up a Christmas tree is an entirely voluntary act. They know that it has some connection with children, but they do not understand that married couples with children of any age are effectively required to have trees and that childless unmarried people are somehow prevented from having them. Middletown people do not consciously perceive the Christmas tree as a symbol of the complete nuclear family (father, mother, and one or more children). Those to whom we suggested that possibility seemed to resent it....

The Wrapping Rule

> Christmas gifts must be wrapped before they are presented.

A subsidiary rule requires that the wrapping be appropriate, that is, emblematic, and another subsidiary rule says that wrapped gifts are appropriately displayed as a set but that unwrapped gifts should not be so displayed. Conformity with these rules is exceedingly high.

An unwrapped object is so clearly excluded as a Christmas gift that Middletown people who wish to give something at that season without defining it as a Christmas gift have only to leave the object unwrapped. Difficult-to-wrap Christmas gifts, like a pony or a piano, are wrapped symbolically by adding a ribbon or bow or card and are hidden until presentation....

In nearly every Middletown household, the wrapped presents are displayed under or around the Christmas tree as a glittering monument to the family's affluence and mutual affection. Picture taking at Christmas gatherings is clearly a part of the ritual; photographs were taken at 65% of the recorded gatherings. In nearly all instances, the pile of wrapped gifts was photographed; and individual participants were photographed opening a gift, ideally at the moment of "surprise." Although the pile of wrapped gifts is almost invariably photographed, a heap of unwrapped gifts is not a suitable subject for the Christmas photographer. Among the 366 gatherings we recorded, there was a single instance in which a participant, a small boy, was photographed with all his unwrapped gifts. To display unwrapped gifts as a set seems to invite the invidious comparison of gifts—and of the relationships they represent.

The Decoration Rule

> Any room where Christmas gifts are distributed should be decorated by affixing Christmas emblems to the walls, the ceiling, or the furniture.

This is done even in nondomestic places, like offices or restaurant dining rooms, if gifts are to be distributed there. Conformity to this rule was perfect in our sample of 366 gatherings at which gifts were distributed, although, once again, the existence of the rule was not recognized by the people who obeyed it.

The same lack of recognition applies to the interesting subsidiary rule that a Christmas tree should not be put up in an undecorated place, although a decorated place need not have a tree. Unmarried, childless persons normally decorate their homes, although they have no trees, and decorations without a tree are common in public places, but a Christmas tree in an undecorated room would be unseemly. . . .

It goes without saying that Christmas decorations must be temporary, installed for the season and removed afterward (with the partial exception of outdoor wreaths, which are sometimes left to wither on the door.) A room painted in red and green, or with a frieze of plaster wreaths, would not be decorated within the meaning of the rule.

The Gathering Rule

> Christmas gifts should be distributed at gatherings where every person gives and receives gifts.

Compliance with this rule is very high. More than nine-tenths of the 1,378 gifts our respondents received, and of the 2,969 they gave, were distributed in gatherings, more than three-quarters of which were family gatherings. Most gifts mailed or shipped by friends and relatives living at a distance were double wrapped, so that the outer unceremonious wrappings could be removed and the inner packages could be placed with other gifts to be opened at a gathering. In the typical family gathering, a number of related persons assemble by prearrangement at the home of one of them where a feast is served; the adults engage in conversation; the children play; someone takes photographs; gifts are distributed, opened, and admired; and the company then disperses. The average Middletown adult fits more than three of these occasions into a 24-hour period beginning at Christmas Eve, often driving long distances and eating several large dinners during that time.

The Dinner Rule

> Family gatherings at which gifts are distributed include a "traditional Christmas dinner."

This is a rule that participants in Middletown's Christmas ritual may disregard if they wish, but it is no less interesting because compliance is only partial. Presumably, this rule acquired its elective character because the pattern of multiple gatherings described above requires many gatherings to be scheduled at odd hours when dinner either would be inappropriate or, if the dinner rule were inflexible, would require participants to overeat beyond the normal expectations of the season. However, 65% of the survey respondents had eaten at least one traditional Christmas dinner the previous year.

There appears to be a subsidiary rule that traditional Christmas dinners served in homes should be prepared exclusively by women. There was not a single reported instance in this survey of a traditional Christmas dinner prepared by a man.

The Gift Selection Rules

> A Christmas gift should (a) demonstrate the giver's familiarity with the receiver's preferences; (b) surprise the receiver, either by expressing more affection—measured by the

aesthetic or practical value of the gift — than the receiver might reasonably anticipate or more knowledge than the giver might reasonably be expected to have; (*c*) be scaled in economic value to the emotional value of the relationship.

The economic values of any giver's gifts are supposed to be sufficiently scaled to the emotional values of relationships that, when they are opened in the bright glare of the family circle, the donor will not appear to have disregarded either the legitimate inequality of some relationships by, for example, giving a more valuable gift to a nephew than to a son, or the legitimate equality of other relationships by, for example, giving conspicuously unequal gifts to two sons.

Individuals participating in these rituals are not free to improvise their own scales of emotional value for relationships. The scale they are supposed to use, together with its permissible variations, is not written down anywhere but is thoroughly familiar to participants. From analysis of the gifts given and received by our survey respondents, we infer the following rules for scaling the emotional value of relationships.

The Scaling Rules

(*a*) A spousal relationship should be more valuable than any other for both husband and wife, but the husband may set a higher value on it than the wife. (*b*) A parent–child relationship should be less valuable than a spousal relationship but more valuable than any other relationship. The parent may set a higher value on it than the child does. (*c*) The spouse of a married close relative should be valued as much as the linking relative. (*d*) Parents with several children should value them equally throughout their lives. (*e*) Children with both parents still living, and still married to each other, may value them equally or may value their mothers somewhat more than their fathers. A married couple with two pairs of living, still-married

parents should value each pair equally. Children of any age with divorced, separated, or remarried parents may value them unequally. (*f*) Siblings should be valued equally in childhood but not later. Adult siblings who live close by and are part of one's active network should be equally valued, along with their respective spouses, but siblings who live farther away may be valued unequally. (*g*) Friends of either sex, aside from sexual partners treated as quasi-spouses, may be valued as much as siblings but should not be valued as much as spouses, parents, or children. (*h*) More distant relatives — like aunts or cousins — may be valued as much as siblings but should not be valued as much as spouses, parents, or children.

It is a formidable task to balance these ratios every year and to come up with a set of Christmas gifts that satisfies them. Small wonder that Middletown people complain that Christmas shopping is difficult and fatiguing. But although they complain, they persist in it year after year without interruption. People who are away from home for Christmas arrange in advance to have their gifts distributed to the usual receivers and to open their own gifts ceremoniously. People confined by severe illness delegate others to do shopping and wrapping. Although our random sample of Middletown adults included several socially isolated persons, even the single most isolated respondent happened to have an old friend with whom he exchanged expensive gifts.

Given the complexity of the rules, errors and failures in gift selection can be expected to occur, and they frequently do. Indeed, the four or five shopping days immediately after Christmas are set aside in Middletown stores for return or exchange of badly selected gifts. A number of respondents described relatives who make a point of being impossible to please, like the grandfather in Renata Adler's story:

The grandfather, who pretended not to care about the holiday, every year, until the precise moment when the door to the study, where the piano stood, was opened and the presents were revealed, became every year, at that moment, hopeful, eager, even zealous and then dejected utterly. No one had ever found a present that actually pleased him. "Very nice," he would say, in a tight voice, as he unwrapped one thing after another. "Very nice. Now I'll just put that away." The year his sons gave him an electric razor, he said, "Very nice. Of course I'll never use it. I'm too old to change the way I shave." When they asked him at least to try it, he said "No, I'm sorry. It's very nice. No I'll just put that away." (Adler 1978, 136–37)

The standard disappointing gift is an article of clothing in the wrong size. Women are particularly resentful of oversized items that seem to say the giver perceives them as "fat." Children are often insulted by inattentive relatives who give them toys that are too "young." The spouse's or lover's gift that is disliked by the receiver is a sign of alienation. Two of the five couples in our sample for whom such gifts were reported at Christmas 1978 had separated by the time of the interview several weeks later.

The rigor of the Selection Rules is softened by several devices—joint gifts from and to married couples, from children to parents, and from two or three siblings to another are common. Such arrangements make it difficult to determine whether the comparative value of relationships has been correctly translated into gifts, and that is the more or less conscious intention. Two families in our sample drew lots for their gifts. That practice is nearly standard at nonfamilial Christmas gatherings, like ward parties for hospitalized children, where presents are distributed without any attempt to particularize relationships.

Fitness Rules

Rules about the fitness of gifts (e.g., women should not give cut flowers to men) are too numerous to specify, but one deserves passing at-

tention. Money is an appropriate gift from senior to junior kin, but an inappropriate gift from junior to senior kin, regardless of the relative affluence of the parties. This is another rule which appears to be unknown to the people who obey it. Of 144 gifts of money given by persons in our sample to those in other generations, 94% went to junior kin, and of the 73 money gifts respondents received from persons in other generations, 93% were from senior kin. A gift certificate may be given to a parent or grandparent to whom an outright gift of money would be improper, but we did not record a single instance of a gift certificate having been given to a child or a grandchild, no substitution being called for.

The Reciprocity Rule

Participants in this gift system should give (individually or jointly) at least one Christmas gift every year to their mothers, fathers, sons, daughters; to the current spouses of these persons; and to their own spouses.

By the operation of this rule, participants expect to receive at least one gift in return from each of these persons excepting infants. Conformity runs about 90% for each relationship separately and for the aggregate of all such relationships. Gifts to grandparents and grandchildren seem to be equally obligatory if these live in the same community or nearby, but not at greater distances (see Caplow 1982, table 6). Christmas gifts to siblings are not required. Only about one-third of the 274 sibling relationships reported by the sample were marked by Christmas gifts. The proportion was no higher for siblings living close than for those farther away. However, gifts to siblings do call for a return gift; this obligation is seldom scanted. Gift giving to siblings' children, and parents' siblings and their respective spouses, appears to be entirely elective; fewer than half of these are reciprocated. We have no way of knowing whether such gifts may be reciprocated at another Christmas, but there were no references to deferred reciprocation in the interviews.

The Reciprocity Rule does not require reciprocated gifts to be of equal value. Parents expect to give more valuable and more numerous gifts to their minor children and to their adult children living at home than they receive in return. This imbalance is central to the entire ritual. The iconography of Middletown's secular Christmas emphasizes unreciprocated giving to children by the emblematic figure of Santa Claus, and the theme of unreciprocated giving provides one of the few connections between the secular and religious iconography of the festival—the Three Wise Men coming from a distant land to bring unreciprocated gifts to a child.

Equivalence of value tends to be disregarded in gift giving between husbands and wives and between parents and their adult children. Husbands often give more valuable gifts to wives than they receive from them. The gifts of parents to adult children are approximately balanced in the aggregate—about the same number of substantial gifts are given in each direction—but there is no insistence on equivalence in particular cases, and when we examine such relationships one by one, we discover many unbalanced exchanges, which seem to be taken for granted.

Only in the relationship between siblings and sibling couples do we find any active concern that the gifts exchanged be of approximately equal value, and even there it is more important to give gifts of approximately equal value to several siblings than to exchange gifts of equal value with each of them.

Empirically, the gift giving between adults and children in our sample was highly unbalanced, in both quantity and value. Respondents gave 946 gifts to persons under 18 and received 145 in return; 89 of these were of substantial value and six of the return gifts were. In about one-third of these relationships, no

gift was returned to the adult either by the child or in the child's name. In most of the remaining relationships, the child returned a single gift of token or modest value.

There is little reciprocity in the gift giving between non-kin. A large number of the gifts in this category are addressed to persons who provide minor services; reciprocation in those cases would be bizarre. Gifts from employers to employees, from grateful patients to physicians, and from pupils to teachers do not call for reciprocation. The Christmas gifts exchanged en masse at club meetings and office parties are reciprocal to the extent that each participant gives and receives some small gift, but there is no direct exchange between giver and receiver.

Discussion

Since the problem is to account for the uniformities of gift-giving behavior revealed by the data, speaking of rules begs the question to some extent. Although we infer from the uniformities observed in Middletown's Christmas gift giving that, somewhere in the culture, there must be statements to which the observed behavior is a response, the crucial point is that we cannot find those statements in any explicit form. Indeed, they are not recognized by participants in the system. In effect, the rules of the game are unfamiliar to the players, even though they can be observed to play meticulously by the rules. Instructions for Christmas gift giving are not found in administrative regulations or popular maxims or books of etiquette; they are not *promulgated*. Neither do they seem to be enforced by what Durkheim called "the public conscience" (Durkheim 1895/ 1964, 2–3). People who scanted their Christmas obligations would not be disapproved of by the public conscience in Middletown because Christmas gift giving is visualized there as both a private and a voluntary activity. We never heard anyone make an even indirect reference to community opinion in connection with Christmas gift giving. As far as we can tell, there are no customary forms of moral disapproval reserved for persons who neglect their Christmas duties (which are not, of course, considered to be duties). The moral drift goes the other way. Among Middletown's Protestant fundamentalists there are still vestiges of the violent Puritan objection to the celebration of Christmas as a "wanton Bacchanalian feast" (Barnett 1954, 1–23), which is commonly expressed in sermons about the "degradation" and "commercialization" of the festival. . . .

Gift exchange, in effect, is a language that employs objects instead of words as its lexical elements. In this perspective, every culture (there may be exotic exceptions, but I am unaware of them) has a language of prestation to express important interpersonal relationships on special occasions, just as it has a verbal language to create and manage meaning for other purposes. The language of prestation, like the verbal language, begins to be learned in early childhood and is used with increasing assurance as the individual matures and acquires social understanding. These "natal" languages are seldom completely forgotten, although new languages may be learned by translation and practice. The problem of accounting for the enforcement of gift-giving rules without visible means is simplified if we take them to be linguistic rules, or at least as similar to them, because linguistic rules, for the most part, are enforced among native speakers of a language without visible means and without being recognized explicitly. It may be objected that school teachers do make linguistic rules explicit and then enforce them by reward and punishment, but that is a rather special case of learning a new language or relearning a natal language in more elegant form. The acquisition of language does not depend on schooling, and the grammatical rules that are made explicit in school are only a small fraction of

the rules that native speakers obey without being aware of their existence. The process whereby grammatical rules acquire consensual support is partly instinctual, partly cultural, and partly social. The tendency to follow linguistic rules without explicit awareness appears to be innate in the construction of new verbal combinations: young children acquire the language of the people who raise them along with other elements of the ambient culture; and linguistic rules are self-enforcing insofar as the effective transmission of messages rewards both senders and receivers.

Visualizing Christmas gift giving as a language — or, more precisely, as a dialect or code (Douglas 1972, 1979) — helps to explain, among other matters, the insistence on wrapping and other signs to identify the objects designated for lexical use and the preference for the simultaneous exchange of gifts at family gatherings rather than in private.

In most cases such a gathering is composed of a parent–child unit containing one or two parents and one or more children together with other persons who are tied to that unit by shared membership in another parent–child unit, such as children's children, children's spouses, parents' siblings, or parents' parents. Although there is room at a family gathering for a friend or distant relative who otherwise might be solitary at Christmas, there is no convenient way of including any large number of persons to whom no gift messages are owed.

Under the Scaling Rules, gift messages are due from every person in a parent–child relationship to every other. The individual message says "I value you according to the degree of our relationship" and anticipates the response "I value you in the same way." But the compound message that emerges from the unwrapping of gifts in the presence of the whole gathering allows more subtle meanings to be conveyed. It permits the husband to say to the wife "I value you more than my parents" or the mother to say to the daughter-in-law "I value you as much as my son so long as you are married to him" or the brother to say to the brother "I value you more than our absent brothers, but less than our parents and much less than my children." These statements, taken together, would define and sustain a social structure, if only because, by their gift messages, both parties to each dyadic relationship confirm that they have the same understanding of the relationship and the bystanders, who are interested parties, endorse that understanding by tacit approval. The compound messages would have a powerful influence even if they were idiosyncratic and each parent–child unit had its own method of scaling relationships. In fact, there are some observable differences in scaling from one Middletown family to another and from one subcultural group to another, but the similarities are much more striking than the differences. We attribute this commonality to the shared dialect of Christmas gift giving, hyperdeveloped in Middletown and elsewhere in the United States in response to commercial promotion, stresses in the family institution, and constant reiteration by the mass media. Once the dialect is reasonably well known, these factors continue to enlarge its vocabulary and its domain.

Another circumstance facilitating the standardization of the dialect is that nearly every individual in this population belongs to more than one parent–child unit for Christmas giftgiving purposes. Because these units are linked and cross-linked to other units in a network that ultimately includes the larger part of the community, they would probably tend to develop a common set of understandings about appropriate kinship behavior, even without the reinforcement provided by domestic rituals.

The most powerful reinforcement remains to be mentioned. In the dialect of Christmas gift giving, the absence of a gift is also a lexical sign, signifying either the absence of a close relation, as in the Christmas contact of cousins, or the desire to terminate a close relationship, as when a husband gives no gift to his wife. People who have once learned the dialect cannot choose to forget it, nor can they pretend to ignore messages they understand. Thus, without any complicated normative machinery, Middletown people find themselves compelled to give Christmas gifts to their close relatives, lest they inadvertently send them messages of hostility. In this community, where most people depend on their relatives for emotional and social support, the consequences of accidentally sending them a hostile message are too serious to contemplate, and few are willing to run the risk.

In sum, we discover that the participants in this gift-giving system are themselves the agents who enforce its complex rules, although they do so unknowingly and without conscious reference to a system. The dialect, once learned, imposes itself by linguistic necessity, and the enforcement of its rules is the more effective for being unplanned.

References

Adler, Renata. 1978. *Speedboat.* New York: Popular Library.

Barnett, James H. 1954. *The American Christmas: A Study of National Culture.* New York: Macmillan.

Caplow, Theodore. 1982. "Christmas Gifts and Kin Networks." *American Sociological Review* 47: 383–392.

Caplow, Theodore, Howard H. Bahr, Bruce A. Chadwick, Reuben Hill, and Margaret Holmes Williamson. 1982. *Middletown Families: Fifty Years of Change and Continuity.* Minneapolis: University of Minnesota Press.

Douglas, Mary. 1972. "Deciphering a Meal." *Daedalus* 101: 31–81.

———. 1979. *The World of Goods.* New York: Basic Books.

Durkheim, Émile. 1895/1964. *Rules of Sociological Method.* New York: Free Press.

Lynd, Robert, and Helen Merell Lynd. 1929/1959. *Middletown: A Study in American Culture.* New York: Harcourt Brace.

———. 1937/1963. *Middletown in Transition: A Study in Cultural Conflicts.* New York: Harcourt Brace.

Questions

1. In your judgment, why is it deemed inappropriate by Middletown families to display or photograph *unwrapped* gifts?

2. Which of the rules mentioned by Caplow are followed by you and your family or (if you don't celebrate the holiday) by others known to you? Which aren't followed?

3. Caplow suggests that people who break the rules regarding gift giving run no risk of sanction. Do you agree? Let us say, for example, that you found shopping to be more trouble than it's worth and decided to give your parents or your partner/spouse gift certificates for generous amounts. Would you be sanctioned in any way? How so? Likewise, suppose you violated the "scaling rule" by giving every person in your family the exact same thing. What would be their response?

4. Consider other special times when gift giving is deemed appropriate — Chanukah or birthdays, for example. What rules govern those sorts of interaction?

·12·

The Code of the Streets

Elijah Anderson

Except in the most general sense, it is wrong to speak of "American" culture as if it were a single entity. American society is not homogeneous, nor is its culture. In this article, Elijah Anderson focuses on a particular *subculture* that exists within the larger culture. In this subculture, the ubiquitous human search for respect creates what has been called a "perverse etiquette of violence," one from which it may well be impossible to escape.

Of all the problems besetting the poor inner-city black community, none is more pressing than that of interpersonal violence and aggression. It wreaks havoc daily in the lives of community residents and increasingly spills over into downtown and residential middle-class areas. Muggings, burglaries, carjackings, and drug-related shootings, all of which may leave their victims or innocent bystanders dead, are now common enough to concern all urban and many suburban residents. The inclination to violence springs from the circumstances of life among the ghetto poor—the lack of jobs that pay a living wage, the stigma of race, the fallout from rampant drug use and drug trafficking, and the resulting alienation and lack of hope for the future.

Simply living in such an environment places young people at special risk of falling victim to aggressive behavior. Although there are often forces in the community which can counteract the negative influences, by far the most powerful being a strong, loving, "decent" (as inner-city residents put it) family committed to middle-class values, the despair is pervasive enough to have spawned an oppositional culture, that of "the streets," whose norms are often consciously opposed to those of mainstream society. These two orientations—decent and street—socially organize the community, and their coexistence has important consequences for residents, particularly children growing up in the inner city. Above all, this environment means that even youngsters whose home lives reflect mainstream values—and the majority of homes in the community do—must be able to handle themselves in a street-oriented environment.

This is because the street culture has evolved what may be called a code of the streets, which amounts to a set of informal rules governing interpersonal public behavior, including violence. The rules prescribe both a proper comportment and a proper way to respond if challenged. They regulate the use of violence and so allow those who are inclined to aggression to precipitate violent encounters in an approved way. The rules have been established and are enforced mainly by the street-oriented, but on the streets the distinction between street and decent is often irrelevant; everybody knows that if the rules are violated, there are penalties. Knowledge of the code is thus largely defensive; it is literally necessary for operating in public. Therefore, even though families with a decency orientation are usually opposed to the values of the code, they often reluctantly encourage their children's familiarity with it to enable them to negotiate the inner-city environment.

At the heart of the code is the issue of respect —loosely defined as being treated "right," or granted the deference one deserves. However, in the troublesome public environment of the inner city, as people increasingly feel buffeted by forces beyond their control, what one deserves in the way of respect becomes more and more problematic and uncertain. This in turn further opens the issue of respect to sometimes intense interpersonal negotiation. In the street culture, especially among young people, respect is viewed as almost an external entity that is hard-won but easily lost, and so must constantly be guarded. The rules of the code in fact provide a framework for negotiating respect. The person whose very appearance— including his clothing, demeanor, and way of moving—deters transgressions feels that he possesses, and may be considered by others to possess, a measure of respect. With the right amount of respect, for instance, he can avoid "being bothered" in public. If he is bothered, not only may he be in physical danger but he has been disgraced or "dissed" (disrespected). Many of the forms that dissing can take might seem petty to middle-class people (maintaining eye contact for too long, for example), but to those invested in the street code, these actions become serious indications of the other person's intentions. Consequently, such people become very sensitive to advances and slights, which could well serve as warnings of imminent physical confrontation.

This hard reality can be traced to the profound sense of alienation from mainstream society and its institutions felt by many poor inner-city black people, particularly the young. The code of the streets is actually a cultural adaptation to a profound lack of faith in the police and the judicial system. The police are most often seen as representing the dominant white society and not caring to protect inner-city residents. When called, they may not respond, which is one reason many residents feel they must be prepared to take extraordinary measures to defend themselves and their loved ones against those who are inclined to aggression. Lack of police accountability has in fact been incorporated into the status system: the person who is believed capable of "taking care of himself" is accorded a certain deference, which translates into a sense of physical and psychological control. Thus the street code emerges where the influence of the police ends and personal responsibility for one's safety is felt to begin. Exacerbated by the proliferation of drugs and easy access to guns, this volatile situation results in the ability of the street-oriented minority (or those who effectively "go for bad") to dominate the public spaces.

Decent and Street Families

Although almost everyone in poor inner-city neighborhoods is struggling financially and therefore feels a certain distance from the rest of America, the decent and the street family in a real sense represent two poles of value orientation, two contrasting conceptual categories. The labels "decent" and "street," which the residents themselves use, amount to evaluative judgments that confer status on local residents. The labeling is often the result of a social contest among individuals and families of the neighborhood. Individuals of the two orientations often coexist in the same extended family. Decent residents judge themselves to be so while judging others to be of the street, and street individuals often present themselves as decent, drawing distinctions between themselves and other people. In addition, there is quite a bit of circumstantial behavior—that is one person may at different times exhibit both decent and street orientations, depending on the circumstances. Although these designations result from so much social jockeying, there do exist concrete features that define each conceptual category.

Generally, so-called decent families tend to accept mainstream values more fully and attempt to instill them in their children. Whether married couples with children or single-parent (usually female) households, they are generally "working poor" and so tend to be better off financially than their street-oriented neighbors. They value hard work and self-reliance and are willing to sacrifice for their children. Because they have a certain amount of faith in mainstream society, they harbor hopes for a better future for their children, if not for themselves. Many of them go to church and take a strong interest in their children's schooling. Rather than dwelling on the real hardships and inequities facing them, many such decent people, particularly the increasing number of grandmothers raising grandchildren, see their difficult situation as a test from God and derive great support from their faith and from the church community.

Extremely aware of the problematic and often dangerous environment in which they reside, decent parents tend to be strict in their child-rearing practices, encouraging children to respect authority and walk a straight moral line. They have an almost obsessive concern about trouble of any kind and remind their children to be on the lookout for people and situations that might lead to it. At the same time, they are themselves polite and considerate of others, and teach their children to be the same way. At home, at work, and in church, they strive hard to maintain a positive mental attitude and a spirit of cooperation.

So-called street parents, in contrast, often show a lack of consideration for other people and have a rather superficial sense of family and community. Though they may love their children, many of them are unable to cope with the physical and emotional demands of parenthood, and find it difficult to reconcile their needs with those of their children. These families, who are more fully invested in the code of the streets than the decent people are, may aggressively socialize their children into it in a normative way. They believe in the code and judge themselves and others according to its values.

In fact the overwhelming majority of families in the inner-city community try to approximate the decent-family model, but there are many others who clearly represent the worst fears of the decent family. Not only are their financial resources extremely limited, but what little they have may easily be misused. The lives of the street-oriented are often marked by disorganization. In the most desperate circumstances people frequently have a limited understanding of priorities and consequences, and so frustrations mount over bills, food, and, at times, drink, cigarettes, and drugs. Some tend toward self-destructive behavior; many street-oriented women are crack-addicted ("on the pipe"), alcoholic, or involved in complicated relationships with men who abuse them. In addition, the seeming intractability of their situation, caused in large part by the lack of well-paying jobs and the persistence of racial discrimination, has engendered deep-seated bitterness and anger in many of the most desperate and poorest blacks, especially young people. The need both to exercise a measure of control and to lash out at somebody is often reflected in the adults' relations with their children. At the least, the frustrations of persistent poverty shorten the fuse in such people — contributing to a lack of patience with anyone, child or adult, who irritates them.

In these circumstances a woman — or a man, although men are less consistently present in children's lives — can be quite aggressive with children, yelling at and striking them for the least little infraction of the rules she has set down. Often little if any serious explanation follows the verbal and physical punishment. This response teaches children a particular lesson. They learn that to solve any kind of interpersonal problem one must quickly resort to hitting or other violent behavior. Actual peace and quiet, and also the appearance of calm, respectful children conveyed to her neighbors and friends, are often what the young mother most desires, but at times she will be very aggressive in trying to get them. Thus she may be quick to beat her children, especially if they defy her law, not because she hates them but because this is the way she knows to control them. In fact, many street-oriented women love their children dearly. Many mothers in the community subscribe to the notion that there is a "devil in the boy" that must be beaten out of him or that socially "fast girls need to be whupped." Thus much of what borders on child abuse in the view of social authorities is acceptable parental punishment in the view of these mothers.

Many street-oriented women are sporadic mothers whose children learn to fend for themselves when necessary, foraging for food and money any way they can get it. The children are sometimes employed by drug dealers or become addicted themselves. These children of the street, growing up with little supervision, are said to "come up hard." They often learn to fight at an early age, sometimes using short-tempered adults around them as role models. The street-oriented home may be fraught with anger, verbal disputes, physical aggression, and even mayhem. The children observe these goings-on, learning the lesson that might makes right. They quickly learn to hit those who cross them, and the dog-eat-dog mentality prevails. In order to survive, to protect oneself, it is necessary to marshal inner resources and be ready to deal with adversity in a hands-on way. In these circumstances physical prowess takes on great significance.

In some of the most desperate cases, a street-oriented mother may simply leave her young children alone and unattended while she goes out. The most irresponsible women can be found at local bars and crack houses, getting high and socializing with other adults. Sometimes a troubled woman will leave very young children alone for days at a time. Reports of crack addicts abandoning their children have become common in drug-infested inner-city communities. Neighbors or relatives discover the abandoned children, often hungry and distraught over the absence of their mother. After repeated absences, a friend or relative, particularly a grandmother, will often step in to care for the young children, sometimes petitioning the authorities to send her, as guardian of the children, the mother's welfare check, if the mother gets one. By this time, however, the children may well have learned the first lesson of the streets: survival itself, let alone respect, cannot be taken for granted; you have to fight for your place in the world.

Campaigning for Respect

These realities of inner-city life are largely absorbed on the streets. At an early age, often even before they start school, children from street-oriented homes gravitate to the streets, where they "hang" — socialize with their peers. Children from these generally permissive homes have a great deal of latitude and are allowed to "rip and run" up and down the street. They often come home from school, put their books down, and go right back out the door. On school nights eight- and nine-year-olds remain out until nine or ten o'clock (and teenagers typically come in whenever they want to). On the streets they play in groups that often become the source of their primary social bonds. Children from decent homes tend to be more carefully supervised and are thus likely to have curfews and to be taught how to stay out of trouble.

When decent and street kids come together, a kind of social shuffle occurs in which children have a chance to go either way. Tension builds as a child comes to realize that he must choose an orientation. The kind of home he comes from influences but does not determine the way he will ultimately turn out—although it is unlikely that a child from a thoroughly street-oriented family will easily absorb decent values on the streets. Youths who emerge from street-oriented families but develop a decency orientation almost always learn those values in another setting—in school, in a youth group, in church. Often it is the result of their involvement with a caring "old head" (adult role model).

In the street, through their play, children pour their individual life experiences into a common knowledge pool, affirming, confirming, and elaborating on what they have observed in the home and matching their skills against those of others. And they learn to fight. Even small children test one another, pushing and shoving, and are ready to hit other children over circumstances not to their liking. In turn, they are readily hit by other children, and the child who is toughest prevails. Thus the violent resolution of disputes, the hitting and cursing, gains social reinforcement. The child in effect is initiated into a system that is really a way of campaigning for respect.

In addition, younger children witness the disputes of older children, which are often resolved through cursing and abusive talk, if not aggression or outright violence. They see that one child succumbs to the greater physical and mental abilities of the other. They are also alert and attentive witnesses to the verbal and physical fights of adults, after which they compare notes and share their interpretations of the event. In almost every case the victor is the person who physically won the altercation, and this person often enjoys the esteem and respect of onlookers. These experiences reinforce the lessons the children have learned at home: might makes right, and toughness is a virtue, while humility is not. In effect they learn the social meaning of fighting. When it is left virtually unchallenged, this understanding becomes an ever more important part of the child's working conception of the world. Over time the code of the streets becomes refined.

Those street-oriented adults with whom children come in contact—including mothers, fathers, brothers, sisters, boyfriends, cousins, neighbors, and friends—help them along in forming this understanding by verbalizing the messages they are getting through experience: "Watch your back." "Protect yourself." "Don't punk out." "If somebody messes with you, you got to pay them back." "If someone disses you, you got to straighten them out." Many parents actually impose sanctions if a child is not sufficiently aggressive. For example, if a child loses a fight and comes home upset, the parent might respond, "Don't you come in here crying that somebody beat you up; you better get back out there and whup his ass. I didn't raise no punks! Get back out there and whup his ass. If you don't whup his ass, I'll whup your ass when you come home." Thus the child obtains reinforcement for being tough and showing nerve.

While fighting, some children cry as though they are doing something they are ambivalent about. The fight may be against their wishes, yet they may feel constrained to fight or face the consequences—not just from peers but also from caretakers or parents, who may administer another beating if they back down. Some adults recall receiving such lessons from their own parents and justify repeating them to their children as a way to toughen them up. Looking capable of taking care of oneself as a form of self-defense is a dominant theme among both street-oriented and decent adults who worry about the safety of their children. There is thus times a convergence in their child-rearing practices, although the rationales behind them may differ.

Self-Image Based on "Juice"

By the time they are teenagers, most youths have either internalized the code of the streets or at least learned the need to comport themselves in accordance with its rules, which chiefly have to do with interpersonal communication. The code revolves around the presentation of self. Its basic requirement is the display of a certain predisposition to violence. Accordingly, one's bearing must send the unmistakable if sometimes subtle message to "the next person" in public that one is capable of violence and mayhem when the situation requires it, that one can take care of oneself. The nature of this communication is largely determined by the demands of the circumstances but can include facial expressions, gait, and verbal expressions—all of which are geared mainly to deterring aggression. Physical appearance, including clothes, jewelry, and grooming, also plays an important part in how a person is viewed; to be respected, it is important to have the right look.

Even so, there are no guarantees against challenges, because there are always people around looking for a fight to increase their share of respect—or "juice," as it is sometimes called on the street. Moreover, if a person is assaulted, it is important, not only in the eyes of his opponent but also in the eyes of his "running buddies," for him to avenge himself. Otherwise he risks being "tried" (challenged) or "moved on" by any number of others. To maintain his honor he must show he is not someone to be "messed with" or "dissed." In general, the person must "keep himself straight" by managing his position of respect among others; this involves in part his self-image, which is shaped by what he thinks others are thinking of him in relation to his peers.

Objects play an important and complicated role in establishing self-image. Jackets, sneakers, gold jewelry, reflect not just a person's taste, which tends to be tightly regulated among adolescents of all social classes, but also a willingness to possess things that may require defending. A boy wearing a fashionable, expensive jacket, for example, is vulnerable to attack by another who covets the jacket and either cannot afford to buy one or wants the added satisfaction of depriving someone else of his. However, if the boy forgoes the desirable jacket and wears one that isn't "hip," he runs the risk of being teased and possibly even assaulted as an unworthy person. To be allowed to hang with certain prestigious crowds, a boy must wear a different set of expensive clothes—sneakers and athletic suit—every day. Not to be able to do so might make him appear socially deficient. The youth comes to covet such items—especially when he sees easy prey wearing them.

In acquiring valued things, therefore, a person shores up his identity—but since it is an identity based on having things, it is highly precarious. This very precariousness gives a heightened sense of urgency to staying even with peers, with whom the person is actually competing. Young men and women who are able to command respect through their presentation of self—by allowing their possessions and their body language to speak for them—may not have to campaign for regard but may, rather, gain it by the force of their manner. Those who are unable to command respect in this way must actively campaign for it—and are thus particularly alive to slights.

One way of campaigning for status is by taking the possessions of others. In this context, seemingly ordinary objects can become trophies imbued with symbolic value that far exceeds their monetary worth. Possession of the trophy can symbolize the ability to violate somebody—to "get in his face," to take something of value from him, to "dis" him, and thus to enhance one's own worth by stealing someone else's. The trophy does not have to be something material. It can be another person's sense of honor, snatched away with a derogatory remark. It can be the outcome of a fight. It can be the imposition of a certain standard, such as a girl's getting herself recognized as the most beautiful. Material things, however, fit easily into the pattern. Sneakers, a pistol, even somebody else's girlfriend, can become a trophy. When a person can take something from another and then flaunt it, he gains a certain regard by being the owner, or the controller, of that thing. But this display of ownership can then provoke other people to challenge him. This game of who controls what is thus constantly being played out on inner-city streets, and the trophy—extrinsic or intrinsic, tangible or intangible—identifies the current winner.

An important aspect of this often violent give-and-take is its zero-sum quality. That is, the extent to which one person can raise himself up depends on his ability to put another person down. This underscores the alienation that permeates the inner-city ghetto community. There is a generalized sense that very little respect is to be had, and therefore everyone competes to get what affirmation he can of the little that is available. The craving for respect that results gives people thin skins. Shows of deference by others can be highly soothing, contributing to a sense of security, comfort, self-confidence, and self-respect. Transgressions by others which go unanswered diminish these feelings and are believed to encourage further transgressions. Hence one must be ever vigilant against the transgressions of others or even *appearing* as if transgressions will be tolerated. Among young people, whose sense of self-esteem is particularly vulnerable, there is an especially heightened concern with being disrespected. Many inner-city young men in particular crave respect to such a degree that they will risk their lives to attain and maintain it.

The issue of respect is thus closely tied to whether a person has an inclination to be violent, even as a victim. In the wider society people may not feel required to retaliate physically after an attack, even though they are aware that they have been degraded or taken advantage of. They may feel a great need to defend themselves *during* an attack, or to be-

have in such a way as to deter aggression (middle-class people certainly can and do become victims of street-oriented youths), but they are much more likely than street-oriented people to feel that they can walk away from a possible altercation with their self-esteem intact. Some people may even have the strength of character to flee, without any thought that their self-respect or esteem will be diminished.

In impoverished inner-city black communities, however, particularly among young males and perhaps increasingly among females, such flight would be extremely difficult. To run away would likely leave one's self-esteem in tatters. Hence people often feel constrained not only to stand up and at least attempt to resist during an assault but also to "pay back"—to seek revenge—after a successful assault on their person. This may include going to get a weapon or even getting relatives involved. Their very identity and self-respect, their honor, is often intricately tied up with the way they perform on the streets during and after such encounters. This outlook reflects the circumscribed opportunities of the inner-city poor. Generally people outside the ghetto have other ways of gaining status and regard, and thus do not feel so dependent on such physical displays. . . .

"Going for Bad"

In the most fearsome youths such a cavalier attitude toward death grows out of a very limited view of life. Many are uncertain about how long they are going to live and believe they could die violently at any time. They accept this fate; they live on the edge. Their manner conveys the message that nothing intimidates them; whatever turn the encounter takes, they maintain their attack—rather like a pit bull, whose spirit many such boys admire. The demonstration of such tenacity "shows heart" and earns their respect.

This fearlessness has implications for law enforcement. Many street-oriented boys are much more concerned about the threat of "justice" at the hands of a peer than at the hands of the police. Moreover, many feel not only that they have little to lose by going to prison but that they have something to gain. The toughening-up one experiences in prison can actually enhance one's reputation on the streets. Hence the system loses influence over the hard core who are without jobs, with little perceptible stake in the system. If mainstream society has done nothing *for* them, they counter by making sure it can do nothing *to* them.

At the same time, however, a competing view maintains that true nerve consists in backing down, walking away from a fight, and going on with one's business. One fights only in self-defense. This view emerges from the decent philosophy that life is precious, and it is an important part of the socialization process common in decent homes. It discourages violence as the primary means of resolving disputes and encourages youngsters to accept nonviolence and talk as confrontational strategies. But "if the deal goes down," self-defense is greatly encouraged. When there is enough positive support for this orientation, either in the home or among one's peers, then nonviolence has a chance to prevail. But it prevails at the cost of relinquishing a claim to being bad and tough, and therefore sets a young person up as at the very least alienated from street-oriented peers and quite possibly a target of derision or even violence.

Although the nonviolent orientation rarely overcomes the impulse to strike back in an encounter, it does introduce a certain confusion and so can prompt a measure of soul-searching, or even profound ambivalence. Did the person back down with his respect intact or did he back down only to be judged a "punk"—a person lacking manhood? Should he or she have acted? Should he or she have hit the other person in the mouth? These questions beset many young men and women during public confrontations. What is the "right" thing to do? In the quest for honor, respect, and local status—which few young people are uninterested in—common sense most often prevails, which leads many to opt for the tough approach, enacting their own particular versions of the display of nerve. The presentation of oneself as rough and tough is very often quite acceptable until one is tested. And then that presentation may help the person pass the test, because it will cause fewer questions to be asked about what he did and why. It is hard for a person to explain why he lost the fight or why he backed down. Hence many will strive to appear to "go for bad," while hoping they will never be tested. But when they are tested, the outcome of the situation may quickly be out of their hands, as they become wrapped up in the circumstances of the moment.

An Oppositional Culture

The attitudes of the wider society are deeply implicated in the code of the streets. Most people in inner-city communities are not totally invested in the code. But the significant minority of hard-core street youths who are have to maintain the code in order to establish reputations because they have—or feel they have—few other ways to assert themselves. For these young people the standards of the street code are the only game in town. The extent to which some children—particularly those who through up-bringing have become most alienated and those lacking in strong and conventional social support—experience, feel, and internalize racist rejection and contempt from mainstream society may strongly encourage them to express contempt for the more conventional society in turn. In dealing with this contempt and rejection, some youngsters will consciously invest themselves and their considerable mental resources in what amounts to an oppositional culture to preserve themselves and their self-respect. Once they do, any respect they might be able to garner in the wider system pales in comparison with the respect available in the local system; thus they often lose interest in even attempting to negotiate the mainstream system.

At the same time, many less alienated young blacks have assumed a street-oriented demeanor as a way of expressing their blackness while really embracing a much more moderate way of life; they, too, want a nonviolent setting in which to live and raise a family. These decent people are trying hard to be part of the mainstream culture, but the racism, real and perceived, that they encounter helps to legitimate the oppositional culture. And so on occasion they adopt street behavior. In fact, depending on the demands of the situation, many people in the community slip back and forth between decent and street behavior.

A vicious cycle has thus been formed. The hopelessness and alienation many young inner-city black men and women feel, largely as a result of endemic joblessness and persistent racism, fuels the violence they engage in. This violence serves to confirm the negative feelings many whites and some middle-class blacks harbor toward the ghetto poor, further legitimating the oppositional culture and the code of the streets in the eyes of many poor young blacks. Unless the cycle is broken, attitudes on both sides will become increasingly entrenched, and the violence, which claims victims black and white, poor and affluent, will only escalate.

Questions

1. How would you define each of the following terms (used by Anderson in his article)?
   a. mayhem
   b. oppositional culture
   c. zero-sum

2. What factors of life on the street make it difficult for people to be "decent"?

3. In your judgment, are young men from more "middle-class" cultural settings at all preoccupied with earning respect? How do young men in middle-class culture earn the respect of others and prove themselves to be properly "manly"?

·13·

The Presentation of Self in Everyday Life

Erving Goffman

In this reading, Erving Goffman introduces what has come to be called the *dramaturgical* approach to the study of social interaction (so called because, in effect, it views social life as theater). Goffman's focus is on what happens when people are in the presence of others, on how they play their roles. As you will see, from Goffman's point of view, routine social interaction is a cooperative effort between the social actor and his or her audience. The actor may play a role, but frequently he or she must be helped along by the complicity of the audience.

When an individual enters the presence of others, they commonly seek to acquire information about him or to bring into play information about him already possessed. They will be interested in his general socio-economic status, his conception of self, his attitude toward them, his competence, his trustworthiness, etc. Although some of this information seems to be sought almost as an end in itself, there are usually quite practical reasons for acquiring it. Information about the individual helps to define the situation, enabling others to know in advance what he will expect of them and what they may expect of him. Informed in these ways, the others will know how best to act in order to call forth a desired response from him.

For those present, many sources of information become accessible and many carriers (or "sign-vehicles") become available for conveying this information. If unacquainted with the individual, observers can glean clues from his conduct and appearance which allow them to apply their previous experience with individuals roughly similar to the one before them or, more important, to apply untested stereotypes to him. They can also assume from past experience that only individuals of a particular kind are likely to be found in a given social setting. They can rely on what the individual says about himself or on documentary evidence he provides as to who and what he is. If they know, or know of, the individual by virtue of experience prior to the interaction, they can rely on assumptions as to the persistence and generality of psychological traits as a means of predicting his present and future behavior.

However, during the period in which the individual is in the immediate presence of the others, few events may occur which directly provide the others with the conclusive information they will need if they are to direct wisely their own activity. Many crucial facts lie beyond the time and place of interaction or lie concealed with it. For example, the "true" or "real" attitudes, beliefs, and emotions of the individual can be ascertained only indirectly, through his avowals or through what appears to be involuntary expressive behavior. Similarly, if the individual offers the others a product or service, they will often find that during the interaction there will be no time and place immediately available for eating the pudding that the proof can be found in. They will be forced to accept some events as conventional or natural signs of something not directly available to the senses. In other terms, the individual will have to act so that he intentionally or unintentionally *expresses* himself, and the others will in turn have to be *impressed* in some way by him (Ichheiser 1949, 6–7).

The expressiveness of the individual (and therefore his capacity to give impressions) appears to involve two radically different kinds of sign activity: the expression that he *gives,* and the expression that he *gives off.* The first involves verbal symbols or their substitutes which he uses admittedly and solely to convey the information that he and the others are known to attach to these symbols. This is communication in the traditional and narrow sense. The second involves a wide range of action that others can treat as symptomatic of the actor, the expectation being that the action was performed for reasons other than the information conveyed in this way. As we shall have to see, this distinction has an only initial validity. The individual does of course intentionally convey misinformation by means of both of these types of communication, the first involving deceit, the second feigning.

Taking communication in both its narrow and broad sense, one finds that when the individual is in the immediate presence of others, his activity will have a promissory character. The others are likely to find that they must accept the individual on faith, offering him a just return while he is present before them in exchange for something whose true value will not be established until after he has left their presence. (Of course, the others also live by inference in their dealings with the physical world, but it is only in the world of social interaction that the objects about which they make inferences will purposely facilitate and hinder this inferential process.) The security that they justifiably feel in making inferences about the individual will vary, of course, de-

pending on such factors as the amount of information they already possess about him, but no amount of such past evidence can entirely obviate the necessity of acting on the basis of inferences. As William I. Thomas suggested:

> It is also highly important for us to realize that we do not as a matter of fact lead our lives, make our decisions, and reach our goals in everyday life either statistically or scientifically. We live in inference. I am, let us say, your guest. You do not know, you cannot determine scientifically, that I will not steal your money or your spoons. But inferentially I will not, and inferentially you have me as a guest (quoted in Volkart 1951, 5).

Let us now turn from the others to the point of view of the individual who presents himself before them. He may wish them to think highly of him, or to think that he thinks highly of them, or to perceive how in fact he feels toward them, or to obtain no clear-cut impression; he may wish to ensure sufficient harmony so that the interaction can be sustained, or to defraud, get rid of, confuse, mislead, antagonize, or insult them. Regardless of the particular objective which the individual has in mind and of his motive for having this objective, it will be in his interests to control the conduct of the others, especially their responsive treatment of him. This control is achieved largely by influencing the definition of the situation which the others come to formulate, and he can influence this definition by expressing himself in such a way as to give them the kind of impression that will lead them to act voluntarily in accordance with his own plan. Thus, when an individual appears in the presence of others, there will usually be some reason for him to mobilize his activity so that it will convey an impression to others which it is in his interests to convey. Since a girl's dormitory mates will glean evidence of her popularity from the calls she receives on the phone, we can suspect that some girls will arrange for calls to be made, and Willard Waller's (n.d., 730) finding can be anticipated.

> It has been reported by many observers that a girl who is called to the telephone in the dormitories will often allow herself to be called several times, in order to give all the other girls ample opportunity to hear her paged.

Of the two kinds of communication—expressions given and expressions given off—this report will be primarily concerned with the latter, with the more theatrical and contextual kind, the non-verbal, presumably unintentional kind, whether this communication be purposely engineered or not. As an example of what we must try to examine, I would like to cite at length a novelistic incident in which Preedy, a vacationing Englishman, makes his first appearance on the beach of his summer hotel in Spain:

> But in any case he took care to avoid catching anyone's eye. First of all, he had to make it clear to those potential companions of his holiday that they were of no concern to him whatsoever. He stared through them, round them, over them—eyes lost in space. The beach might have been empty. If by chance a ball was thrown his way, he looked surprised; then let a smile of amusement lighten his face (Kindly Preedy), looked round dazed to see that there *were* people on the beach, tossed it back with a smile to himself and not a smile *at* the people, and then resumed carelessly his nonchalant survey of space.
>
> But it was time to institute a little parade, the parade of the Ideal Preedy. By devious handlings he gave any who wanted to look a chance to see the title of his book—a Spanish translation of Homer, classic thus, but not daring, cosmopolitan too—and then gathered together his beach-wrap and bag into a neat sand-resistant pile (Methodical and Sensible Preedy), rose slowly to stretch at ease his huge frame (Big-Cat Preedy), and tossed aside his sandals (Carefree Preedy, after all).
>
> The marriage of Preedy and the sea! There were alternative rituals. The first involved the stroll that turns into a run and a dive straight into the water, thereafter smoothing into a strong splashless crawl towards the horizon. But of course not really to the horizon. Quite suddenly he would turn on to his back and thrash great white splashes with his legs, somehow thus showing that he could have swum further had he wanted to, and then would stand up a quarter out of water for all to see who it was.
>
> The alternative course was simpler, it avoided the cold-water shock and it avoided the risk of appearing too high-spirited. The point was to appear to be so used to the sea, the Mediterranean, and this particular beach, that one might as well be in the sea as out of it. It involved a slow stroll down and into the edge of the water—not even noticing his toes were wet, land and water all the same to *him!*—with his eyes up at the sky gravely surveying portents, invisible to others, of the weather (Local Fisherman Preedy). (Samson 1956, 230–232)

The novelist means us to see that Preedy is improperly concerned with the extensive impressions he feels his sheer bodily action is giving off to those around him. We can malign Preedy further by assuming that he has acted merely in order to give a particular impression, that this is a false impression, and that the others present receive either no impression at all, or, worse still, the impression that Preedy is affectedly trying to cause them to receive this particular impression. But the important point for us here is that the kind of impression Preedy thinks he is making is in fact the kind of impression that others correctly and incorrectly glean from someone in their midst.

I have said that when an individual appears before others his actions will influence the definition of the situation which they come to have. Sometimes the individual will act in a thoroughly calculating manner, expressing himself in a given way solely in order to give the kind of impression to others that is likely to evoke from them a specific response he is concerned to obtain. Sometimes the individual will be calculating in his activity but be relatively unaware that this is the case. Sometimes he will intentionally and consciously express himself in a particular way, but chiefly because the tradition of his group or social status requires this kind of expression and not because of any particular response (other than vague acceptance or approval) that is likely to be evoked from those impressed by the expression. Sometimes the traditions of an individual's role will lead him to give a well-designed impression of a particular kind and yet he may be neither consciously nor unconsciously disposed to create such an impression. The others, in their turn, may be suitably impressed by the individual's efforts to convey something, or may misunderstand the situation and come to conclusions that are warranted neither by the individual's intent nor by the facts. In any case, in so far as the others act *as if* the individual had conveyed a particular impression, we may take a functional or pragmatic view and say that the individual has "effectively" projected a given definition of the situation and "effectively" fostered the understanding that a given state of affairs obtains.

There is one aspect of the others' response that bears special comment here. Knowing that the individual is likely to present himself in a light that is favorable to him, the others may divide what they witness into two parts; a part that is relatively easy for the individual to manipulate at will, being chiefly his verbal assertions, and a part in regard to which he seems to have little concern or control, being chiefly derived from the expressions he gives off. The others may then use what are considered to be the ungovernable aspects of his expressive behavior as a check upon the validity of what is conveyed by the governable aspects. In this a fundamental asymmetry is demonstrated in the communication process, the individual presumably being aware of only one stream of his communication, the witnesses of this stream and one other. For example, in

Shetland Isle one crofter's wife, in serving native dishes to a visitor from the mainland of Britain, would listen with a polite smile to his polite claims of liking what he is eating; at the same time she would take note of the rapidity with which the visitor lifted his fork or spoon to his mouth, the eagerness with which he passed food into his mouth, and the gusto expressed in chewing the food, using these signs as a check on the stated feelings of the eater. The same woman, in order to discover what one acquaintance (A) "actually" thought of another acquaintance (B), would wait until B was in the presence of A but engaged in conversation with still another person (C). She would then covertly examine the facial expressions of A as he regarded B in conversation with C. Not being in conversation with B, and not being directly observed by him, A would sometimes relax usual constraints and tactful deceptions, and freely express what he was "actually" feeling about B. This Shetlander, in short, would observe the unobserved observer.

Now given the fact that others are likely to check up on the more controllable aspects of behavior by means of the less controllable, one can expect that sometimes the individual will try to exploit this very possibility, guiding the impression he makes through behavior felt to be reliably informing. For example, in gaining admission to a tight social circle, the participant observer may not only wear an accepting look while listening to an informant, but may also be careful to wear the same look when observing the informant talking to others; observers of the observer will then not as easily discover where he actually stands. A specific illustration may be cited from Shetland Isle. When a neighbor dropped in to have a cup of tea, he would ordinarily wear at least a hint of an expectant warm smile as he passed through the door into the cottage. Since lack of physical obstructions outside the cottage and lack of light within it usually made it possible to observe the visitor unobserved as he approached the house, islanders sometimes took pleasure in watching the visitor drop whatever expression he was manifesting and replace it with a sociable one just before reaching the door. However, some visitors, in appreciating that this examination was occurring, would blindly adopt a social face a long distance from the house, thus ensuring the projection of a constant image.

This kind of control upon the part of the individual reinstates the symmetry of the communication process, and sets the stage for a kind of information game—a potentially infinite cycle of concealment, discovery, false revelation, and rediscovery. It should be added that since the others are likely to be relatively unsuspicious of the presumably unguided aspect of the individual's conduct, he can gain much by controlling it. The others of course may sense that the individual is manipulating the presumably spontaneous aspects of his behavior, and seek in this very act of manipulation some shading of conduct that the individual has not managed to control. This again provides a check upon the individual's behavior, this time his presumably uncalculated behavior, thus re-establishing the asymmetry of the communication process. Here I would like only to add the suggestion that the arts of piercing an individual's effort at calculated unintentionality seem better developed than our capacity to manipulate our own behavior, so that regardless of how many steps have occurred in the information game, the witness is likely to have the advantage over the actor, and the initial asymmetry of the communication process is likely to be retained.

When we allow that the individual projects a definition of the situation when he appears before others, we must also see that the others, however passive their role may seem to be, will themselves effectively project a definition of the situation by virtue of their response to the individual and by virtue of any lines of action they initiate to him. Ordinarily the definitions of the situation projected by the several different participants are sufficiently attuned to one another so that open contradiction will not occur. I do not mean that there will be the kind of consensus that arises when each individual present candidly expresses what he really feels and honestly agrees with the expressed feelings of the others present. This kind of harmony is an optimistic ideal and in any case not necessary for the smooth working of society. Rather, each participant is expected to suppress his immediate heartfelt feelings, conveying a view of the situation which he feels the others will be able to find at least temporarily acceptable. The maintenance of this surface of agreement, this veneer of consensus, is facilitated by each participant concealing his own wants behind statements which assert values to which everyone present feels obliged to give lip service. Further, there is usually a kind of division of definitional labor. Each participant is allowed to establish the tentative official ruling regarding matters which are vital to him but not immediately important to others, e.g., the rationalizations and justifications by which he accounts for his past activity. In exchange for this courtesy he remains silent or noncommittal on matters important to others but not immediately important to him. We have then a kind of interactional *modus vivendi*.[1] Together the participants contribute to a single over-all definition of the situation which involves not so much a real agreement as to what exists but rather a real agreement as to whose claims concerning what issues will be temporarily honored. Real agreement will also exist concerning the desirability of avoiding

---

[1] *Modus vivendi* is Latin and can be literally translated as "a way of living." But generally it refers to "a way of acting" so that people who might not feel positively toward one another can nonetheless get along. —Ed.

an open conflict of definitions of the situation.[2] I will refer to this level of agreement as a "working consensus." It is to be understood that the working consensus established in one interaction setting will be quite different in content from the working consensus established in a different type of setting. Thus, between two friends at lunch, a reciprocal show of affection, respect, and concern for the other is maintained. In service occupations, on the other hand, the specialist often maintains an image of disinterested involvement in the problem of the client, while the client responds with a show of respect for the competence and integrity of the specialist. Regardless of such differences in content, however, the general form of these working arrangements is the same.

In noting the tendency for a participant to accept the definitional claims made by the others present, we can appreciate the crucial importance of the information that the individual *initially* possesses or acquires concerning his fellow participants, for it is on the basis of this initial information that the individual starts to define the situation and starts to build up lines of responsive action. The individual's initial projection commits him to what he is proposing to be and requires him to drop all pretenses of being other things. As the interaction among the participants progresses, additions and modifications in this initial informational state will of course occur, but it is essential that these later developments be related without

contradiction to, and even built up from, the initial positions taken by several participants. It would seem that an individual can more easily make a choice as to what line of treatment to demand from and extend to the others present at the beginning of an encounter than he can alter the line of treatment that is being pursued once the interaction is underway.

In everyday life, of course, there is a clear understanding that first impressions are important. Thus, the work adjustment of those in service occupations will often hinge upon a capacity to seize and hold the initiative in the service relation, a capacity that will require subtle aggressiveness on the part of the server when he is of lower socio-economic status than his client. W. F. Whyte (1946, 132–133) suggests the waitress as an example:

> The first point that stands out is that the waitress who bears up under pressure does not simply respond to her customers. She acts with some skill to control their behavior. The first question to ask when we look at the customer relationship is, "Does the waitress get the jump on the customers, or does the customer get the jump on the waitress?" The skilled waitress realizes the crucial nature of this question. . . .
> The skilled waitress tackles the customer with confidence and without hesitation. For example, she may find that a new customer has seated himself before she could clear off the dirty dishes and change the cloth. He is now leaning on the table studying the menu. She greets him, says, "May I change the cover, please?" and, without waiting for an answer, takes his menu away from him so that he moves back from the table, and she goes about her work. The relationship is handled politely but firmly, and there is never any question as to who is in charge.

When the interaction that is initiated by "first impressions" is itself merely the initial interaction in an extended series of interactions involving the same participants, we speak of

---

[2]An interaction can be purposely set up as a time and place for voicing differences in opinion, but in such cases participants must be careful to agree not to disagree on the proper tone of voice, vocabulary, and degree of seriousness in which all arguments are to be phrased, and upon the mutual respect which disagreeing participants must carefully continue to express toward one another. This debaters' or academic definition of the situation may also be invoked suddenly and judiciously as a way of translating a serious conflict of views into one that can be handled within a framework acceptable to all present.

"getting off on the right foot" and feel that it is crucial that we do so. Thus, one learns that some teachers take the following view:

> "You can't ever let them get the upper hand on you or you're through. So I start out tough. The first day I get a new class in, I let them know who's boss. . . . You've got to start off tough, then you can ease up as you go along. If you start out easy-going, when you try to get tough, they'll just look at you and laugh." (quoted in Becker n.d., 459)

Similarly, attendants in mental institutions may feel that if the new patient is sharply put in his place the first day on the ward and made to see who is boss, much future difficulty will be prevented (Taxel 1953).

Given the fact that the individual effectively projects a definition of the situation when he enters the presence of others, we can assume that events may occur within the interaction which contradict, discredit, or otherwise throw doubt upon this projection. When these disruptive events occur, the interaction itself may come to a confused and embarrassed halt. Some of the assumptions upon which the responses of the participants had been predicated become untenable, and the participants find themselves lodged in an interaction for which the situation has been wrongly defined and is now no longer defined. At such moments the individual whose presentation has been discredited may feel ashamed while the others present may feel hostile, and all the participants may come to feel ill at ease, nonplussed, out of countenance, embarrassed, experiencing the kind of anomy that is generated when the minute social system of face-to-face interaction breaks down.

In stressing the fact that the initial definition of the situation projected by an individual tends to provide a plan for the co-operative activity that follows—in stressing this action point of view—we must not overlook the crucial fact that any projected definition of the sit-

uation also has a distinctive moral character. It is this moral character of projections that will chiefly concern us in this report. Society is organized on the principle that any individual who possesses certain social characteristics has a moral right to expect that others will value and treat him in an appropriate way. Connected with this principle is a second, namely that an individual who implicitly or explicitly signifies that he has certain social characteristics ought in fact to be what he claims he is. In consequence, when an individual projects a definition of the situation and thereby makes an implicit or explicit claim to be a person of a particular kind, he automatically exerts a moral demand upon the others, obliging them to value and treat him in the manner that persons of his kind have a right to expect. He also implicitly forgoes all claims to be things he does not appear to be and hence forgoes the treatment that would be appropriate for such individuals. The others find, then, that the individual has informed them as to what is and as to what they *ought* to see as the "is."

One cannot judge the importance of definitional disruptions by the frequency with which they occur, for apparently they would occur more frequently were not constant precautions taken. We find that preventive practices are constantly employed to avoid these embarrassments and that corrective practices are constantly employed to compensate for discrediting occurrences that have not been successfully avoided. When the individual employs these strategies and tactics to protect his own projections, we may refer to them as "defensive practices"; when a participant employs them to save the definition of the situation projected by another, we speak of "protective practices" or "tact." Together, defensive and protective practices comprise the techniques employed to safeguard the impression fostered by an individual during his presence before others. It should be added that while we may be ready to see that no fostered impression would survive if defensive practices were not employed, we are less ready perhaps to see that few impressions could survive if those who received the impression did not exert tact in their reception of it.

In addition to the fact that precautions are taken to prevent disruption of projected definitions, we may also note that an intense interest in these disruptions comes to play a significant role in the social life of the group. Practical jokes and social games are played in which embarrassments which are to be taken unseriously are purposely engineered. Fantasies are created in which devastating exposures occur. Anecdotes from the past—real, embroidered, or fictitious—are told and retold, detailing disruptions which occurred, almost occurred, or occurred and were admirably resolved. There seems to be no grouping which does not have a ready supply of these games, reveries, and cautionary tales, to be used as a source of humor, a catharsis for anxieties, and a sanction for inducing individuals to be modest in their claims and reasonable in their projected expectations. The individual may tell himself through dreams of getting into impossible positions. Families tell of the time a guest got his dates mixed and arrived when neither the house nor anyone in it was ready for him. Journalists tell of times when an all-too-meaningful misprint occurred, and the paper's assumption of objectivity or decorum was humorously discredited. Public servants tell of times a client ridiculously misunderstood form instructions, giving answers which implied an unanticipated and bizarre definition of the situation (Blau n.d., 127–129). Seamen, whose home away from home is rigorously he-man, tell stories of coming back home and inadvertently asking mother to "pass the fucking butter" (Beattie 1950, 35). Diplomats tell of the time a near-sighted queen asked a republican ambassador about the health of his king (Ponsonby 1952, 46). . . .

It will be convenient to end this introduction with some definitions that are implied in what has gone before and required for what is to follow. For the purpose of this report, interaction (that is, face-to-face interaction) may be roughly defined as the reciprocal influence of individuals upon one another's actions when in one another's immediate physical presence. *An* interaction may be defined as all the interaction which occurs throughout any one occasion when a given set of individuals are in one another's continuous presence; the term "an encounter" would do as well. A "performance" may be defined as all the activity of a given participant on a given occasion which serves to influence in any way any of the other participants. Taking a particular participant and his performance as a basic point of reference, we may refer to those who contribute the other performances as the audience, observers, or co-participants. The pre-established pattern of action which is unfolded during a performance and which may be presented or played through on other occasions may be called a "part" or "routine." These situational terms can easily be related to conventional structural ones. When an individual or performer plays the same part to the same audience on different occasions, a social relationship is likely to arise. Defining social role as the enactment of rights and duties attached to a given status, we can say that a social role will involve one or more parts and that each of these different parts may be presented by the performer on a series of occasions to the same kinds of audience or to an audience of the same persons.

References

Beattie, Walter M., Jr. 1950. "The Merchant Seaman." Unpublished M. A. report, Department of Sociology, University of Chicago.

Becker, Howard S. n.d. "Social Class Variations in the Teacher–Pupil Relationship." *Journal of Educational Sociology* 25.

Blau, Peter. n.d. "Dynamics of Bureaucracy." Ph.D. dissertation, Department of Sociology, Columbia University.

Ichheiser, Gustav. 1949. "Misunderstandings in Human Relations." Supplement to *The American Journal of Sociology* 55 (September).

Ponsonby, Sir Frederick. 1952. *Recollections of Three Reigns*. New York: Dutton.

Sansom, William. 1956. *A Contest of Ladies*. London: Hogarth.

Taxel, Harold. 1953. "Authority Structure in a Mental Hospital Ward." Unpublished M.A. thesis, Department of Sociology, University of Chicago.

Volkart, E. H. (ed.). 1951. "Contributions of W. I. Thomas to Theory and Social Research." In *Social Behavior and Personality*. New York: Social Science Research Council.

Waller, Willard. n.d. "The Rating and Dating Complex." *American Sociological Review* 2.

Whyte, W. F. 1946. "When Workers and Customers Meet." Chap. 7 in W. F. Whyte (ed.), *Industry and Society*. New York: McGraw-Hill.

Questions

1. What is Goffman's distinction between expressions that one gives and expressions that one gives off?

2. Suppose you are about to visit your professor to ask a question about the upcoming exam. Besides information gathering, you would like to influence your professor's definition of the situation such that he or she infers that you are a smart student. How might you do this (both in terms of expressions you give and expressions you give off)?

   Now suppose you are preparing for a date that you've been looking forward to for several days. Your goal this time is to have fun and to influence your date's definition of the situation so that he or she infers that you are a cool person. How might you do this?

   Is there a difference between how you would act in each situation? Which is the "real" you?

3. Think of a time in which you exercised "tact." Using that situation as an example, how might you (as Goffman would say) employ this projective technique in order to save the definition of the situation projected by another?

·14·

The Pathology of Imprisonment

Philip G. Zimbardo

When I was a kid in school, I was very shy. I rarely volunteered answers to questions posed by my teachers, and I cringed whenever I was asked to do an arithmetic problem on the chalk board. That wasn't the best way to fulfill my role as a student, but it was an acceptable way. Now I am a professor, and I am the one who not only asks questions but makes scholarly pronouncements that I expect everyone in the room to write down. My first-grade teacher, who regarded my shyness with despair, would be shocked to see that I actually seem to do these professorial things comfortably. Has my personality changed? Not really. I'm still shy. But the role expectations of a professor evoke a different side of me, one that's "outgoing" and even extroverted. As you will read in this article by Philip Zimbardo, roles—the social scripts that are attached to the statuses people occupy—are powerfully evocative. They can bring out parts of someone's "personality" that the individual never knew existed.

I was recently released from solitary confinement after being held therein for 37 months [months!]. A silent system was imposed upon me and to even whisper to the man in the next cell resulted in being beaten by guards, sprayed with chemical mace, blackjacked, stomped and thrown into a strip-cell naked to sleep on a concrete floor without bedding, covering, wash basin or even a toilet. The floor served as toilet and bed, and even there the silent system was enforced. To let a moan escape your lips because of the pain and discomfort . . . resulted in another beating. I spent not days, but months there during my 37 months in solitary. . . . I have filed every writ possible against the administrative acts of brutality. The state courts have all denied the petitions. Because of my refusal to let the things die down and forget all that happened during my 37 months in solitary . . . I am the most hated prisoner in [this] penitentiary, and called a "hard-core incorrigible."

Maybe I am an incorrigible, but if true, it's because I would rather die than to accept being treated as less than a human being. I have never complained of my prison sentence as being unjustified except through legal means of appeals. I have never put a knife on a guard's throat and demanded my release. I know that thieves must be punished and I don't justify stealing, even though I am a thief myself. But now I don't think I will be a thief when I am released. No, I'm not rehabilitated. It's just that I no longer think of becoming wealthy by stealing. I now only think of killing—killing those who have beaten me and treated me as if I were a dog. I hope and pray for the sake of my own soul and future life of freedom that I am able to overcome the bitterness and hatred which eats daily at my soul, but I know to overcome it will not be easy.

This eloquent plea for prison reform— for humane treatment of human beings, for the basic dignity that is the right of every American— came to me secretly in a letter from a prisoner who cannot be identified because he is still in a state correctional institution. He sent it to me because he read of an experiment I recently conducted at Stanford University. In an attempt to understand just what it means psychologically to be a prisoner or a prison guard, Craig Haney, Curt Banks, Dave Jaffe and I created our own prison. We carefully screened over 70 volunteers who answered an ad in a Palo Alto city newspaper and ended up with about two dozen young men who were selected to be part of this study. They were mature, emotionally stable, normal, intelligent college students from middle-class homes throughout the United States and Canada. They appeared to represent the cream of the crop of this generation. None had any criminal record and all were relatively homogeneous on many dimensions initially.

Half were arbitrarily designated as prisoners by a flip of a coin, the others as guards. These were the roles they were to play in our simulated prison. The guards were made aware of the potential seriousness and danger of the situation and their own vulnerability. They made up their own formal rules for maintaining law, order and respect, and were generally free to improvise new ones during their eight-hour, three-man shifts. The prisoners were unexpectedly picked up at their homes by a city policeman in a squad car, searched, handcuffed, fingerprinted, booked at the Palo Alto station house and taken blindfolded to our jail. There they were stripped, deloused, put into a uniform, given a number and put into a cell with two other prisoners where they expected to live for the next two weeks. The pay was good ($15 a day) and their motivation was to make money.

We observed and recorded on videotape the events that occurred in the prison, and we interviewed and tested the prisoners and guards at various points throughout the study. Some of the videotapes of the actual encounters between the prisoners and guards were seen on the NBC News feature "Chronolog" on November 26, 1971.

At the end of only six days we had to close down our mock prison because what we saw was frightening. It was no longer apparent to most of the subjects (or to us) where reality ended and their roles began. The majority had indeed become prisoners or guards, no longer able to clearly differentiate between role playing and self. There were dramatic changes in virtually every aspect of their behavior, thinking and feeling. In less than a week the experience of imprisonment undid (temporarily) a lifetime of learning; human values were suspended, self-concepts were challenged and the ugliest, most base, pathological side of human nature surfaced. We were horrified because we saw some boys (guards) treat others as if they were despicable animals, taking pleasure in cruelty, while other boys (prisoners) became servile, dehumanized robots who thought only of escape, of their own individual survival and of their mounting hatred for the guards.

We had to release three prisoners in the first four days because they had such acute situational traumatic reactions as hysterical crying, confusion in thinking and severe depression. Others begged to be paroled, and all but three were willing to forfeit all the money they had earned if they could be paroled. By then (the fifth day) they had been so programmed to think of themselves as prisoners that when their request for parole was denied, they returned docilely to their cells. Now, had they been thinking as college students acting in an oppressive experiment, they would have quit once they no longer wanted the $15 a day we used as our only incentive. However, the reality was not quitting an experiment but "being paroled by the parole board from the Stanford County Jail." By the last days, the earlier solidarity among the prisoners (systematically broken by the guards) dissolved into "each man for himself." Finally, when one of their fellows was put in solitary confinement (a small closet) for refusing to eat, the prisoners were given a choice by one of the guards: give up their blankets and the incorrigible prisoner would be let out, or keep their blankets and he would be kept in all night. They voted to keep their blankets and to abandon their brother.

About a third of the guards became tyrannical in their arbitrary use of power, in enjoying their control over other people. They were corrupted by the power of their roles and became quite inventive in their techniques of breaking the spirit of the prisoners and making them feel they were worthless. Some of the guards merely did their jobs as tough but fair correctional officers, and several were good guards from the prisoners' point of view since they did them small favors and were friendly. However, no good guard ever interfered with a command by any of the bad guards; they never intervened on the side of the prisoners, they never told the others to ease off because it was only an experiment, and they never even came to me as prison superintendent or experimenter in charge to complain. In part, they were good because the others were bad; they needed the others to help establish their own egos in a positive light. In a sense, the good guards perpetuated the prison more than the other guards because their own needs to be liked prevented them from disobeying or violating the implicit guards' code. At the same time, the act of befriending the prisoners created a social reality which made the prisoners less likely to rebel.

By the end of the week the experiment had become a reality, as if it were a Pirandello[1] play directed by Kafka[2] that just keeps going after the audience has left. The consultant for our prison, Carlo Prescott, an ex-convict with 16 years of imprisonment in California's jails, would get so depressed and furious each time he visited our prison, because of its psychological similarity to his experiences, that he would have to leave. A Catholic priest who was a former prison chaplain in Washington, D.C., talked to our prisoners after four days and said they were just like the other first-timers he had seen.

But in the end, I called off the experiment not because of the horror I saw out there in the prison yard, but because of the horror of realizing that *I* could have easily traded places with the most brutal guard or become the weakest prisoner full of hatred at being so powerless that I could not eat, sleep or go to the toilet without permission of the authorities. I could have become Calley at My Lai, George Jackson at San Quentin, one of the men at Attica or the prisoner quoted at the beginning of this article.

Individual behavior is largely under the control of social forces and environmental contingencies rather than personality traits, character, will power or other empirically unvalidated constructs. Thus we create an illusion of freedom by attributing more internal control to ourselves, to the individual, than actually exists. We thus underestimate the power and pervasiveness of situational controls over behavior because: (a) they are often non-obvious and subtle, (b) we can often avoid entering situations where we might be so controlled, (c) we label as "weak" or "deviant" people in those situations who do behave differently from how we believe we would.

Each of us carries around in our heads a favorable self-image in which we are essentially

---

[1]Luigi Pirandello (1867–1936) was a Sicilian author. He won the 1934 Nobel Prize for literature. His fame is primarily owing to his grimly humorous plays dealing with the confusions of illusions and reality (for example, *Six Characters in Search of an Author*). —Ed.

[2]The writer Franz Kafka (1883–1924) was born in Prague of Jewish parents. In his novels and short stories, Kafka painted a world that was steeped in illusion and contradiction. His characters suffered from feelings of guilt, anxiety, and despair and an overwhelming sense of futility as they struggled to cope with rigid bureaucracies and totalitarian regimes. Today, similarly tortured visions of society are often referred to as "Kafkaesque." — Ed.

just, fair, humane and understanding. For example, we could not imagine inflicting pain on others without much provocation or hurting people who had done nothing to us, who in fact were even liked by us. However, there is a growing body of social psychological research which underscores the conclusion derived from this prison study. Many people, perhaps the majority, can be made to do almost anything when put into psychologically compelling situations—regardless of their morals, ethics, values, attitudes, beliefs or personal convictions. My colleague, Stanley Milgram, has shown that more than 60 percent of the population will deliver what they think is a series of painful electric shocks to another person even after the victim cries for mercy, begs them to stop and then apparently passes out. The subjects complained that they did not want to inflict more pain but blindly obeyed the command of the authority figure (the experimenter) who said that they must go on. In my own research on violence, I have seen mild-mannered co-eds repeatedly give shocks (which they thought were causing pain) to another girl, a stranger whom they had rated very favorably, simply by being made to feel anonymous and put in a situation where they were expected to engage in this activity.

Observers of these and similar experimental situations never predict their outcomes and estimate that it is unlikely that they themselves would behave similarly. They can be so confident only when they were outside the situation. However, since the majority of people in these studies do act in non-rational, non-obvious ways, it follows that the majority of observers would also succumb to the social psychological forces in the situation.

With regard to prisons, we can state that the mere act of assigning labels to people and putting them into a situation where those labels acquire validity and meaning is sufficient to elicit pathological behavior. This pathology is not predictable from any available diagnostic indicators we have in the social sciences, and is extreme enough to modify in very significant ways fundamental attitudes and behavior. The prison situation, as presently arranged, is guaranteed to generate severe enough pathological reactions in both guards and prisoners as to debase their humanity, lower their feelings of self-worth and make it difficult for them to be part of a society outside of their prison. . . .

Questions

1. What are the similarities between Zimbardo's findings and Milgram's (see reading 7)?

2. Zimbardo's experiment cemented sociologists' conviction that the roles people play have a lot of power to elicit particular behaviors from them. Sociologists refer to the process by which people take on socially constructed roles and carry them out as "role-taking." The men chosen to be prisoners and to be guards were, for all intents and purposes, the same until they took on their respective roles; it was taking on and playing the roles that "changed" them (or elicited new behaviors from them).

    Role-taking is a part of everyday life. When an individual reaches adulthood (or possibly sooner!), he or she may take the status and role of married person—husband or wife. As many women and men have found in recent decades, it is hard to change those roles to fit new understandings of, for example, gender roles. But sociologists are aware that all people, in all cases, do not simply take on conventional roles, that people do not simply do role-taking. In some cases, people adapt the roles to themselves rather than the other way around. Sociologists call that "role-making." It isn't easy; when you do not act the way people expect you to act, you can expect some sort of responses—often, informal negative sanctions. Think of the young man who wishes, for example, to study ballet rather than football. He wants to make the role of young man fit his own proclivities.

Consider how you play the role of student. What things do you do that an observer would judge to be role-taking? What do you do that an observer would judge to be role-making?

·15·

Marked

Women in the Workplace

Deborah Tannen

As I discussed in chapter 9 in *The Practical Skeptic,* a status is a position in a group that an individual may occupy. Each status comes with a role—and a series of expectations about how the individual should carry out the role. But, as Deborah Tannen explains, even when people occupy the same status, the expectations that others have of them may differ depending on seemingly unrelated factors. In this essay, Tannen describes how some status incumbents are "marked" by virtue of their sex and how this makes a difference.

Some years ago I was at a small working conference of four women and eight men. Instead of concentrating on the discussion, I found myself looking at the three other women at the table, thinking how each had a different style and how each style was coherent.

One woman had dark brown hair in a classic style that was a cross between Cleopatra and Plain Jane. The severity of her straight hair was softened by wavy bangs and ends that turned under. Because she was beautiful, the effect was more Cleopatra than plain.

The second woman was older, full of dignity and composure. Her hair was cut in a fashionable style that left her with only one eye, thanks to a side part that let a curtain of hair fall across half her face. As she looked down to read her prepared paper, the hair robbed her of binocular vision and created a barrier between her and the listeners.

The third woman's hair was wild, a frosted blond avalanche falling over and beyond her shoulders. When she spoke, she frequently tossed her head, thus calling attention to her hair and away from her lecture.

Then there was makeup. The first woman wore facial cover that made her skin smooth and pale, a black line under each eye, and mascara that darkened her already dark lashes. The second wore only a light gloss on her lips and a hint of shadow on her eyes. The third had blue bands under her eyes, dark blue shadow, mascara, bright red lipstick, and rouge; her fingernails also flashed red.

I considered the clothes each woman had worn on the three days of the conference: In the first case, man-tailored suits in primary colors with solid-color blouses. In the second, casual but stylish black T-shirt, a floppy collarless jacket and baggy slacks or skirt in neutral colors. The third wore a sexy jumpsuit; tight sleeveless jersey and tight yellow slacks; a dress with gaping armholes and an indulged tendency to fall off one shoulder.

Shoes? The first woman wore string sandals with medium heels; the second, sensible, comfortable walking shoes; the third, pumps with spike heels. You can fill in the jewelry, scarves, shawls, sweaters—or lack of them.

As I amused myself finding patterns and coherence in these styles and choices, I suddenly wondered why I was scrutinizing only the women. I scanned the table to get a fix on the styles of the eight men. And then I knew why I wasn't studying them. The men's styles were unmarked.

The term "marked" is a staple of linguistic theory. It refers to the way language alters the base meaning of a word by adding something—a little linguistic addition that has no meaning on its own. The unmarked form of a word carries the meaning that goes without saying, what you think of when you're not thinking anything special.

The unmarked tense of verbs in English is the present—for example, *visit*. To indicate past, you have to mark the verb for "past" by adding *ed* to yield *visited*. For future, you add a word: *will visit*. Nouns are presumed to be singular until marked for plural. To convey the idea of more than one, we typically add something, usually *s* or *es*. More than one *visit* becomes *visits*, and one *dish* becomes two *dishes*, thanks to the plural marking.

The unmarked forms of most English words also convey "male." Being male is the unmarked case. We have endings, such as *ess* and *ette,* to mark words as female. Unfortunately, marking words for female also, by association, tends to mark them for frivolousness. Would you feel safe entrusting your life to a doctorette? This is why many poets and actors who happen to be female object to the marked forms "poetess" and "actress." Alfre Woodard, an Oscar nominee for Best Supporting Actress, says she identifies herself as an actor because "actresses worry about eyelashes and cellulite, and women who are actors worry about the characters we are playing." Any marked form can pick up extra meaning beyond what the marking is intended to denote. The extra meanings carried by gender markers reflect the traditional associations with the female gender: not quite serious, often sexual.

I was able to identify the styles and types of the women at the conference because each of us had to make decisions about hair, clothing, makeup and accessories, and each of those decisions carried meaning. Every style available to us was marked. Of course, the men in our group had to make decisions too, but their choices carried far less meaning. The men could have chosen styles that were marked, but they didn't have to, and in this group, none did. Unlike the women, they had the option of being unmarked.

I took account of the men's clothes. There could have been a cowboy shirt with string tie or a three-piece suit or a necklaced hippie in jeans. But there wasn't. All eight men wore brown or blue slacks and standard-style shirts of light colors.

No man wore sandals or boots; their shoes were dark, closed, comfortable, and flat. In short, unmarked.

Although no man wore makeup, you couldn't say the men didn't wear makeup in the sense that you could say a woman didn't wear makeup. For men, no makeup is unmarked.

I asked myself what style we women could have adopted that would have been unmarked, like the men's. The answer was: none. There is no unmarked woman.

There is no woman's hairstyle that could be called "standard," that says nothing about her. The range of women's hairstyles is staggering, but if a woman's hair has no particular style, this in itself is taken as a statement that she doesn't care how she looks—an eloquent message that can disqualify a woman for many positions.

Women have to choose between shoes that are comfortable and shoes that are deemed attractive. When our group had to make an unexpected trek, the woman who wore flat laced shoes arrived first. The last to arrive was the woman with spike heels, her shoes in her hand and a handful of men around her.

If a woman's clothes are tight or revealing (in other words, sexy), it sends a message—an intended one of wanting to be attractive but also a possibly unintended one of availability. But if her clothes are not sexy, that too sends a message, lent meaning by the knowledge that they could have been. In her book *Women Lawyers,* Mona Harrington quotes a woman who, despite being a partner in her firm, found herself slipping into this fault line when she got an unexpected call to go to court right away. As she headed out the door, a young (male) associate said to her, "Hadn't you better button your blouse?" She was caught completely off guard. "My blouse wasn't buttoned unusually low," the woman told Harrington. "And this was not a conservative guy. But he thought one more button was necessary for court." And here's the rub: "I started wondering if my authority was being undermined by one button."

A woman wearing bright colors calls attention to herself, but if she avoids bright colors, she has (as my choice of verb in this sentence suggests) avoided something. Heavy makeup calls attention to the wearer as someone who wants to be attractive. Light makeup tries to be attractive without being alluring. There are thousands of products from which makeup must be chosen and myriad ways of applying them. Yet no makeup at all is anything but unmarked. Some men even see it as a hostile refusal to please them. Women who ordinarily do not wear makeup can be surprised by the transforming effect of putting it on. In a book titled *Face Value,* my colleague Robin Lakoff noted the increased attention she got from men when she went forth from a television station still professionally made-up.

Women can't even fill out a form without telling stories about themselves. Most application forms now give four choices for titles. Men have one to choose—"Mr."—so their choice carries no meaning other than to say they are male. But women must choose among three, each of them marked. A woman who checks the box for "Mrs." or "Miss" communi-

cates not only whether she has been married but also that she had conservative tastes in forms of address, and probably other conservative values as well. Checking "Ms." declines to let on about marriage (whereas "Mr." declines nothing since nothing was asked), but it also marks the woman who checks it on her form as either liberated or rebellious, depending on the attitudes and assumptions of the one making the judgment.

I sometimes try to duck these variously marked choices by giving my title as "Dr."—and thereby risk marking myself as either uppity (hence sarcastic responses like "Excuse *me!*") or an over-achiever (hence reactions of congratulatory surprise, like "Good for you!").

All married women's surnames are marked. If a woman takes her husband's name, she announces to the world that she is married and also that she is traditional in her values, according to some observers. To others it will indicate that she is less herself, more identified by her husband's identity. If she does not take her husband's name, this too is marked, seen as worthy of comment: She has *done* something; she has "kept her own name." Though a man can do exactly the same thing—and usually does—he is never said to have "kept his own name," because it never occurs to anyone that he might have given it up. For him, but not for her, using his own name is unmarked.

A married woman who wants to have her cake and eat it too may use her surname plus his. But this too announces that she is or has been married and often results in a tongue-tying string that makes life miserable for anyone who needs to alphabetize it. In a list (Harvey O'Donovan, Jonathan Feldman, Stephanie Woodbury McGillicutty), the woman's multiple name stands out. It is marked.

Pronouns conspire in this pattern as well. Grammar books tell us that "he" means "he or she" and that "she" is used only if a referent is specifically female. But this touting of "he" as the sex-indefinite pronoun is an innovation introduced into English by grammarians in the eighteenth and nineteenth centuries, according to Peter Mühlhäusler and Rom Harré in their book *Pronouns and People*. From at least about the year 1500, the correct sex-indefinite pronoun was "they," as it still is in casual spoken English. In other words, the female was declared by grammarians to be the marked case.

Looking at the men and women sitting around the conference table, I was amazed at how different our worlds were. Though men have to make choices too, and men's clothing styles may be less neutral now than they once were, nonetheless the parameters within which men must choose when dressing for work — the cut, fabric, or shade of jackets, shirts, and pants, and even the one area in which they are able to go a little wild, ties — are much narrower than the riotous range of colors and styles from which women must choose. For women, decisions about whether to wear a skirt, slacks, or a dress is only the start; the length of skirts can range from just above the floor to just below the hips, and the array of colors to choose from would make a rainbow look drab. But even this contrast in the range from which men and women must choose is irrelevant to the crucial point: A man can choose a style that will not attract attention or subject him to any particular interpretation, but a woman can't. Whatever she wears, whatever she calls herself, however she talks, will be fodder for interpretation about her character and competence. In a setting where most of the players are men, there is no unmarked woman.

This does not mean that men have complete freedom when it comes to dress. Quite the contrary — they have much less freedom than women have to express their personalities in their choice of fabrics, colors, styles, and jewelry. But the one freedom they have that women don't is the point of this discussion — the freedom to be unmarked.

That clothing is a metaphor for women's being marked was noticed by David Finkel, a journalist who wrote an article about women in Congress for *The Washington Post Magazine*. He used the contrast between women's and men's dress to open his article by describing the members coming through the doors to the floor of the U.S. House of Representatives:

> So many men, so many suits. Dark suits. Solid suits. Blue suits that look gray, gray suits that look blue. There's Tom Foley — he's in one, and Bob Michel, and Steny Hoyer, and Fred Grandy, and Dick Durbin, and dozens, make that hundreds, more.
>
> So many suits, so many white shirts. And dark ties. And five o'clock shadows. And short haircuts. And loosening jowls. And big, visible ears.
>
> So many, many men.
>
> . . .
>
> And still the members continue to pour through the doors — gray, grayer, grayest — until the moment when, emerging into this humidor, comes a surprise:
>
> The color red.
>
> It is Susan Molinari, a first-termer from New York . . .
>
> Now, turquoise. It is Barbara Boxer . . .
>
> Now, paisley. It is Jill Long . . .

Embroidering his color-of-clothing metaphor, Finkel, whose article appeared in May 1992, concluded, "Of the 435 members of the House of Representatives, 29 are women, which means that if Congress is a gray flannel suit, the women of Congress are no more than a handful of spots on the lapel."

When Is Sexism Realism?

If women are marked in our culture, their very presence in professional roles is, more often than not, marked. Many work settings, just like families, come with ready-made roles prescribed by gender, and the ones women are expected to fill are typically support roles. It was not long ago when medical offices and hospitals were peopled by men who were doctors and orderlies and women who were nurses and clerical workers, just as most offices were composed of men who ran the business and women who served them as receptionists, clerks, and secretaries. All members of Congress were men, and women found in the Capitol Building were aides and staff members. When a woman or man enters a setting in an atypical role, the expectation is always a backdrop to the scene.

All the freshmen women in Congress have had to contend with being mistaken for staff, even though they wear pins on their lapels identifying them as members. For her book *A Woman's Place*, Congresswoman Marjorie Margolies-Mezvinsky interviewed her female colleagues about their experiences. One congresswoman approached a security checkpoint with two congressmen when a guard stopped only her and told her to go through the metal detector. When Congresswoman Maria Cantwell needed to get into her office after hours, the guard wanted to know which member she worked for. But her press secretary, Larry West, has gone through the gate unthinkingly without being stopped. When Congresswoman Lynn Schenk attended a reception with a male aide, the host graciously held out his hand to the aide and said "Oh, Congressman Schenk."

You don't have to be in Congress to have experiences like that. A woman who owned her own business found that if she took any man along on business trips, regardless of whether he was her vice president or her assistant, people she met tended to address themselves to him, certain that he must be the one with power and she his helper. A double-bass player had a similar experience when she arrived for an audition with a male accompanist. The people who greeted them assumed she was the accompanist. A woman who heads a research firm and holds a doctorate finds she is frequently addressed as "Mrs.," while her assistant, who holds only a master's degree, is addressed as "Dr."

One evening after hours, I was working in my office at Georgetown University. Faculty offices in my building are lined up on both sides of a corridor, with cubicles in the corridor for secretaries and graduate-student assistants. Outside each office is a nameplate with the professor's title and last name. The quiet of the after-hours corridor was interrupted when a woman came to my door and asked if she could use my phone. I was surprised but glad to oblige, and explained that she had to dial "9." She made the call, thanked me, and left. A few minutes later, she reappeared and asked if I had any correction fluid. Again surprised, but still happy to be of help, I looked in my desk drawer but had to disappoint her: Since my typewriter was self-correcting, I had none. My patience began to waver, but my puzzlement was banished when the woman bounded into my office for the third and final time to ask if I was Dr. Murphy's secretary, in which case she would like to leave with me the paper she was turning in to him.

I doubt this woman would have imposed on my time and space to use my telephone and borrow correction fluid if she had known I was a professor, even though I would not have minded had she done so. At least she would probably have been more deferential in intruding. And the experience certainly gave me a taste of how hard it must be for receptionists to get any work done, as everyone regards them as perpetually interruptible. But what amused and amazed me was that my being female had overridden so many clues to my position: My office was along the wall, it was fully enclosed like all faculty offices, my name and title were on the door, and I was working after five, the hour when offices close and secretaries go home. But all these clues were nothing next to the master clue of gender: In the university environment, she expected that professors were men and women were secretaries. Statistics were on her side: Of the eighteen members of my department at the time, sixteen were men; of the five members of Dr. Murphy's department, four were men. So she was simply trusting the world to be as she knew it was.

It is not particularly ironic or surprising that the student who mistook me for a secretary was female. Women are no less prone to assume that people will adhere to the norm than are men. And this includes women who themselves are exceptions. A woman physician who works in a specialty in which few of her colleagues are female told me of her annoyance when she telephones a colleague, identifies herself as "Dr. Jones calling for Dr. Smith," and is told by Dr. Smith's receptionist, "I'll go get Dr. Smith while you put Dr. Jones on the line." But this same woman catches herself referring to her patients' general practitioners as "he," even though she ought to know better than anyone that a physician could be a woman.

Children seem to pick up norms as surely as adults do. A woman who was not only a doctor but a professor at a medical school was surprised when her five-year-old said to her, "You're not a doctor, Mommy. You're a nurse." Intent on impressing her daughter, she said, "Yes, I am a doctor. In fact, I teach other doctors how to be doctors." The little girl thought about this as she incorporated the knowledge into her worldview. "Oh," she said. "But you only teach women doctors." (Conversely, male nurses must deal with being mistaken for doctors, and men who work as assistants must deal with being mistaken for their boss.)

Another of my favorite stories in this mode is about my colleague who made a plane reservation for herself and replied to the question "Is that Mrs. or Miss?" by giving her title: "It's Dr." So the agent asked, "Will the doctor be needing a rental car when he arrives?" Her attempt to reframe her answer to avoid revealing her marital status resulted in the agent reframing her as a secretary.

I relate these stories not to argue that sexism is rampant and that we should all try to bear in mind that roles are changing, although I believe these statements to be true. I am inclined to be indulgent of such errors, even though I am made uncomfortable when they happen to me, because I myself have been guilty of them. I recall an occasion when I gave a talk to a gathering of women physicians, and then signed books. The woman who organized the signing told me to save one book because she had met a doctor in the elevator who couldn't make it to the talk but asked to have a book signed nonetheless. I was pleased to oblige and asked, pen poised, to whom I should sign the book—and was surprised when I heard a woman's name. Even though I had just spent the evening with a room full of doctors who were all women, in my mind "a doctor" had called up the image of a man.

So long as women are a minority of professional ranks, we cannot be surprised if people assume the world is as it is. I mention these stories to give a sense of what the world is like for people who are exceptions to expectations—every moment they live in the unexpected role, they must struggle against others' assumptions that do not apply to them, much like gay men and lesbians with regard to their sexual orientation, and, as Ellis Cose documents in his book *The Rage of a Privileged Class*, much like middle-class black professionals in most American settings.

One particular burden of this pattern for a woman in a position of authority is that she must deal with incursions on her time, as others make automatic assumptions that her time is more expendable, although she also may benefit from hearing more information because people find her "approachable." There is a sense in which every woman is seen as a receptionist—available to give information and help, perennially interruptible. A woman surgeon complained that although she has very good relations with the nurses in her hospital, they simply do not wait on her the way they wait on her male colleagues. (The very fact that I must say "woman surgeon" and "male nurse" reflects this dilemma: All surgeons are presumed male, all nurses presumed female, unless proven otherwise. In other words, the unmarked surgeon is male, the unmarked nurse female.)

Questions

1. Tannen asserts that "any marked form [of a word] can pick up extra meaning beyond what the marking is intended to denote." Consider the terms *waitress* and *waiter.* Do these words suggest anything other than a woman who waits on tables and a man who waits on tables?

2. Tannen suggests that in the business world, women do not have the freedom to be "unmarked." Is this only true in the business world? What about among college students? Do female college students have more or less freedom to be unmarked than women in the business world? How about men?

3. Assume that there are three types of jobs in our society: those whose incumbents are expected to be men, those whose incumbents are expected to be women, and those for whom there are no expectations about the sex of incumbents. Try to list a half dozen examples for each category. How difficult is this task?

    Look at your three lists. What do the jobs within each list have in common with one another?

·16·

"Getting" and "Making" a Tip

Greta Foff Paule

In this article, Greta Foff Paule, who received a Ph.D. in cultural anthropology from Princeton University, takes us into the world of the waitress. If you've never waited on tables, you might naturally assume that waitresses (and waiters, for that matter) are there to serve the customers. But as Paule discovered through participant observation, there is a lot more to the customer–waitress relationship than meets the eye. You decide who has what kinds of power in this relationship.

The waitress can't help feeling a sense of personal failure and public censure when she is "stiffed."
—William F. Whyte, "When Workers and Customers Meet"

They're rude, they're ignorant, they're obnoxious, they're inconsiderate. . . . Half of these people don't deserve to come out and eat, let alone try and tip a waitress.

—Route waitress

Making a Tip at Route

A common feature of past research is that the worker's control over the tipping system is evaluated in terms of her efforts to con, coerce, compel, or otherwise manipulate a customer into relinquishing a bigger tip. Because these efforts have for the most part proven futile, the worker has been seen as having little defense against the financial vicissitudes of the tipping system. What these studies have overlooked is that an employee can increase her tip income by controlling the number as well as the size of tips she receives. This oversight has arisen from the tendency of researchers to concentrate narrowly on the relationship between server and served, while failing to take into account

the broader organizational context in which this relationship takes place.

Like service workers observed in earlier studies, waitresses at Route strive to boost the amount of individual gratuities by rendering special services and being especially friendly. As one waitress put it, "I'll sell you the world if you're in my station." In general though, waitresses at Route Restaurant seek to boost their tip income, not by increasing the amount of individual gratuities, but by increasing the number of customers they serve. They accomplish this (a) by securing the largest or busiest stations and working the most lucrative shifts; (b) by "turning" their tables quickly; and (c) by controlling the flow of customers within the restaurant.

Technically, stations at Route are assigned on a rotating basis so that all waitresses, including rookies, work fast and slow stations equally. Station assignments are listed on the work schedule that is posted in the office window where it can be examined by all workers on all shifts, precluding the possibility of blatant favoritism or discrimination. Yet a number of methods exist whereby experienced waitresses are able to circumvent the formal rotation system and secure the more lucrative stations for themselves. A waitress can trade assignments with a rookie who is uncertain of her ability to handle a fast station; she can volunteer to take over a large station when a *call-out*[1] necessitates reorganization of station assignments; or she can establish herself as the only waitress capable of handling a particularly large or chaotic station. Changes in station assignments tend not to be formally recorded, so inconsistencies in the rotation system often do not show up on the schedule. Waitresses on the same shift may notice of course that a co-worker has managed to avoid an especially slow station for many days, or has somehow ended up in the busiest station two weekends in a row, but the waitresses' code of noninterference . . . inhibits them from openly objecting to such irregularities.

A waitress can also increase her tip income by working the more lucrative shifts. Because day is the busiest and therefore most profitable shift at Route, it attracts experienced, professional waitresses who are most concerned and best able to maximize their tip earnings. There are exceptions: some competent, senior-ranking waitresses are unable to work during the day due to time constraints of family or second jobs. Others choose not to work during the day despite the potential monetary rewards, because they are unwilling to endure the intensely competitive atmosphere for which day shift is infamous.

The acutely competitive environment that characterizes day shift arises from the aggregate striving of each waitress to maximize her tip income by serving the greatest possible number of customers. Two strategies are enlisted to this end. First, each waitress attempts to *turn* her tables as quickly as possible. Briefly stated, this means she takes the order, delivers the food, clears and resets a table, and begins serving the next party as rapidly as customer

lingering and the speed of the kitchen allow. A seven-year veteran of Route describes the strategy and its rewards:

> What I do is I prebus my tables. When the people get up and go all I got is glasses and cups, pull off, wipe, set, and I do the table turnover. But see that's from day shift. See the girls on graveyard . . . don't understand the more times you turn that table the more money you make. You could have three tables and still make a hundred dollars. If you turn them tables.

As the waitress indicates, a large part of turning tables involves getting the table cleared and set for the next customer. During a rush, swing and grave waitresses tend to leave dirty tables standing, partly because they are less experienced and therefore less efficient, partly to avoid being given parties, or *sat*, when they are already behind. In contrast, day waitresses assign high priority to keeping their tables cleared and ready for customers. The difference in method reflects increased skill and growing awareness of and concern with money-making strategies.

A waitress can further increase her customer count by controlling the flow of customers within the restaurant. Ideally the hostess or manager running the front house rotates customers among stations, just as stations are rotated among waitresses. Each waitress is given, or *sat*, one party at a time in turn so that all waitresses have comparable customer counts at the close of a shift. When no hostess is on duty, or both she and the manager are detained and customers are waiting to be seated, waitresses will typically seat incoming parties.

Whether or not a formal hostess is on duty, day waitresses are notorious for by-passing the rotation system by racing to the door and directing incoming customers to their own tables. A sense of the urgency with which this strategy is pursued is conveyed in the comment of one five-year veteran, "They'll run you

---

[1] A call-out (which more logically might be termed a "call-in") occurs when an employee calls in sick or with some other reason why he or she can't make it to work that day. — Ed.

down to get that person at the door, to seat them in their station." The competition for customers is so intense during the day that some waitresses claim they cannot afford to leave the floor (even to use the restroom) lest they return to find a co-worker's station filled at their expense. "In the daytime, honey," remarks an eight-year Route waitress, "in the daytime it's like pulling teeth. You got to stay on the floor to survive. To survive." It is in part because they do not want to lose customers and tips to their co-workers that waitresses do not take formal breaks. Instead, they rest and eat between waiting tables or during lulls in business, returning to the floor intermittently to check on parties in progress and seat customers in their stations.

The fast pace and chaotic nature of restaurant work provide a cover for the waitress's aggressive pursuit of customers, since it is difficult for other servers to monitor closely the allocation of parties in the bustle and confusion of a rush. Still, it is not uncommon for waitresses to grumble to management and co-workers if they notice an obvious imbalance in customer distribution. Here again, the waitress refrains from directly criticizing her fellow servers, voicing her displeasure by commenting on the paucity of customers in her own station, rather than the overabundance of customers in the stations of certain co-waitresses. In response to these grumblings, other waitresses may moderate somewhat their efforts to appropriate new parties, and management may make a special effort to seat the disgruntled server favorably.

A waitress can also exert pressure on the manager or hostess to keep her station filled. She may, for instance, threaten to leave if she is not seated enough customers.

I said, "Innes [a manager], I'm in [station] one and two. If one and two is not filled at all times from now until three, I'm getting my coat, my pocketbook, and I'm leaving." And one and two was filled, and I made ninety-five dollars.

Alternatively, she can make it more convenient for the manager or hostess to seat her rather than her co-workers, either by keeping her tables open (as described), or by taking extra tables. If customers are waiting to be seated, a waitress may offer to pick up parties in a station that is closed or, occasionally, to pick up parties in another waitress's station. In attempting either strategy, but especially the latter, the waitress must be adept not only at waiting tables, but in interpersonal restaurant politics. Autonomy and possession are of central concern to waitresses, and a waitress who offers to pick up tables outside her station must select her words carefully if she is to avoid being accused of invading her co-workers' territory. Accordingly, she may choose to present her bid for extra parties as an offer to help—the manager, another waitress, the restaurant, customers—rather than as a request.

The waitress who seeks to increase her tip income by maximizing the number of customers she serves may endeavor to cut her losses by refusing to serve parties that have stiffed her in the past. If she is a low-ranking waitress, her refusal is likely to be overturned by the manager. If she is an experienced and valuable waitress, the manager may ask someone else to take the party, assure the waitress he will take care of her (that is, pad the bill and give her the difference), or even pick up the party himself. Though the practice is far from common, a waitress may go so far as to demand a tip from a customer who has been known to stiff in the past.

This party of two guys come in and they order thirty to forty dollars worth of food . . . and they stiff us. Every time. So Kaddie told them, "If you don't tip us, we're not going to wait on you." They said, "We'll tip you." So Kaddie waited on them, and they tipped her. The next night they came in, I waited on them and they didn't tip me. The third time they came in [the manager] put them in my station and I told [the manager] straight up, "I'm not waiting on them . . ." So he made Hailey pick them up. And they stiffed Hailey. So when they came in the next night . . . [they] said, "Are you going to give us a table?" I said, "You going to tip me? I'm not going to wait on you. You got all that money, you sell all that crack on the streets and you come here and you can't even leave me a couple of bucks?" . . . So they left me a dollar. So when they come in Tuesday night, I'm telling them a dollar ain't enough.

The tactics employed by waitresses, and particularly day-shift waitresses, to increase their customer count and thereby boost their tip earnings have earned them a resounding notoriety among their less competitive co-workers. Day (and some swing) waitresses are described as "money hungry," "sneaky little bitches," "self-centered," "aggressive," "backstabbing bitches," and "cutthroats over tables." The following remarks of two Route waitresses, however, indicate that those who employ these tactics see them as defensive, not aggressive measures. A sense of the waitress's preoccupation with autonomy and with protecting what is hers also emerges from these comments.

> You have to be like that. Because if you don't be like that, people step on you. You know, like as far as getting customers. I mean, you know, I'm sorry everybody says I'm greedy. I guess that's why I've survived this long at Route. Cause I am greedy. . . . *I want what's mine*, and if it comes down to me cleaning your table or my table, I'm going to clean my table. Because see I went through all that stage where I would do your table. To be fair. And you would walk home with seventy dollars, and I'd have twenty-five, cause I was being fair all night. (emphasis added)

> If the customer comes in the door and I'm there getting that door, don't expect me to cover your backside while you in the back smoking a cigarette and I'm here working for myself. You not out there working for me. . . . When I go to the door and get the customers, when I keep my tables clean and your tables are dirty, and you wonder why you only got one person . . . then that's just tough shit. . . . You're damn right my

station is filled. *I'm not here for you.* (emphasis added)

Whether the waitress who keeps her station filled with customers is acting aggressively or defensively, her tactics are effective. It is commonly accepted that determined day waitresses make better money than less competitive co-workers even when working swing or grave. Moreover Nera, the waitress most infamous for her relentless use of "money-hungry tactics," is at the same time most famous for her consistently high daily takes. While other waitresses jingle change in their aprons, Nera is forced to store wads of bills in her shoes and in paper bags to prevent tips from overflowing her pockets. She claims to make a minimum of five hundred dollars a week in tip earnings; her record for one day's work exceeds two hundred dollars and is undoubtedly the record for the restaurant.

Inverting the Symbolism of Tipping

It may already be apparent that the waitress views the customer—not as a master to pamper and appease—but as a substance to be processed as quickly and in as large a quantity as possible. The difference in perspective is expressed in the objectifying terminology of waitresses: a customer or party is referred to as a *table*, or by table number, as *table five* or simply *five*; serving successive parties at a table is referred to as *turning the table*; taking an order is also known as *picking up a table*; and to serve water, coffee, or other beverages is to *water, coffee,* or *beverage* a table, number, or customer. Even personal acquaintances assume the status of inanimate matter, or tip-bearing plants, in the language of the server:

> I got my fifth-grade teacher [as a customer] one time. . . . I kept her coffeed. I kept her boyfriend coked all night. Sodaed. . . . And I kept them filled up.

If the customer is perceived as material that is processed, the goal of this processing is the production or extraction of a finished product: the tip. This image too is conveyed in the language of the floor. A waitress may comment that she "got a good tip " or "gets good tips," but she is more likely to say that she "made" or "makes good tips." She may also say that she "got five bucks out of" a customer, or complain that some customers "don't want to give up on" their money. She may accuse a waitress who stays over into her shift of "tapping on" her money, or warn an aspiring waitress against family restaurants on the grounds that "there's no money in there." In all these comments (and all are actual), the waitress might as easily be talking about mining for coal or drilling for oil as serving customers.

Predictably, the waitress's view of the customer as substance to be processed influences her perception of the meaning of tips, and especially substandard tips. At Route, low tips and stiffs are not interpreted as a negative reflection on the waitress's personal qualities or social status. Rather, they are felt to reveal the refractory nature or poor quality of the raw material from which the tip is extracted, produced, or fashioned. In less metaphorical terms, a low tip or stiff is thought to reflect the negative qualities and low status of the customer who is too cheap, too poor, too ignorant, or too coarse to leave an appropriate gratuity. In this context, it is interesting to note that *stiff*, the term used in restaurants to refer to incidents of nontipping or to someone who does not tip, has also been used to refer to a wastrel or penniless man, a hobo, tramp, vagabond, deadbeat, and a moocher (Wentworth and Flexner 1975).

Evidence that waitresses assign blame for poor tips to the tipper is found in their reaction to being undertipped or stiffed. Rather than breaking down in tears and lamenting her "personal failure," the Route waitress responds to a stiff by announcing the event to her co-workers and managers in a tone of angry disbelief. Co-workers and managers echo the waitress's indignation and typically ask her to identify the party (by table number and physical description), or if she has already done so, to be more specific. This identification is crucial for it allows sympathizers to join the waitress in analyzing the cause of the stiff, which is assumed a priori[2] to arise from some shortcoming of the party, not the waitress. The waitress and her co-workers may conclude that the customers in question were rude, troublemakers, or bums, or they may explain their behavior by identifying them as members of a particular category of customers. It might be revealed for instance, that the offending party was a church group: church groups are invariably tightfisted. It might be resolved that the offenders were senior citizens, Southerners, or businesspeople: all well-known cheapskates. If the customers were European, the stiff will be attributed to ignorance of the American tipping system; if they were young, to immaturity; if they had children, to lack of funds.

These classifications and their attendant explanations are neither fixed nor trustworthy. New categories are invented to explain otherwise puzzling incidents, and all categories are subject to exception. Though undependable as predictive devices, customer typologies serve a crucial function: they divert blame for stiffs and low tips from the waitress to the characteristics of the customer. It is for this reason that it is "important" for workers to distinguish between different categories of customers, despite the fact that such distinctions are based on "unreliable verbal and appearance clues." In fact, it is precisely the unreliability, or more appropriately the flexibility, of customer typologies that makes them valuable to waitresses. When categories can be constructed and dissolved on demand, there is no

---

[2]*A priori* is Latin for "from what comes before," or reasoning from what is already known. —Ed.

danger that an incident will fall outside the existing system of classification and hence be inexplicable.

While waitresses view the customer as something to be processed and the tip as the product of this processing, they are aware that the public does not share their understanding of the waitress–diner–tip relationship. Waitresses at Route recognize that many customers perceive them as needy creatures willing to commit great feats of service and absorb high doses of abuse in their anxiety to secure a favorable gratuity or protect their jobs. They are also aware that some customers leave small tips with the intent to insult the server and that others undertip on the assumption that for a Route waitress even fifty cents will be appreciated. One waitress indicated that prior to being employed in a restaurant, she herself subscribed to the stereotype of the down-and-out waitress "because you see stuff on television, you see these wives or single ladies who waitress and they live in slummy apartments or slummy houses and they dress in rags." It is these images of neediness and desperation, which run so strongly against the waitress's perception of herself and her position, that she attacks when strained relations erupt into open conflict.

> Five rowdy black guys walked in the door and they went to seat themselves at table seven. I said, "Excuse me. You all got to wait to be seated." "We ain't got to do *shit*. We here to eat. . . ." So they went and sat down. And I turned around and just looked at them. And they said, "Well, I hope you ain't our waitress, cause you blew your tip. Cause you ain't getting nothing from us." And I turned around and I said, "You need it more than I do, baby."

This waitress's desire to confront the customer's assumption of her destitution is widely shared among service workers whose status as tipped employees marks them as needy in the eyes of their customers. Davis (1959, 162–163) reports that among cabdrivers "a forever re-peated story is of the annoyed driver, who, after a grueling trip with a Lady Shopper, hands the coin back, telling her, 'Lady, keep your lousy dime. You need it more than I do.'" Mars and Nicod (1984, 75) report a hotel waitress's claim that "if she had served a large family with children for one or two weeks, and then was given a 10p piece,[3] she would give the money back, saying, 'It's all right, thank you, I've got enough change for my bus fare home.'" In an incident I observed (not at Route), a waitress followed two male customers out of a restaurant calling, "Excuse me! You forgot this!" and holding up the coins they had left as a tip. The customers appeared embarrassed, motioned for her to keep the money, and continued down the sidewalk. The waitress, now standing in the outdoor seating area of the restaurant and observed by curious diners, threw the money after the retreating men and returned to her work. Episodes such as these allow the worker to repudiate openly the evaluation of her financial status that is implied in an offensively small gratuity, and permit her to articulate her own understanding of what a small tip says and about whom. If customers can only afford to leave a dime, or feel a 10p piece is adequate compensation for two weeks' service, they must be very hard up or very ignorant indeed.

In the following incident the waitress interjects a denial of her neediness into an altercation that is not related to tipping, demonstrating that the customer's perception of her financial status is a prominent and persistent concern for her.

> She [a customer] wanted a California Burger with mayonnaise. And when I got the mayonnaise, the mayonnaise had a little brown on it. . . . So this girl said to me, she said, "What the fuck is

---

[3]Until it converts to the Eurodollar, the British monetary unit is the pound sterling (£). One pound is worth about $1.65 in U.S. currency. There are 100 pence to the pound. So, 10p (pronounced "10 pea") is worth about 17 cents. — Ed.

this you giving me?" And I turned around, I thought, "Maybe she's talking to somebody else in the booth with her." And I turned around and I said, "Excuse me?" She said, "You hear what I said. I said, What the fuck are you giving me?" And I turned around, I said, "I don't know if you're referring your information to *me*," I said, "but if you're referring your information to *me*," I said, "I don't *need* your bullshit." I said, "I'm not going to even take it. . . . Furthermore, I could care less if you eat or *don't* eat. . . . And you see this?" And I took her check and I ripped it apart. . . . And I took the California Burger and I says, "You don't have a problem anymore now, right?" She went up to the manager. And she says, "That black waitress" —I says, "Oh. By the way, what is my name? I don't have a name, [using the words] 'that black waitress'. . . . My name happens to be Nera. . . . That's N-E-R-A. . . . And I don't need your bullshit, sweetheart. . . . People like you I can walk on, because you don't know how to talk to human beings." And I said, "I don't need you. I don't need your quarters. I don't need your nickels. I don't need your dimes. So if you want service, be my guest. Don't you *ever* sit in my station, cause I won't wait on you." The manager said, "Nera, please. Would you wait in the back?" I said, "No. I don't take back seats no more for nobody."

In each of these cases, the waitress challenges the customer's definition of the relationship in which tipping occurs. By speaking out, by confronting the customer, she demonstrates that she is not subservient or in fear of losing her job; that she is not compelled by financial need or a sense of social hierarchy to accept abuse from customers; that she does not, in Nera's words, "take back seats no more for nobody." At the same time, she reverses the symbolic force of the low tip, converting a statement on her social status or work skills into a statement on the tipper's cheapness or lack of savoir faire.[4] . . .

References

Davis, Fred. 1959. "The Cabdriver and His Fare: Facets of a Fleeting Relationship." *American Journal of Sociology* 65(2): 158–165.

Mars, Gerald, and Michael Nicod. 1984. *The World of Waiters.* London: Allen & Unwin.

Wentworth, Harold, and Stuart Berg Flexner (eds. and comps.). 1975. *Dictionary of American Slang.* 2nd supplemental ed. New York: Crowell.

---

[4]*Savoir faire* is French and means literally "knowing how to do." Generally the phrase is used to mean "a knowledge of how to get around in the world," or simply, tact. —Ed.

Questions

1. You've just been out to dinner at a nice restaurant. Your waitress presented you with a tab for $72.50. Assuming the service was fine, how much did you tip her? How much do you think she might have expected. Where did you learn the appropriate amount to tip?

2. Have you ever tried to send a "message" to a waitperson by leaving no tip or a very small one? What was that message? Whether you've ever sent such a message, based on what you've read in Paule's article, do you think the message was received?

3. One of the techniques for understanding how people interact within a social structure is to look at "role sets" — that is, the set of statuses with which one interacts in carrying out one's role. In the accompanying diagram, I've sketched my role set as a professor. Try your hand at this by sketching the role set of the waitress.

Professor's role set

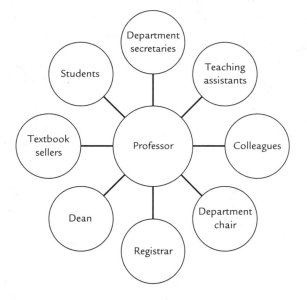

Generally, people within a particular role set have a similar understanding of one another's role—that is, their rights and duties as incumbents in a particular status. As Paule tells it, however, the customer has a different understanding of the waitress's role than the waitress does. To what sorts of complications might this lead? What would be the effect on the relationship if both customer and waitress understood the waitress's role from the waitress's point of view? From the customer's point of view?

·17·

Handling the Stigma
of Handling the Dead

Morticians and Funeral Directors

William E. Thompson

As William Thompson observes in his article on the funeral profession, a individual's occupational status—and the role attached to that status—is central to his or her identity. How, then, do people who do work that others find *repugnant* manage things such that they themselves do not feel repugnant?

In a complex, industrialized society a person's occupation or profession is central to his or her personal and social identity. As Pavalko (1988) pointed out, two strangers are quite ". . . likely to 'break the ice' by indicating the kind of work they do." As a result, individuals often make a number of initial judgments about others based on preconceived notions about particular occupations.

This study examines how morticians and funeral directors handle the stigma associated with their work. Historically, stigma has been attached to those responsible for caring for the dead, and the job typically was assigned to the lower classes (e.g., the Eta of Japan and the Untouchables in India),[1] and in some cases, those who handled the dead were forbidden from touching the living (Bendann 1930; Kearl 1989; Murray 1969). Today, the stigma has grown to new and potentially more threaten-

ing proportions for those engaged in the profession, for during the twentieth century Americans have become preoccupied with the denial of death (Becker 1973; Charmaz 1980; Fulton 1961; Jackson 1980; Kearl 1989; Momeyer 1988; Sudnow 1967).[2] As Stephenson (1985, 223) noted, "In a society which seeks to deny the reality of death, the funeral director is a living symbol of this dreaded subject."

Two major problems faced by members of the funeral industry are that they make their living by doing work considered taboo by most Americans and that they are viewed as

---

[1]The Eta were a people of Japan who—like the scheduled castes (or untouchables) of India—were regarded as ritually polluted. The distinction between Eta and non-Eta was officially outlawed in Japan in the nineteenth century, just as the distinction between the scheduled castes and others was outlawed in India in the mid-twentieth century. In both countries, however, the distinction continues informally — Ed.

[2]The wholesale denial of death in contemporary American society has been seriously questioned by some. For example, Parsons and Lidz (1967) eloquently refuted the "denial of death" thesis, indicating that "American society has institutionalized a broadly stable, though flexible and changing, orientation to death that is fundamentally not a 'denial' but a mode of acceptance appropriate to our primary cultural patterns of activism" (134). In a later article Parsons, Fox, and Lidz (1972, 368) argued that "what is often interpreted as 'denial' is in reality a kind of 'apathy.'" They insist that, in a religious sense, death must be viewed as "a reciprocal gift to God, the consummatory reciprocation of the gift of life" (451). Others counter, however, that death and funerals have become increasingly secularized and that although constantly confronted with the realities of death, most Americans choose to ignore and deny it as much as possible.

profiting from death and grief—a fact from which they must continually attempt to divert public attention. The "7-billion-dollar-a-year American funeral industry" has received much criticism over the past 2 decades and widespread complaints have led to "congressional hearings, new trade practices rules from the Federal Trade Commission, and undercover sting operations by various consumer groups" (Kearl 1989, 271). Those in the funeral business were further stigmatized when it was revealed that 58% of the funeral homes studied by the FTC had committed at least one billing abuse against their bereaved clients, and public testimony revealed "horror stories" of inflated charges for funeral services neither required nor requested (Kearl 1989, 278).

Morticians and funeral directors are fully aware of the stigma associated with their work, so they continually strive to enhance their public image and promote their social credibility. They must work to shift the emphasis of their work from the dead to the living, and away from sales and toward service. As Aries (1976, 99) noted:

> In order to sell death, it had to be made friendly . . . since 1885 . . . [funeral directors have] presented themselves not as simple sellers of services, but as "doctors of grief" who have a mission . . . [which] consists in aiding the mourning survivors to return to normalcy.

Couched within the general theoretical framework of symbolic interactionism, there are a variety of symbolic and dramaturgical methods[3] whereby morticians and funeral directors attempt to redefine their occupations and minimize and/or neutralize negative attitudes toward them and what they do.

---

[3]You may recall that the concept of dramaturgical was introduced at the beginning of reading 13—it developed from the line of sociological analysis followed by Erving Goffman. —Ed.

Method

This study reflects over 2 years of qualitative fieldwork as outlined by Schatzman and Strauss (1973), Spradley (1979) and Berg (1989). Extensive ethnographic interviews were conducted during 1987–1989 with 19 morticians and funeral directors in four states: Kansas, Missouri, Oklahoma, and Texas. The funeral homes included both privately owned businesses and branches of large franchise operations. They were located in communities ranging from less than 1,000 population to cities of over 1 million people.

First contacts were made by telephone, and appointments were made to tour the funeral homes and meet with the directors and morticians. Initial taped interviews ranged from 1½ to a little over 4 hours in duration. In all but two cases, follow-up interviews were used to obtain additional information about the individuals and their work.

Rather than limiting questions to a standardized interview schedule, the researcher soon discovered that, as with most ethnographic fieldwork (Berg, 1989; Spradley 1979), interviewees were much more comfortable and provided more information during casual conversation. Consequently, the structured portion of the interview focused primarily on demographic data, educational credentials, how they decided to enter the profession, how they felt about their jobs, and how they handled the stigma associated with their work. The questions were open-ended, and answers to one question invariably led to a variety of spontaneous follow-up questions.

Respondents

Interviewees included people from different age groups, both sexes, and both whites and nonwhites. There were 16 males and 3 females interviewed for this study, ranging in age from 26 to 64 years. Most of the respondents were between their late 30s and early 50s. Fourteen of the males were both morticians (licensed embalmers) and licensed funeral directors. The other two males were licensed embalmers who were employed in funeral homes, but were not licensed funeral directors. None of the females had been trained or licensed to embalm. Two of the females were licensed funeral directors, and the other woman was neither licensed as an embalmer nor funeral director. She was married to a man who was licensed to do both, and she simply helped out around the funeral home—usually answering the phone and helping with bookkeeping. All the women admitted, however, that they often helped out in the embalming room and in making funeral arrangements.

Seventeen of the people interviewed were white. The other two were African-American brothers who jointly owned and operated a funeral home located in a city of approximately 150 thousand people. Only one was a licensed funeral director and licensed embalmer. They candidly admitted, however, that they both worked in the embalming room and arranged funeral services.

With only one exception, all of the morticians and funeral directors interviewed were more than willing to talk about their occupations. They were aware that the author was conducting research, and several of them commented that the funeral industry was much maligned and stigmatized, and they were anxious to get an opportunity to "set the record straight," or "tell their side of the story" about their jobs. As the interviews progressed, however, the author was struck by the candor with which most of the interviewees responded to questions and provided additional information. Only one of the funeral directors, a single 50-year-old white male, was reluctant to talk about his work, refused to be taped, and was

extremely guarded throughout the interview. He attempted to answer as many questions as possible with short, cryptic responses, and on several occasions became quite defensive and asked: "Why did you ask that?" and "What are you going to do with this information?" Despite his defensiveness, his answers indicated that his experiences as a mortician and funeral director were very similar to the others interviewed. In fact, his reticence about answering some of the questions served to underscore the fact that he believed there was a great deal of stigma attached to his work and he wanted to be careful not to add to it (a point he made verbally during the interview).

Occupational Stigma

Erving Goffman (1963) defined *stigma* as any attribute that sets people apart and discredits them or disqualifies them from full social acceptance. This paper explores what happens when people are discredited (stigmatized) because of the work they perform, and how they attempt to reduce or eliminate the stigma.

People are most likely to be stigmatized because of their work if it is viewed as deviant by other members of society. George Ritzer (1977) cited three criteria, any one of which can cause an occupation to be considered deviant: (a) if it is illegal, (b) if it is considered immoral, and (c) if it is considered improper.

The first category of occupations, those that are illegal, has been widely studied by sociologists. Even a cursory list of studies on organized crime, prostitution, shoplifting, counterfeiting, confidence swindling, professional thievery, and other illegal occupations would be voluminous. The second category of deviant occupations is less straightforward than the first. Although many occupations that are considered immoral also have been made illegal (e.g., prostitution), there is much less agreement on the morality of occupations than on their legality.

The final category is a fascinating one, and perhaps the most ripe for sociological investigation. It includes those jobs that may not be considered "a proper or fitting occupation by society" (Polsky 1969, 32). In any society there are certain jobs that most people prefer not to do. These jobs often require little or no training, pay very little, rank low in occupational prestige, and involve "dirty work" (Garson 1975; Hughes 1971). As Hughes (1971, 344) pointed out:

> . . . the delegation of dirty work to someone else is common among humans. Many cleanliness taboos . . . depend for their practice upon success in delegating the tabooed activity to someone else.

Although the occupations of mortician and funeral director do not fit neatly into any of Ritzer's three categories, preparing the dead for funerals, burial, and/or cremation can be characterized as "dirty work." The stigma associated with these occupations is not so much that they are literally unclean, although embalming can be rather messy. It is, however, no more so than surgery—a highly prestigious profession. Rather, they are figuratively unclean because they violate social taboos against handling the dead.

THE STIGMA OF HANDLING THE DEAD

Ritualistic disposal of dead human bodies is a cultural universal (Bendann 1930; Habenstein and Lamers 1960; Huntington and Metcalf 1979). These ceremonies ". . . manifest the collective image of death—what the larger society thinks and feels about death" (Stephenson 1985). In American society, death is surrounded by mystery and taboos. David Sudnow (1967) pointed out that Americans shun the idea that death is a natural process begun at birth; instead, they view death as a very brief process or an act.

Until the turn of the century, in this country, people died at home and friends and family members prepared the bodies for burial (Lesy 1987). As medical knowledge and technology progressed and became more specialized, more and more deaths occurred outside the home— usually in hospitals. Death became something to be handled by a select group of highly trained professionals—doctors, nurses, and hospital staff. As fewer people witnessed death firsthand, it became surrounded with more mystery, and physically handling the dead became the domain of only a few.

Members or friends of the family relinquished their role in preparing bodies for disposal to an *undertaker*, ". . . a special person who would 'undertake' responsibility for the care and burial of the dead" (Amos 1983, 2). From the beginning stigma was associated with funerary occupations because they were "linked to the American death orientation whereby the industry is the cultural scapegoat for failed immortality" (Kearl 1989, 278).

To counter this stigma, undertakers (later to be called morticians) initially emphasized the scientific aspects of their work. Embalming and preparation for burial were presented as highly technical skills that required scientific knowledge and sophisticated training. Most states began licensing embalmers around the end of the nineteenth century (Amos 1983). These licensed embalmers did not enjoy the prestige accorded to the medical profession, however, and almost immediately were surrounded by mystery and viewed as unusual, if not downright weird. They were not family members or friends of the deceased faced with the unsavory but necessary responsibility for disposing of a loved one's body, but strangers who *chose* to work with dead bodies—for compensation. Although most welcomed the opportunity to relinquish this chore, they also viewed those who willingly assumed it with some skepticism and even disdain. Having failed to gain the desired prestige associated with the scientific aspects of embalming, and realizing that emphasizing embalming only served to increase what was perhaps the most stigmatizing aspect of their work (handling the dead), morticians shifted the focus away from their work on the dead body to their work with the living by emphasizing their roles as funeral directors and bereavement counselors.

In contemporary American society, those who routinely handle the dead have entered what Michael Lesy calls the "forbidden zone." Lesy (1987, 5) points out:

> In some cultures, the dead are ritually unclean and those who touch them must be ritually cleansed. In America, those who deal with the dead have social identities that shift back and forth like stationary objects that seem to move from left to right and back again as one eye is opened and the other is closed. Sometimes they look like pariahs and deviants, sometimes like charlatans. Other times they look like heroes or even adepts, initiates, and priests. Those who deal with death work at an intersection of opposites, tainted by the suffering and decay of the body, transfigured by the plight of the self and the destiny of the soul. The world never considers anyone who routinely deals with death to be "pure." . . .

Sudnow (1967, 51–64) underscored the negative attitudes toward people who work with the dead in describing how those who work in a morgue, for example, are "death-tainted" and work very hard to rid themselves of the social stigma associated with their jobs. Morticians and funeral directors cannot escape from this "taint of death" and they must constantly work to "counteract the stigma" directed at them and their occupations (Charmaz 1980, 182). Warner (1959, 315) described the funeral director as "a private enterpriser who will do the ritually unclean and physically distasteful work

of disposing of the dead in a manner satisfying to the living, at a price which they can pay." Fulton (1961) echoed this definition when he wrote, "In a word, the funeral director, by virtue of his close association with death, and by the 'relative' attitude he takes toward all funerals is, in a religious sense, 'unclean'" (322).

Are morticians and funeral directors really that stigmatized? After all, they generally are well-known and respected members of their communities. In small communities and even many large cities, local funeral homes have been owned and operated by the same family for several generations. These people usually are members of civic organizations, have substantial incomes, and live in nice homes and drive nice automobiles. Most often they are viewed as successful business people. On the other hand, their work is surrounded by mystery, taboos, and stigma, and they often are viewed as cold, detached, and downright morbid for doing it. All the respondents in this study openly acknowledged that stigma was associated with their work. Some indicated that they thought the stigma primarily came from the "misconception" that they were "getting rich" off other people's grief; others believed it simply came from working with the dead. Clearly these two aspects of their work —handling the dead and profiting from death and grief—emerged as the two most stigmatizing features of the funeral industry according to respondents. Pine (1975) noted that funeral directors cannot escape the "contamination by death," and contended:

> . . . people view individuals in such work as different . . . because they feel that they themselves could never do it and that there must be something "strange" about those who voluntarily choose to do it. (38)

Kathy Charmaz (1980, 174–206) discussed the stigma experienced by morticians, funeral directors, and others involved in "death work," and the negative impact that working with the dead can have on self-image. It is important from their perspective, she notes, that "who they are should not be defined by what they do" (174). This idea was confirmed by all the respondents in this study in one way or another. As one funeral director/embalmer noted, "I don't want to be thought of as somebody who likes working with the *dead*—that's morbid—I enjoy what I do because I like working with the *living*."

Managing Stigma

Erving Goffman wrote the most systematic analysis of how individuals manage a "spoiled" social identity in his classic work, *Stigma* (1963). He described several techniques, such as "passing," "dividing the social world," "mutual aid," "physical distance," "disclosure," and "covering," employed by the *discredited* and *discreditable* to manage information and conceal their stigmatizing attributes (41–104). Although these techniques work well for the physically scarred, blind, stammerers, bald, drug addicted, ex-convicts, and many other stigmatized categories of people, they are less likely to be used by morticians and funeral directors.

Except perhaps when on vacation, it is important for funeral directors to be known and recognized in their communities and to be associated with their work. Consequently, most of the morticians and funeral directors studied relied on other strategies for reducing the stigma associated with their work. Paramount among these strategies were: symbolic redefinition of their work, role distance, professionalism, emphasizing service, and enjoying socioeconomic status over occupational prestige. This was much less true for licensed embalmers who worked for funeral directors, especially in chain-owned funeral homes in large cities. In those cases the author found that many embalmers concealed their occupation from their neighbors and others with whom they were not intimately acquainted, by using the techniques of information control discussed by Goffman (1963).

SYMBOLIC REDEFINITION

A rose by any other name may smell as sweet, but death work by almost any other name does not sound quite as harsh. One of the ways in which morticians and funeral directors handle the stigma of their occupations is through symbolically negating as much of it as possible. Language is the most important symbol used by human beings, and Woods and Delisle (1978, 98) revealed how sympathy cards avoid the use of the terms "dead" and "death" by substituting less harsh words such as "loss," "time of sorrow," and "hour of sadness." This technique is also used by morticians and funeral directors to reduce the stigma associated with their work.

Words that are most closely associated with death are rarely used, and the most harsh terms are replaced with less ominous ones. The term *death* is almost never used by funeral directors; rather, they talk of "passing on," "meeting an untimely end," or "eternal slumber." There are no *corpses* or *dead bodies*; they are referred to as "remains," "the deceased," "loved one," or more frequently, by name (e.g., "Mr. Jones"). Use of the term *body* is almost uniformly avoided around the family. Viewing rooms (where the embalmed body is displayed in the casket) usually are given serene names such as "the sunset room," "the eternal slumber room," or, in one case, "the guest room."[4] Thus, when friends or family arrive to view the body, they are likely to be told that "Mr. Jones is lying in re-

---

[4]In this case the denial of death was symbolically enhanced by having the embalmed body lying in bed, as if asleep. The funeral director indicated that this room was used when families had not yet decided on a casket, thus allowing for viewing of the body in what he called a "natural, peaceful surrounding."

pose in the eternal slumber room." This language contrasts sharply with that used by morticians and funeral directors in "backstage" areas (Goffman 1959, 112)[5] such as the embalming room where drowning victims often are called "floaters," burn victims are called "crispy critters," and others are simply referred to as "bodies" (Turner and Edgley 1976).

All the respondents indicated that there was less stigma attached to the term *funeral director* than *mortician* or *embalmer*, underscoring the notion that much of the stigma they experienced was attached to physically handling the dead. Consequently, when asked what they do for a living, those who acknowledge that they are in the funeral business (several indicated that they often do not) referred to themselves as "funeral directors" even if all they did was the embalming. *Embalming* is referred to as "preservation" or "restoration," and in order to be licensed, one must have studied "mortuary arts" or "mortuary science." Embalming no longer takes place in an *embalming room,* but in a "preparation room," or in some cases the "operating room."

Coffins are now "caskets," which are transported in "funeral coaches" (not *hearses*) to their "final resting place" rather than to the *cemetery* or worse yet, *graveyard,* for their "interment" rather than *burial.* Thus, linguistically, the symbolic redefinition is complete, with death verbally redefined during every phase, and the stigma associated with it markedly reduced.

All the morticians and funeral directors in this study emphasized the importance of using the "appropriate" terms in referring to their work. Knowledge of the stigma attached to certain words was readily acknowledged, and all indicated that the earlier terminology was

stigma-laden, especially the term "undertaker," which they believed conjured up negative images in the mind of the public. For example, a 29-year-old male funeral director indicated that his father still insisted on calling himself an "undertaker." "He just hasn't caught up with the twentieth century," the son remarked. Interestingly, when asked why he did not refer to himself as an undertaker, he replied "It just sounds so old-fashioned [pause] plus, it sounds so morbid." As Pine (1975) noted, the special argot of the funeral industry performs an important function in reducing the stigma associated with the work and allows funeral directors to achieve role distance.

In addition to using language to symbolically redefine their occupations, funeral directors carefully attempt to shift the focus of their work away from the care of the dead (especially handling the body), and redefine it primarily in terms of caring for the living. The dead are de-emphasized as most of the funeral ritual is orchestrated for the benefit of the friends and family of the deceased (Turner and Edgley 1976). By redefining themselves as "grief therapists," or "bereavement counselors" their primary duties are associated with making funeral arrangements, directing the services, and consoling the family in their time of need.

ROLE DISTANCE

Because a person's sense of self is so strongly linked to occupation, it is common practice for people in undesirable or stigmatized occupations to practice role distance (e.g., Garson 1975; Pavalko 1988; Ritzer 1977; Terkel 1974; Thompson 1983). Although the specific role-distancing techniques vary across different occupations and among different individuals within an occupation, they share the common function of allowing individuals to violate some of the role expectations associated with the occupation, and to express their individuality within the confines of the occupational role. Although the funeral directors and morticians in this study used a variety of role-distancing techniques, three common patterns emerged: emotional detachment, humor, and countering the stereotype.

Emotional Detachment   One of the ways that morticians and funeral directors overcome their socialization regarding death taboos and the stigma associated with handling the dead is to detach themselves from the body work. Charmaz (1980) pointed out that a common technique used by coroners and funeral directors to minimize the stigma associated with death work is to routinize the work as much as possible. When embalming, morticians focus on the technical aspects of the job rather than thinking about the person they are working on. One mortician explained:

> When I'm in the preparation room I never think about *who* I'm working on, I only think about what has to be done next. When I picked up the body, it was a person. When I get done, clean and dress the body, and place it in the casket, it becomes a person again. But in here it's just something to be worked on. I treat it like a mechanic treats an automobile engine—with respect, but there's no emotion involved. It's just a job that has to be done.

Another mortician described his emotional detachment in the embalming room:

> You can't think too much about this process [embalming], or it'll really get to you. For example, one time we brought in this little girl. She was about four years old—the same age as my youngest daughter at the time. She had been killed in a wreck; had gone through the windshield; was really a mess. At first, I wasn't sure I could do that one—all I could think of was my little girl. But when I got her in the prep room, my whole attitude changed. I know this probably sounds cold, and hard I guess, but suddenly I began to think of the challenge involved. This was gonna be an open-casket ser-

vice, and while the body was in pretty good shape, the head and face were practically gone. This was gonna take a lot of reconstruction. Also, the veins are so small on children that you have to be a lot more careful. Anyway, I got so caught up in the job, that I totally forgot about working on a little girl. I was in the room with her about six hours when ———— [his wife] came in and reminded me that we had dinner plans that night. I washed up and went out to dinner and had a great time. Later that night, I went right back to work on her without even thinking about it. It wasn't until the next day when my wife was dressing the body, and I came in, and she was crying, that it hit me. I looked at the little girl, and I began crying. We both just stood there crying and hugging. My wife kept saying "I know this was tough for you," and "yesterday must have been tough." I felt sorta guilty, because I knew what she meant, and it should've been tough for me, real tough, emotionally, but it wasn't. The only "tough" part had been the actual work, especially the reconstruction—I had totally cut off the emotional part. It sometimes makes you wonder. Am I really just good at this, or am I losing something. I don't know. All I know is, if I'd thought about the little girl the way I did that next day, I never could have done her. It's just part of this job—you gotta just do what has to be done. If you think about it much, you'll never make it in this business.

Humor   Many funeral directors and morticians use humor to detach themselves emotionally from their work.[6] The humor, of course, must be carefully hidden from friends and relatives of the deceased, and takes place in backstage areas such as the embalming room, or in professional group settings such as at funeral directors' conventions.

---

[6]This is a common practice among medical students who are notorious for using "cadaver jokes" and pranks to help overcome the taboos associated with death and to ease the tension experienced when dissecting cadavers (Hafferty 1986, 1988; Knight 1973).

The humor varies from impromptu comments while working on the body to standard jokes[7] told over and over again. Not unexpectedly, all the respondents indicated a strong distaste for necrophilia jokes. One respondent commented, "I can think of nothing less funny —the jokes are sick, and have done a lot of damage to the image of our profession."

Humor is an effective technique of diffusing the stigma associated with handling a dead body, however, and when more than one person is present in the embalming room, it is common for a certain amount of banter to take place, and jokes or comments are often made about the amount of body fat or the overendowment, or lack thereof, of certain body parts. For example, one mortician indicated that a common remark made about males with small genitalia is, "Well, at least he won't be missed."

As with any occupation, levels of humor varied among the respondents. During an interview one of the funeral directors spoke of some of the difficulties in advertising the business, indicating that because of attitudes toward death and the funeral business, he had to be sure that his newspaper advertisements did not offend anyone. He reached into his desk drawer and pulled out a pad with several "fake ads" written on it. They included:

"Shake and Bake Special —
Cremation with No Embalming"
"Business Is Slow, Somebody's Gotta Go"
"Try Our Layaway Plan — Best in the Business"
"Count on Us, We'll Be the Last to Let You Down"
"People Are Dying to Use Our Services"
"Pay Now, Die Later"
"The Buck Really Does Stop Here"

---

[7]The author asked each respondent to tell his/her favorite joke about the occupation. One respondent was very indignant and said he hated all the jokes about the profession. All the others, however, quickly launched into what amounted to almost an amateur comedy routine. The author routinely heard several of the same jokes time and time again. Clearly, the most popular was several variations on the theme of burying someone in a rented tuxedo.

He indicated that he and one of his friends had started making up these fake ads and slogans when they were doing their mortuary internships. Over the years, they occasionally corresponded by mail and saw each other at conventions, and they would always try to be one up on the other with the best ad. He said, "Hey, in this business, you have to look for your laughs where you can find them." Garson (1975, 210) refers to a line from a song from *Mary Poppins,* "In every job that must be done, there is an element of fun."

Countering the Stereotype Morticians and funeral directors are painfully aware of the common negative stereotype of people in their occupations. The women in this study were much less concerned about the stereotype, perhaps because simply being female shattered the stereotype anyway. The men, however, not only acknowledged that they were well aware of the public's stereotypical image of them, but also indicated that they made every effort *not* to conform to it.

One funeral director, for instance, said:

People think we're cold, unfriendly, and unfeeling. I always make it a point to be just the opposite. Naturally, when I'm dealing with a family I must be reserved and show the proper decorum, but when I am out socially, I always try to be very upbeat—very alive. No matter how tired I am, I try not to show it.

Another indicated that he absolutely never wore gray or black suits. Instead, he wore navy blue and usually with a small pinstripe. "I might be mistaken for the minister or a lawyer," he said, "but rarely for an undertaker."

The word "cold," which often is associated with death, came up in a number of interviews. One funeral director was so concerned about the stereotype of being "cold," that he kept a handwarmer in the drawer of his desk. He said, "My hands tend to be cold and clammy. It's just a physical trait of mine, but there's no way that I'm going to shake some-one's hand and let them walk away thinking how cold it was." Even on the warmest of days, he indicated that during services, he carried the handwarmer in his right-hand coat pocket so that he could warm his hand before shaking hands with or touching someone.

Although everyone interviewed indicated that he or she violated the public stereotype, each one expressed a feeling of being atypical. In other words, although they believed that they did not conform to the stereotype, they felt that many of their colleagues did. One funeral director was wearing jeans, a short-sleeved sweatshirt and a pair of running shoes during the interview. He had just finished mowing the lawn at the funeral home. "Look at me," he said, "Do I look like a funeral director? Hell, ——— [the funeral director across the street] wears a suit and tie to mow his grass!— or, at least he would if he didn't hire it done."[8]

Others insisted that very few funeral directors conform to the public stereotype when out of public view, but feel compelled to conform to it when handling funeral arrangements, because it is an occupational role requirement. "I always try to be warm and upbeat," one remarked, "But, let's face it, when I'm working with a family, they're experiencing a lot of grief—I have to respect that, and act accordingly." Another indicated that he always lowered his voice when talking with family and friends of the deceased, and that it had become such a habit, that he found himself speaking softly almost all the time. "One of the occupational hazards, I guess," he remarked.

The importance of countering the negative stereotype was evident, when time after time, persons being interviewed would pause and

ask "I'm not what you expected, am I?" or something similar. It seemed very important for them to be reassured that they did not fit the stereotype of funeral director or mortician.

PROFESSIONALISM

Another method used by morticians and funeral directors to reduce occupational stigma is to emphasize professionalism. Amos (1983, 3) described embalming as:

> . . . an example of a vocation in transition from an occupation to a profession. Until mid-nineteenth century, embalming was not considered a profession and this is still an issue debated in some circles today.

Most morticians readily admit that embalming is a very simple process and can be learned very easily. In all but two of the funeral homes studied, the interviewees admitted that people who were not licensed embalmers often helped with the embalming process. In one case, in which the funeral home was owned and operated by two brothers, one of the brothers was a licensed funeral director and licensed embalmer. The other brother had dropped out of high school and helped their father with the funeral business while his brother went to school to meet the educational requirements for licensure. The licensed brother said:

> By the time I got out of school and finished my apprenticeship, ——— [his brother] had been helping Dad embalm for over three years—and he was damned good at it. So when I joined the business, Dad thought it was best if I concentrated on handling the funeral arrangements and pre-service needs. After Dad died, I was the only licensed embalmer, so "officially" I do it all—all the embalming and the funeral arrangements. But, to tell you the truth, I only embalm every now and then when we have several to do, 'cause ——— usually handles most of it. He's one of the best—I'd match him against any in the business.

---

[8]In many communities (especially small towns) rival funeral homes are located in close proximity, often across the street, or within a block of one another. A colleague, Michael Stein at the University of Missouri, St. Louis, suggests this is not unlike the clustering of other "stigmatized places," such as adult bookstores or adult movie theaters.

Despite the relative simplicity of the embalming process and the open admission by morticians and funeral directors that "almost anyone could do it with a little practice," most states require licensure and certification for embalming. The four states represented in this study (Kansas, Oklahoma, Missouri, and Texas) have similar requirements for becoming a licensed certified embalmer. They include a minimum of 60 college hours with a core of general college courses (English, mathematics, social studies, etc.) plus 1 year of courses in the "mortuary sciences," or "mortuary arts." These consist of several courses in physiology and biology, and a 1-year apprenticeship under a licensed embalmer. To become a licensed funeral director requires the passing of a state board examination, which primarily requires a knowledge of state laws related to burial, cremation, disposal of the body, and insurance.

All the respondents in this study who were licensed and certified embalmers and funeral directors exceeded the minimum educational requirements. In fact, all but one of them had a college degree, and three had advanced degrees. The most common degree held was a Bachelor of Science in mortuary sciences. Two of the males had degrees in business (one held the MBA degree), one male had a Bachelor's degree with a major in biology and had attended one year of medical school, one male had a degree in geology, and one had a degree in music. One of the women had a Bachelor's degree in English; another held a degree in business; and one woman had a degree in Nursing. Although the general consensus among them was that an individual did not need a college education to become a good embalmer, they all stressed the importance of a college education for being a successful funeral director. Most thought that some basic courses in business, psychology, death and dying, and "bereavement counseling" were valuable preparation for the field. Also, most of the funeral directors were licensed insurance agents, which allowed them to sell burial policies.

Other evidence of the professionalization of the funeral industry includes state, regional, and national professional organizations that hold annual conventions and sponsor other professional activities; professional journals; state, regional, and national governing and regulating boards; and a professional code of ethics. Although the funeral industry is highly competitive, like most other professions, its members demonstrate a strong sense of cohesiveness and in-group identification.

Reduction of stigma is not the sole purpose for professionalization among funeral directors and morticians, as other benefits are reaped from the process. Nevertheless, as Charmaz (1980, 182) noted, membership in the professional organizations of coroners and funeral directors is one of the most effective ways to "counteract the stigma conferred upon them." One of the married couples in this study indicated that it was reassuring to attend national conventions where they met and interacted with other people in the funeral industry because it helps to "reassure us that we're not weird." The wife went on to say:

A lot of people ask us how we can stand to be in this business—especially ——— because he does all of the embalming. They act like we must be strange or something. When we go to the conventions and meet with all of the other people there who are just like us—people who like helping other people—I feel *normal* again.

All these elements of professionalization—educational requirements, exams, boards, organizations, codes of ethics, and the rest—lend an air of credibility and dignity to the funeral business while diminishing the stigma associated with it. Although the requirements for licensure and certification are not highly exclusive, they still represent forms of boundary maintenance, and demand a certain level of commitment from those who enter the field.

Thus, professionalization helped in the transition of the funeral business from a vocation that can be pursued by virtually anyone to a profession that can be entered only by those with the appropriate qualifications. As Pine (1975, 28) indicated:

> Because professionalization is highly respected in American society, the word "profession" tends to be used as a symbol by occupations seeking to improve or enhance the lay public's conception of that occupation, and funeral directing is no exception. To some extent, this appears to be because the funeral director hopes to overcome the stigma of "doing death work."

"By claiming professional status, funeral directors claim prestige and simultaneously seek to minimize the stigma they experience for being death workers involved in 'dirty work'" (Charmaz 1980, 192).

THE SHROUD OF SERVICE

One of the most obvious ways in which morticians and funeral directors neutralize the stigma associated with their work is to wrap themselves in a "shroud of service." All the respondents emphasized their service role over all other aspects of their jobs. Although their services were not legally required in any of the four states included in this study, all the respondents insisted that people desperately *needed* them.[9] As one funeral director summarized, "Service, that's what we're all about—we're there when people need us the most."

Unlike the humorous fantasy ads mentioned earlier, actual advertisements in the funeral industry focus on service. Typical ads for the companies in this study read:

"Our Family Serving Yours for Over 60 Years"
"Serving the Community for Four Generations"
"Thoughtful Service in Your Time of Need"

The emphasis on service, especially on "grief counseling" and "bereavement therapy," shifts the focus away from the two most stigmatizing elements of funeral work: the handling and preparation of the body, which already has been discussed at length; and retail sales, which are widely interpreted as profiting from other people's grief. Many of the funeral directors indicated that they believed the major reason for negative public feelings toward their occupation was not only that they handled dead bodies, but the fact that they made their living off the dead, or at least, off the grief of the living.[10]

All admitted that much of their profit came from the sale of caskets and vaults, where markup is usually a minimum of 100%, and often 400–500%, but all played down this aspect of their work. The Federal Trade Commission requires that funeral directors provide their customers with itemized lists of all charges. The author was provided with price lists for all merchandise and services by all the funeral directors in this study. When asked to estimate the "average price" of one of their funerals, respondents' answers ranged from $3,000 to $4,000. Typically, the casket accounted for approximately half of the total expense. Respondents indicated that less than 5% of their business involved cremations, but that even then they often encouraged the purchase of a casket. One said, "A lot of people ask about cremation, because they think it's cheaper, but I usually sell them caskets even

---

[9]In Kansas, Missouri, Oklahoma, and Texas, as in most states, bodies do not have to be embalmed or cremated if a legal death certificate is obtained and the body is disposed of within 24 hours.

[10]Several studies have focused on how unscrupulous members of the funeral industry capitalize on the grief of their customers to reap enormous profits from the sale of caskets, vaults, burial clothing, grave markers, and a variety of unnecessary and often unwanted "services" (e.g., see Consumers' Union 1977; Fulton 1961; Harmer 1963; Mitford 1963).

for cremation; then, if you add the cost of cremation and urn, cremation becomes more profitable than burial."

Despite this denial of the retail aspects of the job, trade journals provide numerous helpful hints on the best techniques for displaying and selling caskets, and great care is given to this process. In all the funeral homes visited, one person was charged with the primary responsibility for helping with "casket selection." In smaller family-operated funeral homes, this person usually was the funeral director's wife. In the large chain-owned companies, it was one of the "associate funeral directors." In either case, the person was a skilled salesperson.

Nevertheless, the sales pitch is wrapped in the shroud of service. During each interview, the author asked to be shown the "selection room," and to be treated as if he were there to select a casket for a loved one. All the funeral directors willingly complied, and most treated the author as if he actually were there to select a casket. Interestingly, most perceived this as an actual sales opportunity, and mentioned their "pre-need selection service" and said that if the author had not already made such arrangements, they would gladly assist him with the process. The words "sell," "sales," "buy," and "purchase," were carefully avoided. Also, although by law the price for each casket must be displayed separately, most funeral homes also displayed a "package price" that included the casket and "full services." If purchased separately, the casket was always more expensive than if it was included in the package of services. This gave the impression that a much more expensive casket could be purchased for less money if bought as part of a service package. It also implied that the services provided by the firm were of more value than the merchandise.

The funeral directors rationalized the high costs of merchandise and funerals by empha-

sizing that they were a small price to pay for the services performed. One insisted, "We don't sell merchandise, we sell service!" Another asked "What is peace of mind worth?" and another "How do you put a price on relieving grief?"

Another rationalization for the high prices was the amount of work involved in arranging and conducting funeral services. When asked about the negative aspects of their jobs, most emphasized the hard work and long hours involved.[11] In fact, all but two of the interviewees said that they did not want their children to follow in their footsteps, because the work was largely misunderstood (stigmatized), too hard, the hours too long, and "the income not nearly as high as most people think."

In addition to emphasizing the service aspect of their work, funeral directors also tend to join a number of local philanthropic and service organizations (Pine 1975, 40). Although many businessmen find that joining such organizations is advantageous for making contacts, Stephenson (1985, 223) contended that the small-town funeral director "may be able to counter the stigma of his or her occupation by being active in the community, thereby counteracting some of the negative images associated with the job of funeral directing."

SOCIOECONOMIC STATUS VERSUS OCCUPATIONAL PRESTIGE

Ritzer (1977, 9) pointed out that some jobs suffer from "occupational status insecurity." This clearly is the case with morticians and funeral directors. They are members of an occupation wrought with "social stigma . . . an occupational group which is extremely sensitive to

---

[11]One funeral director estimated that he spent approximately 125 hours on each funeral, and performed on the average of 100 funerals a year. By his estimate, if he worked 24 hours per day, he would have to work 561 days in a year!

public criticism, and which works hard to enhance its position in society" (Stephenson 1985, 225).

It seems that what funeral directors lack in occupational prestige, they make up for in socioeconomic status. Although interviewees were very candid about the number of funerals they performed every year and the average costs per funeral, most were reluctant to disclose their annual incomes. One exception was a 37-year-old funeral home owner, funeral director, and licensed embalmer in a community of approximately 25,000 who indicated that in the previous year he had handled 211 funerals and had a gross income of just under $750,000. After deducting overhead (three licensed embalmers on staff, a receptionist, a gardener, a student employee, insurance costs, etc.), he estimated his net income to have been "close to $250,000." He quickly added, however, that he worked long hours, had his 5-day vacation cut to two (because of a "funeral call that he had to handle personally") and despite his relatively high income (probably one of the two or three highest incomes in the community), he felt morally, socially, and professionally obligated to hide his wealth in the community. "I have to walk a fine line," he said, "I can live in a nice home, drive a nice car, and wear nice suits, because people know that I am a successful businessman—but, I have to be careful not to flaunt it."

One of the ways he reconciles this dilemma was by enjoying "the finer things in life" outside the community. He owned a condominium in Vail where he took ski trips and kept his sports car. He also said that none of his friends or neighbors there knew that he was in the funeral business. In fact, when they inquired about his occupation, he told them he was in insurance (which technically was true because he also was a licensed insurance agent who sold burial policies). When asked why he did not disclose his true occupational identity, he responded:

When I tell people what I really do, they initially seem "put off," even repulsed. I have literally had people jerk their hands back during a handshake when somebody introduces me and then tells them what I do for a living. Later, many of them become very curious and ask a lot of questions. If you tell people you sell insurance, they usually let the subject drop.

Although almost all the funeral directors in this study lived what they characterized as fairly "conservative lifestyles," most also indicated that they enjoyed many of the material things that their jobs afforded them. One couple rationalized their recent purchase of a very expensive sailboat (which both contended they "really couldn't afford"), by saying, "Hey, if anybody knows that you can't take it with you, it's us—we figured we might as well enjoy it while we can." Another commented, "Most of the people in this community would never want to do what I do, but most of them would like to have my income."

Summary and Conclusion

A person's occupation is an integral component of his or her personal and social identity. This study describes and analyzes how people in the funeral industry attempt to reduce and neutralize the stigma associated with their occupations. Morticians and funeral directors are particularly stigmatized, not only because they perform work that few others would be willing to do (preparing dead bodies for burial), but also because they profit from death. Consequently, members of the funeral industry consciously work at stigma reduction.

Paramount among their strategies are symbolically redefining their work. This especially involves avoiding all language that reminds their customer of death, the body, and retail sales; morticians and funeral directors emphasize the need for their professional services of relieving family grief and bereavement counseling. They also practice role distance, empha-size their professionalism, wrap themselves in a "shroud of service," and enjoy their relatively high socioeconomic status rather than lament their lower occupational prestige.

Stephenson (1985, 231) pointed out an inter-esting paradox:

> In spite of our current preoccupation with death, we have given it a taboo status that im-plies a great deal of underlying fear and anxiety. Anything that will ease our fears is used to pro-tect us from death. We give millions of dollars to fight disease, we occupy our spare time with staying physically fit, and we blunt death's awful impact with the use of the skills of the fu-neral director. While critics may consider such activities as barbaric or in bad taste, they are certainly in harmony with the basic values of American society.

Morticians and funeral directors are in a precarious social situation. They perform work that the majority of society believes is needed (Kastenbaum and Aisenberg 1973), and al-though their services are not legally required, they are socially demanded. Yet, their occupa-tions place them in a paradoxical position of performing duties deemed by larger society as "necessary," but "undesirable." Try as they may, they cannot fully escape the stigma asso-ciated with their work.

All but two of the people in this study indi-cated that if they had it all to do over again, they would choose the same occupation. Yet, only one indicated that he hoped his children pursued the funeral business. And, even he commented, ". . . but, they need to understand that it's hard work, and largely unappreci-ated." All agreed that one of their major tasks was handling the stigma of handling the dead.

Handling the dead will not become any more glamorous in the future, and that aspect of the mortician's work probably will continue to be stigmatized. However, if Americans be-come more comfortable with death and their own mortality, it also is likely that emphasiz-ing morticians' roles as bereavement coun-selors will no longer be sufficient to redefine their work. If that is indeed the case, how will morticians and funeral directors symbolically redefine their work in the future to neutralize the stigma associated with handling the dead and profiting from grief? This research sug-gests that there is a growing tendency for funeral directors to emphasize their roles as "pre-need counselors." Since death is inevit-able, and an aged population is more likely to recognize that, funeral directors may even more prominently tout themselves as akin to financial planners who can help in the advance planning and preparation of funeral arrange-ments. This could be important in neutralizing the two most stigmatizing attributes of their work. First, like previous strategies, it de-emphasizes the body work; secondly, and per-haps more importantly, it may alleviate some of the stigma associated with profiting from death and grief because they would be viewed as helping people to prepare for funeral needs in advance so that they might create a "hedge" against inflation and make important financial decisions at a time when they are not grief-stricken. Future research on the funeral indus-try should focus on this emerging role.

References

Amos, E. P. 1983. *Kansas Funeral Profession Through the Years*. Topeka: Kansas Funeral Directors' Association.

Aries, P. 1976. *Western Attitudes Toward Death: From the Middle Ages to the Present*. Trans. P. M. Ranum. Baltimore: Johns Hopkins University Press, p. 99.

Becker, E. 1973. *The Denial of Death*. New York: Free Press.

Bendann, E. 1930. *Death Customs: An Analytical Study of Burial Rites*. New York: Knopf.

Berg, B. L. 1989. *Qualitative Research Methods for the Social Sciences*. Boston: Allyn & Bacon.

Charmaz, K. 1980. *The Social Reality of Death: Death in Contemporary America*. Reading, MA: Addison-Wesley.

Consumers' Union. 1977. *Funerals: Consumers' Last Rights*. New York: Norton.

Fulton, R. 1961. "The Clergyman and the Funeral Director: A Study in Role Conflict." *Social Forces* 39: 317–323.

Garson, B. 1975. *All the Livelong Day: The Meaning and Demeaning of Routine Work*. Garden City, NY: Doubleday.

Goffman, E. 1959. *The Presentation of Self in Everyday Life*. Garden City, NY: Anchor Doubleday.

———. 1963. *Stigma: Notes on the Management of Spoiled Identity*. Englewood Cliffs, NJ: Prentice-Hall.

Habenstein, R. W., and W. M. Lamers. 1960. *Funeral Customs the World Over*. Milwaukee: Bulfin.

Hafferty, F. W. 1986. "Cadaver Story Humor." Paper presented at the annual meeting of the Midwest Sociological Society, Des Moines, IA.

———. 1988. "Cadaver Stories and the Emotional Socialization of Medical Students." *Journal of Health and Social Behavior* 29: 344–356.

Harmer, R. M. 1963. *The High Cost of Dying*. New York: Collier.

Hughes, E. C. 1979. *The Sociological Eye: Selected Papers*. Chicago: Aldine-Atherton.

Huntington, R., and P. Metcalf. 1979. *Celebrations of Death*. Cambridge: Cambridge University Press.

Jackson, C. O. 1980. "Death Shall Have No Dominion: The Passing of the World of the Dead in America." Pp. 47–55 in R. A. Kalish (ed.), *Death and Dying: Views from Many Cultures*. Farmingdale, NY: Baywood.

Kastenbaum, R. and R. Aisenberg. 1972. *The Psychology of Death*. New York: Springer.

Kearl, M. C. 1989. *Endings: A Sociology of Death and Dying*. New York: Oxford University Press.

Knight, J. A. 1973. *Doctor to Be: Coping with the Trials and Triumphs of Medical School*. New York: Appleton-Century-Crofts.

Lesy, M. 1987. *The Forbidden Zone*. New York: Farrar, Straus & Giroux.

Mitford, J. 1963. *The American Way of Death*. New York: Simon & Schuster.

Momeyer, R. W. 1988. *Confronting Death*. Bloomington: Indiana University Press.

Murray, M. A. 1969. *The Splendor That Was Egypt*, rev. ed. New York: Praeger.

Parsons, T., and V. M. Lidz. 1967. "Death in American Society." Pp. 133–170 in E. Shneidman (ed.), *Essays in Self-Destruction*. New York: Science House.

Parsons, T., R. C. Fox, and V. M. Lidz. 1972. "The 'Gift of Life' and its Reciprocation." *Social Research* 39: 367–415.

Pavalko, R. M. 1988. *Sociology of Occupations and Professions*, 2nd ed. Itasca, IL: Peacock.

Pine, V. R. 1975. *Caretaker of the Dead: The American Funeral Director*. New York: Irvington.

Polsky, N. 1969. *Hustlers, Beats and Others*. Garden City, NY: Anchor.

Ritzer, G. 1977. *Working: Conflict and Change*, 2nd ed. Englewood Cliffs, NJ: Prentice-Hall.

Schatzman, L., and A. L. Strauss. 1973. *Field Research: Strategies for a Natural Sociology*. Englewood Cliffs, NJ: Prentice-Hall.

Spradley, J. P. 1979. *The Ethnographic Interview*. New York: Holt, Rinehart & Winston.

Stephenson, J. S. 1985. *Death, Grief, and Mourning: Individual and Social Realities*. New York: Free Press.

Sudnow, D. 1967. *Passing On: The Social Organization of Dying*. Englewood Cliffs, NJ: Prentice-Hall.

Terkel, S. 1974. *Working: People Talk About What They Do All Day and How They Feel About What They Do*. New York: Pantheon.

Thompson, W. E. 1983. "Hanging Tongues: A Sociological Encounter with the Assembly Line." *Qualitative Sociology* 6 (Fall): 215–237.

Turner, R. E., and D. Edgley. 1976. "Death as Theater: A Dramaturgical Analysis of the American Funeral." *Sociology and Social Research* 60 (July): 377–392.

Warner, W. L. 1959. *The Living and the Dead*. New Haven, CT: Yale University Press.

Wass, H., F. M. Berardo, and R. A. Neimeyer. 1988. "The Funeral in Contemporary Society." In H. Wass, F. M. Berardo, and R. A. Neimeyer (eds.), *Dying: Facing the Facts*, 2nd ed. New York: Hemisphere.

Woods, A. S., and R. G. Delisle. 1978. "The Treatment of Death in Sympathy Cards." Pp. 95–103 in C. Winick (ed.), *Deviance and Mass Media*. Beverly Hills, CA: Sage.

Questions

1. Thompson makes use of Goffman's concept of the backstage to explain how things work in the funeral home. Can you think of other settings that are divided between front and back stage?

2. Recall Goffman's notion of the "definition of the situation." What sort of definition of the situation do funeral workers want to create for their clients and potential clients — the live ones, that is?

3. What techniques do funeral workers utilize as they attempt to manage the stigma of their jobs? How successful are these techniques?

4. Review the definition of "profession" in chapter 7 of the *The Practical Skeptic*. Given what you know about the funeral workers, do you think that, in the sociological sense, they are professionals? Why or why not?

5. Thompson's review of the literature on death suggested that there is some dispute about whether Americans are in "denial" about death. How might this issue be studied empirically?

6. In your town's "yellow pages," what sorts of ads do funeral homes publish? How do these compare to the ones cited by Thompson?

·18·

Gendered Patterns in Family Communication

Carol J. S. Bruess and Judy C. Pearson

Social scientists frequently distinguish between *sex differences* (the physical and biological differences between males and females) and *gender differences* (which have to do with differences in social expectations about how males and females in a particular culture ought to behave). As Carol Bruess and Judy Pearson make clear in their article, men and women do not simply have genders; people *do* gender. People do gender in just about every social arena, but as this article explains, it is principally in the family that people learn to do gender. Learning to carry out one's gender obligations is an important part of the socialization process.

In the conclusion of their article, Bruess and Pearson further suggest that it is in the family arena that gender is reified. That is, that expectations about what women ought to be and what men ought to be are made to seem as if they are somehow "natural" and not merely social constructions. See if you agree.

What kinds of games did you play when you were a 5-year-old? When we were preschoolers, we played "school." The most envied role was "teacher," which we sought so that we could instruct, and perhaps discipline, our siblings. One of us played "church" (wherein a brother was *always* the priest who distributed vanilla wafers as communion, and the two female siblings were either nuns or ushers for imaginary parishioners). For both of us, our favorite activity was the game of "house," with the primary players being Mom, Dad, and baby. "House" involved a mother who cleaned the house, made the meals, and cooed at the baby, and a father who worked all day at the office and read the paper after work.

One of us has helped to raise four children and two stepchildren, and these siblings and stepsiblings also played house. The roles were not as stable, however, as when we were younger. One of the sons asked for a toy oven when he was 6 years old; another son requested a baby doll for Christmas whom he christened "Sophia" after his maternal grandmother. The oldest daughter refused to play games with boys unless she had a chance to win. By contrast, the youngest daughter loved makeup and "dress-up" from the time she knew how to role play. The two stepbrothers, too, enacted more traditional roles.

As our experiences—both past and present—imply, a discussion of family is incomplete without a discussion of gender. From the earliest age, we experience gender in the family in divisions of labor, roles, tasks, play, rules, and communication. In daily interactions, family members impart expectations of us as sons and daughters, mothers and fathers, and husbands and wives, and these expectations influence girls' and boys' identities. These gendered identities, in turn, inspire gendered career choices, communication styles, task expectations, styles of relating, and modes of engaging in the families we form as adults.

This chapter explores the links between gender and understandings of cultural life, ourselves, our communication, and our relationships. We hope you will be challenged to draw connections between images of yourself, the relationships and communication within your family, and your personal role in (re)creating or altering gender relationally, personally, and socially. The purpose of this chapter is to examine three (necessarily interrelated) gendered patterns of family communications; each reveals ways in which families embody —and continuously (re)create—gender. First, *gendered patterns of marital communication* are explored. Second, *gendered patterns of family roles* are examined. Finally, we discuss *gendered patterns of parenting.*

Gendered Patterns of Marital Communication

Gendered understandings of relationship dynamics are manifest in the communication between spouses. Husbands and wives, especially in Western societies, come from two different cultures with different learned behavior and communication styles (Tannen 1990). They are "intimate strangers" (Rubin 1983) with the potential for many gendered misunderstandings.

Women's speech, in general, is based on notions of equality, supportiveness, expression of feelings, inclusivity, responsiveness, and personal disclosures (Pearson, West, and Turner 1995; Wood 1994a). Tentativeness is also characteristic of Caucasian women's communication, although less pronounced in the speech of African American women. With regard to women's speech, Wood (1994a, 142) explains: "Rather than a rigid you-tell-your-ideas-then-I'll-tell-mine sequence, women's speech more characteristically follows an interactive pattern in which different voices weave together to create conversations." Some men learn a very different style of speech, and thus define the goals of talk differently. Men often aim to establish status, maintain the floor (via talkativeness and humor), exhibit knowledge, solve problems, and assert themselves. Emotional and conversational responsiveness, tentativeness, and personal disclosures are typically underplayed in some men's speech (Pearson et al. 1995; Wood 1994a). African American men, however, tend to be more emotionally expressive and responsive than Caucasian men (Gaines 1995). Men and women often operate out of distinctive speech communities, with styles that are different, "but equally valid" (Tannen 1990, 15). . . .

Gendered communication styles might surface in actual, or perceived, self-disclosure, although findings are mixed. Early research suggested that women appear to self-disclose more than men (DeForest and Stone 1980; Greenblatt, Gasenauer, and Freimuth 1980; LeVine and Franco 1981), disclose more negative information than men (Wheeless and Grotz 1976), and disclose more intimate information than men (Gitter and Black 1976). However, Dindia and Allen (1992, 118) recently conducted a meta-analysis of 205 studies involving almost 24,000 subjects published between 1958 and 1989 in which sex differences in self-disclosure were studied. They conclude that actual sex differences in self-disclosure are not as large as researchers and theorists have suggested in the past, noting: "It is time to stop perpetuating the myth that there large sex differences in men's and women's self-disclosure."

Dindia and Allen (1992, 114) found extremely small differences in self-disclosure based on the sex of the discloser and the sex of the target. According to their meta-analysis, women, in general, disclose slightly more than men, although the statistical differences were extremely small. They also found that females disclose more with other females than males tend to disclose with females, but that females together are not more disclosive than males are with other males. Dindia and Allen argue that early research that reports sex differences in self-disclosure might be based on biased interpretations and/or research methods: "We may expect women to disclose more than men because we believe it is more appropriate for women to disclose than men."

Some researchers suggest that gender differences in self-disclosure are simply matters of gendered perception. Although Shimanoff (1985) found that wives *report* disclosing more, and valuing disclosure more, than husbands, observations revealed little actual difference in men's and women's patterns of self-disclosure. Why might this be so? According to Rubin (1983), some women might not recognize their husbands' comments as self-disclosures. A prototypical complaint of men is, "I tell her, but she's never satisfied. . . . No matter how much I say, it's never enough" (Rubin 1983, 71). Gendered styles of communication, as well as gendered expectations of that communication, contribute to this misunderstanding by socializing women and men into different views of what counts as self-disclosure.

The importance of self-disclosure may be overrated, particularly in the enduring relationship (Wood 1995; Wood and Duck 1995). Although self-disclosure plays an important role in the early stages of relational evolution, self-disclosive communication becomes less important than other types of communication in the enduring marriage. Also, couples' *perceptions* of disclosure may be more important than the amount of disclosure in which they actually engage; couples in happy marriages are more likely to positively distort their perceptions of disclosures received (Beach and Arias 1983; Davidson, Balswick, and Halverson 1983; Pearson 1992).

Gendered styles of interacting (including actual or perceived self-disclosure patterns) might better be understood by examining the disparate ways that feminine and masculine individuals often express themselves (Wood 1994a). Researchers have observed that men often do not express themselves and their feelings in feminine ways, just as many women do not use masculine means of expression (Wood 1994a; Wood and Inman 1993). Masculine modes of expressing closeness are different from feminine methods, which often involve "closeness in dialogue" (Wood 1994a). Self-disclosure might represent an undesirable means of expression for many men who prefer instrumental demonstrations (such as doing a favor for a partner), or "closeness in the doing" (Swain 1989). Gendered ways of expressing closeness represent how gendered socialization manifests itself in the communication of intimate partners.

Because men and women often talk at cross-purposes and often have different perceptions of their own and their partner's communication behavior, marital communication is particularly challenging. Do these differences affect marital satisfaction? It appears that gender at least affects one's *assessment* of marital satisfaction. Researchers have found that "her" marriage is not viewed as positively as "his" marriage; that is, when husbands and wives evaluate their marital happiness, husbands are more likely than wives to give it high marks (Bernard 1972; Riessman 1990). Women are more likely than men to perceive problems in communication and other relational dynamics because women, more than men, are socialized to be attentive to relational issues and problems (Tavris 1992; Wood 1993).

Marital satisfaction might be related to many husbands' ability to be expressive, to be clear, and to decode his wife's messages accurately (Balswick 1988; Blumstein and Schwartz 1983; Rubin 1983). Because the masculine speech community does not encourage or value expressiveness, many wives complain that their husbands are deficiently expressive and nurturing (Davidson and Moore 1992; Fitzpatrick and Indvik 1982; Rubin 1983). Men often express their feelings in instrumental (that is, "helping") behaviors like washing and waxing their wives' car (Wood and Inman 1993). Since women, in general, rely on verbal, emotional displays of feelings, they may fail to perceive instrumental actions as expressing emotion.

While gendered communication between spouses may result in misunderstandings, these differences may be improved over time. Sex-role differences are marked among younger people, but they become less salient as people age (Pearson 1995; Sillars and Wilmot 1989). "Sex-role crossover" might begin to occur as early as midlife (Cooper and Gutmann 1987; McGee and Wells 1982). Women often become freer to display more masculine traits, and many men are more likely to incorporate feminine behaviors into their communication repertoires. These relocations provide the opportunity for increased understanding between women and men.

Gendered Patterns of Family Roles

Each person in any system—whether it is a multinational corporation or a family—plays a role. The fulfillment of specific roles is essential to family functioning. Family roles are often linked to necessary family functions such as decision making and nurturance (Pearson 1993) and to gendered expectations. The influence of gender particularly affects and reflects the roles of breadwinning, housework, and child care.

BREADWINNING

Historically, men have been primarily responsible for providing for the financial needs of the family, particularly among Caucasians. Just as the wearing of white wedding dresses, fathers "giving away" their daughters, and wives adopting their husbands' names in marriage, traditions die hard. Although women are increasingly assuming equal breadwinning roles in families, most men and women still *prefer* husbands to be the primary breadwinners and wives to be homemakers, particularly after children are added to the family (Canter and Ageton 1984; Herzog, Bachman, and Johnston 1983; Riessman 1990).

The role of "provider" remains intimately tied to perceptions of power in the family, reflecting continuing gender patterns. Young couples reveal that men and women still believe men should have more power in the arena of personal relationships (Riessman 1990). An example is the fact that despite many of the nontraditional behaviors of dual-career couples, the marital satisfaction of these couples is still related to perceptions that both spouses fit sex-role stereotypes. Both husbands and wives in dual-career couples report more satisfaction if the husband is seen as more intelligent, competent, and of higher professional status than his wife (Yogev 1987). Gender prescriptions require that men earn more and have higher job status than women; essentially, the partner who earns more tends to be the more powerful, particularly in heterosexual and gay relationships (Blumstein and Schwartz 1983). Lesbians often do not embrace or enact a money-equals-power equation (Blumstein and Schwartz 1983). Hence, viewing money and breadwinning as a source of relational power seems to reflect masculine perspectives more than feminine ones.

Straying from dominant prescriptions has relational consequences. As a wife's salary becomes greater than her husband's, marital satisfaction often decreases (Dersch and Pearson 1986; Philliber and Hiller 1979), and the probability of divorce increases (Trent and South 1989). Some researchers estimate that for every $1,000 increase in a wife's salary, the possibility that she will divorce increases by 2% (Philliber and Vannoy-Hiller 1990).

Still, women's participation in the paid work force has risen greatly in the last few decades. One of the most dramatic increases has been among women with children under the age of 6. In 1950, only 12% of women with children under age 6 worked outside the home. In 1988, 57.4% of these women with young children were employed outside the home (U.S. Department of Commerce 1990). The most recent statistics reveal that over 65% of married women with children under 18 are in the labor force (U.S. Department of Commerce 1990).

Reasons for, and the consequences of, women's increased participation in the family breadwinning role clarify the social meanings and consequences of gender ideologies. The most frequently cited reason for wives working outside the home is economic need (Israelson 1989). However, many factors, including a woman's sex role, affect her decision to work (Krogh 1985; Smith 1985). Women who score high on traditionally masculine characteristics such as ambition, task orientation, and aggressiveness tend to be more satisfied if they have jobs outside the home than if they are full-time homemakers.

Husbands' attitudes also affect wives' decisions to work outside the home. The husbands of working women tend to be more profeminist than are the husbands of nonworking women (Smith 1985). Age may be a mediating factor, since younger men report greater sensitivity to their spouses' needs and to the marriage in general, including a greater willingness to negotiate roles (McLeod 1992).

Tied directly to these gendered patterns is another reality: Many employed wives are playing dual rules that require they work an extra shift—the first shift at work or at the office and a "second shift" at home (Hochschild with Machung 1989). The reality, and consequences, of women's second shift, as we will see, are intimately connected to gender ideologies, and to the gendered politics of this particular family role.

HOUSEWORK

Marriage has been criticized for perpetuating sex inequity. In discussing marriage, Johnson, Huston, Gaines, and Levinger (1992, 361) recognized that "[m]arriage *is* about gender . . . and to a large extent about the gendered organization of labor." According to Riessman (1990, 15), "Traditional marriage is a gendered institution—not just because women and men participate in it, but because the gender-based division of labor in it, in turn, creates inequality between women and men." The division of household tasks benefits the husband, often at the wife's expense.

Marriages, and families, do not exist outside of a gendered division of labor (Delphy 1984). The gendered division of household work is central to the study of gender and family relationships, particularly as women increasingly share the breadwinning role.

As indicated earlier, dual-worker/dual-career marriages constitute approximately two-thirds of married families with children under 18 (Silberstein 1992; Wilkie 1991). Despite women's increased participation in the work force, men are not reciprocating by increasing their participation in household tasks. Wives' employment has minimal impact on husbands' involvement in domestic chores (Berk and Berk 1979; Hochschild with Machung 1989). Although some researchers suggest that for every one-dollar increase in the wife's income, the husband increases his household tasks by 20 minutes (Nickols and Metzen 1978), others dispute claims that wives' earnings directly affect housework (Spitze 1986). The bottom line is that only 20% of men in dual-worker families share equally in homemaking and child care (Hochschild with Machung 1989).

The gendered imbalance of work in the home is staggering. Wives employed outside of the home perform three times more household duties than do their husbands (Berk 1985; Kamo 1988; Warner 1986). These tasks amount to women doing approximately 15 additional hours per week of housework and approximately 79% of the total housework (Burley 1991). In sum, wives perform a month more of housework each year than their husbands (Hochschild with Machung 1989). Not only are many women doing more work at home, but the nature of the tasks expected of women is qualitatively different from the chores assigned to men (Bruess, Dellinger, and Sahlman 1993). Men are typically allocated tasklike "projects" (caring for patio furniture or water-sealing the deck), creative jobs (fixing the toaster), and/or responsibilities that are conducted seasonally or monthly (grilling hamburgers or seeding the lawn). Women's jobs include those that are required several times a day (washing dishes), mundane (folding the laundry), time consuming (running errands and making grocery lists), timely (planning and preparing meals), and simultaneous (fixing dinner while helping children with homework) (Beckwith 1992; Hochschild with Machung 1989).

Some couples report equal "sharing" of tasks, buying into the "upstairs/downstairs" or "inside/outside" myth (Hochschild with Machung 1989). For these couples, outside (and/or downstairs) refers to a garage, basement, and/or yard; these are "his" responsibilities. Her responsibilities include the "upstairs" (and/or "inside"), which means the rest of the house (living room, bedrooms, family rooms, bathrooms, kitchen, and all the work associated with these rooms, such as laundry, dishes, and meal preparation). As a way to justify the second shift, many men *and* women in Hochschild and Machung's (1989) research jointly devised and embraced the outside/inside or upstairs/downstairs arrangement. However, such "half and half" arrangements are simply gendered myths that mask what remains a clearly lopsided division of tasks in most families.

The jobs most women assume in the home are many. The burden of their tasks is not only

physical, but psychological as well. In fact, "psychological responsibility" is actually another job for many women (Hochschild with Machung 1989). It involves the often necessary duty of "managing" the many other household jobs — remembering, planning, and coordinating tasks and reminding others of their responsibilities. Not only are women expected to do more tasks, but also they tend to adopt responsibility for making sure others' tasks get done.

Equally gendered are kinship responsibilities in families (Johnson et al. 1992). "Kinkeeping" is the function of maintaining contact with one's extended family and keeping other family members in touch with one another (Rosenthal 1985). Families with kinkeepers report greater extended family interaction and greater emphasis on family rituals within the extended family and within the historical development of the family. Kinkeepers are more often women than men; grandmothers and mothers are more frequently placed in these roles than other family members (Bahr 1976; Rosenthal 1985). Men sometimes participate in the kinship role function by providing economic aid, but women are more likely to be involved in communication and relational activities (Bahr 1976). Women also often assume responsibility for caring for elderly parents and parents-in-law. Again, men often provide instrumental support (money) while women most often assume responsibility for their parents' daily, personal care (Wood 1994b). Family members define such activities as "women's work." The job is frequently passed from mother to daughter, and the position persists over time (Rosenthal 1985).

What are the implications of the imbalance in shared housework and the additional burdens on women? The effects are detrimental for both marriages and families. The overburdening of women is related to dissatisfaction and depression among dual-career wives (Benin and Agostinelli 1988; Ross, Mirowsky, and Huber 1983). Women also suffer from more physical illness and emotional stress as a result of their extra duties (Hochschild with Machung 1989).

Marital satisfaction is also related to task sharing; the happiest wives are in marriages where husbands share equally in household tasks (Yogev and Brett 1985), and in marriages where they are satisfied with the amount of sharing or support they receive from their husbands (Pina and Bengston 1993). Couples in one study reported that sharing tasks has a number of positive outcomes, such as increased communication, heightened intimacy, and improved decision-making abilities (Haas 1980). However, wives who maintain traditional ideologies about marriage seem the least concerned about husbands who share household work. For wives with egalitarian beliefs about marital roles, marital satisfaction is closely linked to their husband's involvement in housework (Pina and Bengston 1993).

More equal sharing of household labor has positive effects on other familial relationships as well. Fathers who share tasks equally in their marriages report experiencing greater satisfaction in the fathering role, being more aware of their children's needs, and developing a maternal sense as they increased their domestic activities (Coltrane 1989). Moreover, egalitarian families provide nonstereotypical role models for children.

How do you achieve an egalitarian marriage, or at least increase your chances for more equal task sharing? According to one study in which husbands and wives shared equally in housework, Coltrane (1989) found that the key factor influencing the equal division of household work was the attitude by both spouses that household work is not "women's" work. Also important is how husbands and wives experience the division of labor and the roles in their primary families (Haas 1980; Koopman-Boyden and Abbot 1985). Husbands who had working mothers, and who were required to

do chores as a child, were more likely to share household work.

Although women are encouraged in our society to "do it all" and be "superwomen" who handle careers, children, husbands, and in-laws with ease and grace, they seldom are warned about (or expect) the extra month of work each year that most men do not experience. Hochschild and Machung (1989, 24) explain the "ironic heroism" of working mothers: "The common portrayal of the supermom working mother suggests that she is 'energetic' and 'competent' because these are her *personal* characteristics, not because she has been forced to adapt to an overly demanding schedule."

The politics of housework are not confined to bed sheets and dustmops; the politics of housework are deeply saturated with images of gender. These conceptions are culturally constructed and reinforced, and then are further supported and enacted on various levels within the family. Next we explore another gendered family role: child care.

CHILD CARE

Add a child to a family and what is the result? In books and movies (and sometimes in our dreams), adding a child is an idyllic time in which a couple experiences the beauty, poetry, and romance of the occasion. In reality, we know that the addition of children to the family increases stress and decreases marital satisfaction (Cox 1985). Bill Cosby (1986, 18) noted: "Having a child is surely the most beautifully irrational act that two people in love can commit."

Child rearing is important, yet, like other family roles, it often follows highly gendered patterns of cultural expectations and behaviors. Although men have increased their participation in the actual births of children, care for infant children is still assigned primarily to mothers. Even in egalitarian marriages, responsibilities regarding child care tend to become more traditional after children are born (Cox 1985).

Many fathers report feeling unskilled in infant care. As compensation, they tend to emphasize their capacities as protectors and providers (Entwisle and Doering 1988). According to researchers Harris and Morgan 1991, 532), a father's breadwinning role mandates a less active, less compassionate role in parenting: "The traditional paternal role is the instrumental role as breadwinner. This role identifies some paternal responsibilities for training and discipline, but father–child relationships need not be close or compassionate," nor need the role involve the constant availability typically expected of mothers.

We might guess that in dual-career marriages, fathers would participate more equally in child care, since well-educated, middle-class men tend to be less sex-role stereotypical than their less-educated, lower class counterparts (Lamb 1982). In fact, fathers in dual-career marriages do "assist" more than other fathers, and fathers' participation in child care has increased over the last few decades (Seward, Yeats, Seward, and Stanley-Stevens 1993). However, "participating" is altogether different from "sharing equally." Fathers—even those in dual-career marriages—do not represent an egalitarian model of parenting (Bird 1979; Hochschild with Machung 1989; Seward et al. 1993).

Fathers' participation in child care is often in the form of recreational activities such as reading to children, playing with them, or teaching them (Thompson and Walker 1989). Women often spend the majority of time taking care of mundane, repetitive child care activities (Bird 1979), such as feeding, bathing, and other activities of primary caregiving (Katsh 1981). The time many fathers spend with children is more occasional and enjoyable (as in a trip to the zoo on Saturday); the time mothers spend with children is more constant and boring (Burns and Hommel 1989).

Some researchers optimistically suggest that fathers in contemporary dual-career families are "in a state of transition—moving from the traditional perspective of fatherhood toward a more egalitarian model" (Jump and Haas 1987, 111). Until such a model is widely adopted—and embraced by a culture resistant to family-oriented men (Cohen 1987)—gendered patterns of family structure, roles, and communication will remain concrete and distinct, reinforced by social expectations and continuously (re)created within and by families. Next, we explore parenting and parental communication as primary agents of children's gender socialization.

Gendered Patterns of Parenting: Children's Socialization

From birth, male and female babies are treated differently both in American culture and around the world (Williams and Best 1982). The process of socialization occurs in a variety of contexts and throughout our lifetime (Stanton 1990), but it is most salient within the family.

Gender creates expectations of family members, as we discussed. The behaviors expected of "mommies and daddies," "sons and daughters," and "sisters and brothers" reflect social meanings of gender being (re)created and reinforced in our family relationships. The expectations parents have for children reflect parents' views of gender.

For instance, America's "boy preference" (Basow 1992; Coombs 1977) may be manifested in fathers' greater interaction with sons than daughters (Rossi 1984). Too, differential descriptors are applied to babies within hours of their birth: Parents describe boys as "strong," "solid," and "independent," and depict girls as "cute," "sweet," and "delicate" (Handel 1988; Stern and

Karraker 1989). In general, both mothers and fathers encourage, teach, question, and talk explicitly to their sons more than their daughters (Bronstein 1988; Weitzman, Birns, and Friend 1985). Males are valued more than females in almost every country in the world (Basow 1992), a value that parents communicate, often unconsciously, to their children. In these ways, families foster, and children learn, social understandings of gender.

To understand the family is to understand the deeply embedded meanings of gender continuously communicated by parents. Parents' differential expectations for their daughters and sons are communicated both directly and indirectly. For example, parents often decorate children's rooms and bodies distinctively; gendered identities are fostered by the Power Ranger wallpaper and replicas of large machinery used to decorate a 2-year-old boy's room, and in the leggings and the black patent leather shoes strapped on the feet of a 3-year-old girl (Pomerleau et al. 1990; Richardson 1988; Shakin, Shakin, and Sternglanz 1985). After examining over 170 articles on sex-role stereotyping, Lytton and Romney (1991) concluded that sex- and gender-typing are the only areas in which mothers, fathers, and parents combined actually have an impact on children.

Because gendered prescriptions are pervasive and begin so early, it is surprising that children do not develop specific sex-role orientations earlier than they do. For instance, Doyle (1991) found that mothers begin to withdraw touch behaviors from sons around the age of 6 months. However, before the age of 3, children are rather flexible in their orientation: Boys are not yet doing only "little boy" things; girls have not yet learned to do only "little girl" things (Fine 1987; Handel 1988; Seegmiller 1980). Around the age of about 3, the tendency to see oneself as consistently male or female (gender constancy) appears to develop in most children (Wood 1994a).

Gendered identities are learned as families enact gendered patterns of behavior and communication in their everyday, mundane interactions. For instance, parents encourage traditional sex roles for their female children when assigning chores. Daughters are routinely asked to perform more household jobs than are sons (Cloch 1987; Mietus-Sanik and Stafford 1985). Children also learn about gender by watching the roles and the relationship of their parents, such as who assumes the majority of child care and housework responsibilities (Hochschild with Machung 1989), and who acts as the "relationship expert" (Wood 1993).

Parents also shape understandings of gender in their communication, and their playful interaction, with children. Routinely, fathers emphasize independence and autonomy in their sons, while mothers encourage politeness, nurturance, and mutual activities in their daughters (Power and Shanks 1989; Thompson and Walker 1989). Fathers and their boys participate in more "dangerous and exciting" leisure activities (Lundgren and Cassedy 1993); mothers are more likely to engage in social play (Belsky 1980), tending toward more verbal and didactic interaction.

Parenting and gender-role research has been focused on heterosexual relationships. Families with gay or lesbian parents, too, are confronted with complexities of gender socialization. Lesbians, however, often hold less stereotypical perceptions of feminine behavior, believing their sons and daughters to be more similar in qualities than do heterosexual mothers (Hill 1988). Lesbian mothers also tend to promote more traditionally masculine characteristics in their daughters. Gay men and lesbian women may be more sensitive to the constraints related to role restrictions and thus maximize nontraditional role modeling (Martin 1993). However, both gay and lesbian parents note that the strength of cultural stereotypes often overwhelms their earnest attempts to minimize children's gendered attitudes and behaviors (Martin 1993).

Conclusion

In this chapter, we explored gendered patterns of marital communication, family roles, and parenting. We learned that gender seeps into almost every aspect of our families, filtering our perceptions of the world, our views of family roles and relationships, and our expectations. We also learned that family communication is not immune to social meanings of gender, just as we, as individuals, are not immune to our families' prescriptions of, and influences on, who we are as women and men, girls and boys, mothers and fathers, and daughters and sons. Our jointly constructed gender ideologies—often those we learn and enact within the family—influence how we relate to and communicate with others. Indeed, you might recognize how your family has shaped your gendered participation in intimate, extended family, friendship, and even professional relationships. . . . We conclude this chapter by emphasizing that families cannot be understood without a consideration of gender. In multiple ways, each and every day, families normalize, reify, and ultimately embody social understandings of gender.

References

Bahr, H. 1976. "The Kinship Role." Pp. 360–367 in F. Ivan Nye (ed.), *Role Structure and Analysis of the Family*. Beverly Hills, CA: Sage.

Balswick, J. 1988. *The Inexpressive Male*. Lexington, MA: Lexington Books.

Basow, S. 1992. *Gender Stereotypes and Roles*, 3rd ed. Pacific Grove, CA: Brooks/Cole.

Beach, S., and I. Arias, 1983. "Assessment of Perceptual Discrepancy: Utility of the Primary Communication Inventory." *Family Process* 22: 309–316.

Beckwith, J. 1992. "Stereotypes and Reality in the Division of Household Labor." *Social Behavior and Personality* 20: 283–288.

Belsky, J. 1980. "A Family Analysis of Parental Influence on Infant Exploratory Competence." Pp. 87–101 in F. A. Pederson (ed.), *The Father–Infant Relationship: Observational Studies in a Family Setting*. New York: Praeger.

Benin, M. H., and J. Agostinelli. 1988. "Husbands' and Wives' Satisfaction with the Division of Labor." *Journal of Marriage and the Family* 50: 349–361.

Berk, R., and S. Berk. 1979. *Labor and Leisure at Home: Content and Organization of the Household Day*. Beverly Hills, CA: Sage.

Berk, S. F. 1985. *The Gender Factory: The Apportionment of Work in American Households*. New York: World.

Bernard, J. 1972. *The Future of Marriage*. New York: Bantam Books.

Bird, C. 1979. *The Two Paycheck Marriage*. New York: Rosen & Wade.

Blumstein, P., and P. Schwartz. 1983. *American Couples*. New York: Morrow.

Bronstein, P. 1988. "Father–Child Interaction." Pp. 107–124 in P. Bronstein and C. Cowan (eds.), *Fatherhood Today: Men's Changing Role in the Family*. New York: Wiley.

Bruess, C., C. Dellinger, and J. Sahlman. 1993. "I'll Mow the Grass, You Fix Dinner: Engaged Couples' Expectations of Task-Sharing in Marriage." Paper presented at the meeting of the International Network on Personal Relationships, Milwaukee, WI, May.

Burley, K. A. 1991. "Family-Work Spillover in Dual-Career Couples: A Comparison of Two Time Perspectives," *Psychological Reports* 68: 471–480.

Burns, A., and R. Hommel. 1989. "Gender Division of Tasks by Parents and Their Children." *Psychology of Women Quarterly* 13: 113–125.

Canter, R., and S. Ageton. 1984. "The Epidemiology of Adolescent Sex-Role Attitudes." *Sex Roles* 11: 657–676.

Cloch, M. 1987. "The Development of Sex Differences in Young Children's Activities at Home: The Effect of the Social Context." *Sex Roles* 16: 279–302.

Cohen, T. 1987. "Remaking Men." *Journal of Family Issues* 8: 57–77.

Coltrane, S. 1989. "Household Labor and the Routine Production of Gender." *Social Problems* 36: 473–490.

Coombs, L. 1977. "Preferences for Sex of Children Among U.S. Couples." *Family Planning Perspectives* 9: 259–265.

Cooper, K., and D. Gutmann. 1987. "Gender Identity and Ego Mastery Style in Middle-Aged, Pre- and Post–Empty Nest Women." *The Gerontologist* 27: 347–352.

Cosby, B. 1986. *Fatherhood.* New York: Berkley.

Cox, M. 1985. "Progress and Continued Challenges in Understanding the Transition to Parenthood." *Journal of Family Issues* 6: 395–408.

Davidson, B., J. Balswick, and C. Halverson. 1983. "Affective Self-Disclosure and Marital Adjustment: A Test of Equity Theory." *Journal of Marriage and the Family* 45: 93–102.

Davidson, K., and N. Moore. 1992. *Marriage and Family.* Dubuque, IA: Brown.

DeForest, C., and G. Stone. 1980. "Effects of Sex and Intimacy Level on Self-Disclosure." *Journal of Counseling Psychology* 27: 93–96.

Delphy, C. 1984. *Close to Home: A Materialist Analysis of Women's Oppression.* Amherst: University of Massachusetts Press.

Dersch, C., and J. C. Pearson. 1986. "Interpersonal Communication Competence and Marital Adjustment Among Dual Career and Dual Worker Women." Paper presented at the annual meeting of the Central States Speech Communication Association, Cincinnati, OH, April.

Dindia, K., and M. Allen. 1992. "Sex Difference in Self-Disclosure: A Meta-Analysis." *Psychological Bulletin* 112: 106–124.

Doyle, J. 1991. *The Male Experience.* Dubuque, IA: Brown.

Entwisle, D., and S. Doering. 1988. "The Emergent Father Role." *Sex Roles* 18: 119–142.

Fine, G. 1987. *With the Boys: Little League Baseball and Preadolescent Culture.* Chicago: University of Chicago Press.

Fitzpatrick, M. A., and J. Indvik. 1982. "The Instrumental and Expressive Domains of Marital Communication." *Human Communication Research* 8: 195–213.

Gaines, S. 1995. "Relationships Between Members of Cultural Minorities." Pp. 51–88 in J. T. Woods and S. W. Duck (eds.), *Understanding Relationship Processes, 6: Off the Beaten Track: Understudied Relationships.* Thousand Oaks, CA: Sage.

Gitter, G., and H. Black. 1976. "Is Self-Disclosing Revealing?" *Journal of Counseling Psychology* 23: 327–332.

Greenblatt, J., J. Gasenauer, and V. Freimuth. 1980. "Psychological Sex Type and Androgyny in the Study of Communication Variables: Self-Disclosure and Communication Apprehension." *Human Communication Research* 6: 117–129.

Haas, L. 1980. "Role-Sharing Couples: A Study of Egalitarian Marriages." *Family Relations* 29: 289–296.

Handel, G. 1988. *Childhood Socialization.* Hawthorne, NY: Aldine de Gruyter.

Harris, J., and S. Morgan. 1991. "Fathers, Sons, and Daughters: Differential Paternal Involvement in Parenting." *Journal of Marriage and the Family* 53: 531–544.

Herzog, A., J. Bachman, and L. Johnston. 1983. "Paid Work, Child Care, and Housework: A National Survey of High School Seniors' Preferences for Sharing Responsibilities Between Husband and Wife." *Sex Roles* 9: 109–135.

Hill, M. 1988. "Child-Rearing Attitudes of Black Lesbian Mothers." In Boston Lesbian Psychologies Collective (ed.), *Lesbian Psychologies: Explorations and Challenges.* Urbana: University of Illinois Press.

Hochschild, A., with A. Machung. 1989. *The Second Shift: Working Parents and Revolution at Home.* New York: Viking Press.

Israelson, C. 1989. "Family Resource Management." *Family Perspectives* 23: 311–331.

Johnson, M., T. Huston, S. Gaines, and G. Levinger. 1992. "Patterns of Married Life Among Young Couples." *Journal of Social and Personal Relationships* 9: 343–364.

Jump, T., and L. Haas. 1987. "Fathers in Transition: Dual-Career Fathers Participating in Child Care." Pp. 98–114 in M. Kimmel (ed.), *Changing Men: New Directions in Research on Men and Masculinity.* Newbury Park, CA: Sage.

Kamo, Y. 1988. "Determinants of the Household Division of Labor: Resources, Power, and Ideology." *Journal of Family Issues* 9: 177–200.

Katsh, B. 1981. "Fathers and Infants." *Journal of Family Issues* 2: 275–296.

Koopman-Boyden, P., and M. Abbott. 1985. "Expectations for Household Task Allocation and Actual Task Allocation: A New Zealand Study." *Journal of Marriage and the Family* 47: 211–219.

Krogh, K. 1985. "Women's Motives to Achieve and to Nurture in Different Life Stages." *Sex Roles* 12: 75–90.

Lamb, M. 1982. *Nontraditional Families: Parenting and Child Development.* Hillsdale, NJ: Erlbaum.

LeVine, E., and J. Franco. 1981. "A Reassessment of Self-Disclosure Patterns Among Anglo-Americans and Hispanics." *Journal of Counseling Psychology* 28: 522–524.

Lundgren, D., and A. Cassedy, 1993. "Girls' and Boys' Activity Patterns in Family Leisure Settings." In C. Berryman-Fink, D. Ballard-Reisch, and L. Newman (eds.), *Communication and Sex-Role Socialization.* New York: Garland.

Lytton, H., and D. Romney. 1991. "Parents' Differential Socialization of Boys and Girls: A Meta-Analysis." *Psychological Bulletin* 109: 267–296.

Martin, A. 1993. *The Lesbian and Gay Parenting Handbook.* New York: HarperCollins.

McGee, J., and K. Wells. 1982. "Gender Typing and Androgyny in Later Life." *Human Development* 25: 116–139.

McLeod, R. 1992. "Poll on Male Attitudes Finds 90's Men Sensitive, Caring." *Austin American-Statesman,* March 14, pp. A1, A15.

Mietus-Sanik, M., and K. Stafford. 1985. "Adolescents' Contributions to Household Production: Male and Female Differences." *Adolescence* 20: 207–215.

Nickols, S., and E. Metzen. 1978. "Household Time for Husband and Wife." *Home Economics Research Journal* 7: 85–97.

Pearson, J. C. 1992. *Lasting Love: What Keeps Couples Together.* Dubuque, IA: Brown.

———. 1993. *Communication in the Family: Seeking Satisfaction in Changing Times.* New York: HarperCollins.

———. 1995. "Forty-Forever Years? Primary Relationships and Senior Citizens." In N. Vanzetti and S. Duck (eds.), *A Lifetime of Relationships.* Pacific Grove, CA: Brooks/Cole.

Pearson, J. C., R. L. West, and L. Turner. 1995. *Gender and Communication.* Dubuque, IA: Brown & Benchmark.

Philliber, W., and D. Hiller. 1979. "A Research Note:

Occupational Attainments and Perceptions of Status among Working Wives." *Journal of Marriage and the Family* 41: 59–62.

Philliber, W., and D. Vannoy-Hiller. 1990. "The Effect of Husband's Occupational Attainment on Wife's Achievement." *Journal of Marriage and the Family* 52: 323–329.

Pina, D., and V. Bengston. 1993. "The Division of Household Labor and Wives' Happiness: Ideology, Employment, and Perceptions of Support." *Journal of Marriage and the Family.* 55: 901–912.

Pomerleau, A., D. Bolduc, G. Malcuit, and L. Cossette. 1990. "Pink or Blue: Environmental Stereotypes in the First Two Years of Life." *Sex Roles* 22: 359–367.

Power, T., and J. Shanks. 1989. "Parents as Socializers: Maternal and Paternal Views." *Journal of Youth and Adolescence* 18: 203–217.

Richardson, L. 1988. *The Dynamics of Sex and Gender: A Sociological Perspective.* New York: Harper & Row.

Riessman, C. 1990. *Divorce Talk: Women and Men Make Sense of Personal Relationships.* New Brunswick, NJ: Rutgers University Press.

Rosenfeld, L. 1979. "Self-Disclosure Avoidance: Why I Am Afraid to Tell You Who I Am." *Communication Monographs* 46: 63–74.

Rosenthal, C. 1985. "Kinkeeping in the Familial Division of Labor." *Journal of Marriage and the Family* 47: 965–974.

Ross, C. E., J. Mirowsky, and J. Huber. 1983. "Dividing Work, Sharing Work, and In-Between: Marriage Patterns and Depression." *American Sociological Review* 48: 809–823.

Rossi, A. 1984. "Gender and Parenthood." *American Sociological Review* 49: 1–19.

Rubin, L. 1983. *Intimate Strangers: Men and Women Together.* New York: Harper & Row.

Seegmiller, B. 1980. "Sex Typed Behavior in Pre-Schoolers: Sex, Age, and Social Class Effects." *Journal of Psychology* 104: 31–33.

Seward, R., D. Yeats, J. Seward, and L. Stanley-Stevens. 1993. "Fathers' Time Spent with Their Children: A Longitudinal Assessment." *Family Perspectives* 27: 275–283.

Shakin, M., D. Shakin, and S. Sternglanz. 1985. "Infant Clothing: Sex Labeling for Strangers." *Sex Roles* 12: 955–964.

Shimanoff, S. 1985. "Rules Governing the Verbal Expression of Emotions Between Married Couples."

Western Journal of Speech Communication 49: 147–165.

Silberstein, L. 1992. *Dual-Career Marriage: A System in Transition.* Hillsdale, NJ: Erlbaum.

Sillars, A., and W. Wilmot. 1989. "Marital Communication Across the Life Span." Pp. 225–253 in J. F. Nussbaum (ed.), *Life-Span Communication: Normative Processes.* Hillsdale, NJ: Erlbaum.

Smith, D. 1985. "Wife Employment and Marital Adjustment: A Cumulation of Results." *Family Relations* 34: 483–490.

Spitze, G. 1986. "The Division of Task Responsibility in U.S. Households: Longitudinal Adjustments to Change." *Social Forces* 64: 689–701.

Stanton, A. 1990. *Communication and Student Socialization.* Norwood, NJ: Ablex.

Stern, M., and K. Karraker. 1989. "Sex Stereotyping of Infants: A Review of Gender Labeling Studies." *Sex Roles* 20: 501–522.

Swain, S. 1989. "Covert Intimacy: Closeness in Men's Friendships." Pp. 71–86 in B. J. Risman and P. Schwartz (eds.), *Gendered Intimate Relationships.* Belmont, CA: Wadsworth.

Tannen, D. 1990. *You Just Don't Understand: Women and Men in Conversation.* New York: Morrow.

Tavris, C. 1992. *The Mismeasure of Woman.* New York: Simon & Schuster.

Thompson, K., and A. Walker. 1989. "Women and Men in Marriage, Work and Parenthood." *Journal of Marriage and the Family* 51: 845–872.

Trent, K., and S. South. 1989. "Structural Determinants of the Divorce Rate: A Cross-Societal Analysis." *Journal of Marriage and the Family* 51: 391–404.

U.S. Department of Commerce, Bureau of the Census. 1990. *Statistical Abstract of the United States, 1990.* Washington, DC: U.S. Government Printing Office.

Warner, R. L. 1986. "Alternative Strategies for Measuring Household Division of Labor: A Comparison." *Journal of Family Issues* 7: 179–195.

Weitzman, N., B. Birns, and R. Friend. 1985. "Traditional and Nontraditional Mothers' Communication with Their Daughters and Sons." *Child Development* 56: 894–896.

Wheeless, L., and J. Grotz. 1976. "Conceptualization and Measurement of Reported Self-Disclosure." *Human Communication Research* 2: 338–346.

Wilkie, J. 1991. "The Decline in Men's Labor Force Participation and Income and the Changing Structure of Family Economic Support." *Journal of Marriage and the Family* 53: 111–122.

Williams, J., and D. Best. 1982. *Measuring Sex Stereotypes: A Thirty Nation Study.* Beverly Hills, CA: Sage.

Wood, J. T. 1993. "Engendered Relationships: Interaction, Caring, Power, and Responsibility in Close Relationships." In S. Duck (ed.), *Processes in Close Relationships: Contexts of Close Relationships*, Vol. 3. Beverly Hills, CA: Sage.

———. 1994a. *Gendered Lives: Communication, Gender, and Culture.* Belmont, CA: Wadsworth.

———. 1994b. *Who Cares? Women, Care and Culture.* Carbondale: Southern Illinois University Press.

———. 1995. *Relational Communication: Change and Continuity in Personal Relationships.* Belmont, CA: Wadsworth.

Wood, J. T., and S. W. Duck. 1995. "Off the Beaten Track: New Frontiers in Relational Research." Pp. 1–21 in J. T. Wood and S. W. Duck (eds.), *Understanding Relationship Processes, 6: Off the Beaten Track: Understudied Relationships.* Thousand Oaks, CA: Sage.

Wood, J. T., and C. Inman. 1993. "In a Different Mode: Masculine Styles of Communicating Closeness." *Journal of Applied Communication Research* 21: 279–295.

Yogev, S. 1987. "Marital Satisfaction and Sex Role Perceptions Among Dual-Earner Couples." *Journal of Social and Personal Relationships* 4: 35–46.

Yogev, S., and J. Brett. 1985. "Perceptions of Division of Housework and Child Care and Marital Satisfaction." *Journal of Marriage and the Family* 47: 609–619.

Questions

1. Bruess and Pearson begin their article by recalling the types of games they played when they were 5 years old. Take your own trek down memory lane. As far as you can recall, what sorts of games did you play as a preschooler? What *roles* did you take in these games? If you are a male, can you remember taking a role that traditionally would have been taken on by a female? If you are a female, can you remember taking a role that traditionally would have been taken on by a male? How much impact do you think these early games might have had on your life?

2. What do Bruess and Pearson say are the primary differences in feminine and masculine means of expressing closeness? To what degree do your own experiences confirm their conclusions about how men and women express closeness?

3. Bruess and Pearson suggest that "sex-role differences are marked among younger people, but they become less salient as people age." In your judgment, why might "sex-role crossover" be more likely among older than younger people?

4. What is the "second shift"?

5. The authors of this article cite Hochschild and Machung's point about the "ironic heroism" of working mothers: "The common portrayal of the supermom working mother suggests that she is 'energetic' and 'competent' because these are her *personal* characteristics, not because she has been forced to adapt to an overly demanding schedule." Why would it have required these authors to have what Mills would have called a "sociological imagination" to make this point?

6. The bottom line, according to Bruess and Pearson is that "in multiple ways, each and every day, families normalize, reify, and ultimately embody social understandings of gender." Using examples drawn from the article, explain what they meant by this statement.

·19·

Hidden Lessons

Myra Sadker and David Sadker

Myra and David Sadker are frequently asked how they found their mutual interest in gender bias in education. They reply that it came to them when they were in graduate school where, as wife and husband, they were enrolled in the same program: "We attended the same classes, prepared the same assignments, read the same books—and realized that we were getting two very different educations." The turning point, they explain, came in a meeting of students and professors in the program.

> About fifty participants, almost all men, were discussing civil rights for minorities in education. One male voice after another joined in the discussion until Myra made a suggestion and waited for a reaction. But the men kept right on talking. "Perhaps they didn't hear me," she thought, so she tried again. But the discussion rambled on as if she had not uttered a word. Then a loud, deep voice boomed out, the kind of powerful voice that causes eyes to look skyward searching for Charlton Heston to bring down the tablets. All eyes turned to six-foot Mike from Utah as he slowly repeated Myra's idea. The talking stopped, there was complete silence, and then the room exploded with praise. "That's what we've been looking for! Great idea!"
>
> As a result of Myra's good idea that was attributed to Mike, a professor assigned the task of writing grant proposals to improve education for minorities. We worked together and signed our names as coauthors. The faculty member began the next meeting with this announcement: "There's one paper that stands out," he said. "I'd like to talk with you about David's proposal. He has some ideas I think we can pursue." There was enthusiasm for our proposal, our ideas, but "our" had become "David's." "I wrote it, too," Myra said lightly so as not to appear petty. The faculty member looked surprised and concerned. "Of course when we say David, we mean you, too. You know that, don't you?"

Sitting in the same classroom, reading the same textbook, listening to the same teacher, boys and girls receive very different educations. From grade school through graduate school female students are more likely to be invisible members of classrooms. Teachers interact with males more frequently, ask them better questions, and give them more precise and helpful feedback. Over the course of years the uneven distribution of teacher time, energy, attention, and talent, with boys getting the lion's share, takes its toll on girls. Since gender bias is not a noisy problem, most people are unaware of the secret sexist lessons and the quiet losses they engender.

Girls are the majority of our nation's schoolchildren, yet they are second-class educational citizens. The problems they face—loss of self-esteem, decline in achievement, and elimination of career options—are at the heart of the educational process. Until educational sexism is eradicated, more than half our children will be shortchanged and their gifts lost to society.

Award-winning author Susan Faludi discovered that backlash "is most powerful when it goes private, when it lodges inside a woman's mind and turns her vision inward, until she imagines the pressure is all in her head, until she begins to enforce the backlash too—on herself" (Faludi 1991). Psychological backlash internalized by adult women is a frightening concept, but what is even more terrifying is a curriculum of sexist school lessons becoming secret mind games played against female children, our daughters, tomorrow's women.

After almost two decades of research grants and thousands of hours of classroom observation, we remain amazed at the stubborn persistence of these hidden sexist lessons. When we began our investigation of gender bias, we looked first in the classrooms of one of Washington, D.C.'s elite and expensive private schools. Uncertain of exactly what to look for, we wrote nothing down; we just observed. The classroom was a whirlwind of activity, so fast paced we could easily miss the quick but vital phrase or gesture, the insidious incident, the tiny inequity that held a world of meaning. As we watched, we had to push ourselves beyond the blind spots of socialization and gradually focus on the nature of the interaction between teacher and student. On the second day we saw our first example of sexism, a quick, jarring flash within the hectic pace of the school day:

Two second graders are kneeling beside a large box. They whisper excitedly to each other as they pull out wooden blocks, colored balls, counting sticks. So absorbed are these two small children in examining and sorting the materials, they are visibly startled by the teacher's impatient voice as she hovers over them. "Ann! Julia! Get your cotton-pickin' hands out of the math box. Move over so the boys can get in there and do their work."

Isolated here on the page of a book, this incident is not difficult to interpret. It becomes even more disturbing if you think of it with the teacher making a racial distinction. Picture Ann and Julia as African-American children moved away so white children can gain access to the math materials. If Ann and Julia's parents had observed this exchange, they might justifiably wonder whether their tuition dollars were well spent. But few parents actually watch teachers in action, and fewer still have learned to interpret the meaning behind fast-paced classroom events.

The incident unsettles, but it must be considered within the context of numerous interactions this harried teacher had that day. While she talked to the two girls, she was also keeping a wary eye on fourteen other active children. Unless you actually shadowed the teacher, stood right next to her as we did, you might not have seen or heard the event. After all, it lasted only a few seconds.

It took us almost a year to develop an observation system that would register the hundreds of daily classroom interactions, teasing out the gender bias embedded in them. Trained raters coded classrooms in math, reading, English, and social studies. They observed students from different racial and ethnic backgrounds. They saw lessons taught by women and by men, by teachers of different races. In short, they analyzed America's classrooms. By the end of the year we had thousands of observation sheets, and after another year of statistical analysis, we discovered a syntax of sexism so elusive that most teachers and students were completely unaware of its influence (Sadker, Sadker, and Klein 1991).[1]

[1]Our first study, which analyzed gender bias in elementary and secondary classrooms, lasted more than three years and was funded by the National Institute of Education. The report submitted to the government was Myra Sadker and David Sadker, *Year 3: Final Report: Promoting Effectiveness in Classroom Instruction*, Washington, DC: National Institute of Education, 1984.

Recently a producer of NBC's "Dateline" contacted us to learn more about our discovery that girls don't receive their fair share of education. Jane Pauley, the show's anchorwoman, wanted to visit classrooms, capture these covert sexist lessons on videotape, and expose them before a television audience. The task was to extricate sound bites of sexism from a fifth-grade classroom where the teacher, chosen to be the subject of the exposé, was aware she was being scrutinized for sex bias.

"Dateline" had been taping in her class for two days when we received a concerned phone call. "This is a fair teacher," the producer said. "How can we show sexism on our show when there's no gender bias in this teacher's class?" We drove to the NBC studio in Washington, D.C., and found two "Dateline" staffers, intelligent women concerned about fair treatment in school, sitting on the floor in a darkened room staring at the videotape of a fifth-grade class. "We've been playing this over and over. The teacher is terrific. There's no bias in her teaching. Come watch."

After about twenty minutes of viewing, we realized it was a case of déjà vu: The episodal sexist themes and recurring incidents were all too familiar. The teacher was terrific, but she was more effective for half of the students than she was for the other. She was, in fact, a classic example of the hundreds of skillful well-intentioned professionals we have seen who inadvertently teach boys better than girls.

We had forgotten how difficult it was to recognize subtle sexism before you learn how to look. It was as if the "Dateline" staff members were wearing blinders. We halted the tape, pointed out the sexist behaviors, related them to incidents in our research, and played the tape again. There is a classic "aha!" effect in education when people finally "get it." Once the hidden lessons of unconscious bias are understood, classrooms never look the same again to the trained observer.

Much of the unintentional gender bias in that fifth-grade class could not be shown in the short time allowed by television, but the sound bites of sexism were also there. "Dateline" chose to show a segregated math group: boys sitting on the teacher's right side and girls on her left. After giving the math book to a girl to hold open at the page of examples, the teacher turned her back to the girls and focused on the boys, teaching them actively and directly. Occasionally she turned to the girls' side, but only to read the examples in the book. This teacher, although aware that she was being observed for sexism, had unwittingly transformed the girls into passive spectators, an audience for the boys. All but one, that is: The girl holding the math book had become a prop.

"Dateline" also showed a lively discussion in the school library. With both girls' hands and boys' hands waving for attention, the librarian chose boy after boy to speak. In one interaction she peered through the forest of girls' hands waving directly in front of her to acknowledge the raised hand of a boy in the back of the room. Startled by the teacher's attention, the boy muttered, "I was just stretching."

The next day we discussed the show with future teachers, our students at The American University. They were bewildered. "Those teachers really were sexist. They didn't mean to be, but they were. How could that happen—with the cameras and everyone watching?" When we took those students into classrooms to discover the hidden lessons for themselves, they began to understand. It is difficult to detect sexism unless you know precisely how to observe. And if a lifetime of socialization makes it difficult to spot gender bias even when you're looking for it, how much harder it is to avoid the traps when you are the one doing the teaching.

Among Schoolchildren

Subtle sexism is visible to only the most astute readers of *Among Schoolchildren*, Tracy Kidder's chronicle of real-life educator Chris Zajac. A thirty-four-year-old teacher in Mt. Holyoke, Massachusetts, Mrs. Zajac is a no-nonsense veteran of the classroom. She does not allow her fifth-grade students to misbehave, forget to do their homework, or give up without trying their hardest. Underlying her strict exterior is a woman who cares about schoolchildren. Our students admired her dedication and respected her as a good human being, and it took several readings and discussions before they discovered her inadvertent gender bias. Then came the questions: Does Mrs. Zajac work harder teaching boys than girls? Does she know there is sex bias in her classroom?

These questions probably do not occur to most readers of *Among Schoolchildren* and might jolt both Chris Zajac and the author who so meticulously described the classroom. Here's how Tracy Kidder begins the story of a year in the life of this New England teacher:

"Mrs. Zajac wasn't born yesterday. She knows you didn't do your best work on this paper, Clarence. Don't you remember Mrs. Zajac saying that if you didn't do your best, she'd make you do it over? As for you, Claude, God forbid that you should ever need brain surgery. But Mrs. Zajac hopes that if you do, the doctor won't open up your head and walk off saying he's almost done, as you said when Mrs. Zajac asked you for your penmanship, which, by the way, looks like who did it and ran. Felipe, the reason you have hiccups is, your mouth is always open and the wind rushes in. You're in fifth grade now. So, Felipe, put a lock on it. Zip it up. Then go get a drink of water. Mrs. Zajac means business, Robert. The sooner you realize she never said everybody in the room has to do the work except for Robert, the sooner you'll get along with her. And . . . Clarence. Mrs. Zajac knows you didn't try. You don't just hand in junk to Mrs. Zajac. She's been teaching an awful lot of years. She didn't fall off the turnip cart yesterday. She told you she was an old-lady teacher" (Kidder 1989).

Swiftly, adroitly, Kidder introduces the main characters in the classroom—Clarence, Claude, Felipe, Robert, and back to Clarence, the boy in whom Mrs. Zajac invests most. But where are the girls?

As our students analyzed the book and actually examined who Mrs. Zajac was speaking to, they saw that page after page she spent time with the boys—disciplining them, struggling to help them understand, teaching them with all the energy and talent she could muster. In contrast, the pages that showed Mrs. Zajac working with girls were few and far between.

When we ask teachers at our workshops why they spend more time helping boys, they say, "Because boys need it more" or "Boys have trouble reading, writing, doing math. They can't even sit still. They need me more." In *Among Schoolchildren*, Chris Zajac feels that way, too. Kidder describes how she allows boys to take her over because she thinks they need her.

So teachers of good intention, such as Chris Zajac, respond to boys and teach them more actively, but their time and attention are not limitless. While the teachers are spending time with boys, the girls are being ignored and shortchanged. The only girl clearly realized in *Among Schoolchildren* is Judith, a child who is so alert that she has a vast English vocabulary even though her parents speak only Spanish. But while Judith is a girl of brilliant potential, she rarely reaps the benefit of Mrs. Zajac's active teaching attention. In fact, rather than trouble her teacher and claim time and attention for herself, Judith helps Mrs. Zajac, freeing her to work with the more demanding boys. Mrs. Zajac knows she isn't giving this talented girl what she needs and deserves: "If only I had more time," she thinks as she looks at Judith.

On a field trip to Old Sturbridge Village, the children have segregated themselves by sex on the bus, with the boys claiming the back. In a moment of quiet reflection, Chris realizes that in her classroom "the boys rarely give her a chance to spend much time with her girls." She changes her seat, joins the girls, and sings jump rope songs with them for the remainder of the trip.

But her time spent with the girls is short-lived—the length of the day-long field trip—and her recognition of the gender gap in time and attention is brief: a paragraph-long flash of understanding in a book of more than three hundred pages. On the whole, Chris Zajac does not invest her talent in girls. But nurturing children is not unlike tending a garden: Neglect, even when benign, is withering; time and attention bear fruit. Mrs. Zajac and other caring teachers across the country are unaware of the full impact of uneven treatment. They do not realize the high academic and emotional price many girls pay for being too good.

Drawn from years of research, the episodes that follow demonstrate the sexist lessons taught daily in America's classrooms.[2] Pulled out of the numerous incidents in a school day, these inequities become enlarged, as if observed through a magnifying glass, so we can see clearly how they extinguish learning and shatter self-esteem. Imagine yourself in a sixth-grade science class like the one we observed in Maryland.

The teacher is writing a list of inventors and their discoveries on the board:

Elias Howe	sewing machine
Robert Fulton	steamboat
Thomas A. Edison	light bulb
James Otis	elevator
Alexander Graham Bell	telephone
Cyrus McCormick	reaper
Eli Whitney	cotton gin
Orville and Wilbur Wright	airplane

A girl raises her hand and asks, "It looks like all the inventors were men. Didn't women invent anything?" The teacher does not add any female inventors to the list, nor does he discuss new scholarship recognizing the involvement of women in inventions such as the cotton gin. He does not explain how hard it was in times past for women to obtain patents in their own names, and therefore we may never know how many female inventors are excluded from the pages of our history books.[3] Instead he grins, winks, and says, "Sweetheart, don't worry about it. It's the same with famous writers and painters. It's the man's job to create things and the woman's job to look beautiful so she can inspire him." Several boys laugh. A few clown around by flexing their muscles as they ex-

---

[2]These episodes are drawn primarily from our three-year study of sex bias in elementary and secondary classrooms. They are also taken from classroom observations conducted as we supervised student teachers at The American University and as we consulted with schools around the country and assessed their classrooms for gender bias.

---

[3]We may never know how many women inventors are excluded from the pages of history books, but we do know the names of some. For example, Russell Conwell (1843–1925) published accounts of the role played by women in several important inventions:

Who was it that invented the sewing machine? If I would go to school tomorrow and ask your children, they would say "Elias Howe." He was in the Civil War with me, and often in my tent, and I often heard him say that he worked fourteen years to get up that sewing machine. But his wife [Elizabeth J. Ames Howe] made up her mind one day that they would starve to death if there wasn't something or other invented pretty soon, and so in two hours she invented the sewing machine. Of course he took out the patent in his name. Men always do that. (296)

Conwell also published an interview with Cyrus McCormick, "in which the inventor admitted that after he and his father had tried to create the reaper and failed 'a West Virginia woman . . . took a lot of shears and nailed them together on the edge of a board [with one blade of each pair loose]. Then she wired them so that when she pulled the wire one way it closed them, and . . . the other way it opened them. And there she had the principle of the mowing machine. If you look at the mowing-machine, you will see that it is nothing but a lot of shears'"(80).

Eli Whitney (whom history records as the inventor of the cotton gin, the machine that revolutionized life in the southern United States) admitted that the idea for the gin was given him by Catherine Littlefield Green. While working on the gin Whitney was living in her home. Although he tended to underplay her contribution in public, Whitney paid her a share of his royalties for the machine (82–83). [See Autumn Stanley, *Mothers and Daughters of Invention: Notes for a Revised History of Technology*, New Brunswick, NJ: Rutgers University Press, 1993. —Ed.]

claim, "Yes!" One girl rolls her eyes toward the ceiling and shakes her head in disgust. The incident lasts less than a minute, and the discussion of male inventors continues.

We sometimes ask our students at The American University to list twenty famous women from American history. There are only a few restrictions. They cannot include figures from sports or entertainment. Presidents' wives are not allowed unless they are clearly famous in their own right. Most students cannot do it. The seeds of their ignorance were sown in their earliest years of schooling.

In the 1970s, analyses of best-selling history books showed a biological oddity, a nation with only founding fathers (Trecker 1971). More space was given to the six-shooter than to the women's suffrage movement. In fact, the typical history text gave only two sentences to enfranchising half the population. Science texts continued the picture of a one-gender world, with the exception of Marie Curie who was permitted to stand behind her husband and peer over his shoulder as he looked into a microscope. Today's history and science texts are better — but not much (Weitzman and Rizzo 1976).

At our workshops we ask teachers and parents to tell or write about any sexism they have seen in their schools. We have been collecting their stories for years (Trecker 1971). A Utah teacher told us: "Last year I had my U.S. history classes write biographies about famous Americans. When I collected all one hundred and fifty, I was dismayed to find only five on women. When I asked my kids why, they said they didn't know any famous women. When I examined their textbook more closely, I saw there were few females in it. And there were even fewer books on famous American women in our school library."

Teachers add to textbook bias when they produce sexist materials of their own. One parent described her efforts to stop a teacher-made worksheet that perpetuated stereotypes of yesteryear:

A few years ago my daughter came home upset over her grade. When I looked at her paper, I got more angry than she was. At the top of the worksheet were the faces of a man and a woman. At the bottom were different objects — nails, a saw, a sewing needle, thread, a hammer, a screwdriver, a broom. The directions said to draw a line from the man to the objects that belong to him and a line from the woman to the objects that go with her. In our house my husband does the cooking and I do the repair work, so you can imagine what the lines on my daughter's paper looked like. There was a huge red F in the middle of her worksheet. I called the teacher right away. She was very understanding and assured me the F wouldn't count. A small victory, I thought, and forgot about it.

This year my son is in her class. Guess what he brought home last week. Same worksheet — same F. Nothing had changed at all.

When girls do not see themselves in the pages of textbooks, when teachers do not point out or confront the omissions, our daughters learn that to be female is to be an absent partner in the development of our nation. And when teachers add their stereotypes to the curriculum bias in books, the message becomes even more damaging.

In a 1992 survey in *Glamour*, 74 percent of those responding said that they had "a teacher who was biased against females or paid more attention to the boys." Math class was selected as the place where inequities were most likely to occur. Fifty-eight percent picked it as their most sexist subject. Physical education was second, and science came in third, selected by 47 percent of the respondents (*Glamour* 1992). Women at our workshops recall remarks made by math and science teachers that years later still leave them upset and angry:

In my A.P. physics class in high school in 1984 there were only three girls and twenty-seven boys. The three girls, myself included, consistently scored at the top end of the scale. On one test I earned a 98. The next closest boy earned an 88. The teacher handed the tests back saying,

"Boys, you are failing. These three pretty cookies are outscoring you guys on every test." He told the boys it was embarrassing for them to be beaten by a girl. He always referred to us (the girls) as "Cookie" or made our names sound very cutesy!

Sometimes the humiliating lessons come not from school policies, teachers, or books but from boys, the very individuals that adolescent girls most want to impress:

The New England high school was having an assembly during the last period on Friday, and the auditorium was packed with more than a thousand students, who were restless as they listened to announcements. A heavy, awkward tenth grader made her way across the stage to reach the microphone located in the center. As she walked, several male students made loud barking noises to signify she was a dog. Others oinked like pigs. Later a slender long-haired senior walked to the mike; she was greeted by catcalls and whistles. Nobody attempted to stop the demeaning and hurtful public evaluation of the appearance of these teenage girls.

Tolerated under the assumptions that "boys will be boys" and hormone levels are high in high school, sexual harassment is a way of life in America's schools. While teachers and administrators look the other way, sexually denigrating comments, pinching, touching, and propositioning happen daily. Sensitive and insecure about their appearance, some girls are so intimidated they suffer in silence. Others fight back only to find this heightens the harassment. Many girls don't even realize they have a right to protest. And when they do come forward, bringing school sexual harassment into the open, it is often dealt with quickly and nervously; it is swept under the rug, turned aside, or even turned against the girl who had the courage to complain. A teacher at a workshop in Indiana told us: "In our school a girl was pinched on the derriere by two boys and verbally harassed. When she reported the incident to the principal, she was told that her dress was inappropriate and that she had asked for it."

Intimidating comments and offensive sexual jokes are even more common in college and sometimes are even made public as part of a classroom lecture and discussion. A female faculty member, teaching at a university that was historically all male, told us about one of the most popular teachers on campus, an economics professor:

He would show slides illustrating an economic theory and insert women in bikinis in the middle "to keep the students interested."[4] He illustrated different phases of the economic cycle by showing a slide of a woman's breast and pointed out how far away from the nipple each phase was. When a number of female students complained, the local newspaper supported the professor and criticized the "ultrasensitive coeds." That semester the university gave the professor the Teacher of the Year award.

Although sexually harassing remarks, stories, and jokes occur only occasionally in classrooms, female silence is the norm. During our two-year study of colleges, our raters found that girls grow quieter as they grow older. In coeducational classes, college women are even less likely to participate in discussions than elementary and secondary school girls. In the typical college classroom, 45 percent of students do not speak; the majority of these voiceless students are women.

Breaking the Sound Barrier

Women who have spent years learning the lessons of silence in elementary, secondary, and college classrooms have trouble regaining their voices. In our workshops we often set up a role play to demonstrate classroom sex bias. Four volunteers, two women and two men, are

---

[4]One wonders just which group of students he was concerned about here. — Ed.

asked to pretend to be students in a middle school social studies lesson. They have no script; their only direction is to take a piece of paper with them as David, playing the part of the social studies teacher, ushers them to four chairs in front of the room. He tells the audience that he will condense all the research on sexism in the classroom into a ten-minute lesson, so the bias will look blatant, even overwhelming. The job of the parents and teachers in the audience is to detect the different forms of egregious sexism. He begins the lesson.

"Today we're going to discuss the chapter in your book, 'The Gathering Clouds of War,' about the American Revolution. But first I'd like you to take out your homework so I can check it." David walks over to Sarah, the first student in the line of four. (In real life she is an English teacher at the local high school.)

"Let's see your paper, Sarah." He pauses to look it over. "Questions three and seven are not correct." Sarah looks concerned.

David moves to Peggy (who is a communications professor at a state college). "Oh, Peggy, Peggy, Peggy!" She looks up as everyone stares. David holds up Peggy's paper. "Would you all look at this. It is sooo neat. You print just like a typewriter. This is the kind of paper I like to put on the bulletin board for open school night." Peggy looks down, smiles, blushes, looks up wide-eyed, and bats her eyelashes. She is not faking or exaggerating these behaviors. Before our eyes she has returned to childhood as the stereotypical good girl with pretty penmanship. The lessons have been well learned.

Next David stops by Tony (who is a vocational education teacher) and looks at the blank paper he is holding. "Tony, you've missed questions three, seven, and eleven. I think you would do better on your assignments if you used the bold headings to guide your reading. I know you can get this if you try harder." Tony nods earnestly as David moves to Roy. Sarah, who missed questions three and seven, looks perplexed.

David scans Roy's paper and hands it back. "Roy, where's your homework?"

Roy (a college physics teacher) stammers, "Here it is," and again offers the blank paper that served as homework for the others in the role play.

"Roy, that's not your history homework. That's science." Roy still looks puzzled. "Trust me, Roy," David says. "No matter what you come up with, it won't be history homework. Now, where is it?"

"The dog ate it," Roy mutters, getting the picture and falling into the bad boy role.

Next David discusses revolutionary battles, military tactics, and male leaders—George Washington, John and Samuel Adams, Paul Revere, Benjamin Franklin, Thomas Jefferson, and more. He calls on Roy and Tony more than twenty times each. When they don't know the answer, he probes, jokes, challenges, offers hints. He calls on Sarah only twice. She misses both her questions because David gives her less than half a second to speak. After effusively praising Peggy's pretty paper, David never calls on her again. As the lesson progresses, Sarah's face takes on a sad, almost vacant expression. Peggy keeps on smiling.

When the scene of blatant sexism is over, many in the audience want to know how the two women felt.

"That was me all through school," Peggy blurts out. "I did very well. My work was neat. I was always prepared. I would have the right answer if someone had called on me. But they never did."

"Why did you watch the two males get all the attention?" we ask. "If you weren't called on, why didn't you call out?"

"I tried. I just couldn't do it."

"Why? You weren't wearing a muzzle. The men were calling out."

"I know. I felt terrible. It reminded me of all those years in school when I wanted to say something but couldn't."

"What about you, Sarah?" we ask. "Why didn't you just shout out an answer?"

"It never occurred to me to do it," Sarah says, then pauses. "No, that's not true. I thought about it, but I didn't want to be out there where I might get laughed at or ridiculed."

David has taught this role play class hundreds and hundreds of times in workshops in big cities and small towns all across the United States. Each time he demonstrates sex bias by blatantly and offensively ignoring female students, and almost always the adult women, put back into the role of twelve-year-olds, sit and say nothing; once again they become the nice girls watching the boys in action. Inside they may feel sad or furious or relieved, but like Sarah and Peggy, they remain silent.

When women try to get into classroom interaction, they rarely act directly. Instead they doodle, write letters, pass notes, and wait for the teacher to notice them. In a California workshop one parent who was playing the part of a student developed an elaborate pantomime. She reached into her large purse, pulled out a file, and began to do her nails. When that failed to attract David's attention, she brought out a brush, makeup, and a mirror. But David continued to ignore her, talking only with the two males.

"I was so mad I wanted to hit you," the woman fumed at the end of the role play when she was invited to express her feelings.

"What did you do to show your anger?" David asked.

"I didn't do anything." Then she paused, realizing the passive-aggressive but ultimately powerless strategy she had pursued. "No, I did do something—my nails," she said sadly.

After hundreds of these role plays, we are still astonished at how quickly the veneer of adulthood melts away. Grown women and men replay behavior they learned as children at school. The role plays are always reveal-

ing—funny, sad, and sometimes they even have a troubling twist.

At a workshop for college students at a large university in the Midwest, one of the young women ignored in the role play did not exhibit the usual behavior of silence or passive hostility. Instead, in the middle of the workshop in front of her classmates, she began to sob. She explained later in private that as one of only a few girls in the university's agricultural program, she had been either ignored or harassed. That week in an overenrolled course an instructor had announced, "There are too many students in this class. Everyone with ovaries—out!"

"What did you do?"

"What could I do? I left. Later I told my adviser about it. He was sympathetic but said if there was no room, I should consider another major."

Silent Losses

Each time a girl opens a book and reads a womanless history, she learns she is worth less. Each time the teacher passes over a girl to elicit the ideas and opinions of boys, that girl is conditioned to be silent and to defer. As teachers use their expertise to question, praise, probe, clarify, and correct boys, they help these male students sharpen ideas, refine their thinking, gain their voice, and achieve more. When female students are offered the leftovers of teacher time and attention, morsels of amorphous feedback, they achieve less.

Then girls and women learn to speak softly or not at all; to submerge honest feelings, withhold opinions, and defer to boys; to avoid math and science as male domains; to value neatness and quiet more than assertiveness and creativity; to emphasize appearance and hide intelligence. Through this curriculum in sexism they are turned into educational spectators instead of players; but education is not a spectator sport.

When blatantly sexual or sexist remarks become an accepted part of classroom conversation, female students are degraded. Sexual harassment in business and the military now causes shock waves and legal suits. Sexual harassment in schools is dismissed as normal and unavoidable "boys will be boys" behavior; but by being targeted, girls are being intimidated and caused to feel like members of an inferior class.

Like a thief in school, sexist lessons subvert education, twisting it into a system of socialization that robs potential. Consider this record of silent, devastating losses (Sadker, Sadker, and Klein 1991):

- In the early grades girls are ahead of or equal to boys on almost every standardized measure of achievement and psychological well-being. By the time they graduate from high school or college, they have fallen back. Girls enter school ahead but leave behind.

- In high school, girls score lower on the SAT and ACT tests, which are critical for college admission. The greatest gender gap is in the crucial areas of science and math.

- Girls score far lower on College Board Achievement tests, which are required by most of the highly selective colleges.

- Boys are much more likely to be awarded state and national college scholarships.

- The gap does not narrow in college. Women score lower on all sections of the Graduate Record Exam, which is necessary to enter many graduate programs.

- Women also trail on most tests needed to enter professional schools: The GMAT for business school, the LSAT for law school, and the MCAT for medical school.

- From elementary school through higher education, female students receive less active instruction, both in the quantity and in the quality of teacher time and attention.

In addition to the loss of academic achievement, girls suffer other difficulties:

- Eating disorders among girls in middle and secondary schools and in college are rampant and increasing.

- Incidents of school-based sexual harassment are now reported with alarming frequency.

- One in ten teenage girls becomes pregnant each year. Unlike boys, when girls drop out, they usually stay out.

- As girls go through school, their self-esteem plummets, and the danger of depression increases.

- Economic penalties follow women after graduation. Careers that have a high percentage of female workers, such as teaching and nursing, are poorly paid. And even when women work in the same jobs as men, they earn less money. Most of America's poor live in households that are headed by women.

If the cure for cancer is forming in the mind of one of our daughters, it is less likely to become a reality than if it is forming in the mind of one of our sons. Until this changes, everybody loses.

References

Faludi, Susan. 1991. *Backlash: The Undeclared War Against American Women.* New York: Crown.

Glamour. 1992. "This Is What You Thought: Were Any of Your Teachers Biased Against Females?" August, p. 157.

Kidder, Tracy. 1989. *Among Schoolchildren.* Boston: Houghton Mifflin.

Sadker, Myra, David Sadker, and Susan Klein. 1991. "The Issue of Gender in Elementary and Secondary Education." In Gerald Grant (ed.), *Review of Research in Education,* Vol 17. Washington, DC: American Educational Research Association.

Trecker, Janice Law. 1971. "Women in U.S. History High School Textbooks." *Social Education* 35: 249–260.

Weitzman, Lenore, and Diane Rizzo. 1976. *Biased Textbooks: Image of Males and Females in Elementary School Textbooks.* Washington, DC: Resource Center on Sex Roles in Education.

Questions

1. Consider the exercise that the Sadkers said they routinely gave their students— to list twenty famous women from American history ("not including figures from sports or entertainment. President's wives are not allowed unless they are clearly famous in their own right"). Can you do better on this assignment than the Sadkers' students did? Why or why not?

2. On various occasions, I have assigned the Sadkers' book to students in my introductory sociology classes. Regardless of their gender, students most commonly respond by denying that any similar sorts of things happened in their schools. After extensive discussion, however, many students (especially women students) can recall some incidents of sexism they encountered.

   Why is sexism in the schools so difficult for people to notice? Is it because there is no sexism in schools? How would the Sadkers respond to questions about why sexism is hard to spot?

·20·

Anybody's Son Will Do

Gwynne Dyer

Ordinary people would be loathe to do the sorts of things that soldiers may be called upon to do—but societies seem to need soldiers. As Dyer explains in this chapter excerpted from his book *War*, the means of socializing men out of the civilian role and into the soldier/killer role has become institutionalized as a result of centuries of experience.

... All soldiers belong to the same profession, no matter what country they serve, and it makes them different from everybody else. They have to be different, for their job is ultimately about killing and dying, and those things are not a natural vocation for any human being. Yet all soldiers are born civilians. The method for turning young men into soldiers—people who kill other people and expose themselves to death—is basic training. It's essentially the same all over the world, and it always has been, because young men everywhere are pretty much alike.

Human beings are fairly malleable, especially when they are young, and in every young man there are attitudes for any army to work with: the inherited values and postures, more or less dimly recalled, of the tribal warriors who were once the model for every young boy to emulate. Civilization did not involve a sudden clean break in the way people behave, but merely the progressive distortion and redirection of all the ways in which people in the old tribal societies used to behave, and modern definitions of maleness still contain a great deal of the old warrior ethic. The anarchic machismo of the primitive warrior is not what modern armies really need in their soldiers, but it does provide them with promising raw material for the transformation they must work in their recruits.

Just how this transformation is wrought varies from time to time and from country to country. In totally militarized societies—ancient Sparta, the samurai class of medieval Japan, the areas controlled by organizations like the Eritrean People's Liberation Front today[1]—it begins at puberty or before, when the young boy is immersed in a disciplined society in which only the military values are allowed to penetrate. In more sophisticated modern societies, the process is briefer and more concentrated, and the way it works is much more visible. It is, essentially, a conversion process in an almost religious sense—and as in all conversion phenomena, the emotions are far more important than the specific ideas....

> When I was going to school, we used to have to recite the Pledge of Allegiance every day. They don't do that now. You know, we've got kids that come in here now, when they first get here, they don't know the Pledge of Allegiance to the flag. And that's something—that's like a cardinal sin.... My daughter will know that stuff by the time she's three; she's two now and she's working on it.... You know, you've got to have

---

[1]Eritrea, an Italian colony from 1885 to 1941, was annexed by Ethiopia in 1962. After a 30-year civil war, Eritrea gained its independence in 1992.—Ed.

your basics, the groundwork where you can start to build a child's brain from. . . .
— USMC drill instructors, Parris Island recruit training depot, 1981

That is what the rhetoric of military patriotism sounds like, in every country and at every level — and it is virtually irrelevant so far as the actual job of soldiering is concerned. Soldiers are not just robots; they are ordinary human beings with national and personal loyalties, and many of them do feel the need for some patriotic or ideological justification for what they do. But which nation, which ideology, does not matter: men will fight as well and die as bravely for the Khmer Rouge as for "God, King, and Country." Soldiers are the instruments of politicians and priests, ideologues and strategists, who may have high national or moral purposes in mind, but the men down in the trenches fight for more basic motives. The closer you get to the front line, the fewer abstract nouns you hear.

Armies know this. It is their business to get men to fight, and they have had a long time to work out the best way of doing it. All of them pay lip service to the symbols and slogans of their political masters, though the amount of time they must devote to this activity varies from country to country. It is less in the United States than in the Soviet Union, and it is still less in a country like Israel, which actually fights frequent wars. Nor should it be thought that the armies are hypocritical — most of their members really do believe in their particular national symbols and slogans. But their secret is that they know these are not the things that sustain men in combat.

What really enables men to fight is their own self-respect, and a special kind of love that has nothing to do with sex or idealism. Very few men have died in battle, when the moment actually arrived, for the United States of America or for the sacred cause of Communism, or even for their homes and families; if

they had any choice in the matter at all, they chose to die for each other and for their own vision of themselves. . . .

The way armies produce this sense of brotherhood in a peacetime environment is basic training: a feat of psychological manipulation on the grand scale which has been so consistently successful and so universal that we fail to notice it as remarkable. In countries where the army must extract its recruits in their late teens, whether voluntarily or by conscription, from a civilian environment that does not share the military values, basic training involves a brief but intense period of indoctrination whose purpose is not really to teach the recruits basic military skills, but rather to change their values and their loyalties. "I guess you could say we brainwash them a little bit," admitted a U.S. Marine drill instructor, "but you know they're good people." . . .

It's easier if you catch them young. You can train older men to be soldiers; it's done in every major war. But you can never get them to believe that they like it, which is the major reason armies try to get their recruits before they are twenty. There are other reasons too, of course, like the physical fitness, lack of dependents, and economic dispensability of teenagers, that make armies prefer them, but the most important qualities teenagers bring to basic training are enthusiasm and naiveté. Many of them actively want the discipline and the closely structured environment that the armed forces will provide, so there is no need for the recruiters to deceive the kids about what will happen to them after they join.

There is discipline. There is drill. . . . When you are relying on your mates and they are relying on you, there's no room for slackness or sloppiness. If you're not prepared to accept the rules, you're better off where you are.
— British army recruiting advertisement, 1976

People are not born soldiers, they become soldiers. . . . And it should not begin at the moment when a new recruit is enlisted into the ranks, but rather much earlier, at the time of the first signs of maturity, during the time of adolescent dreams.

— *Red Star* (Soviet army newspaper), 1973

Young civilians who have volunteered and have been accepted by the Marine Corps[2] arrive at Parris Island, the Corps's East Coast facility for basic training, in a state of considerable excitement and apprehension: most are aware that they are about to undergo an extraordinary and very difficult experience. But they do not make their own way to the base; rather they trickle in to Charleston airport on various flights throughout the day on which their training platoon is due to form, and are held there, in a state of suppressed but mounting nervous tension, until late in the evening. When the buses finally come to carry them the seventy-six miles to Parris Island, it is often after midnight—and this is not an administrative oversight. The shock treatment they are about to receive will work most efficiently if they are worn out and somewhat disoriented when they arrive.

The basic training organization is a machine, processing several thousand young men every month, and every facet and gear of it has been designed with the sole purpose of turning civilians into Marines as efficiently as possible. Provided it can have total control over their bodies and their environment for approximately three months, it can practically guarantee converts. Parris Island provides that controlled environment, and the recruits do not set foot outside it again until they graduate as Marine privates eleven weeks later.

They're allowed to call home, so long as it doesn't get out of hand—every three weeks or so they can call home and make sure every-

thing's all right, if they haven't gotten a letter or there's a particular set of circumstances. If it's a case of an emergency call coming in, then they're allowed to accept that call; if not, one of my staff will take the message. . . .

In some cases I'll get calls from parents who haven't quite gotten adjusted to the idea that their son had cut the strings—and in a lot of cases that's what they're doing. The military provides them with an opportunity to leave home but they're still in a rather secure environment.

—Captain Brassington, USMC

For the young recruits, basic training is the closest thing their society can offer to a formal rite of passage,[3] and the institution probably stands in an unbroken line of descent from the lengthy ordeals by which young males in pre-civilized groups were initiated into the adult community of warriors. But in civilized societies it is a highly functional institution whose product is not anarchic warriors, but trained soldiers.

Basic training is not really about teaching people skills; it's about changing them, so that they can do things they wouldn't have dreamt of otherwise. It works by applying enormous physical and mental pressure to men who have been isolated from their normal civilian environment and placed in one where the only right way to think and behave is the way the Marine Corps wants them to. The key word the men who run the machine use to describe this process is *motivation*.

I can motivate a recruit and in third phase, if I tell him to jump off the third deck, he'll jump off the third deck. Like I said before, it's a captive audience and I can train that guy; I can get him to do anything I want him to do. . . . They're good kids and they're out to do the right thing. We get some bad kids, but you know, we weed those out. But as far as motivation—here, we

---

[2]Something you might not know if you have no military experience and don't watch war movies or attend the ballet is that the word *corps* is pronounced "core" (from the Latin *corpus*, meaning "body"). — Ed.

[3]The concept of rite of passage (or *rites de passage*) is discussed in *The Practical Skeptic,* chapter 10.

can motivate them to do anything you want, in recruit training.

—USMC drill instructor, Parris Island

The first three days the raw recruits spend at Parris Island are actually relatively easy, though they are hustled and shouted at continuously. It is during this time that they are documented and inoculated, receive uniforms, and learn the basic orders of drill that will enable young Americans (who are not very accustomed to this aspect of life) to do everything simultaneously in large groups. But the most important thing that happens in "forming" is the surrender of the recruits' own clothes, their hair—all the physical evidence of their individual civilian identities.

During a period of only seventy-two hours, in which they are allowed little sleep, the recruits lay aside their former lives in a series of hasty rituals (like being shaven to the scalp) whose symbolic significance is quite clear to them even though they are quite deliberately given absolutely no time for reflection, or any hint that they might have the option of turning back from their commitment. The men in charge of them know how delicate a tightrope they are walking, though, because at this stage the recruits are still newly caught civilians who have not yet made their ultimate inward submission to the discipline of the Corps.

Forming Day One makes me nervous. You've got a whole new mob of recruits, you know, sixty or seventy depending, and they don't know anything. You don't know what kind of a reaction you're going to get from the stress you're going to lay on them, and it just worries me the first day.

Things could happen, I'm not going to lie to you. Something might happen. A recruit might decide he doesn't want any part of this stuff and maybe take a poke at you or something like that. In a situation like that it's going to be a spur-of-the-moment thing and that worries me.

—USMC drill instructor

But it rarely happens. The frantic bustle of forming is designed to give the recruit no time to think about resisting what is happening to him. And so the recruits emerge from their initiation into the system, stripped of their civilian clothes, shorn of their hair, and deprived of whatever confidence in their own identity they may previously have had as eighteen-year-olds, like so many blanks ready to have the Marine identity impressed upon them.

The first stage in any conversion process is the destruction of an individual's former beliefs and confidence, and his reduction to a position of helplessness and need. It isn't really as drastic as all that, of course, for three days cannot cancel out eighteen years; the inner thoughts and the basic character are not erased. But the recruits have already learned that the only acceptable behavior is to repress any unorthodox thoughts and to mimic the character the Marine Corps wants. Nor are they, on the whole, reluctant to do so, for they *want* to be Marines. From the moment they arrive at Parris Island, the vague notion that has been passed down for a thousand generations that masculinity means being a warrior becomes an explicit article of faith, relentlessly preached: to be a man means to be a Marine.

There are very few eighteen-year-old boys who do not have highly romanticized ideas of what it means to be a man, so the Marine Corps has plenty of buttons to push. And it starts pushing them on the first day of real training: the officer in charge of the formation appears before them for the first time, in full dress uniform with medals, and tells them how to become men.

The United States Marine Corps has 205 years of illustrious history to speak for itself. You have made the most important decision in your life . . . by signing your name, your life, your pledge to the Government of the United States, and even more importantly, to the United States Marine Corps—a brotherhood, an elite unit.

In 10.3 weeks you are going to become a member of that history, those traditions, this organization—if you have what it takes.

All of you want to do that by virtue of your signing your name as a man. The Marine Corps says that we build men. Well, I'll go a little bit further. We develop the tools that you have—and everybody has those tools to a certain extent right now. We're going to give you the blueprints, and we are going to show you how to build a Marine. *You've* got to build a Marine—you understand?

—Captain Pingree, USMC

The recruits, gazing at him with awe and adoration, shout in unison, "Yes sir!" just as they have been taught. They do it willingly, because they are volunteers—but even conscripts tend to have the romantic fervor of volunteers if they are only eighteen years old. Basic training, whatever its hardships, is a quick way to become a man among men, with an undeniable status, and beyond the initial consent to undergo it, it doesn't even require any decisions.

I had just dropped out of high school and I wasn't doing much on the street except hanging out, as most teenagers would be doing. So they gave me an opportunity—a recruiter picked me up, gave me a good line, and said that I could make it in the Marines, that I have a future ahead of me. And since I was living with my parents, I figured that I could start my own life here and grow up a little.

—USMC recruit, 1982

I like the hand-to-hand combat and . . . things like that. It's a little rough going on me, and since I have a small frame I would like to become deadly, as I would put it. I like to have them words, especially the way they've been teaching me here.

—USMC recruit (from Brooklyn), Parris Island, 1982

The training, when it starts, seems impossibly demanding physically for most of the recruits—and then it gets harder week by week. There is a constant barrage of abuse and insults aimed at the recruits, with the deliberate purpose of breaking down their pride and so destroying their ability to resist the transformation of values and attitudes that the Corps intends them to undergo. At the same time the demands for constant alertness and for instant obedience are continuously stepped up, and the standards by which the dress and behavior of the recruits are judged become steadily more unforgiving. But it is all carefully calculated by the men who run the machine, who think and talk in terms of the stress they are placing on the recruits: "We take so many c.c.'s of stress and we administer it to each man—they should be a little bit scared and they should be unsure, but they're adjusting." The aim is to keep the training arduous but just within most of the recruits' capability to withstand. One of the most striking achievements of the drill instructors is to create and maintain the illusion that basic training is an extraordinary challenge, one that will set those who graduate apart from others, when in fact almost everyone can succeed.

There has been some preliminary weeding out of potential recruits even before they begin training, to eliminate the obviously unsuitable minority, and some people do "fail" basic training and get sent home, at least in peacetime. The standards of acceptable performance in the U.S. armed forces, for example, tend to rise and fall in inverse proportion to the number and quality of recruits available to fill the forces to the authorized manpower levels. (In 1980, about 15 percent of Marine recruits did not graduate from basic training.) But there are very few young men who cannot be turned into passable soldiers if the forces are willing to invest enough effort in it.

Not even physical violence is necessary to effect the transformation, though it has been used by most armies at most times.

It's not what it was fifteen years ago down here. The Marine Corps still occupies the position of a tool which the society uses when it feels like that is a resort that they have to fall to. Our society changes as all societies do, and our society felt that through enlightened training methods we could still produce the same product—and when you examine it, they're right. . . . Our 100 c.c.'s of stress is really all we need, not two gallons of it, which is what used to be.[4] . . . In some cases with some of the younger drill instructors it was more an initiation than it was an acute test, and so we introduced extra officers and we select our drill instructors to "fine-tune" it.

—Captain Brassington, USMC

There is, indeed, a good deal of fine-tuning in the roles that the men in charge of training any specific group of recruits assume. At the simplest level, there is a sort of "good cop—bad cop" manipulation of the recruits' attitudes toward those applying the stress. The three younger drill instructors with a particular serial are quite close to them in age and unremittingly harsh in their demands for ever higher performance, but the senior drill instructor, a man almost old enough to be their father, plays a more benevolent and understanding part and is available for individual counseling. And generally offstage, but always looming in the background, is the company commander, an impossibly austere and almost godlike personage.

At least these are the images conveyed to the recruits, although of course all these men cooperate closely with an identical goal in view. It works: in the end they become not just role models and authority figures, but the focus of the recruits' developing loyalty to the organization.

I imagine there's some fear, especially in the beginning, because they don't know what to expect. . . . I think they hate you at first, at least for a week or two, but it turns to respect. . . . They're seeking discipline, they're seeking someone to take charge, 'cause at home they never got it. . . . They're looking to be told what to do and then someone is standing there enforcing what they tell them to do, and it's kind of like the father-and-son game, all the way through. They form a fatherly image of the DI[5] whether they want to or not.

—Sergeant Carrington, USMC

Just the sheer physical exercise, administered in massive doses, soon has the recruits feeling stronger and more competent than ever before. Inspections, often several times daily, quickly build up their ability to wear the uniform and carry themselves like real Marines, which is a considerable source of pride. The inspections also help to set up the pattern in the recruits of unquestioning submission to military authority: standing stock-still, staring straight ahead, while somebody else examines you closely for faults is about as extreme a ritual act of submission as you can make with your clothes on.

But they are not submitting themselves merely to the abusive sergeant making unpleasant remarks about the hair in their nostrils. All around them are deliberate reminders—the flags and insignia displayed on parade, the military music, the marching formations and drill instructors' cadenced calls—of the idealized organization, the "brotherhood" to which they will be admitted as full members if they submit and conform. Nowhere in the armed forces are the military courtesies so elaborately observed, the staffs' uniforms so immaculate (some DIs change several times a day), and the ritual aspects of military life so highly visible as on a basic training establishment.

Even the seeming inanity of close-order drill has a practical role in the conversion

---

[4]As a point of information, there are 4 c.c.'s in a teaspoon. —Ed.

[5]Drill instructor. —Ed.

process. It has been over a century since mass formations of men were of any use on the battlefield, but every army in the world still drills its troops, especially during basic training, because marching in formation, with every man moving his body in the same way at the same moment, is a direct physical way of learning two things a soldier must believe: that orders have to be obeyed automatically and instantly, and that you are no longer an individual, but part of a group.

The recruits' total identification with the other members of their unit is the most important lesson of all, and everything possible is done to foster it. They spend almost every waking moment together—a recruit alone is an anomaly to be looked into at once—and during most of that time they are enduring shared hardships. They also undergo collective punishments, often for the misdeed or omission of a single individual (talking in the ranks, a bed not swept under during barracks inspection), which is a highly effective way of suppressing any tendencies toward individualism. And, of course, the DIs place relentless emphasis on competition with other "serials" in training: there may be something infinitely pathetic to outsiders about a marching group of anonymous recruits chanting, "Lift your heads and hold them high, 3313 is a-passin' by," but it doesn't seem like that to the men in the ranks.

Nothing is quite so effective in building up a group's morale and solidarity, though, as a steady diet of small triumphs. Quite early in basic training, the recruits begin to do things that seem, at first sight, quite dangerous: descend by ropes from fifty-foot towers, cross yawning gaps hand-over-hand on high wires (known as the Slide for Life, of course), and the like. The common denominator is that these activities are daunting but not really dangerous: the ropes will prevent anyone from falling to his death off the rappelling tower, and there is a pond of just the right depth—deep enough

to cushion a falling man, but not deep enough that he is likely to drown—under the Slide for Life. The goal is not to kill recruits, but to build up their confidence as individuals and as a group by allowing them to overcome apparently frightening obstacles.

> You have an enemy here at Parris Island. The enemy that you're going to have at Parris Island is in every one of us. It's in the form of cowardice. The most rewarding experience you're going to have in recruit training is standing on line every evening, and you'll be able to look into each other's eyes, and you'll be able to say to each other with your eyes: "By God, we've made it one more day! We've defeated the coward."
>
> —Captain Pingree, USMC

> Number on deck, sir, forty-five . . . highly motivated, truly dedicated, rompin', stompin', bloodthirsty, kill-crazy United States Marine Corps recruits, SIR!
>
> —Marine chant, Parris Island, 1982

If somebody does fail a particular test, he tends to be alone, for the hurdles are deliberately set low enough that most recruits can clear them if they try. In any large group of people there is usually a goat: someone whose intelligence or manner or lack of physical stamina marks him for failure and contempt. The competent drill instructor, without deliberately setting up this unfortunate individual for disgrace, will use his failure to strengthen the solidarity and confidence of the rest. When one hapless young man fell off the Slide for Life into the pond, for example, his drill instructor shouted the usual invective—"Well, get out of the water. Don't contaminate it all day"—and then delivered the payoff line: "Go back and change your clothes. You're useless to your unit now."

"Useless to your unit" is the key phrase, and all the recruits know that what it means is "useless *in battle*." The Marine drill instructors at Parris Island know exactly what they are doing to the recruits, and why. They are not rear-echelon people filling comfortable jobs, but the most dedicated and intelligent NCOs[6] the Marine Corps can find: even now, many of them have combat experience. The Corps has a clear-eyed understanding of precisely what it is training its recruits for—combat—and it ensures that those who do the training keep that objective constantly in sight.

The DIs "stress" the recruits, feed them their daily ration of synthetic triumphs over apparent obstacles, and bear in mind all the time that the goal is to instill the foundations for the instinctive, selfless reactions and the fierce group loyalty that is what the recruits will need if they ever see combat. They are arch-manipulators, fully conscious of it, and utterly unashamed. These kids have signed up as Marines, and they could well see combat; this is the way they have to think if they want to live. . . .

Combat is the ultimate reality that Marines—or any other soldiers, under any flag—have to deal with. Physical fitness, weapons training, battle drills, are all indispensable elements of basic training, and it is absolutely essential that the recruits learn the attitudes of group loyalty and interdependency which will be their sole hope of survival and success in combat. The training inculcates or fosters all of those things, and even by the halfway point in the eleven-week course, the recruits are generally responding with enthusiasm to their tasks.

But there is nothing in all this (except the weapons drill) that would not be found in the training camp of a professional football team. What sets soldiers apart is their willingness to kill. But it is not a willingness that comes easily to most men—even young men who have been provided with uniforms, guns, and official approval to kill those whom their government has designated as enemies. They will, it

is true, fall very readily into the stereotypes of the tribal warrior group. Indeed, most of them have had at least a glancing acquaintance in their early teens with gangs (more or less violent, depending on, among other things, the neighborhood), the modern relic of that ancient institution.

And in many ways what basic training produces is the uniformed equivalent of a modern street gang: a bunch of tough, confident kids full of bloodthirsty talk. But gangs don't actually kill each other in large numbers. If they behaved the way armies do, you'd need trucks to clean the bodies off the streets every morning. They're held back by the civilian belief—the normal human belief—that killing another person is an awesome act with huge consequences.

There is aggression in all of us—men, women, children, babies. Armies don't have to create it, and they can't even increase it. But most of learn to put limits on our aggression, especially physical aggression, as we grow up. . . .

There is such a thing as a "natural soldier": the kind of man who derives his greatest satisfaction from male companionship, from excitement, and from the conquering of physical and psychological obstacles. He doesn't necessarily want to kill people as such, but he will have no objections if it occurs within a moral framework that gives him a justification—like war—and if it is the price of gaining admission to the kind of environment he craves. Whether such men are born or made, I do not know, but most of them end up in armies (and many move on again to become mercenaries, because regular army life in peacetime is too routine and boring).

But armies are not full of such men. They are so rare that they form only a modest fraction even of small professional armies, mostly congregating in the commando-type special forces. In large conscript armies they virtually disappear beneath the weight of numbers of more ordinary men. And it is these ordinary

---

[6]Noncommissioned officers. —Ed.

men, who do not like combat at all, that the armies must persuade to kill. Until only a generation ago, they did not even realize how bad a job they were doing.

Armies had always assumed that, given the proper rifle training, the average man would kill in combat with no further incentive than the knowledge that it was the only way to defend his own life. After all, there are no historical records of Roman legionnaires refusing to use their swords, or Marlborough's infantrymen[7] refusing to fire their muskets against the enemy. But then dispersion hit the battlefield, removing each rifleman from the direct observation of his companions—and when U.S. Army Colonel S. L. A. Marshall finally took the trouble to inquire into what they were doing in 1943–45, he found that on average only 15 percent of trained combat riflemen fired their weapons at all in battle. The rest did not flee, but they would not kill—even when their own position was under attack and their lives were in immediate danger.

> The thing is simply this, that out of an average one hundred men along the line of fire during the period of an encounter, only fifteen men on average would take any part with the weapons. This was true whether the action was spread over a day, or two days or three. . . . In the most aggressive infantry companies, under the most intense local pressure, the figure rarely rose above 25% of total strength from the opening to the close of an action.
>
> —Col. S. L. A. Marshall

Marshall conducted both individual interviews and mass interviews with over four hundred infantry companies, both in Europe and in the Central Pacific, immediately after they had been in close combat with German or Japanese troops, and the results were the same each time. They were, moreover, as astonish-

---

[7]John Churchill (1650–1722), first Duke of Marlborough, British general, supreme commander of the British forces in the War of the Spanish Succession. — Ed.

ing to the company officers and the troops themselves as they were to Marshall; each man who hadn't fired his rifle thought he had been alone in his defection from duty.

Even more indicative of what was going on was the fact that almost all the crew-served weapons had been fired. Every man had been trained to kill and knew it was his duty to kill, and so long as he was in the presence of other soldiers who could see his actions, he went ahead and did it. But the great majority of the riflemen, each unobserved by the others in his individual foxhole, had chosen not to kill, even though it increased the likelihood of his own death. . . .

But the question naturally arises: if the great majority of men are not instinctive killers, and if most military killing these days is in any case done by weapons operating from a distance at which the question of killing scarcely troubles the operators—then why is combat an exclusively male occupation? The great majority of women, everyone would agree, are not instinctive killers either, but so what? If the remote circumstances in which the killing is done or the deliberate conditioning supplied by the military enable most men to kill, why should it be any different for women?

My own guess would be that it probably wouldn't be different; it just hasn't been tried very extensively. But it is an important question, because it has to do with the causes and possible cure of war. If men fight wars because that is an intrinsic part of the male character, then nothing can abolish the institution of warfare short of abolishing the male half of the human race (or at least, as one feminist suggested, disfranchising it for a hundred years).

If, on the other hand, wars are a means of allocating power between civilized human groups, in which the actual soldiers have always been male simply because men were more suited to it by their greater physical strength and their freedom from the burden of childbearing, then what we are discussing is not Original Sin, but simply a mode of social behavior. The fact that almost every living male for thousands of generations has imbibed some of the warrior mystique is no proof of a genetic predisposition to be warlike. The cultural continuity is quite enough to transmit such attitudes, and men were specialized in the hunting and warrior functions for the same physical reasons long before civilized war was invented.

It was undoubtedly men, the "hunting" specialists, who invented civilized war, just as it was probably women, specializing in the "gathering" part of the primitive economy, who invented agriculture. That has no necessary relevance today: we all eat vegetables, and we can all die in war. It is a more serious allegation against males to say that all existing forms of political power have been shaped predominantly by men, so that even if wars are about power and not about the darker side of the masculine psyche, war is still a male problem. That has unquestionably been true through all of history (although it remains to be proven that women exercising power respond very differently to its temptations and obsessions). But there is no need to settle that argument: if war and masculinity are not inseparable, then we have already moved onto negotiable ground. For the forms of political power, unlike psyches, are always negotiable.

Unfortunately there is little direct support for this optimistic hypothesis in the prevailing current of opinion among soldiers generally, where war and maleness are indeed seen as inseparable. To say that the combat branches of the armed forces are sexist is like remarking that gravity generally pulls downward, and nowhere is the contempt for women greater than at a recruit training base like Parris Island. The DIs are quite ruthless in exploiting every prejudice and pushing every button that will persuade the recruits to accept the value system they are selling, and one of those buttons (quite a large one) is the conviction of young males—or at least the desire to be convinced—that they are superior to young females. (After all, even recruits want to feel superior to somebody, and it certainly isn't going to be anybody in their immediate vicinity at Parris Island.)

When it's all boys together, especially among the younger men, Marine Corps slang for any woman who isn't the wife, mother, or daughter of anyone present is "Suzie." It is short for "Suzie Rottencrotch"—and Suzie crops up a lot in basic training. Even when the topic of instruction is hand and arm signals in combat.

> Privates, if you don't have a little Suzie now, maybe you're going to find one when you get home. You bet. You'll find the first cheap slut you can get back home. What do you mean, "No"? You're a Marine, you're going to do it.
>
> If we get home with little Suzie . . . we're in a nice companionship with little Suzie and here you are getting hot and heavy and then you're getting ready to go down there and make that dive, privates, and Suzie says . . . Suzie says it's the wrong time of the month. Privates, if you don't want to get back home and indulge in this little adventure, you can show your girlfriend the hand and arm signal for "close it up."
>
> And you want her to close up those nasty little thighs of hers, do you not, privates? The hand and arm signal: the arms are laterally shoulder height, the fingers are extended, and the palms are facing toward the front. This is the starting position for "close it up" [tighten up the formation]: just like closing it up, bring the arms together just like that.
>
> Privates, in addition, I want you to dedicate all this training to one very special person. Can anyone tell me who that is, privates?
>
> (Voice) The Senior Drill Instructor, sir?
>
> No, not your Senior Drill Instructor. You're going to dedicate all this training, privates, to your enemy . . . to your enemy. To your enemy: the reason being, so *he* can die for *his* country. So who are we going to dedicate all this training to, privates?
>
> —lecture on hand and arm signals, Parris Island, 1982

And they shouted enthusiastically: "The enemy, sir! The enemy, sir!" It would not be instantly clear to the disinterested observer from Mars, however, why these spotty-faced male eighteen-year-olds are uniquely qualified to kill the enemy, while their equally spotty-faced female counterparts get to admire them from afar (or so the supposition goes), and get called Suzie Rottencrotch for their trouble.

Interestingly, it isn't entirely clear either to the senior military and civilian officials whose responsibility it is to keep the organization filled up with warm bodies capable of doing the job. Women are not employed in combat roles in the regular armed forces of any country (though increasing numbers of women have been admitted to the noncombat military jobs in the course of this century). But in the last decade the final barrier has come under serious consideration. It was, unsurprisingly, in the United States, where the problems of getting enough recruits for the all-volunteer armed forces converged with the changes of attitude flowing from the women's liberation movement, that the first serious proposals to send women into combat were entertained, during the latter years of the Carter administration.

> There is no question but that women could do a lot of things in the military. So could men in wheelchairs. But you couldn't expect the services to want a whole company of people in wheelchairs.
>
> —Gen. Lewis B. Hershey,
> former director, Selective Service System, 1978

> If for no other reason than because women are the bearers of children, they should not be in combat. Imagine your daughter as a ground soldier sleeping in the fields and expected to do all the things that soldiers do. It represents to me an absolute horror.
>
> —Gen. Jacqueline Cochran, U.S. Air Force

Despite the anguished cries of military conservatives, both male and female, the reaction of younger officers in the combat branches (all male, of course) was cautious but not entirely negative. The more intelligent ones dismissed at once arguments about strength and stamina —the average American woman, one pointed out, is bigger than the average Vietnamese man—and were as little impressed by the alleged special problems arising from the fact that female soldiers may become pregnant. In the noncombat branches, the army loses less time from its women soldiers due to pregnancy than it loses from desertion, drug abuse, and alcoholism in its male soldiers.

More important, few of the male officers involved in the experimental programs giving combat training to women recruits in the late 1970s had any doubt that the women would function effectively in combat. Neither did the women themselves. Despite their lack of the traditional male notions about the warrior stereotype, the training did its job. As one female trainee remarked: "I don't like the idea of killing anything . . . [and] I may not at this moment go into combat. But knowing that I can fire as well as I can fire now, knowing that today, I'd go in. I believe in my country . . . I'd fight to keep it."

The one major reservation the male officers training the "infantrywomen" had was about how the presence of women in combat would affect the men. The basic combat unit, a small group of men bound together by strong male ties of loyalty and trust, was a time-tested system that worked, and they were reluctant to tamper with it by adding an additional, unknown factor to the equation.

In the end a more conservative administration canceled the idea of introducing women to American combat units, and it may be some years yet before there are female soldiers in the infantry of any regular army. But it is manifestly sheer social conservatism that is retarding this development. Hundreds of thousands, if not millions, of women have fought in combat as irregular infantry in the past half-century, from the Yugoslav and Soviet partisans of World

War II to Nicaragua in 1978–79. They performed quite satisfactorily, and so did the mixed units of which they were members. There are numerous differences of detail between guerrilla and regular army units, but none of them is of the sort to suggest that women would not fight just as well in a regular infantry battalion, or that the battalion would function less well if women were present.

The point of all this is not that women should be allowed (or indeed compelled) to take their fair share of the risks in combat. It is rather that war has moved a very long way from its undeniably warrior male origins, and that human behavior, male or female, is extremely malleable. Combat of the sort we know today, even at the infantryman's level — let along the fighter pilot's — simply could not occur unless military organizations put immense effort into reshaping the behavior of individuals to fit their unusual and exacting requirements. The military institution, for all its imposing presence, is a highly artificial structure that is maintained only by constant endeavor. And if ordinary people's behavior is malleable in the direction the armed forces require, it is equally open to change in other directions. . . .

Questions

1. Why did Dyer entitle his article "*Anybody's* Son Will Do"?

2. "To be a man means to be a marine" — or so recruits are taught. In what ways does the success of basic training seem to rely on the additional idea that if one cannot perform as a marine, one is no better than a woman? How might the presence of female marines in boot camp complicate the job of socializing males into their soldier role?

3. Erving Goffman (1961) defined "total institution" as "a place of residence and work where a large number of like-situated individuals, cut off from the wider society for an appreciable period of time, together lead an enclosed, formally administered round of life." Imagine that you've been put in charge of creating a total institution that has the goal of radically changing people's behavior. Military boot camp is one of the most successful types of total institutions. Based on what you've learned from Dyer's description of the way this total institutional resocializes men, what sorts of procedures would you institute in your total institution to help ensure its success? For example, what sorts of things would you do to your "recruits" when they first arrived at your total institution?

·21·

País de Mis Sueños

Reflections on Ethnic Labels, Dichotomies, and Ritual Interactions

Gisela Ernst

As a young adult, Gisela Ernst left her homeland of Peru to find a new life in the United States. Her recollections of the process by which she was transformed from a Peruvian into a Hispanic remind us of the power of social structure to put us in our place: Who we think we are is often less important than who others think we are. But Ernst's tale of her experiences in the United States conveys another important lesson—that what transpires during routine, face-to-face interaction is not always what it appears to be.

Like Saint Paul, I have seen the light. It happened while I was finishing my master's degree, when I was introduced to sociolinguistics; what I learned about language, language use, and culture literally changed the direction of my career. I had found an area of study that allowed me to grapple with the interplay of linguistic, social, and cultural factors in human communication. During my doctoral program at the University of Florida, I had the opportunity to think more deeply about why people use language the way they use it and why language can be clear and precise. At the same time, language often can be characterized by vagueness, ambiguity, and imprecision.

Perhaps nowhere is the interplay of language and culture more "fuzzy" than in the labels we use to define ourselves and others. In this chapter I will share some of my experiences, and my subsequent reflections upon those experiences, with the use of labels and terms used to refer to a person's ethnic, cultural, and racial background. Within this context I will share my feelings about, and explore the connotations of, the made-in-the-U.S.A. label "Hispanic." Then I will explore the use of dichotomies and negative constructions in English. These structures will be better understood by contrasting them to Spanish. This comparison will illustrate that the existence in English of extreme dichotomies can often influence how native English speakers voice and manage their relations with others. Finally, I would like to illustrate how some of us "foreigners" can often be taken in by the friendliness of people in the United States.

Ethnic Labels: "I Came as a Peruvian and Immediately Became a Hispanic"

I was a fortunate child who grew up in Lima, Peru. I was brought up in an upper-middle-class environment, attended private schools, lived in a handsome neighborhood, and was surrounded by a protected haven of mostly well-educated friends and acquaintances. Like many others in Peru, I was a *mestiza,* the daughter of an Austrian father and a Peruvian mother, the product of an encounter of two continents, of two races. Like many others, I had European names and Peruvian looks, spoke more than one language, and was proud to be a Peruvian who also had knowledge about and appreciation for her father's homeland.

In spite of my good fortune, I also encountered my share of problems, sorrow, and broken dreams. This is why, like many others who leave their familiar lands in search of better lives, I too left mine in search of *el país de mis sueños* (the land of my dreams). I had little money but lots of hope, confidence, and a clear sense of national identity as a Peruvian woman. Therefore I set off happily, in June of 1985, unaware of the need for "clear" labels to identify my ethnicity, race, and culture. Soon after my arrival in Florida, I did what many other foreign students have to do if they want to get into graduate school in the United States: fill out multiple forms. Throughout this process I discovered two things: first, the momentousness of the written work in this society, and second, the importance of race and ethnicity as forms of social classification in the United States. It quickly dawned on me that my avowed national identity was of little relevance to the society at large. I realized that I was seldom considered a Peruvian but was most often either "Hispanic, "legal alien," "Latino," "Spanish-speaking," "South American," "Spanish," or, what is worse, "Other"! Within the context of official forms, institutionalized inquiries, and government requirements, I was faced with having to find the appropriate label to describe my nationality, culture, and background. The following question about ethnic origin will help illustrate my feeling of dubiousness, doubtfulness, and diffidence as I attempted to answer what, for some, might be just another question on a form.

Ethnic Origin (mark one)
__ White (not Hispanic origin)
__ Asian or Pacific Islanders
__ Black (not Hispanic origin)
__ American Indian or Alaskan Native
__ Hispanic
__ Other

Not only did I find the emphasis on racial categorizations in the United States perplexing, but I felt that the selection offered was limited and problematic. I felt that I had to summarize my nationality, ethnicity, upbringing, language, culture—in sum, my whole existence—in one fixed and unappealing label. I was not only appalled but also confused. For example, given the categories mentioned above, I could have marked the first option since I appeared "white" in both of my passports (Peruvian and Austrian). Yet, at the same time, that option would be incorrect since I am also what could be called "Hispanic."

I thought about marking "American Indian or Alaskan Native" since, in fact, I was born in (South) America and there is some Indian blood in my mother's ancestry (even though she might not want to admit to it). But these labels did not reflect all my other influences: my mother's descent from Spain, my father's Austrian and German blood, the fact that I do not speak the languages nor share the cultures of Peruvian Indians. Because I had to use my European passport, on which I appeared as "white" (it included my visa and my "alien" number), I felt that no available categories encompassed my national and cultural identity.

My confusion grew as the smorgasbord of categories changed—from form to form and from institution to institution, and I often found myself spending considerable time trying to select the most appropriate label. After several months and many more forms, I opted to leave the question unmarked (when possible) or to mark "Other" (if there was such an option). On some occasions, depending on my mood, when the question asked for "race," I would write "Cocker Spaniel," "German Shepherd," or "unknown" on the blank line next to "Other." Because there often was an indication that this information was optional, I did not feel any remorse for perhaps skewing some demographic data. On the contrary, this simple act provided me with an opportunity to show my dissent toward questions that limited my individuality to a generic label.

Do the classifications recognized by the U.S. Census Bureau offer us a useful way of understanding our national and cultural experiences? Do terms such as *black, Asian American, Hispanic* have any real substance to them, or are they the creation of media czars and political impresarios? Let's examine the official definition of Hispanic (according to the 1990 U.S. census):

> A person is of Spanish/Hispanic origin if the person's origin (ancestry) is Mexican, Mexican-American, Chicano, Puerto Rican, Dominican, Ecuadorian, Guatemalan, Honduran, Nicaraguan, Peruvian, Salvadoran; from other Spanish-speaking countries of the Caribbean or Central or South America; or from Spain.

The ethnic label "Hispanic" began to be used heavily by state agencies in the early 1970s to refer to all people in this country whose ancestry is predominantly from one or more Spanish-speaking countries. As a result, millions of people of a variety of national and cultural backgrounds are put into a single arbitrary category. No allowances are made for our varied racial, linguistic, and national experiences, nor for whether we are recent immigrants, long-time residents, or belong to an associated territory. Furthermore, using "Hispanic" to refer to those who are of Spanish-speaking origin can be problematic in that it excludes a considerable sector of the population in Latin America for whom Spanish is not a first language. Many "Hispanic" immigrants come from regions that are not necessarily pre-

dominantly Spanish. This is the case of those who speak Nahuatl and Tiwa in Indian villages in Mexico; Kanjobal and Jacaltec in the southern part of Guatemala; Quechua and Aymara in the highlands of Peru and Bolivia; Guarani, Chulupi, and Mascoi in the Chaco region of Paraguay; Tukano and Tuyukaf in the swamps of Venezuela and Columbia; and others from predominantly non-Spanish-speaking regions. Thus, given that their native language may not be Spanish, it is inaccurate to call these people of "Spanish-speaking origin."

Furthermore, as Berkeley social scientist Carlos Muñoz writes, the term *Hispanic* is derived from *Hispania*, which was the name the Romans gave to the Iberian peninsula, most of which became Spain, and "implicitly emphasizes the white European culture of Spain at the expense of the nonwhite cultures that have profoundly shaped the experience of all Latin Americans" through its refusal to acknowledge "the nonwhite indigenous cultures of the Americas, Africa, and Asia, which historically have produced multicultural and multiracial peoples in Latin America and the United States" (1989, 11). It is a term that ignores the complexities within and throughout these various groups.[1]

Dichotomies and Negative Constructions: "I Didn't Realize I Was a Minority Until I Came to the United States"

As mentioned earlier, I always felt special and different among my fellow Peruvians. However, it was only until I came to this country that a label for being different was assigned to

---

[1]Ernst's analysis of her transformation from Peruvian to Hispanic is a nice illustration of what the sociologist Andrew Greeley called "ethnogenesis." This concept is discussed in chapter 14 of *The Practical Skeptic: Core Concepts in Sociology.* —Ed.

me: I became a minority! I must say that being labeled as such has not always been that bad; on occasion I have received some special treatment just because I fit the category of minority. However, the term *minority* has heavy connotations, especially when we realize that it signifies differences from those who make up the majority in this country. In other words, my status was assigned to me because I am not part of the majority, so therefore I should be part of the minority. The term *minority,* like other terms used to identify people's racial, ethnic, and cultural backgrounds, is defined in opposition to another term.[2]

The same can be said about the term *Hispanic.* In contemporary discourse the term *Hispanic* has come to be used as a nonwhite racial designation. It is not unusual to read or hear people use the terms *whites, blacks,* and *Hispanics* as if they were mutually exclusive when, in fact, the 1990 census states that 52 percent of Hispanics identify themselves as white, 3 percent as black, and 43 percent as "other race."

The English language is constructed as a system of differences organized as extreme dichotomies—white/black, majority/minority, good/bad, dark/fair, and so on. The existence of this polarization influences how English speakers manage their relations with others. Consider the case of qualifiers or adjectives. The heavy emphasis on opposites often compels speakers of English to use one of the two opposite adjectives when formulating questions. As a result, people in the United States commonly use evaluative terms in questions and descriptions, and find it easier to be critical rather than positive or neutral. For example, let's compare pairs of adjectives in English and in Spanish:

English		*Spanish*	
old	young	viejo	joven
long	short	largo	corto
far	near	cerca	lejos

At first, it may seem as if both the English and Spanish pairs contain words that are opposite in meaning but equal in their power to describe a point on a continuum. However, this is not the case. Consider how the English adjectives are used in asking questions: "How old is he?" "How long is that ruler?" and "How far do we have to go?" Questions are not phrased using the secondary term, as in "How young is he?" (unless in reference to a baby or small child), "How short is that ruler?" and "How near do we have to go?" In all of these questions one of the terms is designated as the defining term—for age, *old*; for size, *long*; for distance, *far*.

To the Spanish speaker, these same dichotomies do not have the same dependent hierarchy; rather, these pairs enjoy symmetry. This weaker polarization of Spanish pairs is evident in the way questions are phrased. In Spanish, "How old is he?" becomes "*¿Qué edad tiene él?*" which can be literally translated as "What is his age?" The question "How long is that ruler?" becomes "*¿Cuánto mide esa regla?*"—that is, "What's the measurement of that ruler?"—and so on. In Spanish, the emphasis is placed on the middle ground of the continuum rather than on one of its ends.

Thus, one important aspect of opposing adjectives in English is that the primary term appears as the defining term or the norm of cultural meaning, while the secondary term is much more specific or derives its meaning from its relation to the first one. Examples of the "good–bad" dichotomy help to illustrate this point. If you ask a friend to help you with a new software program, you will probably say, "How good are you with MacMisha 5.1?" rather than "How bad are you with MacMisha 5.1?" That is, the use of the term *good* reflects a

---

[2]The sociological concept of "minority group" is discussed in detail in chapter 14 of *The Practical Skeptic: Core Concepts in Sociology.* —Ed.

more general qualifier, while the use of the term *bad* already suggests that something is not good; thus this latter term is more specific (in a negative sense).

This same polarity can be applied to some of the qualifiers used in discussing issues of race and ethnicity. For example, in the case of pairs of labels, as in white/black, majority/minority, resident/nonresident, white/colored, American/other, the defining term of the norm is given by the primary term; the secondary term represents what is different, alien, or abnormal.

The negative precision of English qualifiers yields a linguistic base for qualifying as negative whatever appears to be different. Thus, the labels and distinctions made among different ethnic and racial groups perpetuate a hierarchical system where some groups are the norm while the others, by default, do not fit the norm.

Ritual Interactions: *"People Are Incredibly Friendly!"*

My brother, who recently visited me from Peru, shared with me his thoughts about American friendliness after spending two days wandering around a large northwestern city. He was taken aback by the Pacific Northwest because he found people to be "incredibly friendly." He went on to say that during his three-week stay in this part of the country, a number of people on the street, on the road, and in the parks had smiled or said "hello" to him. He found it "kind of strange because you just don't see that in Lima, New York, Vienna, or Paris." I was a bit taken aback myself when I heard the story, thinking to myself, "Is the difference tangible?" After pondering a moment, I answered my own question "Absolutely!" There's a unique, friendly spirit you find throughout the Pacific Northwest. I think we sometimes lose sight of that fact. When you live something every day, there's a chance you'll start taking it for

granted. My brother's comments were somewhat of a wake-up call for me and reminded me of my first months in the United States.

Although at that time I was in northern Florida, I can recall having similar feelings about this unusual kind of friendliness. I clearly remember feeling incredibly special when someone would welcome me to the town, ask me how I was feeling, and wish me a pleasant day. Furthermore, I still remember how shocked I was when an auto mechanic spent almost two hours trying to install a tiny plastic hook in the door of my 1966 VW bug and charged me only $1.50 for the part. And, in perhaps the most startling demonstration of American "friendliness," I vividly recall how, just two months after my arrival in this country, a smiling police officer said, "Welcome to America" after she gave me two (undeserved, I must add) traffic tickets.

Instances like these remind me of an incident recounted by British-born journalist Henry Fairlie in an article entitled "Why I Love America":

> One spring day, shortly after my arrival, I was walking down the long, broad street of a suburb, with its sweeping front lawns (all that space), its tall trees (all that sky), and its clumps of azaleas (all that color). The only other person on the street was a small boy on a tricycle. As I passed him, he said "Hi" —just like that. No four-year-old boy had ever addressed me without an introduction before. Yet here was this one, with his cheerful "Hi!" Recovering from the culture shock, I tried to look down stonily at his flaxen head, but instead, involuntarily, I found myself saying in return: "Well—hi!" He pedaled off, apparently satisfied. He had begun my Americanization. (1983, 12)

For Fairlie the word "Hi!" had an important meaning:

> (I come from a country where one can tell someone's class by how they say "Hallo!" or "Hello!" or "Hullo," or whether they say it at all.) But [in America] anyone can say "Hi!" Anyone does.

Like my brother and Henry Fairlie, I was also very impressed with the friendliness of people in this part of the globe, in particular the friendliness and concern of store clerks and waiters, who would often introduce themselves by their first names and treat me in a casual, friendly manner, even asking how I was feeling today. I was really taken by this caring manner. I remember thinking, How can you not feel special in this great nation if everyone is always trying to see if you are okay? In Lima, where everyone is in a hurry (and sometimes trying to take advantage of others), store clerks and waiters barely say "thank you," if they speak to you at all. And of course, as a customer, you would not spend time chatting or exchanging greetings with those who are in such unsuccessful positions.

One day, however, I was struck by a somewhat sad discovery: What I thought was true concern and friendliness was just a ritual interaction. On that day, I had just learned that Max, my roommate's Golden Retriever, was at a veterinary hospital; he had been run over by a car. On my way home, I stopped by the grocery store to get some milk. As on other days, a friendly clerk checked my groceries, and when she asked me, "How are you?" I responded, "A bit sad," To my surprise, the friendly clerk said, "Great! Have a nice day." After a few seconds of puzzlement, I grabbed my paper sack and left the store. Later, my roommate, a native Floridian, explained that this type of greeting was routine and that stores often require their employees to display "extreme friendliness" with customers. It was only after this explanation that I realized that the caring tone used by clerks and others working with the public was routine chat, part of a ritual exchange.

Ritual exchanges such as "How are you?" "I'm fine, thank you," "Nice meeting you," "Hope you have a nice day," and other similar phrases are, like any ritual exchange, more about form than substance. In other words,

questions and answers are (or should be) the same, regardless of the participants in the interactions and their feelings. In the above incident, even though I responded candidly with an unscripted answer to the customary "How are you" questions, I got a conventional short and scripted answer.

The brevity and formulaic aspects of these ritual exchanges, I believe, have little to do with whether people are friendly or not. Rather, this behavior might be related to an informal, egalitarian approach to others characteristic of American culture. It might also have to do with the brevity, informality, and practicality that characterizes the American style of communication (which, by the way, reminds me of the typical monosyllabic answers that I receive from my students when I ask even complex questions: "Sure," "OK," or "Nope").

Ritual interactions, like many other aspects of language and communication, vary from culture to culture and from country to country. This becomes evident when contrasting the little and often impersonal ritual exchanges of Americans with the long and personal ritual interactions of Peruvians. In Peru, ritual exchanges like those mentioned above are not as common as in the United States. When they do occur, however, one generally asks about family members' health. On these occasions, one needs to be accurate in one's questioning and attentive in one's listening, not only in terms of asking about the appropriate family members (for instance, not asking a widow about her husband's health), but also in relation to the substance of the answer (for example, showing some empathy when someone mentions an illness in the family).

Some Final Thoughts

The study of communication and miscommunication across cultures is a relatively new area of research and one that holds much promise in terms of what it can teach us about language and intercultural communication. In this piece I have shared my experiences and reflections about the powerful role played by some terms and ethnic labels in the construction of people's social identity. In addition, I have also discussed some aspects of face-to-face interaction that vary from culture to culture and, as in the case of ritual interactions, provide fertile ground for miscommunication. My intent has been not only to illustrate how individual misunderstandings emerge but also to signal how these interactional processes reproduce and reinforce larger patterns within a society.

All in all, my years in the United States have for the most part unfolded like a dream. Sure, I encountered some problems, misunderstandings, and barriers, and often I had to adjust my expectations and appeal to my flexibility in order to keep going. But then, that is life. I am still learning about how to survive in this, my new home, and in the process I am trying to figure out why we use language the way we use it and why language can make things fuzzier and or less fuzzy.

References

Fairlie, H. 1983. "Why I Love America." *The New Republic,* July 4, p.12.

Lakoff, G. 1972. "Hedges: A Study in Meaning Criteria and the Logic of Fuzzy Concepts." In *Chicago Linguistic Society Papers.* Chicago: Chicago Linguistic Society.

Muñoz, C. 1989. *Youth, Identity, Power.* London: Verso.

Oboler, S. 1995. *Ethnic Labels, Latino Lives: Identity and the Politics of (Re)presentation in the United States.* Minneapolis: University of Minnesota Press.

Questions

1. Ernst argues that, at least compared to some other languages, the "negative precision of English yields a linguistic base for qualifying as negative whatever appears to be different." What does she mean by this statement? What might be the functions of this sort of precision? What about the dysfunctions?

2. Ernst observes that "ritual exchanges such as 'How are you?' 'I'm fine, thank you' . . . and other similar phrases are, like any ritual exchanges, more about form than substance." Provide an example of some ritual exchange in which you routinely participate, and explain the degree to which it is more about form than substance.

3. Some people have suggested that if people had little computers that could translate exactly words from one language into another, travelers could easily interact with people from other cultures. Based on what you learned from Ernst's experiences, do you agree or disagree with this? Explain.

4. Suppose that in the spirit of cultural diversity, a club to which you belong picks "Hispanic" as the theme for its annual banquet. Why might this be a difficult theme to carry out?

·22·

Suspended Identity

Identity Transformation
in a Maximum Security Prison

Thomas J. Schmid and Richard S. Jones

Schmid and Jones look closely at the resocialization process that new prison inmates undergo — but from the point of view of the prisoner and his concerns
about his identity. As you read this article, consider how experiences in this sort
of total institution differ from those undergone by men in boot camp.

... A prison sentence constitutes a "massive assault" on the identity of those imprisoned (Berger 1963, 100–101). This assault is especially severe on first-time inmates, and we might expect radical identity changes to ensue from their imprisonment. At the same time, a prisoner's awareness of the challenge to his identity affords some measure of protection against it. As part of an ethnographic analysis of the prison experiences of first-time, short-term inmates, this article presents an identity transformation model that differs both from the gradual transformation processes that characterize most adult identity changes and from such radical transformation processes as brainwashing or conversion.

Data for the study are derived principally from ten months of participant observation at a maximum security prison for men in the upper midwest of the United States. One of the authors was an inmate serving a felony sentence for one year and one day, while the other participated in the study as an outside observer. Relying on traditional ethnographic data collection and analysis techniques, this approach offered us general observations of hundreds of prisoners, and extensive field-notes that were based on repeated, often daily, contacts with about fifty inmates, as well as on personal relationships established with a smaller number of inmates. We subsequently returned to the prison to conduct focused interviews with other prisoners; using information provided by prison officials, we were able to identify and interview twenty additional first-time inmates who were serving sentences of two years or less. See Schmid and Jones (1987) for further description of this study.

Three interrelated research questions guided our analysis: How do first-time, short-term inmates define the prison world, and how do their definitions change during their prison careers? How do these inmates adapt to the prison world, and how do their adaptation strategies change during their prison careers? How do their self-definitions change during their prison careers? Our analyses of the first two questions are presented in detail elsewhere (Schmid and Jones 1987, 1990); an abbreviated outline of these analyses, to which we will allude throughout this article, is presented in Figure 1. The identity transformation model presented here, based on our analysis of the third question, is outlined in Figure 2.

194

Figure 1 Prison Images
and Strategies of New
Inmates

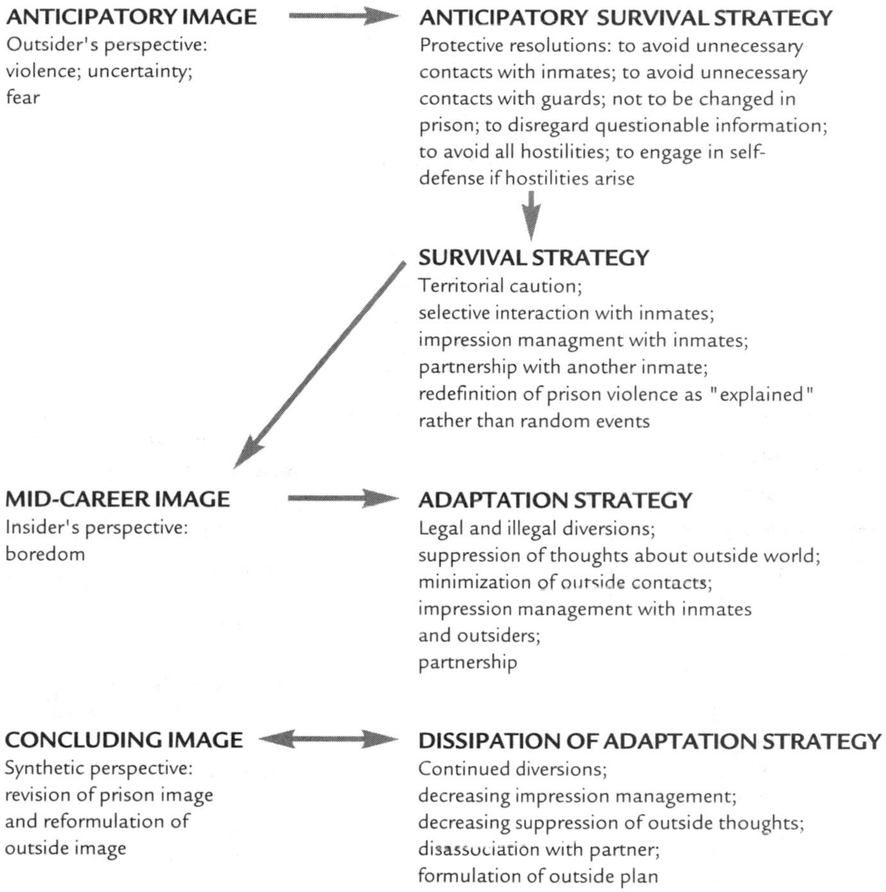

ANTICIPATORY IMAGE
Outsider's perspective:
violence; uncertainty;
fear

ANTICIPATORY SURVIVAL STRATEGY
Protective resolutions: to avoid unnecessary
contacts with inmates; to avoid unnecessary
contacts with guards; not to be changed in
prison; to disregard questionable information;
to avoid all hostilities; to engage in self-
defense if hostilities arise

SURVIVAL STRATEGY
Territorial caution;
selective interaction with inmates;
impression managment with inmates;
partnership with another inmate;
redefinition of prison violence as "explained"
rather than random events

MID-CAREER IMAGE
Insider's perspective:
boredom

ADAPTATION STRATEGY
Legal and illegal diversions;
suppression of thoughts about outside world;
minimization of outside contacts;
impression management with inmates
and outsiders;
partnership

CONCLUDING IMAGE
Synthetic perspective:
revision of prison image
and reformulation of
outside image

DISSIPATION OF ADAPTATION STRATEGY
Continued diversions;
decreasing impression management;
decreasing suppression of outside thoughts;
disassociation with partner;
formulation of outside plan

Preprison Identity

Our data suggest that the inmates we studied have little in common before their arrival at prison, except their conventionality. Although convicted of felonies, most do not possess "criminal" identities (cf. Irwin 1970, 29–34). They begin their sentences with only a vague, incomplete image (Boulding 1961) of what prison is like, but an image that nonetheless stands in contrast to how they view their own social worlds. Their prison image is dominated by the theme of violence: they see prison inmates as violent, hostile, alien human beings, with whom they have nothing in common. They have several specific fears about what will happen to them in prison, including fears of assault, rape, and death. They are also concerned about their identities, fearing that—if they survive prison at all—they are in danger of changing in prison, either through the intentional efforts of rehabilitation personnel or through the unavoidable hardening effects of the prison environment. Acting on this imagery (Blumer 1969)—or, more precisely, on the inconsonance of their self-images with this prison image—they develop an anticipatory survival strategy (see Figure 1) that consists primarily of protective resolutions: a resolve to avoid all hostilities; a resolve to avoid all nonessential contacts with inmates and guards; a resolve to defend themselves in any

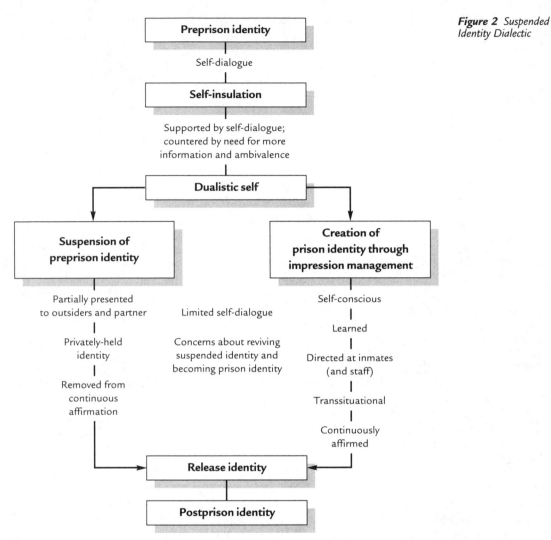

Figure 2 *Suspended Identity Dialectic*

way possible; and a resolve not to change, or to be changed, in prison.

A felon's image and strategy are formulated through a running self-dialogue, a heightened state of reflexive awareness (Lewis 1979) through which he ruminates about his past behavior and motives, and imaginatively projects himself into the prison world. This self-dialogue begins shortly after his arrest, continues intermittently during his trial or court hearings, and becomes especially intense at the time of his transfer to prison.

> You start taking a review—it's almost like your life is passing before your eyes. You wonder how in the heck you got to this point and, you know, what are—what's your family gonna think about it—your friends, all the talk, and how are you going to deal with that—and the kids, you know, how are they gonna react to it? . . . All those things run through your

head. . . . The total loss of control — the first time in my life that some other people were controlling my life.

• • •

My first night in the joint was spent mainly on kicking myself in the butt for putting myself in the joint. It was a very emotional evening. I thought a lot about all my friends and family, the good-byes, the things we did the last couple of months, how good they had been to me, sticking by me. I also thought about my fears: Am I going to go crazy? Will I end up fighting for my life? How am I going to survive in here for a year? Will I change? Will things be the same when I get out?

His self-dialogue is also typically the most extensive self-assessment he has ever conducted; thus, at the same time that he is resolving not to change, he is also initiating the kind of introspective analysis that is essential to any identity transformation process.

Self-Insulation

A felon's self-dialogue continues during the initial weeks and months of his sentence, and it remains a solitary activity, each inmate struggling to come to grips with the inconsonance of his established (preprison) identity and his present predicament. Despite the differences in their preprison identities, however, inmates now share a common situation that affects their identities. With few exceptions, their self-dialogues involve feelings of vulnerability, discontinuity, and differentiation from other inmates, emotions that reflect both the degradations and deprivations of institutional life (cf. Garfinkel 1956; Goffman 1961; and Sykes 1958) and their continuing outsiders' perspective on the prison world. These feelings are obviously the result of everything that has happened to the inmates, but they are something else as well: they are the conditions in which every first-time, short-term inmate finds himself. They might even be called the common

attributes of the inmates' selves-in-prison, for the irrelevance of their preprison identities within the prison world reduces their self-definitions, temporarily, to the level of pure emotion. These feelings, and a consequent emphasis on the "physical self" (Zurcher 1977, 176), also constitute the essential motivation for the inmates' self-insulation strategies.[1]

An inmate cannot remain wholly insulated within the prison world, for a number of reasons. He simply spends too much of his time in the presence of others to avoid all interaction with them. He also recognizes that his prison image is based on incomplete and inadequate information, and that he must interact with others in order to acquire first-hand information about the prison world. His behavior in prison, moreover, is guided not only by his prison image but by a fundamental ambivalence he feels about his situation, resulting from his marginality between the prison and outside social worlds (Schmid and Jones 1987). His ambivalence has several manifestations throughout his prison career, but the most important is his conflicting desires for self-insulation and for human communication.

Managing a Dualistic Self

An inmate is able to express both directions of his ambivalence (and to address his need for more information about the prison) by drawing a distinction between his "true" identity (i.e.,

---

[1]There are four principal components to the survival strategies of the inmates we studied, in the early months of their prison sentences. "Selective interaction" and "territorial caution" are essentially precautionary guidelines that allow inmates to increase their understanding of the prison world while minimizing danger to themselves. "Partnership" is a special friendship bond between two inmates, typically based on common backgrounds and interests (including a shared uncertainty about prison life) and strengthened by the inmates' mutual exploration of a hostile prison world. The fourth component of their strategies, impression management, is discussed in subsequent sections of this article.

his outside, preprison identity) and a "false" identity he creates for the prison world. For most of a new inmate's prison career, his preprison identity remains a "subjective" or "personal" identity while his prison identity serves as his "objective" or "social" basis for interaction in prison (see Goffman 1963; Weigert 1986). This bifurcation of his self (Figure 2) is not a conscious decision made at a single point in time, but it does represent two conscious and interdependent identity-preservation tactics, formulated through self-dialogue and refined through tentative interaction with others.

First, after coming to believe that he cannot "be himself" in prison because he would be too vulnerable, he decides to "suspend" his preprison identity for the duration of his sentence. He retains his resolve not to let prison change him, protecting himself by choosing not to reveal himself (his "true" self) to others. Expressions of a suspension of identity emerged repeatedly and consistently in both the fieldwork and interview phases of our research through such statements as

> I was reserved. . . . I wouldn't be very communicative, you know. I'd try to keep conversation to a minimum. . . . I wasn't interested in getting close to anybody . . . or asking a lot of questions. You know, try to cut the conversation short . . . go my own way back to my cell or go to the library or do something.
>
> • • •
>
> I didn't want nobody to know too much about me. That was part of the act.

An inmate's decision to suspend his preprison identity emanates directly from his feelings of vulnerability, discontinuity and differentiation from other inmates. These emotions foster something like a "proto-sociological attitude" (Weigert, 1986, 173; see also Zurcher 1977), in which new inmates find it necessary to step outside their taken-for-granted preprison identities. Rather than viewing these identities and the everyday life experience in which they are

grounded as social constructions, however, inmates see the *prison* world as an artificial construction, and judge their "naturally occurring" preprison identities to be out of place within this construction. By attempting to suspend his preprison identity for the time that he spends in prison an inmate believes that he will again "be his old self" after his release.

While he is in confinement, an inmate's decision to suspend his identity leaves him with little or no basis for interaction. His second identity tactic, then, is the creation of an identity that allows him to interact, however cautiously, with others. This tactic consists of his increasingly sophisticated impression management skills (Goffman 1959;[2] Schlenker 1980), which are initially designed simply to hide his vulnerability, but which gradually evolve into an alternative identity felt to be more suitable to the prison world. The character of the presented identity is remarkably similar from inmate to inmate:

> Well, I learned that you can't act like—you can't get the attitude where you are better than they are. Even where you might be better than them, you can't strut around like you are. Basically, you can't stick out. You don't stare at people and things like that. I knew a lot of these things from talking to people and I figured them out by myself. I sat down and figured out just what kind of attitude I'm going to have to take.
>
> • • •
>
> Most people out here learn to be tough, whether they can back it up or not. If you don't learn to be tough, you will definitely pay for it. This toughness can be demonstrated through a mean look, tough language, or an extremely big build. . . . One important thing is never to let your guard down.

An inmate's prison identity, as an inauthentic presentation of self, is not in itself a form of

[2]Recall from reading 13 Goffman's concepts of expressions given and expressions given off—these are important components of impression management. —Ed.

identity transformation but is rather a form of identity construction. His prison identity is simply who he must pretend to be while he is in prison. It is a false identity created for survival in an artificial world. But this identity nonetheless emerges in the same manner as any other identity: it is learned from others, and it must be presented to, negotiated with, and validated by others. A new inmate arrives at prison with a general image of what prisoners are like, and he begins to flesh out this image from the day of his arrival, warily observing others just as they are observing him. Through watching others, through eavesdropping, through cautious conversation and selective interaction, a new inmate refines his understanding of what maximum security prisoners look like, how they talk, how they move, how they act. Despite his belief that he is different from these other prisoners, he knows that he cannot appear to be too different from them, if he is to hide his vulnerability. His initial image of other prisoners, his early observations, and his concern over how he appears to others thus provide a foundation for the identity he gradually creates through impression management.

Impression management skills, of course, are not exclusive to the prison world; a new inmate, like anyone else, has had experience in presenting a "front" to others, and he draws upon his experience in the creation of his prison identity. He has undoubtedly even had experience in projecting the very attributes— strength, stoicism, aplomb—required by his prison identity. Impression management in prison differs, however, in the totality with which it governs interactions and in the perceived costs of failure: humiliation, assault, or death. For these reason the entire impression management process becomes a more highly conscious endeavor. When presenting himself before others, a new inmate pays close attention to such minute details of his front as eye contact, posture, and manner of walking:

I finally got out of orientation. I was going out with the main population, going down to get my meals and things. The main thing is not to stare at a bunch of people, you know. I tried to just look ahead, you know, not stare at people. 'Cause I didn't really know; I just had to learn a little at a time.

• • •

The way you look seems to be very important. The feeling is you shouldn't smile, that a frown is much more appropriate. The eyes are very important. You should never look away; it is considered a sign of weakness. Either stare straight ahead, look around, or look the person dead in the eyes. The way you walk is important. You shouldn't walk too fast; they might think you were scared and in a hurry to get away.

To create an appropriate embodiment (Stone 1962; Weigert 1986) of their prison identities, some new inmates devote long hours to weightlifting or other body-building exercises, and virtually all of them relinquish their civilian clothes—which might express their preprison identities—in favor of the standard issue clothing that most inmates wear. Whenever a new inmate is open to the view of other inmates, in fact, he is likely to relinquish most overt symbols of his individuality, in favor of a standard issue "prison inmate" appearance.

By acting self-consciously, of course, a new inmate runs the risk of exposing the fact that he *is* acting. But he sees no alternative to playing his part better; he cannot "not act" because that too would expose the vulnerability of his "true" identity. He thus sees every new prison experience, every new territory that he is allowed to explore, as a test of his impression management skills. Every nonconfrontive encounter with another inmate symbolizes his success at these skills, but it is also a social validation of his prison identity. Eventually he comes to see that many, perhaps most, inmates are engaging in the same kind of inauthentic presentations of self (cf. Glaser and Strauss 1964). Their identities are as "false" as his, and their validations of his identity may be equally false. But he realizes that he is powerless to change this state of affairs, and that he must continue to present his prison identity for as long as he remains in prison.

A first-time inmate enters prison as an outsider, and it is from an outsider's perspective that he initially creates his prison identity. In contrast to this suspended preprison identity, his prison identity is a *shared* identity, because it is modeled on his observations of other inmates. Like those of more experienced prisoners, his prison identity is tied directly to the social role of "prison inmate" (cf. Scheff 1970; Solomon 1970); because he is an outsider, however, his prison identity is also severely limited by his narrow understanding of that role. It is based on an outsider's stereotype of who a maximum security inmate is and what he acts like. It is, nonetheless, a *structural* identity (Weigert 1968), created to address his outsider's institutional problems of social isolation and inadequate information about the prison world.

By the middle of his sentence, a new inmate comes to adopt what is essentially an insider's perspective on the prison world. His prison image has evolved to the point where it is dominated by the theme of boredom rather than violence. (The possibility of violence is still acknowledged and feared, but those violent incidents that do occur have been redefined as the consequences of prison norm violations rather than as random predatory acts; see Schmid and Jones 1990.) His survival strategy, although still extant, has been supplemented by such general adaptation techniques as legal and illegal diversionary activities and conscious efforts to suppress his thoughts about the outside world (Figure 1). His impression management tactics have become second nature rather than self-conscious, as he routinely interacts with others in terms of his prison identity.

An inmate's suspension of his preprison identity, of course, is never absolute, and the separation between his suspended identity and his prison identity is never complete. He continues to interact with his visitors at least partially in terms of his preprison identity, and he is likely to have acquired at least one inmate "partner" with whom he interacts in terms of his preprison as well as his prison identity. During times of introspection, however—which take place less frequently but do not disappear—he generally continues to think of himself as being the same person he was before he came to prison. But it is also during these periods of self-dialogue that he begins to have doubts about his ability to revive his suspended identity.

> That's what I worry about a lot. Because I didn't want to change. . . . I'm still fighting it, 'cause from what I underst ood, before, I wasn't that bad—I wasn't even violent. But I have people say stuff to me now, before I used to say "O.k., o.k."—but now it seems like I got to eye them back, you know.
>
> • • •
>
> I don't know, but I may be losing touch with the outside. I am feeling real strange during visits, very uncomfortable. I just can't seem to be myself, although I am not really sure what myself is all about. My mind really seems to be glued to the inside of these walls. I can't even really comprehend the outside. I haven't even been here three months, and I feel like I'm starting to lose it. Maybe I'm just paranoid. But during these visits I really feel like I'm acting. I'm groping for the right words, always trying to keep the conversation going. Maybe I'm just trying to present a picture that will relieve the minds of my visitors, I just don't know.
>
> • • •
>
> I realized that strength is going to be an important factor whether I'm going to turn into a cold person or whether I'm going to keep my humanitarian point of view. I know it is going to be an internal war. It's going to take a lot of energy to do that. . . . I just keep telling myself that you

gotta do it and sometimes you get to the point where you don't care anymore. You just kinda lose it and you get so full of hate, so full of frustration, it gets wound up in your head a lot.

At this point, both the inmate's suspended preprison identity and his created prison identity are part of his "performance consciousness" (Schechner 1985), although they are not given equal value. His preprison identity is grounded primarily in the memory of his biography (Weigert 1986) rather than in self-performance. His concern, during the middle of his sentence, is that he has become so accustomed to dealing with others in terms of his prison identity — that he has been presenting and receiving affirmation of this identity for so long — that it is becoming his "true" identity.[3]

An inmate's fear that he is becoming the character he has been presenting is not unfounded. All of his interactions within the prison world indicate the strong likelihood of a "role-person merger" (Turner 1978). An inmate views his presentation of his prison identity as a necessary expression of his inmate status. Unlike situational identities presented through impression management in the outside world, performance of the inmate role is transsituational and continuous. For a new inmate, prison consists almost exclusively of front regions, in which he must remain in character. As long as he is in the maximum security institution, he remains in at least partial view of the audience for which his prison identity

is intended: other prison inmates. Moreover, because the stakes of his performance are so high, there is little room for self-mockery or other forms of role distance (Coser 1966; Ungar 1984) from his prison identity, and there is little possibility that an inmate's performance will be "punctured" (Adler and Adler 1989) by his partner or other prison acquaintances. And because his presentation of his prison identity is continuous, he also receives continuous affirmation of his identity from others — affirmation that becomes more significant in light of the fact that he also remains removed from day-to-day reaffirmation of his preprison identity by his associates in the outside world. The inauthenticity of the process is beside the point: Stone's (1962, 93) observation that "one's identity is established when others *place* him as a social object by assigning him the same words of identity that he appropriates for himself or *announces*" remains sound even when both the announcements and the placements are recognized as false.

Standing against these various forms of support for a inmate's prison identity are the inmate's resolve not to be changed in prison, the fact that his sentence is relatively brief (though many new inmates lose sight of this brevity during the middle of their careers) and the limited reaffirmation of his preprison identity that he receives from outsiders and from his partner. These are not insubstantial resources, but nor do they guarantee an inmate's future ability to discard his prison identity and revive the one he has suspended.

Identity Dialectic

When an inmate's concerns about his identity first emerge, there is little that he can do about them. He recognizes that he has no choice but to present his prison identity so, following the insider's perspective he has now adopted, he

---

[3]Clemmer (1958, 299) has defined "prisonization" as the "taking on in greater or less degree of the folkways, mores, customs, and general culture of the penitentiary." Yet new inmates begin to "take on" these things almost immediately, as part of the impression they are attempting to present to other inmates. Thus, we would argue instead that prisonization (meaning assimilation to the prison world) begins to occur for these inmates when their prison identities become second nature — when their expressions of prison norms and customs are no longer based on self-conscious acting. A new inmate's identity concerns, during the middle of his sentence, are essentially a recognition of this assimilation.

consciously attempts to suppress his concerns. Eventually, however, he must begin to consider seriously his capacity to revive his suspended identity: his identity concerns, and his belief that he must deal with them, become particularly acute if he is transferred to the minimum security unit of the prison for the final months of his sentence.[4] At the conclusion of his prison career, an inmate shifts back toward an outsider's perspective on the prison world (see Figure 1); this shift involves the dissipation of his maximum security adaptation strategy, further revision of his prison image, reconstruction of an image of the outside world, and the initial development of an outside plan.[5] The inmate's efforts to revive his suspended identity are part of his shift in perspectives.

It is primarily through a renewed self-dialogue that the inmate struggles to revive his suspended identity — a struggle that amounts to a dialectic between his suspended identity and his prison identity. Through self-dialogue he recognizes, and tries to confront, the extent to which these two identities really do differ. He again tries to differentiate himself from maximum security inmates.

> There seems to be a concern with the inmates here to be able to distinguish . . . themselves from the other inmates. That is — they feel they are above the others. . . . Although they may associate with each other, it still seems important to degrade the majority here.

---

[4]Not all prisoners participate in this unit; inmates must apply for transfer to the unit, and their acceptance depends both on the crimes for which they were sentenced and staff evaluation of their potential for success in the unit. Our analysis focuses on those inmates who are transferred.

[5]There are three features of the minimum security unit that facilitate this shift in perspectives: a more open physical and social environment; the fact that the unit lies just outside the prison wall (so that an inmate who is transferred is also physically removed from the maximum security prison); and greater opportunity for direct contact with the outside world, through greater access to telephones, an unrestricted visitor list, unrestricted visiting hours and, eventually, weekend furloughs.

And he does have some success in freeing himself from his prison identity.

> Well, I think I am starting to soften up a little bit. I believe the identity I picked up in the prison is starting to leave me now that I have left the world of the [maximum security] joint. I find myself becoming more and more involved with the happenings of the outside world. I am even getting anxious to go out and see the sights, just to get away from this place.

But he recognizes that he *has* changed in prison, and that these changes run deeper than the mask he has been presenting to others. He has not returned to his "old self" simply because his impression management skills are used less frequently in minimum security. He raises the question — though he cannot answer it — of how permanent these changes are. He wonders how much his family and friends will see him as having changed. As stated by one of our interview respondents:

> I know I've changed a little bit. I just want to realize how the people I know are going to see it, because they [will] be able to see it more than I can see it. . . . Sometimes I just want to go somewhere and hide.

He speculates about how much the outside world — especially his own network of outside relationships — has changed in his absence. (It is his life, not those of his family and friends, that has been suspended during his prison sentence; he knows that changes have occurred in the outside world, and he suspects that some of these changes may have been withheld from him, intentionally or otherwise.) He has questions, if not serious doubts, about his ability to "make it" on the outside, especially concerning his relationships with others; he knows, in any case, that he cannot simply return to the outside world as if nothing has happened. Above all, he repeatedly confronts the question of who he is, and who he will be in the outside world.

An inmate's struggle with these questions, like his self-dialogue at the beginning of his prison career, is necessarily a solitary activity. The identity he claims at the time of his release, in contrast to his prison identity, cannot be learned from other inmates. Also like his earlier periods of self-dialogue, the questions he considers are not approached in a rational systematic manner. The process is more one of rumination—of pondering one question until another replaces it, and then contemplating the new question until it is replaced by still another, or suppressed from his thoughts. There is, then, no final resolution to any of the inmate's identity questions. Each inmate confronts these questions in his own way, and each arrives at his own understanding of who he is, based on this unfinished, unresolved self-dialogue. In every case, however, an inmate's release identity is a synthesis of his suspended preprison identity and his prison identity.[6]

Postprison Identity

Because each inmate's release identity is the outcome of his own identity dialectic, we cannot provide a profile of the "typical" release identity. But our data do allow us to specify some of the conditions that affect this outcome. Reaffirmations of his preprison identity by outsiders—visits and furloughs during which others interact with him as if he has not changed—provide powerful support for his efforts to revive his suspended identity. These efforts are also promoted by an inmate's recollection of his preprison identity (i.e., his attempts, through self-dialogue, to assess who he was before he came to prison), by his desire to abandon his prison identity, and by his gen-

eral shift back toward an outsider's perspective. But there are also several factors that favor his prison identity, including his continued use of diversionary activities; his continued periodic efforts to suppress thoughts about the outside world; his continued ability to use prison impression management skills; and his continuing sense of injustice about the treatment he has received. Strained or cautious interactions with outsiders, or unfulfilled furlough expectations, inhibit the revival of his preprison identity. And he faces direct, experiential evidence that he has changed: when a minimum security resident recognizes that he is now completely unaffected by reports of violent incidents in maximum security, he acknowledges that he is no longer the same person that he was when he entered prison. Turner (1978, 1) has suggested three criteria for role-person merger: "failure of role compartmentalization, resistance to abandoning a role in the face of advantageous alternative roles, and the acquisition of role-appropriate attitudes"; at the time of their release from prison, the inmates we studied had already accrued some experience with each of these criteria.

Just as we cannot define a typical release identity, we cannot predict these inmates' future, postprison identities, not only because we have restricted our analysis to their prison experiences but because each inmate's future identity is inherently unpredictable. What effect an ex-inmate's prison experience has on his identity depends on how he, in interaction with others, defines this experience. Some of the men we have studied will be returned to prison in the future; others will not. But all will have been changed by their prison experiences. They entered the prison world fearing for their lives; they depart with the knowledge that they have survived. On the one hand, these men are undoubtedly stronger persons by virtue of this accomplishment. On the other hand, the same tactics that enabled them to survive the prison world can be called upon,

---

[6]This is an important parallel with our analysis of the inmate's changing prison definitions: his concluding prison image is a synthesis of the image he formulates before coming to prison and the image he holds at the middle of his prison career; see Schmid and Jones, 1990.

appropriately or not, in difficult situations in the outside world. To the extent that these men draw upon their prison survival tactics to cope with the hardships of the outside world — to the extent that their prison behavior becomes a meaningful part of their "role repertoire" (Turner 1978) in their everyday lives — their prison identities will have become inseparable from their "true" identities. . . .

References

Adler, Patricia A., and Peter Adler. 1989. "The Gloried Self: The Aggrandizement and the Construction of Self." *Social Psychology Quarterly* 52: 299–310.

Berger, Peter L. 1963. *Invitation to Sociology: A Humanistic Perspective.* Garden City, NY: Doubleday Anchor Books.

Blumer, Herbert. 1972. "Action vs. Interaction: Review of *Relations in Public* by Erving Goffman." *Transaction* 9: 50–53.

Boulding, Kenneth. 1961. *The Image.* Ann Arbor: University of Michigan Press.

Clemmer, Donald. 1958. *The Prison Community.* New York: Holt, Rinehart & Winston.

Coser, R. 1966. "Role Distance, Sociological Ambivalence and Traditional Status Systems." *American Journal of Sociology* 72: 173–187.

Goffman, Erving. 1961. *Asylums.* Garden City, NY: Doubleday Anchor Books.

———. 1959. *The Presentation of Self in Everyday Life.* Garden City, NY: Doubleday Anchor Books.

———. 1963. *Stigma: Notes on the Management of Spoiled Identity.* Englewood Cliffs, NJ: Prentice-Hall.

Irwin, John. 1970. *The Felon.* Englewood Cliffs, NJ: Prentice-Hall.

Lewis, David J. 1979. "A Social Behaviorist Interpretation of the Median I." *American Journal of Sociology* 84: 261–287.

Schechner, Richard. 1985. *Between Theater and Anthropology.* Philadelphia: University of Pennsylvania Press.

Scheff, Thomas. 1970. "On the Concepts of Identity and Social Relationships." Pp. 193–207 in T. Shibutani (ed.), *Human Nature and Collective Behavior.* Englewood Cliffs, NJ: Prentice-Hall.

Schlenker, B. 1980. *Impression Management: The Self Concept, Social Identity and Interpersonal Relations.* Belmont, CA: Wadsworth.

Schmid, Thomas, and Richard Jones. 1987. "Ambivalent Actions: Prison Adaptation Strategies of New Inmates." American Society of Criminology, annual meetings, Montreal, Quebec.

Schmid, Thomas, and Richard Jones. 1990. "Experiential Orientations to the Prison Experience: The Case of First-Time, Short-Term Inmates." Pp. 189–210 in Gale Miller and James A. Holstein (eds.), *Perspectives on Social Problems.* Greenwich, CT: JAI Press.

Solomon, David N. 1970. "Role and Self-Conception: Adaptation and Change in Occupations." Pp. 286–300 in T. Shibutani (ed.), *Human Nature and Collective Behavior.* Englewood Cliffs, NJ: Prentice-Hall.

Stone, Gregory P. 1962. "Appearance and the Self." Pp. 86–118 in Arnold Rose (ed.), *Human Behavior and Social Processes.* Boston: Houghton Mifflin.

Sykes, Gresham. 1958. *The Society of Captives: A Study of a Maximum Security Prison.* Princeton, NJ: Princeton University Press.

Turner, Ralph H. 1978. "The Role and the Person." *American Journal of Sociology* 84: 1–23.

Ungar, Sheldon. 1984. "Self-Mockery: An Alternative Form of Self-Presentation." *Symbolic Interaction* 7: 121–133.

Weigert, Andrew J. 1986. "The Social Production of Identity: Metatheoretical Foundations." *Sociological Quarterly* 27: 165–183.

Zurcher, Louis A. 1977. *The Mutable Self.* Beverly Hills, CA: Sage.

Questions

1. Define the following terms, as used by Schmid and Jones in the article.
    a. rumination
    b. inauthentic presentation of self

    c. performance consciousness
    d. identity dialectic
    e. proto-sociological attitude

2. How do Schmid and Jones distinguish between "identity transformation" and "identity construction"?

3. In what ways, if any, do you think prison might have a different effect on women's identity than on men's identity? Explain.

4. Identify the parallels between identity and transformation in prison and the implicit identity transformation undergone by kids as they are introduced to street culture (as described by Anderson in reading 12).

·23·

The Active Worker

Compliance and Autonomy at the Workplace

Randy Hodson

As Randy Hodson observes in this reading, many social scientists (and managers) traditionally have viewed workers as some sort of automaton—subject to the whims of their employers' conceptions of their (the workers') roles. As we saw in reading 16 on waitresses working at The Route, however, the roles of workers can be much more complex than they might seem. In this article, Hodson explores how workers more generally can and do resist being made slaves to the patterns laid down by their employers. To put it in Goffman's terms, the workers are as much in charge of defining the situation as the employers are. (As you read this article, consider how it relates to your own experience as a worker.)

Workers do not leave creative activity behind when they enter the workplace. A brief behind-the-scenes look at any workplace reveals an intricate world of creative, purposive activity, some of it related to the ongoing tasks of the organization and some of it not (Homans 1950; Mars and Nicod 1984; Van Maanen 1977). Indeed, workers' autonomous creative abilities are being called on today to rescue American productivity from its pattern of secular decline (Parker 1985; Rothschild and Russell 1986). Workers' creativity is being solicited under such banners as Quality of Work Life Programs, Group Centered Responsibility, and Participative Management.

Unfortunately, current theories of the workplace provide inadequate guidance in understanding workers' creative activities. Most theories of the workplace anesthetize workers, considering them merely as objects of manipulation. This is equally true of management theories from scientific management to human relations (Argyle 1972; Mayo 1945) as it is of radical theories which focus on the structural determination (or overdetermination) of workers' actions and consciousness (Braverman 1974; Edwards 1979; Poulantzas 1975). Those theories that do include a role for workers' autonomous actions typically place workers' behaviors in theoretical straitjackets. From the management side, workers are seen as engaged in output restriction and foot-dragging (Crozier 1964; Etzioni 1971; Organ 1988). Even research sympathetic to workers has been constrained by a focus on output restriction as the central problematic (Ditton 1976; Gardner and Whyte 1946).[1] From a radical perspective, workers' behaviors are forced into a theoretical straitjacket of acquiescence ("false consciousness")[2] or resistance to capitalist control

---

[1] That is, the ways in which workers act to intentionally slow down the production process. —Ed.

[2] The concept of false consciousness refers to ways of thinking that are not in keeping with an individual's actual economic situation in life. False consciousness is a product of the vision of reality perpetrated by the rich and powerful. Marxists use this term to explain why economic minorities do not rise up and revolt. The idea is that minorities are conditioned to

of the workplace (Edwards and Scullion 1982; Shaiken 1984; Wood 1982). These visions cast workers' actions within very narrow theoretical constraints that have limited and distorted our understanding of workers' actions. Over time, these limitations have led to a restricted set of questions being asked about workers: How are workers controlled by management and when and how do they resist this control? Other, more diverse questions and problematics have been largely ignored. As Hughes (1958) noted over 3 decades ago, the term "'restriction of production'. . . contains a value assumption . . . namely, that there is someone *who knows and has a right* to determine the right amount of work for other people to do. . . . But I think we might better understand the social interaction which determines the measure of effort if we keep ourselves free of terms which suggest that it is abnormal to do less than one is asked by some reasonable authority" (47–48, emphasis added).

Some contemporary researchers argue for a more active view of the worker, but even this vision is typically a very constrained one. For example, Burawoy (1979) argued that workers are centrally concerned with "making out"—devising a way to meet production goals without completely exhausting themselves in the process. Burawoy also argued, however, that contemporary industrial relations are based on hegemonic control[3] of the economic and political relations of production by the capitalist

class. Thus workers' efforts to make out operate within the overriding "logic of the capitalist system" (see also Beynon 1973, 208). Such theories accept the view that the Fordist[4] logic of mass production has created a situation in which workers' creative efforts make little or no difference. Thus even the small range of creative activity allowed workers in these models is rendered theoretically inconsequential.

Only a few contemporary researchers view workers' behaviors in a fashion that cannot be reduced to the single dimension of struggle between capital[5] and labor over control of the labor process (see, e.g., Jermier 1988; Van Maanen 1977). These researchers view workers' activities as multidimensional and hence not easily reducible to any single dimension, including that posed by the imposition of managerial control. Such research is based on the assumption that functional autonomy is widespread in the workplace and that understanding the prerogatives of autonomy is key to understanding worker behavior (Hughes 1958).

Since the dominant theories of the workplace do not adequately address the diversity of worker behaviors, I relied on in-depth interviews and observations of workers and inductive theory building[6] to uncover and further conceptualize these activities. I anticipated that I would find that workers were neither passive objects of manipulation nor intransigent resisters of every management and organizational goal. The question before us therefore becomes: What sorts of resistance do workers engage in, under what conditions, and toward what ends?

accept the rightness of the status quo. Part of this conditioning may come from religious beliefs encouraged by the rich and powerful. Marx, for example, referred to religion as "the opium of the people"—so-called because religion, with its promises of salvation and rewards in the afterlife, is used by the rich to help keep poor people in line. —Ed.

[3]The word *hegemony* (derived from the Greek *hegemonia,* meaning "leader") refers to the heavy influence of some group or nation over another. The Italian sociologist Antonio Gramsci (1891–1937) adapted the word to a more precise sociological meaning; hegemony refers to the capacity of one group to persuade others that its ideas, beliefs, values, and norms are legitimate and thus ought to be accepted. —Ed.

[4]That is, production technology of the sort made famous by Henry Ford. Also known as "assembly line production," this sort of technology emphasizes efficiency and the reduction of worker creativity and autonomy. —Ed.

[5]That is, capitalists, or the owners of the factories. —Ed.

[6]That is, theory built from the ground up. Building theory through induction requires the researcher to explore the world and collect data. From these data, the theory is constructed. —Ed.

In the following section, I discuss the nature of the data collected to address these questions. Next, I present an interpretation of the data and develop a typology of forms of resistance. The article concludes with a discussion of how the analysis presented here can be used to inform current theories of the workplace.

Method

Ethnographic methods provide tools that allow researchers to release workers from the theoretical straitjackets of existing theoretical agendas (Glaser and Strauss 1967). The analysis of data from field research can yield genuinely new concepts and theoretical propositions. For example, I started this investigation into workers' behavior with the idea that I was studying sabotage. After preliminary observations and interviews, I developed a less restrictive focus on subtle noncompliance, foot-dragging, and conditional effort. As the research progressed, so too did these concepts. Eventually, they expanded into a fuller model of the multidimensional nature of the effort bargain.

I started by interviewing clerical workers and then moved to the paraprofessions and semiprofessions and finally to service and manual workers. The reason for this progression was a desire to avoid restricting conceptual development by an overemphasis on the manual occupations which have provided the backdrop for so much of the conceptual work in this area. My initial contacts for securing interviews were mainly through students who had been in continuing studies classes that I have taught on the sociology of work. Although none of these students were themselves included in the study, they provided access to networks that enabled me to select respondents from a wide range of occupations. At each stage in the process, I was guided by the principle of theoretical sampling in which

the next respondent is chosen in order to answer the most pressing theoretical question (McCall and Simmons 1969).

My goal throughout the research was to understand the nature of effort at the workplace and the ways it is elicited and stymied. The interviews are largely unstructured and took place in a variety of settings chosen by respondents. These settings included respondents' workplaces, restaurants, parks, and homes. I established a basis for conversation by asking about what motivated them to work hard and what caused them to feel unmotivated. The interviews typically lasted from 1.5 to 2.5 hours. Besides talking with workers, in most cases, I also visited their workplaces, some repeatedly. I thus had the opportunity to observe most of the workplaces directly and to talk further with the workers and sometimes with their coworkers. The respondents ranged in age from 19 to 54 years. They were employed in jobs arrayed across the major occupational categories and made salaries ranging from poverty-level earnings to earnings about two times the national average. . . .

Compliance and Autonomy

The diagram presented in Figure 1 summarizes the data and will help organize the discussion by providing a visual referent. However, the reader should bear in mind that social reality is not well depicted by a two-dimensional diagram. Many of the spheres of behavior depicted have overlap with other spheres of behavior that the two-dimensional nature of this diagram does not allow to be displayed. These relationships will become clearer in the following discussion. The model of workers' behaviors presented in Figure 1 is built around the central categories of enthusiastic compliance and conditional effort. The goal of the following sections will be to motivate this typology of

Figure 1 *Behavioral Modes at the Workplace*

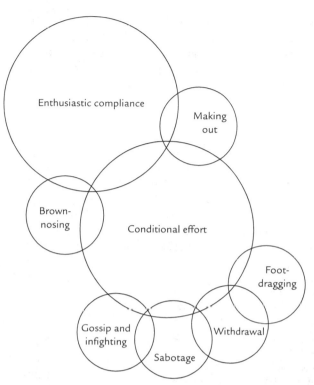

behaviors and to derive some preliminary hypotheses about the conditions under which the different options are selected.

ENTHUSIASTIC COMPLIANCE

Let us begin with the sphere labeled "Enthusiastic Compliance." Enthusiastic effort may rest on a number of bases, including pride in doing quality work, a strong service orientation to clients, friendship and allegiance to co-workers, or a commitment to help carry the collective work load. Pride in work has been identified as a central orientation among those who must work for a living, both those in and outside the traditional working class (Montgomery 1979; Reinarman 1987). Pride is a particularly strong motivation and was voiced in a variety of contexts during the interviews. An accounts clerk at an auto parts store reported that "I'm the

type of person that likes to make sure that my desk is done. I can't stand half-completed work." A mental health paraprofessional reported that "I work especially hard when it is something that personally interests me; that gets my creative juices going. I feel like doing research on it, expanding my knowledge and being more helpful to people." Enthusiastic compliance to organizational goals is not reducible to a lockstep adherence to organizational rules. Worker initiative and autonomous activity are involved in determining the specifics of the nature and direction of effort even where the worker fully subscribes to the goals and dictates of the organization (Becker et al. 1961, 12).

Workers often evaluated the quality of their jobs in terms of the degree of flexibility allowed. Jobs that were flexible enough so that workers could exercise creativity in their work provided the structural preconditions for the emergence of pride, enthusiasm, and extra effort. The worker I interviewed who had the least job flexibility was a long-distance telephone operator. The work involved was too repetitive and too closely supervised, both electronically and by direct supervision, to have a significant sphere of autonomy and flexibility; hence this was one of the most alienated and cynical workers I interviewed. Other jobs had greater spheres of flexibility, and gradations in the autonomy that this allowed provided one of the most important determinants of differential enthusiasm and extra effort. For example, a metal fabrications worker reported that

> free rein implies responsibility and people excel if they think they have responsibility. I know I do. My boss said at the beginning that "I'm not going to stand over you and there are no set breaks, but as long as you get the job done, you'll find time to rest or talk to somebody." So he put the responsibility of knowing what to do and when to do it to me, and I thought it was good.

Similarly, a maintenance worker on night shift at an automated factory reported that "I can do it any way I want to do it as long as it is fixed in the morning. As long as it is fixed in the morning, they don't care how it got fixed—if I snap my fingers, do a rain dance, or whatever."

Worker control over pace and work rules is increased where workers are expected to devise the details of their own procedures as a matter of standard practice. Having responsibility for devising their own work procedures gives workers immense power (see Lipsky 1981). Often, workers have to figure out how to do required tasks with little or no instruction from management. Workers' most frequent source of information is other workers who are currently doing the job or who have done similar work in the past. Hughes (1958)

noted that the right to make judgments about the details of work practices is "most jealously guarded" by workers (94).

Having a job that enables one to construct a positive personal identity is also important in motivating extra effort. An administrative secretary reported: "I like to solve problems and in this job you can do a lot of that. And I like working with people. I like meeting people. I wouldn't ever like to work by myself. If I opened my own business, I would want something where the public was involved. I'm just that kind of person." Some work settings facilitate the development of a positive personal identity. Other settings make the development of a viable identity extremely difficult. For example, Snow and Anderson (1987) discussed the problems of establishing viable personal identities among the homeless whose occupational roles are largely restricted to jobs contracted on a day-labor basis.

Somewhere on the borderline between enthusiastic compliance and conditional effort are two additional types of workplace behavior that I have categorized as "making out" and "brownnosing." Making out and brownnosing lie partly within the field of enthusiastic compliance and partly within the field of conditional effort and therefore have somewhat ambiguous interpretations. Brownnosing, in particular, is an ambiguous behavior and its interpretation may vary across observers who attribute different meanings to the behaviors involved.

Making Out   Making out means finding ways to satisfy organizational demands while simultaneously meeting one's own needs. To successfully make out, one must meet organizational standards. But because tending to one's own needs is a central concern in making out, such behaviors cannot be considered solely as examples of enthusiastic compliance. Goffman (1961) referred to such behaviors in the context of total institutions as "secondary adjustments" (189). Burawoy (1979) argued that workers' attempts to make out are the key to understanding worker behavior.

Workers are immensely creative in devising strategies that preserve their autonomy and dignity in the face of excessive or inappropriate demands. Probably the most common behavioral strategy is to withhold enthusiasm and become detached from work. Depending on the nature of the work and the degree of the perceived managerial offenses, this detachment may mean that workers take an extra 10 minutes on breaks or that they avoid work 80% of the time. Along with giving only partial effort comes the creation of smoke screens to obscure this strategy. A worker at a sewage treatment plant reported that many workers neglect to take readings in the tanks at regular intervals and have learned to predict these readings reasonably well by taking recent rainfall amounts into account: "There is no way anyone can tell definitely whether or not we have actually taken the readings." Sometimes managers are fooled by such stratagems. More often, they are not, but the cost of challenging the scam is prohibitively large or the rewards for overturning it are too low. Thus many situations in which workers limit their efforts involve some degree of complicity or at least acquiescence by supervisors and management.

Appearances are key to successfully making out. A teacher reported the following practices at his school:

> The principal can in some schools ask to see the lesson plans every week. What you do is make lesson plans but just don't do them. So if they ask you what you did that week, you show them lessons plans that you never used. And have a whole bunch of grades. It looks like you did all that grading, but these can be based on attendance or on oral quizzes. Come up with some flashy thing once a month so everybody thinks something is going on. Open your curtains and then the principal walks by and sees this wonderful thing going on this 1 week out

of the month that you do it and then the rest of the time actually close your curtains. Really advertise when you're doing something good and when you're not, close up shop.

Such image manipulation is not limited to professional settings. According to a commentator on work practices in a skilled blue-collar setting, "[Workers] become well versed in concealing information and practices from management so as to manipulate them. The distinction between rhetoric and practice is one they are experienced in maintaining" (Halle 1984, 146).

Brownnosing   Brownnosing is being ingratiating toward one's supervisors and receiving favors or privileges in return. Brownnosing is something other people do: Reports of brownnosing are always in the third person. When a worker had engaged in a behavior that someone else might call brownnosing, they will tend to interpret their behavior as "making out" or as successfully manipulating management. Brownnosing *is* akin to making out in that it rests on an overlap between managerial and worker interests. However, brownnosing is a tainted behavior because it violates the workplace norm of solidarity with other workers and opposition to management.

The attribution of brownnosing to others is not an everyday occurrence. Only about a third of the respondents made any mention of such issues, and none dwelt on this as a major concern. More complaints are made against coworkers for slackness than for brownnosing. While brownnosing itself was not frequently noted, what was commonly condemned was managers treating workers differently. Thus the blame was placed on management for treating workers differently rather than on workers for seeking to brownnose management. A kitchen worker in a nursing home reported that

> if the boss catches someone slacking off, he gets really upset, really. He expects you to have a rag in your hand and be wiping some grease up or

he will bite your ear off. You have to look busy. Unless you are one of his favorites—he has a couple of those. If he likes an individual employee, they get better treatment. It's perfectly obvious. They get more free rein. They don't have to look so busy all the time. You will see them in the break room smoking a cigarette a little bit more often.

Favoritism may simply be the way in which what I have called brownnosing is socially constructed by workers. The social construction of such behaviors as favoritism maintains the image of solidarity against an unjust and manipulative management. The implicit consensus seems to be that everyone tries to get ahead; some just have different strategies than others. The crime seems to be more in management inappropriately rewarding ingratiating behavior than in workers attempting it as a strategy.

CONDITIONAL EFFORT

Infringements on autonomy and flexibility were the most common basis for workers saying that they were not enthusiastic about their work. These infringements could take the form of bureaucratic rules or overly strict supervision. Workers seemed much less concerned with machine pacing and instead took it as part of the invisible background against which their roles at the workplace were played out. Human infringements and autonomy were experienced with considerably less tolerance. A waitress whose boss started holding time cards until the waitresses rolled the mandatory two trays of silverware and napkins before checking out at night identified this experience as a pivotal one in coming to dislike her job: "I felt like Larry was trying to babysit or something. A lot of people don't think it should even be our job. That's another reason we're really reluctant to do it. It's like holding our time cards to make us do something we shouldn't have to do in the first place." The

reason this episode so irritated the waitress was that it undermined the dignity and honor of her position. As Hughes (1974) noted, honor derives from being granted and upholding the prerogatives of one's position in society, something that the waitress felt was violated in this situation. Violations of the dignity with which people expect to be treated leads to cynicism, rebellion, and conditional effort (Becker et al. 1961, 114). Where opportunities for the attainment of honor in work are perceived as absent, withdrawal of effort is likely to follow (Becker, Geer, and Hughes 1968, 102).

A significant share of behaviors at the workplace entail an element of deviation from some aspect of the formal organizational agenda. Relevant behaviors include the pursuit of alternative tasks, the avoidance of unpleasant tasks through delay, and physical withdrawal from work through absenteeism, tardiness, or hiding from work while on the job. Delay is a particularly common strategy. The operational theory behind delay is that work delayed is work avoided. Someone else may do the work or the work may not get done, and the consequences may be within the range of management tolerance. A clerical worker reported the following responses to work she dislikes:

> Find something else to do. Some other kind of work that you like better. Goof off. Do my checkbook, play computer games, take a walk with somebody else in the building. I'd rather goof off and do it right later at the last minute if it still has to be done than do a poor job on it now.

Doing poor-quality work appears to be distasteful in most circumstances; it violates the principle of taking pride in one's own work. Delaying unnecessary or undesirable work, however, not only avoids such work but simultaneously realizes the principle of autonomy and creativity in arranging one's schedule, even if one must do so through subterfuge (Fine 1984; Roy 1960).

There are often some things about work that directly anger workers. Frequently, these relate to management. Management provides a good target for discontents no matter what the complex causality of the issues involved. After all, they are in charge. Complaints against management are myriad but conform to two general themes: abuse styles and incompetence. Willis (1977) argued that such complaints arise from a basic human dislike of subordination. However, a lack of leadership can be equally infuriating. As Crawford (1989) noted, workers resent nothing more than an incompetent manager. This dislike for subordination and managerial incompetence opens the door to a variety of forms of resistance in the effort to create personal and social space for autonomous, self-directed activity.

Managers are condemned for such faults as inability to provide needed materials, laziness, stupidity, lack of leadership in crisis situations ("management by drift"), and destructive infighting with other managers. A waitress reported the following evaluation of her supervisor: "I'm not even sure what he does but give you a bad time. Sometimes, we sit around and wonder how this restaurant ever goes anywhere. I think the managers have no idea what is really going on." A cook at another restaurant was even harsher in his evaluation of management: "The man who owns this place was busted for cocaine. He's dumb as a rock." A telephone worker complained about the continuing disruptions and deteriorating conditions caused by divestiture in the telephone industry:

> We don't take as much pride in our work in that we don't ever know what is going on. It is chaotic since 1983. Nobody knows what is going on. If you have any experience getting your phone fixed since divestiture, you call, and nobody knows what's going on. Sometimes you can talk to as many as 20 people. The right hand doesn't know what the left is doing. If they can't get their own act together and give decent service, why should *you* try?

Juravich (1985) noted similar damaging effects of chaotic management styles on worker morale in a manufacturing setting. And in their research on college undergraduates, Becker, Geer, and Hughes (1968) noted that a central complaint about faculty is that they are not clear enough about what they want students to learn (111).

A female operator at a chemical plant condemned managers for laziness:

> The lower managers tend to drive around the plant—they'll spend the whole day driving around the plant, listening to the radio or park somewhere. They'll say they're doing an inspection of the plant and walk around the plant for 2 hours and not do anything. The higher management tends to disappear into their offices all day. They essentially do nothing, or they say they're going to lunch and to a meeting and then they are gone for 6 hours and don't come back. They pretty much do what they want because there's no one to see what they're doing.

This operator interpreted management behavior in terms of the "free rider" problem which is a common focus of concern at the workplace: Someone gets their share of rewards without doing an appropriate share of work.

Fears associated with job insecurity also figured heavily into complaints against management. A retail store worker employed in a company in the midst of a union busting drive (which included the company filing Chapter 11 bankruptcy papers) said: "If you are worried about whether or not you are going to have a job next week, it's hard to keep a smile on your face for customers. . . . I have a wife and a son and for me to just be out of a job, it's going to be tough. . . . I'm scared."

Managers were also condemned for being abusive, for not valuing and respecting workers and their contributions, for favoritism, and for being paid so much when workers are paid so little. An administrative secretary in a not-for-profit organization reported painful experiences of status degradation:

> In many instances the whole tag of being a secretary is degrading. I think people don't look at you with the respect you deserve. They think that you are some kind of clerical person that can perform miracles but that you don't have any brains in your head. I think a lot of the lack of motivation here comes from being made fun of for grammar being corrected; there are a lot of cracks in this office about being [local bumpkins], and there are some of us who may be. But after a while it gets old.

Given the apparently light duties of management and the onerousness of their own duties, many workers also experienced steep pay differentials in favor of management as a direct slap in the face.

Along with learning the organizational rules about their jobs, workers simultaneously learn how to bend these rules to maintain their own autonomy and dignity (Willis 1977). Even the experience of learning rules whose main purpose is to limit the autonomy of workers thus becomes an opportunity to exercise creativity through the development of counterstrategies of productivity that create spheres of autonomous activity. These spheres of activity at the workplace are analogous to the "underlife" of activity observed in total institutions (Goffman 1961).

Workers report that managers' responses to restricted effort vary dramatically. Some managers try to run a tighter ship. Sometimes, this eliminates a sphere of restricted activity, but it can also provoke additional restrictions on activity as a response to perceived managerial abuse. Some managers implement new rules or accounting systems, but often these are ineffective in the face of workers applying their full creative efforts to restricting their output and not getting caught or sanctioned (see Ditton 1976). Sometimes, managers are simply unaware of restricted output because they do not care enough to find out about it. They have

their hands full with problems with customers, suppliers, or superiors and have simply delegated so much authority and autonomy that workers are pretty much able to write their own rules. Managers may also be limited in their ability to respond to restricted activity by the possibility that workers will retaliate if management seeks to discipline workers. A public school teacher reported that

> it's much easier for the principal to look the other way than to confront a teacher with a disciplinary issue. If they confront the teacher, they are going to be unpopular. Then, they are not going to have the support of the teachers, and their job is going to be made miserable. Teachers have a lot of power over administrators.

Strategies of control by management elicit strategies of resistance by workers. Resistance by workers elicits strategies of counterresistance by management which in turn may elicit further strategies of counter-counterresistance by workers. . . .

There appear to be at least four separate clusters of behavior within the general category of conditional effort. The diversity of these behaviors is what makes conditional effort such a robust and interesting phenomenon. These behaviors include foot-dragging, withdrawal, sabotage, and gossip and infighting. There is substantial overlap between some of these behaviors. I have listed them in an order that places more closely related behaviors in adjacent positions but there are areas of overlap between many of these specific behaviors. We will discuss each of these behavioral clusters in turn.

Foot-dragging Foot-dragging is differentiated from other types of conditional effort by its heavy reliance on delay, playing dumb, and sometimes rudeness. A waitress reported that if customers were rude or she did not anticipate a good tip, she would not bother to take their dirty plates away but would relax instead:

If they're nasty, you leave things and don't take them away early. Also, if you're in a bad section and people aren't tipping, you tend not to do any of your other duties either. You keep saying to yourself: "I am only getting paid $2.01 an hour, that's not enough to deal with this."

Selective foot-dragging can also be used to manipulate the work environment so that it more closely matches the workers' preferences. For instance, the waitress just quoted routinely failed to bus tables that had less desirable locations so that the hostess would be forced to seat new customers in more favorable locations (typically window seats), thus increasing the likelihood of good tips. Similar behaviors among nurses are reported by Strauss (1975): In response to doctors who countermanded nurses' orders or gave inconsistent instructions for patient therapy, nurses would seek to get these doctors' patients transferred off the floor.

Playing dumb is one of the most frequently used strategies to avoid unpleasant tasks in preference for other tasks or for non-work-related activities. A teacher reported it as a favored strategy in the school setting:

Certain teachers would act like they can't run the audio-visual equipment so they get somebody else to do it 'cuz they are just too lazy to do it. . . . Nobody wants to give a presentation in the faculty meetings about whatever is going on in their department or in their classroom — so they just act like they don't know about anything to get out of making a presentation. . . .

Withdrawal   Absenting oneself from work is the most drastic form of limiting work effort. It is, however, a common response, though generally in measured doses. In describing how his colleagues dealt with work they wanted to avoid, a public school teacher made the following observations: "they drink and they do drugs, including on the job. They rush home and turn on the TV at night and they play like they are not at work when they are actually here, busying themselves with gossip or sneak-

ing magazines into the classroom and reading them." Active hiding is also a commonly used option, according to a nursing home worker who spoke somewhat "tongue in cheek": "We got people who will actually bring their sleeping bag and camp out in the restroom, I think. Sometimes, it is hard to figure out a bathroom to go to. Some places out there they should almost charge rent." Finally, a chemical plant worker reported that workers intentionally hurt themselves to draw sick leave, including inflicting cuts on their hands and reporting back injuries that are hard to disprove. Avoidance of work appears to be most common where there is a breakdown in the normative social order. Such a breakdown is likely to occur where the "individual's anticipated future in the organization looks empty or grim" (Van Maanen 1977, 163). Commitment to the ongoing enterprise is so attenuated in such situations that workers simply distance themselves from it in whatever way possible (Kolchin 1978).

Absenting oneself from work is also associated with poor wages and/or limited flexibility on the job. As a production worker in a metal-fabricating plant reported: "They don't give me the money or the security or benefits or any of the things other jobs have. So I don't feel I owe them anything.". . .

Sabotage   Machine wrecking is a heady experience, chiefly reserved for those who have both limited attachment to the job and a great deal of resentment against the organization or their immediate boss (Genovese 1974; Scott 1985). Other types of conditional effort are more common on a daily basis because correctly functioning equipment is necessary for the efficient performance of required tasks. Workers therefore have an interest in protecting machinery and maintaining its performance. Defective machinery may limit workers' latitude to do those parts of the job that they enjoy doing or may otherwise limit their ability to control the conditions of their work. Breaking machinery is simply too abrupt and total an interruption for most situations. Where it does occur, it generally involves tension-reducing destruction of peripheral equipment. For instance, at a chemical plant, golf carts were used to access some of the outlying buildings. The plant had four of these carts, so if one was damaged there would generally be another one available. As a result, workers drove them hard, laid skid marks, and banged the carts into each other. This is intentional destruction of equipment, but it does not interfere with other options the worker may want to pursue in negotiating the details of the level and direction of their effort. Such seemingly pointless activities can have significant social and symbolic payoffs for workers as they engage in playful collective activity at the expense of management. Sabotage is fun. Sabotage of all types, including the relatively playful type just discussed, occurs most frequently where, as a hospital orderly stated simply but eloquently, "workers disrespect the job because the job disrespects them." In such settings, being destructive is one of the few ways in which one can find genuine pleasure in work.

Petty theft is also a common response to felt grievances. Theft of small items occurs at most workplaces and is an important mechanism through which grievances are vented. Some degree of retribution and equity can be achieved through a small theft. At a nursing home, this involved stealing serving-size boxes of breakfast cereal. In white-collar settings, it involved stealing paper, pencils, and envelopes for home use. In situations involving food preparation or serving, it involved eating food on the job beyond what was allowed. These activities are not identified as theft by their practitioners (Mars 1982). Rather, they are the particular fringe benefits offered by the job or they are faint and often symbolic compensation for inadequate salary or excessive work demands (Hollinger and Clark 1983). Such activities often involve a certain degree of collaborative effort with other workers, or, at a minimum, an implicit agreement to look the other way. As a result, petty theft can be an important mechanism through which group solidarity is heightened and management is defined as the outgroup. Mars and Nicod (1984) reported that maitre'ds in expensive restaurants differentiate between customers whose bills can be padded and those who cannot be so bilked and seat customers that can be cheated in a specific waiter's section as a reward for services rendered or in exchange for complimentary favors. Goffman (1961) included the theft of work materials as an important type of "secondary adjustment" to institutional norms and rules. Larger thefts occur, too, but here the motivations, while building on the issue of retribution, also include illicit gain on a more substantial scale. For example, an expensive generator was taken from a chemical plant. Here, the motivation included the desire to have the generator itself as well as a desire for retribution arising from workplace grievances. Dalton (1959) noted that the difference between such thefts and the "abuse of privilege" by those higher placed in the organizational structure is only a matter of scale (197).

Gossip and Infighting I have argued that work practices generally involve a negotiated consensus about the details of the effort bargain. Group mechanisms thus play a central role in developing norms about appropriate levels of effort. It was noted above that gossip about bosses is a key mechanism for defining the nature of the effort bargain. Such gossip operates through defining bosses as part of the outgroup and, conversely, workers as members of the in-group whose definitions of the effort bargain are given greater credibility (Hughes 1974).

Gossip is also commonly used within work groups to create ongoing interpretations of appropriate levels of effort for the members of the group. One particularly common line of discussion among respondents focused on the problem of lazy co-workers and the upholding of group standards. In settings with task interdependence, workers who dragged their feet caused other workers extra effort and were ostracized for their laziness. A computer accounts clerk reported that "people who do not do their share find that they have fewer friends at break time."

In settings with less task interdependence, poor workers are condemned not because they cause others extra effort but because they are getting paid the same but are putting in less effort than other workers. Even slight nuances of reduced effort can evoke strong negative responses. A substantial share of the material from an interview with an operator at a waste water treatment plant involved discussions of workers who abused sick leave policies by declaring fictitious injuries or exaggerating minor ones:

> We earn 8 hours of sick leave per month. Some people use up all their sick time and you wonder about the motivation involved. You never see anyone with 100 hours of sick time on the books get hurt. You always see the people who use all their vacation time, and now they're hurt. That happens time and time again. It seems like you can predict who is going to be hurt and when. For example, tomorrow is the first day of the month and we earn 8 hours. Tomorrow, there will be a tremendous number of sick people. It will be the people who have zero now and will have 8 tomorrow. You won't have a person who has 100 hours today be sick tomorrow.

Workers indicated that management often appeared to be aware of conflict among workers and relied on pressure from co-workers as the first line of control. A strong reliance on peer pressure has been noted in the analysis of work groups in Japan (Lillrank and Kano 1989). Observers of current industrial relations in the United States seem less attuned to this aspect of social control.

Gossip is pervasive at the workplace because it serves so many functions. These include providing an outlet for boredom and stress, social control and boundary maintenance, bragging and self-glorification, and disseminating information. Gossip is most pervasive in settings where there is strong competition between workers and in settings with a lack of leadership or with strong organizational ambiguities. Gossip is a key mechanism for developing and enforcing norms in such settings (Eder and Enke 1988; Moore 1962). Gossip also becomes an important means of disseminating information in situations of ambiguity (Kanter 1977, 97).

The social control functions of gossip are evidenced in the following comments by a teacher:

> I guess some teachers who just did everything were seen as brownnosers and as goody-two-shoes and they were often the victim or the butt of a lot of the social gossip. So, in a sense, they pay socially for being good 'cuz everybody is jealous, and so anytime there was any scuttlebutt possible to spread about them, it was out in force.

The importance of infighting and cliques in the social order of the factory has been known for some time (see Homans 1950), but it has not been widely developed in the literature on the workplace.

The social outlet functions of gossip were also evidenced by a teacher's comments:

> People are so bored and burnt out by these kids that they have to do something to just kill the time, so they'll go to the teachers' lounge during their planning period instead of doing lessons and get caught up on the latest and who hates who. Getting embroiled in conflicts somehow makes it more bearable because you have some sort of social agenda that you are working as opposed to just your damn work.

Gossip is also an important mechanism whereby workers can learn about working conditions and wages for other workers. A waitress reports that "I heard that people at [another restaurant] can make their whole rent in one weekend." Similarly, a worker at a retail store learned that his employer was filing Chapter 11 bankruptcy papers from a truck driver bringing supplies from the main warehouse. Gossip is not all fun, however. For many workers, it can also be a source of stress and is something to be avoided. A night shift worker reported that being out of the gossip circuit was one of the things he appreciated most about the night shift. For those seeking to minimize and de-emphasize their involvement in work, gossip may threaten their strategy of withdrawal and nonalignment.

Gossip and character assassination are the primary weapons in interpersonal conflicts at the workplace. Character assassination is popular because it inflicts damage on the target with minimal risk to the attacker. Taking more concrete actions to antagonize co-workers or disrupt their work runs the risk of being called to task by other workers or by management for intentionally disrupting production.

Beside character assassination, the most common tactic in infighting is to intentionally shift work to another person. A food service worker at a nursing home reported chronic attempts by the nursing and food service staffs to shift responsibilities to each other:

> Nursing doesn't like dietary. Dietary doesn't like nursing. Neither one likes housekeeping. Because there is a grey area of responsibility between them. Nursing doesn't want to bother feeding a particularly nasty resident, even though the person should be in their room because they are a distraction and a nuisance and a burden on other people in the dining room— other residents and their families. They will continually try to pawn off that person on the dining room staff. It's not good for the business to have someone who is extremely aggressive, is vulgar, has no control over their bowels or bladder in the dining room.

Outright interference with others' work is rare but not unknown. A waitress reported the following skirmish: "Sometimes other waitresses have even been known to take their tip from the table and then they'll just leave, and, when the customers leave, you're left with clearing off their tables. You don't mind helping but you don't like being taken advantage of."

Infighting may also involve snitching on co-workers to management. A telephone operator reported that "a certain group of employees think they can get ahead by reporting other employees." It is ugly, but it happens. Workers also sometimes try to make other workers appear as fools by pointing out their weaknesses in awkward situations.

Discussion and Conclusions

As Marxists have argued, the struggle for control of work is a central activity at the workplace. However, this struggle rarely takes place as a head-on clash between management and labor. Instead, the conflict is waged by individual workers and small groups of workers against managers and supervisors and also against other workers over the details of the effort bargain. These struggles are often symbolic in nature with gossip and character assassination playing central roles. . . .

References

Argyle, M. 1972. *The Social Psychology of Work.* London: Penguin Books.

Becker, H. S., B. Geer, and E. C. Hughes. 1968. *Making the Grade: The Academic Side of College Life.* New York: Wiley.

Becker, H. S., B. Geer, E. C. Hughes, and A. L. Strauss. 1961. *Boys in White.* Chicago: University of Chicago Press.

Beynon, H. 1973. *Working for Ford.* London: Penguin Books.

Braverman, H. 1974. *Labor and Monopoly Capital.* New York: Monthly Review Press.

Burawoy, M. 1979. *Manufacturing Consent*. Chicago: University of Chicago Press.

Crawford, S. 1989. *Technical Workers in an Advanced Society*. New York: Cambridge University Press.

Crozier, M. 1964. *The Bureaucratic Phenomena*. Chicago: University of Chicago Press.

Dalton, M. 1959. *Men Who Manage*. New York: Wiley.

Ditton, J. 1976. "Moral Horror Versus Folk Terror: Output Restriction, Class, and the Social Organization of Exploitation." *Sociological Review* 24: 519–544.

Eder, D., and J. Enke. 1988. "Gossip as a Means for Transmitting and Developing Social Structure." Paper presented at the annual meetings of the American Sociological Society, Atlanta, GA, August.

Edwards, P. K., and H. Scullion. 1982. *The Social Organization of Industrial Conflict*. Oxford: Basil Blackwell.

Edwards, R. C. 1979. *Contested Terrain*. New York: Basic Books.

Etzioni, A. 1971. *A Comparative Analysis of Complex Organizations*. New York: Free Press.

Fine, G. A. 1984. "Negotiated Orders and Organizational Cultures." Pp. 239–262 in R. H. Turner and J. F. Short, Jr. (eds.), *The Annual Review of Sociology*, Vol. 10. Palo Alto, CA: Annual Reviews.

Gardner, B. B., and W. F. Whyte. 1946. "Methods for the Study of Human Relations in Industry." *American Sociological Review* 11: 506–511.

Genovese, E. D. 1974. *Roll, Jordon, Roll: The World the Slaves Made*. New York: Pantheon Books.

Glaser, B. G., and A. L. Strauss. 1967. *The Discovery of Grounded Theory*. Chicago: Aldine.

Goffman, E. 1961. *Asylums*. Garden City, NY: Anchor.

Halle, D. 1984. *America's Working Man*. Chicago: University of Chicago Press.

Hollinger, R. C., and J. P. Clark. 1983. *Theft by Employees*. Lexington, MA: Heath.

Homans, G. 1950. *The Human Group*. New York: Harcourt, Brace & World.

Hughes, E. C. 1958. *Men and Their Work*. Glencoe, IL: Free Press.

———. 1974. "Comments on 'Honor in Dirty Work'" *Work and Occupations* 1: 284–287.

Jermier, J. M. 1988. "Sabotage at Work." Pp. 101–135 in Nancy DiTomaso (ed.), *Research in the Sociology of Organizations*, Vol. 6. Greenwich, CT: JAI.

Juravich, T. 1985. *Chaos on the Shop Floor*. Philadelphia: Temple University Press.

Kanter, R. M. 1977. *Men and Women of the Corporation*. New York: Basic Books.

Kolchin, P. 1978. "The Process of Confrontation: Patterns of Resistance to Bondage in Nineteenth-Century Russia and the United States." *Journal of Social History* 11: 457–490.

Lillrank, P., and N. Kano. 1989. *Continuous Improvement: Quality Control Circles in Japanese Industry*. Ann Arbor: Center for Japanese Studies, University of Michigan.

Lipsky, M. 1981. *Street-Level Bureaucracy*. New York: Russell Sage.

Mars, G. 1982. *Cheats at Work*. London: Unwin.

Mars, G., and M. Nicod. 1984. *The World of Waiters*. London: Allen & Unwin.

Mayo, E. 1945. *The Social Problems of an Industrial Civilization*. Cambridge, MA: Harvard University Press.

McCall, G. J., and J. L. Simmons (eds.). 1969. *Issues in Participant Observation*. New York: Random House.

Montgomery, D. 1979. *Workers' Control in America*. Cambridge: Cambridge University Press.

Moore, W. 1962. *The Conduct of the Corporation*. New York: Random House.

Organ, D. W. 1988. A restatement of the satisfaction-performance hypothesis. *Journal of Management* 14: 547–557.

Parker, M. 1985. *Inside the Circle: A Union Guide to QWL*. Boston: South End Press.

Poulantzas, N. 1975. *Classes in Contemporary Capitalism*. London: New Left Books.

Reinarman, C. 1987. *American States of Mind: Political Beliefs and Behavior Among Private and Public Workers*. New Haven, CT: Yale University Press.

Rothschild, J., and R. Russell. 1986. "Alternatives to Bureaucracy: Democratic Participation in the Economy." Pp. 307–328 in R. H. Turner and J. F. Short, Jr. (eds.), *The Annual Review of Sociology*, Vol. 12. Palo Alto, CA: Annual Reviews.

Roy, D. 1960. "'Banana time': Job Satisfaction and Informal Interaction." *Human Organization* 18: 158–168.

Scott, J. C. 1985. *Weapons of the Weak: Everyday Forms of Peasant Resistance*. New Haven, CT: Yale University Press.

Shaiken, H. 1984. *Work Transformed*. New York: Holt, Rinehart & Winston.

Snow, D. A., and L. Anderson. 1987. "Identity Work Among the Homeless: The Verbal Construction and Avowal of Personal Identities." *American Journal of Sociology* 92: 1336–1371.

Strauss, A. L. 1975. *Professions, Work and Careers*. New Brunswick, NJ: Transaction Books.

Van Maanen, J. 1977. *Organizational Careers*. London: Wiley.

Willis, P. 1977. *Learning to Labor: How Working Class Kids Get Working Class Jobs*. New York: Columbia University Press.

Wood, S. (ed.). 1982. *The Degradation of Work?* London: Hutchinson.

Questions

1. What are some examples of ways in which workers can impose their own definition of the situation on their jobs (even when this definition of the situation is contrary to the employer's definition)?

2. Among some of the less enthusiastically compliant workers that Hodson interviewed were schoolteachers. Do you recall seeing any evidence that teachers are engaging in such behaviors?

3. Assume that you are the manager of some business that employs other people. Given what you have learned from this article, what two steps could you take to ensure that you receive what Hodson calls "enthusiastic compliance"?

4. Although Hodson focused specifically on workers, much of what he says might be generalizable to other situations in which there is a hierarchical power structure. For example, what Hodson found to be true of workers with respect to their employers might also apply to children with respect to their parents or to students with respect to teachers. Using either the parent–child or teacher–student example, discuss which tactics, similar to those used by workers, might come into play. (You might entitle your analysis "Compliance and Autonomy in the Home" or "Compliance and Autonomy in the Classroom.")

·24·

The Normality of Crime

Émile Durkheim

The following excerpt is from Émile Durkheim's *Rules of the Sociological Method.* The excerpt is brief but (like much of what people wrote in the nineteenth century) fairly complex. Durkheim begins by pointing out that crime—or acts that offend the collective conscience—is normal in every society. In other words, every society can expect some of its members occasionally to do things that offend that society's shared values and beliefs. According to Durkheim's analysis, the only way to completely do away with murder, for example, would be for every single person in the society to develop intense respect for all other members. If that happened, Durkheim points out, then the crime of murder might disappear, but previously minor offenses would then seem more serious. In a society of saints, he says, the crime of murder would not be a problem, but perhaps the "crime" of insulting others would be.

Here we are, then, in the presence of a conclusion in appearance quite paradoxical. Let us make no mistake. To classify crime among the phenomena of normal sociology is not to say merely that it is an inevitable, although regrettable phenomenon, due to the incorrigible wickedness of men; it is to affirm that it is a factor in public health, an integral part of all healthy societies. This result is, at first glance, surprising enough to have puzzled even ourselves for a long time. Once this first surprise has been overcome, however, it is not difficult to find reasons explaining this normality and at the same time confirming it.

In the first place crime is normal because a society exempt from it is utterly impossible. Crime, we have shown elsewhere, consists of an act that offends certain very strong collective sentiments. In a society in which criminal acts are no longer committed, the sentiments they offend would have to be found without exception in all individual consciousnesses, and they must be found to exist with the same degree as sentiments contrary to them. Assum-

ing that this condition could actually be realized, crime would not thereby disappear; it would only change its form, for the very cause which would thus dry up the sources of criminality would immediately open up new ones.

Indeed, for the collective sentiments which are protected by the penal law[1] of a people at a specific moment of its history to take possession of the public conscience or for them to acquire a stronger hold where they have an insufficient grip, they must acquire an intensity greater than that which they had hitherto had. The community as a whole must experience them more vividly, for it can acquire from no other source the greater force necessary to control these individuals who formerly were the most refractory. For murderers to disappear, the horror of bloodshed must become greater in those social strata from which murderers are recruited; but, first it must become greater throughout the entire society. Moreover, the very absence of crime would directly

---

[1]Penal law is criminal law.

contribute to produce this horror; because any sentiment seems much more respectable when it is always and uniformly respected.

One easily overlooks the consideration that these strong states of the common consciousness cannot be thus reinforced without reinforcing at the same time the more feeble states, whose violation previously gave birth to mere infraction of convention—since the weaker ones are only the prolongation, the attenuated form, of the stronger. Thus robbery and simple bad taste injure the same single altruistic sentiment, the respect for that which is another's. However, this same sentiment is less grievously offended by bad taste than by robbery; and since, in addition, the average consciousness has not sufficient intensity to react keenly to the bad taste, it is treated with greater tolerance. That is why the person guilty of bad taste is merely blamed, whereas the thief is punished. But, if this sentiment grows stronger, to the point of silencing in all consciousnesses the inclination which disposes man to steal, he will become more sensitive to the offenses which, until then, touched him but lightly. He will react against them, then, with more energy; they will be the object of greater oppro-

brium, which will transform certain of them from the simple moral faults that they were and give them the quality of crimes. For example, improper contracts, or contracts improperly executed, which only incur public blame or civil damages, will become offenses in law.

Imagine a society of saints, a perfect cloister of exemplary individuals. Crimes, properly so called, will there be unknown; but faults which appear venial to the layman will create there the same scandal that the ordinary offense does in ordinary consciousnesses. If, then, this society has the power to judge and punish, it will define these acts as criminal and will treat them as such. For the same reason, the perfect and upright man judges his smallest failings with a severity that the majority reserve for acts more truly in the nature of an offense. Formerly, acts of violence against persons were more frequent than they are today, because respect for individual dignity was less strong. As this has increased, these crimes have become more rare; and also, many acts violating this sentiment have been introduced into the penal law which were not included there in primitive times. . . .

Questions:

1. Durkheim argues that crime is "normal." What does he mean by this?

2. Does Durkheim believe that it is either possible or desirable for a society to exist in which there is no crime? Why or why not?

·25·

The Saints and the Roughnecks

William J. Chambliss

Robert K. Merton was inspired by the "Thomas theorem"—the notion (from W. I. Thomas) that if people "define situations as real, they are real in their consequences." Merton observed that Thomas was pointing out that people "not only respond to the objective features of a situation" but to the "meaning this situation has for them." One implication of the Thomas theorem was something that Merton called the "self-fulfilling prophecy": "The self-fulfilling prophecy is, in the beginning, a *false* definition of the situation evoking a new behavior which makes the originally false conception come *true*." For example, if a rumor circulates that the town bank is about to fail, that rumor, even if initially false, can come true simply because it's there. That is, the rumor may worry people sufficiently that they hurry to the bank and withdraw their funds. Ultimately, the bank *does* fail. Then, the rumormonger can say "See, I told you the bank was going to fail."[1]

The following reading, by William Chambliss, explores some of the ways in which public definitions of a situation come into being with respect to two small groups of high school kids. As you read this article, look for examples of how the ways in which people define the situation have real consequences for the people involved.

Eight promising young men—children of good, stable, white upper-middle-class families, active in school affairs, good pre-college students—were some of the most delinquent boys at Hanibal High School. While community residents and parents knew that these boys occasionally sowed a few wild oats, they were totally unaware that sowing wild oats completely occupied the daily routine of these young men. The Saints were constantly occupied with truancy, drinking, wild driving, petty theft and vandalism. Yet not one was officially arrested for any misdeed during the two years I observed them.

This record was particularly surprising in light of my observations during the same two years of another gang of Hanibal High School students, six lower-class white boys known as the Roughnecks. The Roughnecks were constantly in trouble with police and community even though their rate of delinquency was about equal with that of the Saints. What was the cause of this disparity? the result? The following consideration of the activities, social class and community perceptions of both gangs may provide some answers.

The Saints from Monday to Friday

The Saints' principal daily concern was with getting out of school as early as possible. The

[1]From Robert Merton, *Social Theory and Social Structure* (New York: Free Press, 1968), p. 477. —Ed.

223

boys managed to get out of school with minimum danger that they would be accused of playing hookey through an elaborate procedure for obtaining "legitimate" release from class. The most common procedure was for one boy to obtain the release of another by fabricating a meeting of some committee, program or recognized club. Charles might raise his hand in his 9:00 chemistry class and asked to be excused—a euphemism for going to the bathroom. Charles would go to Ed's math class and inform the teacher that Ed was needed for a 9:30 rehearsal of the drama club play. The math teacher would recognize Ed and Charles as "good students" involved in numerous school activities and would permit Ed to leave at 9:30. Charles would return to his class, and Ed would go to Tom's English class to obtain his release. Tom would engineer Charles' escape. The strategy would continue until as many of the Saints as possible were freed. After a stealthy trip to the car (which had been parked in a strategic spot), the boys were off for a day of fun.

Over the two years I observed the Saints, this pattern was repeated nearly every day. There were variations on the theme, but in one form or another, the boys used this procedure for getting out of class and then off the school grounds. Rarely did all eight of the Saints manage to leave school at the same time. The average number avoiding school on the days I observed them was five.

Having escaped from the concrete corridors the boys usually went either to a pool hall on the other (lower-class) side of town or to a cafe in the suburbs. Both places were out of the way of people the boys were likely to know (family or school officials), and both provided a source of entertainment. The pool hall entertainment was the generally rough atmosphere, the occasional hustler, the sometimes drunk proprietor and, of course, the game of pool. The cafe's entertainment was provided by the owner. The boys would "accidentally" knock a glass on the floor or spill cola on the counter—not all the time, but enough to be sporting. They would also bend spoons, put salt in sugar bowls and generally tease whoever was working in the cafe. The owner had opened the cafe recently and was dependent on the boys' business which was, in fact, substantial since between the horsing around and the teasing they bought food and drinks.

The Saints on Weekends

On weekends the automobile was even more critical than during the week, for on weekends the Saints went to Big Town—a large city with a population of over a million 25 miles from Hanibal. Every Friday and Saturday night most of the Saints would meet between 8:00 and 8:30 and would go into Big Town. Big Town activities included drinking heavily in taverns or nightclubs, driving drunkenly through the streets, and committing acts of vandalism and playing pranks.

By midnight on Fridays and Saturdays the Saints were usually thoroughly high, and one or two of them were often so drunk they had to be carried to the cars. Then the boys drove around town, calling obscenities to women and girls; occasionally trying (unsuccessfully so far as I could tell) to pick girls up; and driving recklessly through red lights and at high speeds with their lights out. Occasionally they played "chicken." One boy would climb out the back window of the car and across the roof to the driver's side of the car while the car was moving at high speed (between 40 and 50 miles an hour); then the driver would move over and the boy who had just crawled across the car roof would take the driver's seat.

Searching for "fair game" for a prank was the boys' principal activity after they left the tavern. The boys would drive alongside a foot patrolman and ask directions to some street. If the policeman leaned on the car in the course of answering the question, the driver would speed away, causing him to lose his balance. The Saints were careful to play this prank only in an area where they were not going to spend much time and where they could quickly disappear around a corner to avoid having their license plate number taken.

Construction sites and road repair areas were the special province of the Saints' mischief. A soon-to-be-repaired hole in the road inevitably invited the Saints to remove lanterns and wooden barricades and put them in the car, leaving the hole unprotected. The boys would find a safe vantage point and wait for an unsuspecting motorist to drive into the hole. Often, though not always, the boys would go up to the motorist and commiserate with him about the dreadful way the city protected its citizenry.

Leaving the scene of the open hole and the motorist, the boys would then go searching for an appropriate place to erect the stolen barricade. An "appropriate place" was often a spot on a highway near a curve in the road where the barricade would not be seen by an oncoming motorist. The boys would wait to watch an unsuspecting motorist attempt to stop and (usually) crash into the wooden barricade. With saintly bearing the boys might offer help and understanding.

A stolen lantern might well find its way onto the back of a police car or hang from a street lamp. Once a lantern served as a prop for a reenactment of the "midnight ride of Paul Revere" until the "play," which was taking place at 2:00 AM in the center of a main street of Big Town, was interrupted by a police car several blocks away. The boys ran, leaving the lanterns on the street, and managed to avoid being apprehended.

Abandoned houses, especially if they were located in out-of-the-way places, were fair game for destruction and spontaneous vandalism. The boys would break windows, remove furniture to the yard and tear it apart,

urinate on the walls and scrawl obscenities inside.

Through all the pranks, drinking and reckless driving the boys managed miraculously to avoid being stopped by police. Only twice in two years was I aware that they had been stopped by a Big City policeman. Once was for speeding (which they did every time they drove whether they were drunk or sober), and the driver managed to convince the policeman that it was simply an error. The second time they were stopped they had just left a nightclub and were walking through an alley. Aaron stopped to urinate and the boys began making obscene remarks. A foot patrolman came into the alley, lectured the boys and sent them home. Before the boys got to the car one began talking in a loud voice again. The policeman, who had followed them down the alley, arrested this boy for disturbing the peace and took him to the police station where the other Saints gathered. After paying a $5.00 fine, and with the assurance that there would be no permanent record of the arrest, the boy was released.

The boys had a spirit of frivolity and fun about their escapades. They did not view what they were engaged in as "delinquency," though it surely was by any reasonable definition of that word. They simply viewed themselves as having a little fun and who, they would ask, was really hurt by it? The answer had to be no one, although this fact remains one of the most difficult things to explain about the gang's behavior. Unlikely though it seems, in two years of drinking, driving, carousing and vandalism no one was seriously injured as a result of the Saints' activities.

The Saints in School

The Saints were highly successful in school. The average grade for the group was "B," with two of the boys having close to a straight "A" average. Almost all of the boys were popular and many of them held offices in the school. One of the boys was vice-president of the student body one year. Six of the boys played on athletic teams.

At the end of their senior year, the student body selected ten seniors for special recognition as the "school wheels"; four of the ten were Saints. Teachers and school officials saw no problem with any of these boys and anticipated that they would all "make something of themselves."

How the boys managed to maintain this impression is surprising in view of their actual behavior while in school. Their technique for covering truancy was so successful that teachers did not even realize that the boys were absent from school much of the time. Occasionally, of course, the system would backfire and then the boy was on his own. A boy who was caught would be most contrite, would plead guilty and ask for mercy. He inevitably got the mercy he sought.

Cheating on examinations was rampant, even to the point of orally communicating answers to exams as well as looking at one another's papers. Since none of the group studied, and since they were primarily dependent on one another for help, it is surprising that grades were so high. Teachers contributed to the deception in their admitted inclination to give these boys (and presumably others like them) the benefit of the doubt. When asked how the boys did in school, and when pressed on specific examinations, teachers might admit that they were disappointed in John's performance, but would quickly add that they "knew that he was capable of doing better," so John was given a higher grade than he had actually earned. How often this happened is impossible to know. During the time that I observed the group, I never saw any of the boys take homework home. Teachers may have been "understanding" very regularly.

One exception to the gang's generally good performance was Jerry, who had a "C" average in his junior year, experienced disaster the next year and failed to graduate. Jerry had always been a little more nonchalant than the others about the liberties he took in school. Rather than wait for someone to come get him from class, he would offer his own excuse and leave. Although he probably did not miss any more classes than most of the others in the group, he did not take the requisite pains to cover his absences. Jerry was the only Saint whom I ever heard talk back to a teacher. Although teachers often called him a "cut up" or a "smart kid," they never referred to him as a troublemaker or as a kid headed for trouble. It seems likely, then, that Jerry's failure his senior year and his mediocre performance his junior year were consequences of his not playing the game the proper way (possibly because he was disturbed by his parents' divorce). His teachers regarded him as "immature" and not quite ready to get out of high school.

The Police and the Saints

The local police saw the Saints as good boys who were among the leaders of the youth in the community. Rarely, the boys might be stopped in town for speeding or for running a stop sign. When this happened the boys were always polite, contrite and pled for mercy. As in school, they received the mercy they asked for. None ever received a ticket or was taken into the precinct by the local police.

The situation in Big City, where the boys engaged in most of their delinquency, was only slightly different. The police there did not know the boys at all, although occasionally the boys were stopped by a patrolman. Once they were caught taking a lantern from a construction site. Another time they were stopped for running a stop sign, and on several occasions they were stopped for speeding. Their behavior was as before: contrite, polite and penitent. The urban police, like the local police, accepted their demeanor as sincere. More important, the urban police were convinced that these were good boys just out for a lark.

The Roughnecks

Hanibal townspeople never perceived the Saints' high level of delinquency. The Saints were good boys who just went in for an occasional prank. After all, they were well dressed, well mannered and had nice cars. The Roughnecks were a different story. Although the two gangs of boys were the same age, and both groups engaged in an equal amount of wild-oat sowing, everyone agreed that the not-so-well-dressed, not-so-well-mannered, not-so-rich boys were heading for trouble. Townspeople would say, "You can see the gang members at the drugstore, night after night, leaning against the storefront (sometimes drunk) or slouching around inside buying cokes, reading magazines, and probably stealing old Mr. Wall blind. When they are outside and girls walk by, even respectable girls, these boys make suggestive remarks. Sometimes their remarks are downright lewd."

From the community's viewpoint, the real indication that these kids were in for trouble was that they were constantly involved with the police. Some of them had been picked up for stealing, mostly small stuff, of course, "but still it's stealing small stuff that leads to big time crimes." "Too bad," people said. "Too bad that these boys couldn't behave like the other kids in town; stay out of trouble, be polite to adults, and look to their future."

The community's impression of the degree to which this group of six boys (ranging in age from 16 to 19) engaged in delinquency was somewhat distorted. In some ways the gang was more delinquent than the community thought; in other ways they were less.

The fighting activities of the group were fairly readily and accurately perceived by almost everyone. At least once a month, the boys would get into some sort of fight, although most fights were scraps between members of the group or involved only one member of the group and some peripheral hanger-on. Only three times in the period of observation did the group fight together: once against a gang from across town, once against two blacks and once against a group of boys from another school. For the first two fights the group went out "looking for trouble" — and they found it both times. The third fight followed a football game and began spontaneously with an argument on the football field between one of the Roughnecks and a member of the opposition's football team.

Jack had a particular propensity for fighting and was involved in most of the brawls. He was a prime mover of the escalation of arguments into fights.

More serious than fighting, had the community been aware of it, was theft. Although almost everyone was aware that the boys occasionally stole things, they did not realize the extent of the activity. Petty stealing was a frequent event for the Roughnecks. Sometimes they stole as a group and coordinated their efforts; other times they stole in pairs. Rarely did they steal alone.

The thefts ranged from very small things like paperback books, comics and ballpoint pens to expensive items like watches. The nature of the thefts varied from time to time. The gang would go through a period of systematically shoplifting items from automobiles or school lockers. Types of thievery varied with the whim of the gang. Some forms of thievery were more profitable than others, but all thefts were for profit, not just thrills.

Roughnecks siphoned gasoline from cars as often as they had access to an automobile, which was not very often. Unlike the Saints, who owned their own cars, the Roughnecks would have to borrow their parents' cars, an event which occurred only eight or nine times a year. The boys claimed to have stolen cars for joy rides from time to time.

Ron committed the most serious of the group's offenses. With an unidentified associate the boy attempted to burglarize a gasoline station. Although this station had been robbed twice previously in the same month, Ron denied any involvement in either of the other thefts. When Ron and his accomplice approached the station, the owner was hiding in the bushes beside the station. He fired both barrels of a double-barreled shotgun at the boys. Ron was severely injured; the other boy ran away and was never caught. Though he remained in critical condition for several months, Ron finally recovered and served six months of the following year in reform school. Upon release from reform school, Ron was put back a grade in school, and began running around with a different gang of boys. The Roughnecks considered the new gang less delinquent than themselves, and during the following year Ron had no more trouble with the police.

The Roughnecks, then, engaged mainly in three types of delinquency: theft, drinking and fighting. Although community members perceived that this gang of kids was delinquent, they mistakenly believed that their illegal activities were primarily drinking, fighting and being a nuisance to passersby. Drinking was limited among the gang members, although it did occur, and theft was much more prevalent than anyone realized.

Drinking would doubtless have been more prevalent had the boys had ready access to liquor. Since they rarely had automobiles at their disposal, they could not travel very far, and the bars in town would not serve them. Most of the boys had little money, and this, too, inhibited their purchase of alcohol. Their major source of liquor was a local drunk who would buy them a fifth if they would give him enough extra to buy himself a pint of whiskey or a bottle of wine.

The community's perception of drinking as prevalent stemmed from the fact that it was the most obvious delinquency the boys engaged in. When one of the boys had been drinking, even a casual observer seeing him on the corner would suspect that he was high.

There was a high level of mutual distrust and dislike between the Roughnecks and the police. The boys felt very strongly that the police were unfair and corrupt. Some evidence existed that the boys were correct in their perception.

The main source of the boys' dislike for the police undoubtedly stemmed from the fact that the police would sporadically harass the group. From the standpoint of the boys, these acts of occasional enforcement of the law were whimsical and uncalled for. It made no sense to them, for example, that the police would come to the corner occasionally and threaten them with arrest for loitering when the night before the boys had been out siphoning gasoline from cars and the police had been nowhere in sight. To the boys, the police were stupid on the one hand, for not being where they should have been and catching the boys in a serious offense, and unfair on the other hand, for trumping up "loitering" charges against them.

From the viewpoint of the police, the situation was quite different. They knew, with all the confidence necessary to be a policeman, that these boys were engaged in criminal activities. They knew this partly from occasionally catching them, mostly from circumstantial evidence ("the boys were around when those tires were slashed"), and partly because the police shared the view of the community in general that this was a bad bunch of boys. The best the police could hope to do was to be sensitive to the fact that these boys were engaged in illegal acts and arrest them whenever there was some evidence that they had been involved. Whether or not the boys had in fact committed a particular act in a particular way was not especially important. The police had a broader view: their job was to stamp out these kids' crimes; the tactics were not as important as the end result.

Over the period that the group was under observation, each member was arrested at least once. Several of the boys were arrested a number of times and spent at least one night in jail. While most were never taken to court, two of the boys were sentenced to six months' incarceration in boys' schools.

The Roughnecks in School

The Roughnecks' behavior in school was not particularly disruptive. During school hours they did not all hang around together, but tended instead to spend most of their time with one or two other members of the gang who were their special buddies. Although every member of the gang attempted to avoid school as much as possible, they were not particularly successful and most of them attended school with surprising regularity. They considered school a burden—something to be gotten through with a minimum of conflict. If they were "bugged" by a particular teacher, it could lead to trouble. One of the boys, Al, once threatened to beat up a teacher and, according to the other boys, the teacher hid under a desk to escape him.

Teachers saw the boys the way the general community did, as heading for trouble, as being uninterested in making something of themselves. Some were also seen as being incapable of meeting the academic standards of the school. Most of the teachers expressed concern for this group of boys and were willing to pass them despite poor performance, in the belief that failing them would only aggravate the problem.

The group of boys had a grade point average just slightly above "C". No one in the group failed either grade, and no one had bet-ter than a "C" average. They were consistent in their achievement or, at least, the teachers were consistent in their perception of the boys' achievement.

Two of the boys were good football players. Herb was acknowledged to be the best player in the school and Jack was almost as good. Both boys were criticized for their failure to abide by training rules, for refusing to come to practice as often as they should, and for not playing their best during practice. What they lacked in sportsmanship they made up for in skill, apparently, and played every game no matter how poorly they had performed in practice or how many practice sessions they had missed.

Two Questions

Why did the community, the school and the police react to the Saints as though they were good, upstanding, nondelinquent youths with bright futures but to the Roughnecks as though they were tough, young criminals who were headed for trouble? Why did the Roughnecks and the Saints in fact have quite different careers after high school—careers which, by and large, lived up to the expectations of the community?

The most obvious explanation for the differences in the community's and law enforcement agencies' reactions to the two gangs is that one group of boys was "more delinquent" than the other. Which group *was* more delinquent? The answer to this question will determine in part how we explain the differential responses to these groups by the members of the community and, particularly, by law enforcement and school officials.

In sheer number of illegal acts, the Saints were the more delinquent. They were truant from school for at least part of the day almost every day of the week. In addition, their drinking and vandalism occurred with surprising regularity. The Roughnecks, in contrast, engaged sporadically in delinquent episodes. While these episodes were frequent, they certainly did not occur on a daily or even a weekly basis.

The difference in frequency of offenses was probably caused by the Roughnecks' inability to obtain liquor and to manipulate legitimate excuses from school. Since the Roughnecks had less money than the Saints, and teachers carefully supervised their school activities, the Roughnecks' hearts may have been as black as the Saints', but their misdeeds were not nearly as frequent.

There are really no clear-cut criteria by which to measure qualitative differences in antisocial behavior. The most important dimension of the difference is generally referred to as the "seriousness" of the offenses.

If seriousness encompasses the relative economic costs of delinquent acts, then some assessment can be made. The Roughnecks probably stole an average of about $5.00 worth of goods a week. Some weeks the figure was considerably higher, but these times must be balanced against long periods when almost nothing was stolen.

The Saints were more continuously engaged in delinquency but their acts were not for the most part costly to property. Only their vandalism and occasional theft of gasoline would so qualify. Perhaps once or twice a month they would siphon a tankful of gas. The other costly items were street signs, construction lanterns and the like. All of these acts combined probably did not quite average $5.00 a week, partly because much of the stolen equipment was abandoned and presumably could be recovered. The difference in cost of stolen property between the two groups was trivial, but the Roughnecks probably had a slightly more expensive set of activities than did the Saints.

Another meaning of seriousness is the potential threat of physical harm to members of the community and to the boys themselves. The Roughnecks were more prone to physical violence; they not only welcomed an opportunity to fight; they went seeking it. In addition, they fought among themselves frequently. Although the fighting never included deadly weapons, it was still a menace, however minor, to the physical safety of those involved.

The Saints never fought. They avoided physical conflict both inside and outside the group. At the same time, though, the Saints frequently endangered their own and other people's lives. They did so almost every time they drove a car, especially if they had been drinking. Sober, their driving was risky; under the influence of alcohol it was horrendous. In addition, the Saints endangered the lives of others with their pranks. Street excavations left unmarked were a very serious hazard.

Evaluating the relative seriousness of the two gangs' activities is difficult. The community reacted as though the behavior of the Roughnecks was a problem, and they reacted as though the behavior of the Saints was not. But the members of the community were ignorant of the array of delinquent acts that characterized the Saints' behavior. Although concerned citizens were unaware of much of the Roughnecks' behavior as well, they were much better informed about the Roughnecks' involvement in delinquency than they were about the Saints'.

Visibility

Differential treatment of the two gangs results in part because one gang was infinitely more visible than the other. This differential visibility was a direct function of the economic standing of the families. The Saints had access to automobiles and were able to remove themselves from the sight of the community. In as routine a decision as to where to go to have a milkshake after school, the Saints stayed away from the mainstream of community life. Lacking transportation, the Roughnecks could not make it to the edge of town. The center of town was the only practical place for them to meet since their homes were scattered throughout the town and any noncentral meeting place put an undue hardship on some members. Through necessity the Roughnecks congregated in a crowded area where everyone in the community passed frequently, including teachers and law enforcement officers. They could easily see the Roughnecks hanging around the drugstore.

The Roughnecks, of course, made themselves even more visible by making remarks to passersby and by occasionally getting into fights on the corner. Meanwhile, just as regularly, the Saints were either at the cafe on one edge of town or in the pool hall at the other edge of town. Without any particular realization that they were making themselves inconspicuous, the Saints were able to hide their time-wasting. Not only were they removed from the mainstream of traffic, but they were almost always inside a building.

On their escapades the Saints were also relatively invisible, since they left Hanibal and travelled to Big City. Here, too, they were mobile, roaming the city, rarely going to the same area twice.

Demeanor

To the notion of visibility must be added the difference in the responses of group members to outside intervention with their activities. If one of the Saints was confronted with an accusing policeman, even if he felt he was truly innocent of a wrongdoing, his demeanor was apologetic and penitent. A Roughneck's attitude was almost the polar opposite. When confronted with a threatening adult authority, even one who tried to be pleasant, the Roughneck's hostility and disdain were clearly observable. Sometimes he might attempt to put up a veneer of respect, but it was thin and was not accepted as sincere by the authority.

School was no different from the community at large. The Saints could manipulate the system by feigning compliance with the school norms. The availability of cars at school meant that once free from the immediate sight of the teacher, the boys could disappear rapidly. And this escape was well enough planned that no administrator or teacher was nearby when the boys left. A Roughneck who wished to escape for a few hours was in a bind. If it were possible to get free from class, downtown was still a mile away, and even if he arrived there, he was still very visible. Truancy for the Roughnecks meant almost certain detection, while the Saints enjoyed almost complete immunity from sanctions.

Bias

Community members were not aware of the transgressions of the Saints. Even if the Saints had been less discreet, their favorite delinquencies would have been perceived as less serious than those of the Roughnecks.

In the eyes of the police and school officials, a boy who drinks in an alley and stands intoxicated on the street corner is committing a more serious offense than is a boy who drinks to inebriation in a nightclub or a tavern and drives around afterwards in a car. Similarly, a boy who steals a wallet from a store will be viewed as having committed a more serious offense than a boy who steals a lantern from a construction site.

Perceptual bias also operates with respect to the demeanor of the boys in the two groups when they are confronted by adults. It is not simply that adults dislike the posture affected by boys of the Roughneck ilk; more important

232 WILLIAM J. CHAMBLISS

is the conviction that the posture adopted by the Roughnecks is an indication of their devotion and commitment to deviance as a way of life. The posture becomes a cue, just as the type of the offense is a cue, to the degree to which the known transgressions are indicators of the youths' potential for other problems.

Visibility, demeanor and bias are surface variables which explain the day-to-day operations of the police. Why do these surface variables operate as they do? Why did the police choose to disregard the Saints' delinquencies while breathing down the backs of the Roughnecks?

The answer lies in the class structure of American society and the control of legal institutions by those at the top of the class structure. Obviously, no representative of the upper class drew up the operational chart for the police which led them to look in the ghettoes and on streetcorners—which led them to see the demeanor of lower-class youth as troublesome and that of upper-middle-class youth as tolerable. Rather, the procedures simply developed from experience—experience with irate and influential upper-middle-class parents insisting that their son's vandalism was simply a prank and his drunkenness only a momentary "sowing of wild oats"—experience with cooperative or indifferent, powerless, lower-class parents who acquiesced to the law's definition of their son's behavior.

Adult Careers of the Saints and the Roughnecks

The community's confidence in the potential of the Saints and the Roughnecks apparently was justified. If anything, the community members underestimated the degree to which these youngsters would turn out "good" or "bad."

Seven of the eight members of the Saints went on to college immediately after high school. Five of the boys graduated from college in four years. The sixth one finished college after two years in the army, and the seventh spent fours years in the air force before returning to college and receiving a B.A. degree. Of these seven college graduates, three went on for advanced degrees. One finished law school and is now active in state politics, one finished medical school and is practicing near Hanibal, and one boy is now working for a Ph.D. The other four college graduates entered submanagerial, managerial or executive training positions with larger firms.

The only Saint who did not complete college was Jerry. Jerry had failed to graduate from high school with the other Saints. During his second senior year, after the other Saints had gone on to college, Jerry began to hang around with what several teachers described as a "rough crowd"—the gang that was heir apparent to the Roughnecks. At the end of his second senior year, when he did graduate from high school, Jerry took a job as a used-car salesman, got married and quickly had a child. Although he made several abortive attempts to go to college by attending night school, when I last saw him (ten years after high school) Jerry was unemployed and had been living on unemployment for almost a year. His wife worked as a waitress.

Some of the Roughnecks have lived up to community expectations. A number of them were headed for trouble. A few were not.

Jack and Herb were the athletes among the Roughnecks and their athletic prowess paid off handsomely. Both boys received unsolicited athletic scholarships to college. After Herb received his scholarship (near the end of his senior year), he apparently did an about-face. His demeanor became very similar to that of the Saints. Although he remained a member in good standing of the Roughnecks, he stopped participating in most activities and did not hang on the corner as often.

Jack did not change. If anything, he became more prone to fighting. He even made excuses for accepting the scholarship. He told the gang members that the school had guaranteed him a "C" average if he would come to play football—an idea that seems far-fetched, even in this day of highly competitive recruiting.

During the summer after graduation from high school, Jack attempted suicide by jumping from a tall building. The jump would certainly have killed most people trying it, but Jack survived. He entered college in the fall and played four years of football. He and Herb graduated in four years, and both are teaching and coaching in high schools. They are married and have stable families. If anything, Jack appears to have a more prestigious position in the community than does Herb, though both are well respected and secure in their positions.

Two of the boys never finished high school. Tommy left at the end of his junior year and went to another state. That summer he was arrested and placed on probation on a manslaughter charge. Three years later he was arrested for murder; he pleaded guilty to second degree murder and is serving a 30-year sentence in the state penitentiary.

Al, the other boy who did not finish high school, also left the state in his senior year. He is serving a life sentence in a state penitentiary for first degree murder.

Wes is a small-time gambler. He finished high school and "bummed around." After several years he made contact with a bookmaker who employed him as runner. Later he acquired his own area and has been working it ever since. His position among the bookmakers is almost identical to the position he had in the gang; he is always around but no one is really aware of him. He makes no trouble and he does not get into any. Steady, reliable, capable of keeping his mouth closed, he plays the game by the rules, even though the game is an illegal one.

That leaves only Ron. Some of his former friends reported that they had heard he was "driving a truck up north," but no one could provide any concrete information.

Reinforcement

The community responded to the Roughnecks as boys in trouble, and the boys agreed with that perception. Their pattern of deviancy was reinforced, and breaking away from it became increasingly unlikely. Once the boys acquired an image of themselves as deviants, they selected new friends who affirmed that self-image. As that self-conception became more firmly entrenched, they also became willing to try new and more extreme deviances. With their growing alienation came freer expression of disrespect and hostility for representatives of the legitimate society. This disrespect increased the community's negativism, perpetuating the entire process of commitment to deviance. Lack of a commitment to deviance works the same way. In either case, the process will perpetuate itself unless some event (like a scholarship to college or a sudden failure) external to the established relationship intervenes. For two of the Roughnecks (Herb and Jack), receiving college athletic scholarships created new relations and culminated in a break with the established pattern of deviance. In the case of one of the Saints (Jerry), his parents' divorce and his failing to graduate from high school changed some of his other relations. Being held back in school for a year and losing his place among the Saints had sufficient impact on Jerry to alter his self-image and virtually to assure that he would not go on to college as his peers did. Although the experiments of life can rarely be reversed, it seems likely in view of the behavior of the other boys who did not enjoy this special treatment by the school that Jerry, too, would have

234   WILLIAM J. CHAMBLISS

"become something" had he graduated as anticipated. For Herb and Jack outside intervention worked to their advantage; for Jerry it was his undoing.

Selective perception and labelling—finding, processing and punishing some kinds of criminality and not others—means that visible, poor, nonmobile, outspoken, undiplomatic "tough" kids will be noticed, whether their actions are seriously delinquent or not. Other kids, who have established a reputation for being bright (even though underachieving), disciplined and involved in respectable activities, who are mobile and monied, will be invisible when they deviate from sanctioned activities. They'll sow their wild oats—perhaps even wider and thicker than their lower-class cohorts—but they won't be noticed. When it's time to leave adolescence most will follow the expected path, settling into the ways of the middle class, remembering fondly the delinquent but unnoticed fling of their youth. The Roughnecks and others like them may turn around, too. It is more likely that their noticeable deviance will have been so reinforced by police and community that their lives will be effectively channelled into careers consistent with their adolescent background.

Questions

1. Why were the Saints seen as good boys and the Roughnecks seen as bad boys?

2. The conventional wisdom is that criminals are different from noncriminals, that bad things are done by bad people. To what extent does the information presented in Chambliss's article contradict the conventional wisdom?

3. In what specific way did differences in social class (for example, economic resources and cultural capital) contribute to the community's different treatment of and regard for the Saints and the Roughnecks?

4. What evidence do you find in this article that supports Merton's ideas about the self-fulfilling prophecy? What evidence seems to contradict it?

·26·

On Being Sane in Insane Places

D. L. Rosenhan

Although the following selection was written by a professor of psychology and law at Stanford University, it seems that everyone who publishes a reader for introductory sociology students includes this article (obviously, including me). There's a reason. Rosenhan's exploration of what happens to sane people in mental hospitals contains some important lessons about the impact of people's definition of the situation—especially the impact of the definitions of people in authority.

If sanity and insanity exist, how shall we know them?

The question is neither capricious nor itself insane. However much we may be personally convinced that we can tell the normal from the abnormal, the evidence is simply not compelling. It is commonplace, for example, to read about murder trials wherein eminent psychiatrists for the defense are contradicted by equally eminent psychiatrists for the prosecution on the matter of the defendant's sanity. More generally, there are a great deal of conflicting data on the reliability, utility, and meaning of such terms as "sanity," "insanity," "mental illness," and "schizophrenia." Finally, as early as 1934, Benedict suggested that normality and abnormality are not universal. What is viewed as normal in one culture may be seen as quite aberrant in another. Thus, notions of normality and abnormality may not be quite as accurate as people believe they are.

To raise questions regarding normality and abnormality is in no way to question the fact that some behaviors are deviant or odd. Murder is deviant. So, too, are hallucinations. Nor does raising such questions deny the existence of the personal anguish that is often associated with "mental illness." Anxiety and depression exist. Psychological suffering exists. But normality and abnormality, sanity and insanity, and the diagnoses that flow from them may be less substantive than many believe them to be.

At its heart, the question of whether the sane can be distinguished from the insane (and whether degrees of insanity can be distinguished from each other) is a simple matter: do the salient characteristics that lead to diagnoses reside in the patients themselves or in the environments and contexts in which observers find them? From Bleuler[1] through the formulators of the recently revised *Diagnostic and Statistical Manual* of the American Psychiatric Association, the belief has been strong that patients present symptoms, that those symptoms can be categorized, and, implicitly, that the sane are distinguishable from the insane. More recently, however, this belief has

---

[1]Paul Eugen Bleuler (1857–1939) was a Swiss psychiatrist who, in 1911, introduced the term *schizophrenia* (from the Greek *shizo*, "split or cleave," and *phren*, "mind") to refer to a form of dementia (madness). Today, schizophrenia refers to a general pathology characterized by disturbance of thinking, mood, and behavior (including inappropriate emotional responses and lack of empathy), and sometimes hallucinations and delusions. It is thought to afflict more than 2 million Americans, and "about half of the available hospital beds for the mentally ill (or about one-quarter of available beds in all U.S. hospitals) are occupied by patients diagnosed as schizophrenic" (Philip M. Groves and George V. Rebec, *Introduction to Biological Psychology*. [Dubuque, IA: Brown, 1988], p. 479). —Ed.

been questioned. Based in part on theoretical and anthropological considerations, but also on philosophical, legal, and therapeutic ones, the view has grown that psychological categorization of mental illness is useless at best and downright harmful, misleading, and pejorative at worst. Psychiatric diagnoses, in this view, are in the minds of the observers and are not valid summaries of characteristics displayed by the observed.

Gains can be made in deciding which of these is more nearly accurate by getting normal people (that is, people who do not have, and have never suffered, symptoms of serious psychiatric disorders) admitted to psychiatric hospitals and then determining whether they were discovered to be sane and, if so, how. If the sanity of such pseudopatients were always detected, there would be prima facie[2] evidence that a sane individual can be distinguished from the insane context in which he is found. Normality (and presumably abnormality) is distinct enough that it can be recognized wherever it occurs, for it is carried within the person. If, on the other hand, the sanity of the pseudopatients were never discovered, serious difficulties would arise for those who support traditional modes of psychiatric diagnosis. Given that the hospital staff was not incompetent, that the pseudopatient had been behaving as sanely as he had been outside of the hospital, and that it had never been previously suggested that he belonged in a psychiatric hospital, such an unlikely outcome would support the view that psychiatric diagnosis betrays little about the patient but much about the environment in which an observer finds him.

This article describes such an experiment. Eight sane people gained secret admission to 12 different hospitals. . . .

---

[2]*Prima facie*, from the Latin, means "at first sight." Prima facie evidence of something is regarded as apparently valid evidence. — Ed.

Pseudopatients and Their Settings

The eight pseudopatients were a varied group. One was a psychology graduate student in his 20's. The remaining seven were older and "established." Among them were three psychologists, a pediatrician, a psychiatrist, a painter, and a housewife. Three pseudopatients were women, five were men. All of them employed pseudonyms, lest their alleged diagnoses embarrass them later. Those who were in mental health professions alleged another occupation in order to avoid the special attentions that might be accorded by staff, as a matter of courtesy or caution, to ailing colleagues. With the exception of myself (I was the first pseudopatient and my presence was known to the hospital administrator and chief psychologist and, so far as I can tell, to them alone), the presence of pseudopatients and the nature of the research program was not known to the hospital staffs.

The settings were similarly varied. In order to generalize the findings, admission into a variety of hospitals was sought. The 12 hospitals in the sample were located in five different states on the East and West coasts. Some were old and shabby, some were quite new. Some were research-oriented, others not. Some had good staff–patient ratios, others were quite understaffed. Only one was a strictly private hospital. All of the others were supported by state or federal funds or, in one instance, by university funds.

After calling the hospital for an appointment, the pseudopatient arrived at the admissions office complaining that he had been hearing voices. Asked what the voices said, he replied that they were often unclear, but as far as he could tell they said "empty," "hollow," and "thud." The voices were unfamiliar and were of the same sex as the pseudopatient. The choice of these symptoms was occasioned by their apparent similarity to existential symptoms. Such symptoms are alleged to arise from painful concerns about the perceived meaninglessness of one's life. It is as if the hallucinating person were saying, "My life is empty and hollow." The choice of these symptoms was also determined by the *absence* of a single report of existential psychoses in the literature.

Beyond alleging the symptoms and falsifying name, vocation, and employment, no further alterations of person, history, or circumstances were made. The significant events of the pseudopatient's life history were presented as they had actually occurred. Relationships with parents and siblings, with spouse and children, with people at work and in school, consistent with the aforementioned exceptions, were described as they were or had been. Frustrations and upsets were described along with joys and satisfactions. These facts are important to remember. If anything, they strongly biased the subsequent results in favor of detecting sanity, since none of their histories or current behaviors were seriously pathological in any way.

Immediately upon admission to the psychiatric ward, the pseudopatient ceased simulating *any* symptoms of abnormality. In some cases, there was a brief period of mild nervousness and anxiety, since none of the pseudopatients really believed that they would be admitted so easily. Indeed, their shared fear was that they would be immediately exposed as frauds and greatly embarrassed. Moreover, many of them had never visited a psychiatric ward; even those who had, nevertheless had some genuine fears about what might happen to them. Their nervousness, then, was quite appropriate to the novelty of the hospital setting, and it abated rapidly.

Apart from that short-lived nervousness, the pseudopatient behaved on the ward as he "normally" behaved. The pseudopatient spoke to patients and staff as he might ordinarily. Because there is uncommonly little to do on a psychiatric ward, he attempted to engage others in conversation. When asked by staff how he was feeling, he indicated that he was fine, that he no longer experienced symptoms. He responded to instructions from attendants, to calls for medication (which was not swallowed),[3] and to dining-hall instructions. Beyond such activities as were available to him on the admissions ward, he spent his time writing down his observations about the ward, its patients, and the staff. Initially these notes were written "secretly," but as it soon became clear that no one much cared, they were subsequently written on standard tablets of paper in such public places as the dayroom. No secret was made of these activities.

The pseudopatient, very much as a true psychiatric patient, entered a hospital with no foreknowledge of when he would be discharged. Each was told that he would have to get out by his own devices, essentially by convincing the staff that he was sane. The psychological stresses associated with hospitalization were considerable, and all but one of the pseudopatients desired to be discharged almost immediately after being admitted. They were, therefore, motivated not only to behave sanely, but to be paragons of cooperation. That their behavior was in no way disruptive is confirmed by nursing reports, which have been obtained on most of the patients. These

---

[3]In part of the article not included in this excerpt, Rosenhan notes that over the course of their hospitalization, "the pseudopatients were administered nearly 2100 pills, including Elavil, Stelazine, Compazine, and Thorazine, to name a few. (That such a variety of medications should have been administered to patients presenting identical symptoms is itself worthy of note.) Only two were swallowed. The rest were either pocketed or deposited in the toilet. The pseudopatients were not alone in this. Although I have no precise records on how many patients rejected their medications, the pseudopatients frequently found the medications of other patients in the toilets before they deposited their own. As long as they were cooperative, their behavior and the pseudopatients' own in this matter, as in other important matters, went unnoticed throughout." — Ed.

reports uniformly indicate that the patients were "friendly," "cooperative," and "exhibited no abnormal indications."

The Normal Are Not Detectably Sane

Despite their public "show" of sanity, the pseudopatients were never detected. Admitted, except in one case, with a diagnosis of schizophrenia, each was discharged with a diagnosis of schizophrenia "in remission." The label "in remission" should in no way be dismissed as a formality, for at no time during any hospitalization had any question been raised about any pseudopatient's simulation. Nor are there any indications in the hospital records that the pseudopatient's status was suspect. Rather, the evidence is strong that, once labeled schizophrenic, the pseudopatient was stuck with that label. If the pseudopatient was to be discharged, he must naturally be "in remission"; but he was not sane, nor, in the institution's view, had he ever been sane.

The uniform failure to recognize sanity cannot be attributed to the quality of the hospitals, for, although there were considerable variations among them, several are considered excellent. Nor can it be alleged that there was simply not enough time to observe the pseudopatients. Length of hospitalization ranged from 7 to 52 days, with an average of 19 days. The pseudopatients were not, in fact, carefully observed, but this failure clearly speaks more to traditions within psychiatric hospitals than to lack of opportunity.

Finally, it cannot be said that the failure to recognize the pseudopatients' sanity was due to the fact that they were not behaving sanely. While there was clearly some tension present in all of them, their daily visitors could detect no serious behavioral consequences—nor, indeed, could other patients. It was quite common for the patients to "detect" the pseudopatients' sanity. During the first three hospitalizations, when

accurate counts were kept, 35 of a total of 118 patients on the admissions ward voiced their suspicions, some vigorously. "You're not crazy. You're a journalist, or a professor [referring to the continual note-taking]. You're checking up on the hospital." While most of the patients were reassured by the pseudopatient's insistence that he had been sick before he came in but was fine now, some continued to believe that the pseudopatient was sane throughout his hospitalization. The fact that the patients often recognized normality when staff did not raises important questions.

Failure to detect sanity during the course of hospitalization may be due to the fact that physicians . . . are more inclined to call a healthy person sick (a false positive) than a sick person healthy (a false negative). The reasons for this are not hard to find: it is clearly more dangerous to misdiagnose illness than health. Better to err on the side of caution, to suspect illness even among the healthy.

But what holds for medicine does not hold equally well for psychiatry. Medical illnesses, while unfortunate, are not commonly pejorative. Psychiatric diagnoses, on the contrary, carry with them personal, legal, and social stigmas. It was therefore important to see whether the tendency toward diagnosing the sane insane could be reversed. The following experiment was arranged at a research and teaching hospital whose staff had heard these findings but doubted that such an error could occur in their hospital. The staff was informed that at some time during the following 3 months, one or more pseudopatients would attempt to be admitted into the psychiatric hospital. Each staff member was asked to rate each patient who presented himself at admissions or on the ward according to the likelihood that the patient was a pseudopatient. A 10-point scale was used, with a 1 and 2 reflecting high confidence that the patient was a pseudopatient.

Judgments were obtained on 193 patients who were admitted for psychiatric treatment.

All staff who had had sustained contact with or primary responsibility for the patient— attendants, nurses, psychiatrists, physicians, and psychologists—were asked to make judgments. Forty-one patients were alleged, with high confidence, to be pseudopatients by at least one member of the staff. Twenty-three were considered suspect by at least one psychiatrist. Nineteen were suspected by one psychiatrist *and* one other staff member. Actually, no genuine pseudopatient (at least from my group) presented himself during this period.

The experiment is instructive. It indicates that the tendency to designate sane people as insane can be reversed when the stakes (in this case, prestige and diagnostic acumen) are high. But what can be said of the 19 people who were suspected of being "sane" by one psychiatrist and another staff member? Were these people truly "sane," or was it rather the case that in the course of avoiding the false positive error the staff tended to make more errors of the false negative sort—calling the crazy "sane"? There is no way of knowing. But one thing is certain: any diagnostic process that lends itself so readily to massive errors of this sort cannot be a very reliable one.

The Stickiness of Psychodiagnostic Labels

Beyond the tendency to call the healthy sick— a tendency that accounts better for diagnostic behavior on admission than it does for such behavior after a lengthy period of exposure— the data speak to the massive role of labeling in psychiatric assessment. Having once been labeled schizophrenic, there is nothing the pseudopatient can do to overcome the tag. The tag profoundly colors others' perceptions of him and his behavior.

From one viewpoint, these data are hardly surprising, for it has long been known that elements are given meaning by the context in which they occur. Gestalt psychology made this point vigorously, and Asch demonstrated that there are "central" personality traits (such as "warm" versus "cold") which are so powerful that they markedly color the meaning of other information in forming an impression of a given personality. "Insane," "schizophrenic," "manic-depressive," and "crazy" are probably among the most powerful of such central traits. Once a person is designated abnormal, all of his other behaviors and characteristics are colored by that label. Indeed, that label is so powerful that many of the pseudopatients' normal behaviors were overlooked entirely or profoundly misinterpreted. Some examples may clarify this issue.

Earlier I indicated that there were no changes in the pseudopatient's personal history and current status beyond those of name, employment, and, where necessary, vocation. Otherwise, a veridical description of personal history and circumstances was offered. Those circumstances were not psychotic. How were they made consonant with the diagnosis of psychosis? Or were those diagnoses modified in such a way as to bring them into accord with the circumstances of the pseudopatient's life, as described by him?

As far as I can determine, diagnoses were in no way affected by the relative health of the circumstances of a pseudopatient's life. Rather, the reverse occurred: the perception of his circumstances was shaped entirely by the diagnosis. A clear example of such translation is found in the case of a pseudopatient who had had a close relationship with his mother but was rather remote from his father during his early childhood. During adolescence and beyond, however, his father became a close friend, while his relationship with his mother cooled. His present relationship with his wife was characteristically close and warm. Apart from occasional angry exchanges, friction was minimal. The children had rarely been spanked. Surely there is nothing especially pathological about such a history. Indeed, many readers may see a similar pattern in their own experiences with no markedly deleterious consequences. Observe, however, how such a history was translated in the psychopathological context, this from the case summary prepared after the patient was discharged.

> This white 39-year-old male . . . manifests a long history of considerable ambivalence in close relationships, which begins in early childhood. A warm relationship with his mother cools during his adolescence. A distant relationship to his father is described as becoming very intense. Affective[4] stability is absent. His attempts to control emotionality with his wife and children are punctuated by angry outbursts and, in the case of the children, spankings. And while he says that he has several good friends, one senses considerable ambivalence embedded in those relationships also. . . .

The facts of the case were unintentionally distorted by the staff to achieve consistency with a popular theory of the dynamics of a schizophrenic reaction. Nothing of an ambivalent nature had been described in relations with parents, spouse, or friends. To the extent that ambivalence could be inferred, it was probably not greater than is found in all human relationships. It is true the pseudopatient's relationships with his parents changed over time, but in the ordinary context that would hardly be remarkable—indeed, it might very well be expected. Clearly, the meaning ascribed to his verbalizations (that is, ambivalence, affective instability) was determined by the diagnosis: schizophrenia. An entirely different meaning would have been ascribed if it were known that the man was "normal."

All pseudopatients took extensive notes publicly. Under ordinary circumstances, such behavior would have raised questions in the minds of observers, as, in fact, it did among patients. Indeed, it seemed so certain that the

notes would elicit suspicion that elaborate precautions were taken to remove them from the ward each day. But the precautions proved needless. The closest any staff member came to questioning these notes occurred when one pseudopatient asked his physician what kind of medication he was receiving and began to write down the response. "You needn't write it," he was told gently. "If you have trouble remembering, just ask me again."

If no questions were asked of the pseudopatients, how was their writing interpreted? Nursing records for three patients indicate that the writing was seen as an aspect of their pathological behavior. "Patient engages in writing behavior" was the daily nursing comment on one of the pseudopatients who was never questioned about his writing. Given that the patient is in the hospital, he must be psychologically disturbed. And given that he is disturbed, continuous writing must be a behavioral manifestation of that disturbance, perhaps a subset of the compulsive behaviors that are sometimes correlated with schizophrenia.

One tacit characteristic of psychiatric diagnosis is that it locates the sources of aberration within the individual and only rarely within the complex of stimuli that surrounds him. Consequently, behaviors that are stimulated by the environment are commonly misattributed to the patient's disorder. For example, one kindly nurse found a pseudopatient pacing the long hospital corridors. "Nervous, Mr. X?" she asked. "No, bored," he said.

The notes kept by pseudopatients are full of patient behaviors that were misinterpreted by well-intentioned staff. Often enough, a patient would go "berserk" because he had, wittingly or unwittingly, been mistreated by, say, an attendant. A nurse coming upon the scene would rarely inquire even cursorily into the environmental stimuli of the patient's behavior. Rather, she assumed that his upset derived from his pathology, not from his present interactions with other staff members. Occasion-

---

[4]*Affective* means "emotional." — Ed.

ally, the staff might assume that the patient's family (especially when they had recently visited) or other patients had stimulated the outburst. But never were the staff found to assume that one of themselves or the structure of the hospital had anything to do with a patient's behavior. One psychiatrist pointed to a group of patients who were sitting outside the cafeteria entrance half an hour before lunchtime. To a group of young residents he indicated that such behavior was characteristic of the oral-acquisitive nature of the syndrome. It seemed not to occur to him that there were very few things to anticipate in a psychiatric hospital besides eating.

A psychiatric label has a life and an influence of its own. Once the impression has been formed that the patient is schizophrenic, the expectation is that he will continue to be schizophrenic. When a sufficient amount of time has passed, during which the patient has done nothing bizarre, he is considered to be in remission and available for discharge. But the label endures beyond discharge, with the unconfirmed expectation that he will behave as a schizophrenic again. Such labels, conferred by mental health professionals, are as influential on the patient as they are on his relatives and friends, and it should not surprise anyone that the diagnosis acts on all of them as a self-fulfilling prophecy.[5] Eventually, the patient himself accepts the diagnosis, with all of its surplus meanings and expectations, and behaves accordingly.

The inferences to be made from these matters are quite simple. Much as Zigler and Phillips have demonstrated that there is enormous overlap in the symptoms presented by patients who have been variously diagnosed, so there is enormous overlap in the behaviors of the sane and the insane. The sane are not "sane" all of the time. We lose our tempers "for

no good reason." We are occasionally depressed or anxious, again for no good reason. And we may find it difficult to get along with one or another person—again for no reason that we can specify. Similarly, the insane are not always insane. Indeed, it was the impression of the pseudopatients while living with them that they were sane for long periods of time—that the bizarre behaviors upon which their diagnoses were allegedly predicated constituted only a small fraction of their total behavior. . . .

The Consequences of Labeling and Depersonalization

Whenever the ratio of what is known to what needs to be known approaches zero, we tend to invent "knowledge" and assume that we understand more than we actually do. We seem unable to acknowledge that we simply don't know. The needs for diagnosis and remediation of behavioral and emotional problems are enormous. But rather than acknowledge that we are just embarking on understanding, we continue to label patients "schizophrenic," "manic-depressive," and "insane," as if in those words we had captured the essence of understanding. The facts of the matter are that we have known for a long time that diagnoses are often not useful or reliable, but we have nevertheless continued to use them. We now know that we cannot distinguish insanity from sanity. It is depressing to consider how that information will be used.

Not merely depressing, but frightening. How many people, one wonders, are sane but not recognized as such in our psychiatric institutions? How many have been needlessly stripped of their privileges of citizenship, from the right to vote and drive to that of handling their own accounts? How many have feigned insanity in order to avoid the criminal consequences of their behavior, and, conversely,

---

[5]See the introductory notes to reading 25, "The Saints and the Roughnecks," for an explanation of this concept. —Ed.

how many would rather stand trial than live interminably in a psychiatric hospital — but are wrongly thought to be mentally ill? How many have been stigmatized by well-intentioned, but nevertheless erroneous, diagnoses? On the last point, recall again that a false positive error in psychiatric diagnosis does not have the same consequences it does in medical diagnosis. A diagnosis of cancer that has been found to be in error is cause for celebration. But psychiatric diagnoses are rarely found to be in error. The label sticks, a mark of inadequacy forever. . . .

Questions

1. With which of the following statements would Rosenhan agree, and why?
   a. In this study, the symptoms observed by the psychiatric staff led to the diagnosis.
   b. In this study, the diagnosis led to the symptoms observed by the psychiatric staff.

2. What might be the significance of the fact that many *patients* managed to detect pseudopatients while none of the staff did?

3. Why does a false diagnosis of mental illness generally have more serious repercussions than a false diagnosis of physical illness?

· 27 ·

Fraternities and Collegiate Rape Culture

Why Are Some Fraternities More Dangerous Places for Women?

A. Ayres Boswell and Joan Z. Spade

In the mid-1980s, social scientific researchers began to identify college fraternities as places where women were in special jeopardy of being raped. In 1985, for example, Julie Ehrhart and Bernice Sandler published a study entitled "Campus Gang Rape: Party Games?" (in the Association of American Colleges, *Project on the Status and Education of Women*.) In 1989, Patricia Martin and Robert Hummer published their study, "Fraternities and Rape on Campus," in which they concluded that "the organization and membership of fraternities contribute heavily to coercive and often violent sex. . . . Brotherhood norms require 'sticking together' regardless of right or wrong; thus rape episodes are unlikely to be stopped or reported to outsiders, even when witnesses disapprove" (*Gender and Society*, December). In 1990, anthropologist Peggy Reeves Sanday published *Fraternity Gang Rape: Sex, Brotherhood, and Privilege on Campus,* in which she described her research finding that in many fraternities, gang rape was practiced as a "male bonding ritual."

The conclusion was building that fraternities were places in which a "rape culture" prevailed. In their more recent study, A. Ayres Boswell and Joan Spade report that although fraternities can be dangerous places for women, some are more dangerous than others. Their findings bolster the sociological theory that it is not the members of the fraternity, but rather the social structure of the fraternity, that makes the difference.

Date rape and acquaintance rape on college campuses are topics of concern to both researchers and college administrators. Some estimate that 60 to 80 percent of rapes are date or acquaintance rape (Koss et al. 1988). Further, 1 out of 4 college women say they were raped or experienced an attempted rape, and 1 out of 12 college men say they forced a woman to have sexual intercourse against her will (Koss, Gidycz, and Wisniewski 1985).

Although considerable attention focuses on the incidence of rape, we know relatively little about the context or the *rape culture* surrounding date and acquaintance rape. Rape culture is a set of values and beliefs that provide an environment conducive to rape (Buchwald,

Fletcher, and Roth 1993; Herman 1984). The term applies to a generic culture surrounding and promoting rape, not the specific settings in which rape is likely to occur. We believe that the specific settings also are important in defining relationships between men and women.

Some have argued that fraternities are places where rape is likely to occur on college campuses (Martin and Hummer 1989; O'Sullivan 1993; Sanday 1990) and that the students most likely to accept rape myths and be more sexually aggressive are more likely to live in fraternities and sororities, consume higher doses of alcohol and drugs, and place a higher value on social life at college (Gwartney-Gibbs and Stockard 1989; Kalof and Cargill 1991). Others suggest that sexual aggression is learned in settings such as fraternities and is not part of predispositions or preexisting attitudes (Boeringer, Shehan, and Akers 1991). To prevent further incidences of rape on college campuses, we need to understand what it is about fraternities in particular and college life in general that may contribute to the maintenance of a rape culture on college campuses.

Our approach is to identify the social contexts that link fraternities to campus rape and promote a rape culture. Instead of assuming that all fraternities provide an environment conducive to rape, we compare the interactions of men and women at fraternities identified on campus as being especially *dangerous* places for women, where the likelihood of rape is high, to those seen as *safer* places, where the perceived probability of rape occurring is lower. Prior to collecting data for our study, we found that most women students identified some fraternities as having more sexually aggressive members and a higher probability of rape. These women also considered other fraternities as relatively safe houses, where a woman could go and get drunk if she wanted to and feel secure that the fraternity men would not take advantage of her. We compared parties at houses identified as high-risk and low-risk houses as well as at two local bars frequented by college students. Our analysis provides an opportunity to examine situations and contexts that hinder or facilitate positive social relations between undergraduate men and women.

The abusive attitudes toward women that some fraternities perpetuate exist within a general culture where rape is intertwined in traditional gender scripts. Men are viewed as initiators of sex and women as either passive partners or active resisters, preventing men from touching their bodies (LaPlante, McCormick, and Brannigan 1980). Rape culture is based on the assumptions that men are aggressive and dominant whereas women are passive and acquiescent (Buchwald et al. 1993; Herman 1984). What occurs on college campuses is an extension of the portrayal of domination and aggression of men over women that exemplifies the double standard of sexual behavior in U.S. society (Barthel 1988; Kimmel 1993).

Sexually active men are positively reinforced by being referred to as "studs," whereas women who are sexually active or report enjoying sex are derogatorily labeled as "sluts" (Herman 1984; O'Sullivan 1993). These gender scripts are embodied in rape myths and stereotypes such as "She really wanted it; she just said no because she didn't want me to think she was a bad girl" (Burke, Stets, and Pirog-Good 1989; Jenkins and Dambrot 1987; Lisak and Roth 1988; Malamuth 1986; Muehlenhard and Linton 1987; Peterson and Franzese 1987). Because men's sexuality is seen as more natural, acceptable, and uncontrollable than women's sexuality, many men and women excuse acquaintance rape by affirming that men cannot control their natural urges (Miller and Marshall 1987).

Whereas some researchers explain these attitudes toward sexuality and rape using an individual or a psychological interpretation, we argue that rape has a social basis, one in which both men and women create and re-create masculine and feminine identities and relations. Based on the assumption that rape is part of the social construction of gender, we examine how men and women "do gender" on a college campus (West and Zimmerman 1987). We focus on fraternities because they have been identified as settings that encourage rape (Sanday 1990). By comparing fraternities that are viewed by women as places where there is a high risk of rape to those where women believe there is a low risk of rape as well as two local commercial bars, we seek to identify characteristics that make some social settings more likely places for the occurrence of rape.

Method

We observed social interactions between men and women at a private coeducational school in which a high percentage (49.4 percent) of students affiliate with Greek organizations. The university has an undergraduate population of approximately 4,500 students, just more than one third of whom are women; the students are primarily from upper-middle-class families. The school, which admitted only men until 1971, is highly competitive academically.

We used a variety of data collection approaches: observations of interactions between men and women at fraternity parties and bars, formal interviews, and informal conversations. The first author, a former undergraduate at this school and a graduate student at the time of the study, collected the data. She knew about the social life at the school and had established rapport and trust between herself and undergraduate students as a teaching assistant in a human sexuality course.

The process of identifying high- and low-risk fraternity houses followed Hunter's (1953) reputational approach. In our study, 40 women students identified fraternities that they considered to be high risk, or to have more sexually aggressive members and higher incidence of rape, as well as fraternities that they considered to be safe houses. The women represented all four years of undergraduate college and different living groups (sororities, residence halls, and off-campus housing). Observations focused on the four fraternities named most often by these women as high-risk houses and the four identified as low-risk houses.

Throughout the spring semester, the first author observed at two fraternity parties each weekend at two different houses (fraternities could have parties only on weekends at this campus). She also observed students' interactions in two popular university bars on weeknights to provide a comparison of students' behavior in non-Greek settings. The first local bar at which she observed was popular with seniors and older students; the second bar was popular with first-, second-, and third-year undergraduates because the management did not strictly enforce drinking age laws in this bar.

The observer focused on the social context as well as interaction among participants at each setting. In terms of social context, she observed the following: ratio of men to women, physical setting such as the party decor and theme, use and control of alcohol and level of intoxication, and explicit and implicit norms. She noted interactions between men and women (i.e., physical contact, conversational style, use of jokes) and the relations among men (i.e., their treatment of pledges and other men at fraternity parties). Other than the observer, no one knew the identity of the high- or low-risk fraternities. Although this may have introduced bias into the data collection, students on this campus who read this article before it was submitted for publication commented on how accurately the social scene is described.

In addition, 50 individuals were interviewed including men from the selected fraternities, women who attended those parties, men not affiliated with fraternities, and self-identified rape victims known to the first author. The first author approached men and women by telephone or on campus and asked them to participate in interviews. The interviews included open-ended questions about gender relations on campus, attitudes about date rape, and their own experiences on campus.

To assess whether self-selection was a factor in determining the classification of the fraternity, we compared high-risk houses to low-risk houses on several characteristics. In terms of status on campus, the high- and low-risk houses we studied attracted about the same number of pledges; however, many of the high-risk houses had more members. There was no difference in grade point averages for the two types of houses. In fact, the highest and lowest grade point averages were found in the high-risk category. Although both high- and low-risk fraternities participated in sports, brothers in the low-risk houses tended to play intramural sports whereas brothers in the high-risk houses were more likely to be varsity athletes. The high-risk houses may be more aggressive, as they had a slightly larger number of disciplinary incidents and their reports were more severe, often with physical harm to others and damage to property. Further, in year-end reports, there was more property damage in the high-risk houses. Last, more of the low-risk houses participated in a campus rape-prevention program. In summary, both high- and low-risk fraternities seem to be equally attractive to freshmen men on this campus, and differences between the eight fraternities we studied were not great; however, the high-risk houses had a slightly larger number of reports of aggression and physical destruction in the houses and the low-risk houses were more likely to participate in a rape-prevention program.

Results

THE SETTINGS

Fraternity Parties   We observed several differences in the quality of the interaction of men and women at parties at high-risk fraternities compared to those at low-risk houses. A typical party at a low-risk house included an equal number of women and men. The social atmosphere was friendly, with considerable interaction between women and men. Men and women danced in groups and in couples, with many of the couples kissing and displaying affection toward each other. Brothers explained that, because many of the men in these houses had girlfriends, it was normal to see couples kissing on the dance floor. Coed groups engaged in conversations at many of these houses, with women and men engaging in friendly exchanges, giving the impression that they knew each other well. Almost no cursing and yelling was observed at parties in low-risk houses; when pushing occurred, the participants apologized. Respect for women extended to the women's bathrooms, which were clean and well supplied.

At high-risk houses, parties typically had skewed gender ratios, sometimes involving more men and other times involving more women. Gender segregation also was evident at these parties, with the men on one side of a room or in the bar drinking while women gathered in another area. Men treated women differently in the high-risk houses. The women's bathrooms in the high-risk houses were filthy, including clogged toilets and vomit in the sinks. When a brother was told of the mess in the bathroom at a high-risk house, he replied, "Good, maybe some of these beer wenches will leave so there will be more beer for us."

Men attending parties at high-risk houses treated women less respectfully, engaging in jokes, conversations, and behaviors that degraded women. Men made a display of assessing women's bodies and rated them with thumbs up or thumbs down for the other men in the sight of the women. One man attending a party at a high-risk fraternity said to another, "Did you know that this week is Women's Awareness Week? I guess that means we get to abuse them more this week." Men behaved more crudely at parties at high-risk houses. At one party, a brother dropped his pants, including his underwear, while dancing in front of several women. Another brother slid across the dance floor completely naked.

The atmosphere at parties in high-risk fraternities was less friendly overall. With the exception of greetings, men and women rarely smiled or laughed and spoke to each other less often than was the case at parties in low-risk houses. The few one-on-one conversations between women and men appeared to be strictly flirtatious (lots of eye contact, touching, and very close talking). It was rare to see a group of men and women together talking. Men were openly hostile, which made the high-risk parties seem almost threatening at times. For example, there was a lot of touching, pushing, profanity, and name calling, some done by women.

Students at parties at the high-risk houses seemed self-conscious and aware of the presence of members of the opposite sex, an awareness that was sexually charged. Dancing early in the evening was usually between women. Close to midnight, the sex ratio began to balance out with the arrival of more men or more women. Couples began to dance together but in a sexual way (close dancing with lots of pelvic thrusts). Men tried to pick up women using lines such as "Want to see my fish tank?" and "Let's go upstairs so that we can talk; I can't hear what you're saying in here."

Although many of the same people who attended high-risk parties also attended low-risk parties, their behavior changed as they moved from setting to setting. Group norms differed across contexts as well. At a party that was held jointly at a low-risk house with a high-

risk fraternity, the ambience was that of a party at a high-risk fraternity with heavier drinking, less dancing, and fewer conversations between women and men. The men from both high- and low-risk fraternities were very aggressive; a fight broke out, and there was pushing and shoving on the dance floor and in general.

As others have found, fraternity brothers at high-risk houses on this campus told about routinely discussing their sexual exploits at breakfast the morning after parties and sometimes at house meetings (cf. Martin and Hummer 1989; O'Sullivan 1993; Sanday 1990). During these sessions, the brothers we interviewed said that men bragged about what they did the night before with stories of sexual conquests often told by the same men, usually sophomores. The women involved in these exploits were women they did not know or knew but did not respect, or *faceless victims*. Men usually treated girlfriends with respect and did not talk about them in these storytelling sessions. Men from low-risk houses, however, did not describe similar sessions in their houses.

The Bar Scene   The bar atmosphere and social context differed from those of fraternity parties. The music was not as loud, and both bars had places to sit and have conversations. At all fraternity parties, it was difficult to maintain conversations with loud music playing and no place to sit. The volume of music at parties at high-risk fraternities was even louder than it was at low-risk houses, making it virtually impossible to have conversations. In general, students in the local bars behaved in the same way that students did at parties in low-risk houses with conversations typical, most occurring between men and women.

The first bar, frequented by older students, had live entertainment every night of the week. Some nights were more crowded than others, and the atmosphere was friendly, relaxed, and conducive to conversation. People laughed and smiled and behaved politely toward each other. The ratio of men to women was fairly equal, with students congregating in mostly coed groups. Conversation flowed freely and people listened to each other.

Although the women and men at the first bar also were at parties at low- and high-risk fraternities, their behavior at the bar included none of the blatant sexual or intoxicated behaviors observed at some of these parties. As the evenings wore on, the number of one-on-one conversations between men and women increased and conversations shifted from small talk to topics such as war and AIDS. Conversations did not revolve around picking up another person, and most people left the bar with same-sex friends or in coed groups.

The second bar was less popular with older students. Younger students, often under the legal drinking age, went there to drink, sometimes after leaving campus parties. This bar was much smaller and usually not as crowded as the first bar. The atmosphere was more mellow and relaxed than it was at the fraternity parties. People went there to hang out and talk to each other.

On a couple of occasions, however, the atmosphere at the second bar became similar to that of a party at a high-risk fraternity. As the number of people in the bar increased, they removed chairs and tables, leaving no place to sit and talk. The music also was turned up louder, downing out conversation. With no place to dance or sit, most people stood around but could not maintain conversations because of the noise and crowds. Interactions between women and men consisted mostly of flirting. Alcohol consumption also was greater than it was on the less crowded nights, and the number of visibly drunk people increased. The more people drank, the more conversation and socializing broke down. The only differences between this setting and that of a party at a high-risk house were that brothers no longer controlled the territory and bedrooms were not available upstairs.

GENDER RELATIONS

Relations between women and men are shaped by the contexts in which they meet and interact. As is the case on other college campuses, *hooking up* has replaced dating on this campus, and fraternities are places where many students hook up. Hooking up is a loosely applied term on college campuses that had different meaning for men and women on this campus.

Most men defined hooking up similarly. One man said it was something that happens

> when you are really drunk and meet up with a woman you sort of know, or possibly don't know at all and don't care about. You go home with her with the intention of getting as much sexual, physical pleasure as she'll give you, which can range anywhere from kissing to intercourse, without any strings attached.

The exception to this rule is when men hook up with women they admire. Men said they are less likely to press for sexual activity with someone they know and like because they want the relationship to continue and be based on respect.

Women's version of hooking up differed. Women said they hook up only with men they cared about and described hooking up as kissing and petting but not sexual intercourse. Many women said that hooking up was disappointing because they wanted longer-term relationships. First-year women students realized quickly that hook-ups were usually one-night stands with no strings attached, but many continued to hook up because they had few opportunities to develop relationships with men on campus. One first-year woman said that "70 percent of hook-ups never talk again and try to avoid one another; 26 percent may actually hear from them or talk to them again, and 4 percent may actually go on a date, which can lead to a relationship." Another first-year woman said, "It was fun in the beginning. You get a lot of attention and kiss a lot of boys and think this is what college is about, but it gets tiresome fast."

Whereas first-year women get tired of the hook-up scene early on, many men do not become bored with it until their junior or senior year. As one upperclassman said, "The whole game of hooking up became really meaningless and tiresome for me during my second semester of my sophomore year, but most of my friends didn't get bored with it until the following year."

In contrast to hooking up, students also described monogamous relationships with steady partners. Some type of commitment was expected, but most people did not anticipate marriage. The term *seeing each other* was applied when people were sexually involved but free to date other people. This type of relationship involved less commitment than did one of boyfriend/girlfriend but was not considered to be a hook-up.

The general consensus of women and men interviewed on this campus was that the Greek system, called "the hill," set the scene for gender relations. The predominance of Greek membership and subsequent living arrangements segregated men and women. During the week, little interaction occurred between women and men after their first year in college because students in fraternities or sororities live and dine in separate quarters. In addition, may non-Greek upper-class students move off campus into apartments. Therefore, students see each other in classes or in the library, but there is no place where students can just hang out together.

Both men and women said that fraternities dominate campus social life, a situation that everyone felt limited opportunities for meaningful interactions. One senior Greek man said,

> This environment is horrible and so unhealthy for good male and female relationships and interactions to occur. It is so segregated and male dominated. . . . It is our party, with our rules

and our beer. We are allowing these women and other men to come to our party. Men can feel superior in their domain.

Comments from a senior woman reinforced his views: "Men are dominant; they are the kings of the campus. It is their environment that they allow us to enter; therefore, we have to abide by their rules." A junior woman described fraternity parties as

> good for meeting acquaintances but almost impossible to really get to know anyone. The environment is so superficial, probably because there are so many social cliques due to the Greek system. Also, the music is too loud and the people are too drunk to attempt to have a real conversation anyway.

Some students claim that fraternities even control the dating relationships of their members. One senior woman said, "Guys dictate how dating occurs on this campus, whether it's cool, who it's with, how much time can be spent with the girlfriend and with the brothers." Couples either left campus for an evening or hung out separately with their own same-gender friends at fraternity parties, finally getting together with each other at about 2 A.M. Couples rarely went together to fraternity parties. Some men felt that a girlfriend was just a replacement for a hook-up. According to one junior man, "Basically a girlfriend is someone you go to at 2 A.M. after you've hung out with the guys. She is the sexual outlet that the guys can't provide you with."

Some fraternity brothers pressure each other to limit their time with and commitment to their girlfriends. One senior man said, "The hill [fraternities] and girlfriends don't mix," A brother described a constant battle between girlfriends and brothers over who the guy is going out with for the night, with the brothers usually winning. Brothers teased men with girlfriends with remarks such as "whipped" or "where's the ball and chain?" A brother from a high-risk house said that few brothers at his house had girlfriends; some did, but it was uncommon. One man said that from the minute he was a pledge he knew he would probably never have a girlfriend on this campus because "it was just not the norm in my house. No one has girlfriends; the guys have too much fun with [each other]."

The pressure on men to limit their commitment to girlfriends, however, was not true of all fraternities or of all men on campus. Couples attended low-risk fraternity parties together, and men in the low-risk houses went out on dates more often. A man in one low-risk house said that about 70 percent of the members of his house were involved in relationships with women, including the pledges (who were sophomores).

TREATMENT OF WOMEN

Not all men held negative attitudes toward women that are typical of a rape culture, and not all social contexts promoted the negative treatment of women. When men were asked whether they treated the women on campus with respect, the most common response was "On an individual basis, yes, but when you have a group of men together, no." Men said that, when together in groups with other men, they sensed a pressure to be disrespectful toward women. A first-year man's perception of the treatment of women was that "they are treated with more respect to their faces, but behind closed doors, with a group of men present, respect for women is not an issue." One senior man stated, "In general, college-aged men don't treat women their age with respect because 90 percent of them think of women as merely a means to sex." Women reinforced this perception. A first-year woman stated, "Men here are more interested in hooking up and drinking beer than they are in getting to know women as real people." Another woman said, "Men here use and abuse women."

Characteristic of rape culture, a double standard of sexual behavior for men versus women was prevalent on this campus. As one Greek senior man stated, "Women who sleep around are sluts and get bad reputations; men who do are champions and get a pat on the back from their brothers." Women also supported a double standard for sexual behavior by criticizing sexually active women. A first-year woman spoke out against women who are sexually active: "I think some girls here make it difficult for the men to respect women as a whole."

One concrete example of demeaning sexually active women on this campus is the "walk of shame." Fraternity brothers come out on the porches of their houses the night after parties and heckle women walking by. It is assumed that these women spent the night at fraternity houses and that the men they were with did not care enough about them to drive them home. Although sororities now reside in former fraternity houses, this practice continues and sometimes the victims of hecklings are sorority women on their way to study in the library.

A junior man in a high-risk fraternity described another ritual of disrespect toward women called "chatter." When an unknown woman sleeps over at the house, the brothers yell degrading remarks out the window at her as she leaves the next morning such as "Fuck that bitch" and "Who is that slut?" He said that sometimes brothers harass the brothers whose girlfriends stay over instead of heckling those women.

Fraternity men most often mistreated women they did not know personally. Men and women alike reported incidents in which brothers observed other brothers having sex with unknown women or women they knew only casually. A sophomore woman's experience exemplifies this anonymous state: "I don't mind if 10 guys were watching or it was videotaped. That's expected on this campus. It's the fact that he didn't apologize or even offer to drive me home that really upset me." Descriptions of sexual encounters involved the satisfaction of men by nameless women. A brother in a high-risk fraternity described a similar occurrence:

A brother of mine was hooking up upstairs with an unattractive woman who had been pursuing him all night. He told some brothers to go outside the window and watch. Well, one thing led to another and they were almost completely naked when the woman noticed the brothers outside. She was then unwilling to go any further, so the brother went outside and yelled at the other brothers and then closed the shades. I don't know if he scored or not, because the woman was pretty upset. But he did win the award for hooking up with the ugliest chick that weekend.

ATTITUDES TOWARD RAPE

The sexually charged environment of college campuses raises many questions about cultures that facilitate the rape of women. How women and men define their sexual behavior is important legally as well as interpersonally. We asked students how they defined rape and had them compare it to the following legal definition: the perpetration of an act of sexual intercourse with a female against her will and consent, whether her will is overcome by force or fear resulting from the threat of force, or by drugs or intoxicants; or when, because of mental deficiency, she is incapable of exercising rational judgment. (Brownmiller 1975, 368)

When presented with this legal definition, most women interviewed recognized it as well as the complexities involved in applying it. A first-year woman said, "If a girl is drunk and the guy knows it and the girl says, 'Yes, I want to have sex,' and they do, that is still rape because the girl can't make a conscious, rational decision under the influence of alcohol." Some women disagreed. Another first-year woman stated, "I don't think it is fair that the guy gets blamed when both people involved are drunk."

The typical definition men gave for rape was "when a guy jumps out of the bushes and forces himself sexually onto a girl." When asked what date rape was, the most common answer was "when one person has sex with another person who did not consent." Many men said, however, that "date rape is when a woman wakes up the next morning and regrets having sex." Some men said that date rape was too gray an area to define. "Consent is a fine line," said a Greek senior man student. For the most part, the men we spoke with argued that rape did not occur on this campus. One Greek sophomore man said, "I think it is ridiculous that someone here would rape someone." A first-year man stated, "I have a problem with the word rape. It sounds so criminal, and we are not criminals; we are sane people."

Whether aware of the legal definitions of rape, most men resisted the idea that a woman who is intoxicated is unable to consent to sex. A Greek junior man said, "Men should not be responsible for women's drunkenness." One first-year man said, "If that is the legal definition of rape, then it happens all the time on this campus." A senior man said, "I don't care whether alcohol is involved or not; that is not rape. Rapists are people that have something seriously wrong with them." A first-year man even claimed that when women get drunk, they invite sex. He said, "Girls get so drunk here and then come on to us. What are we supposed to do? We are only human."

Discussion and Conclusion

These findings describe the physical and normative aspects of one college campus as they relate to attitudes about and relations between men and women. Our findings suggest that an explanation emphasizing rape culture also must focus on those characteristics of the social setting that play a role in defining heterosexual relationships on college campuses (Kalof and

Cargill 1991). The degradation of women as portrayed in rape culture was not found in all fraternities on this campus. Both group norms and individual behavior changed as students went from one place to another. Although individual men are the ones who rape, we found that some settings are more likely places for rape than are others. Our findings suggest that rape cannot be seen only as an isolated act and blamed on individual behavior and proclivities, whether it be alcohol consumption or attitudes. We also must consider characteristics of the settings that promote the behaviors that reinforce a rape culture.

Relations between women and men at parties in low-risk fraternities varied considerably from those in high-risk houses. Peer pressure and situational norms influenced women as well as men. Although many men in high- and low-risk houses shared similar views and attitudes about the Greek system, women on this campus, and date rape, their behaviors at fraternity parties were quite different.

Women who are at highest risk of rape are women whom fraternity brothers did not know. These women are faceless victims, nameless acquaintances—not friends. Men said their responsibility to such persons and the level of guilt they feel later if the hook-ups end in sexual intercourse are much lower if they hook up with women they do not know. In high-risk houses, brothers treated women as subordinates and kept them at a distance. Men in high-risk houses actively discouraged ongoing heterosexual relationships, routinely degraded women, and participated more fully in the hook-up scene; thus, the probability that women would become faceless victims was higher in these houses. The flirtatious nature of the parties indicated that women go to these parties looking for available men, but finding boyfriends or relationships was difficult at parties in high-risk houses. However, in the low-risk houses, where more men had long-term relationships, the women were not strangers and were less likely to become faceless victims.

The social scene on this campus, and on most others, offers women and men few other options to socialize. Although there may be no such thing as a completely safe fraternity party for women, parties at low-risk houses and commercial bars encouraged men and women to get to know each other better and decreased the probability that women would become faceless victims. Although both men and women found the social scene on this campus demeaning, neither demanded different settings for socializing, and attendance at fraternity parties is a common form of entertainment.

These findings suggest that a more conducive environment for conversation can promote more positive interactions between men and women. Simple changes would provide the opportunity for men and women to interact in meaningful ways such as adding places to sit and lowering the volume of music at fraternity parties or having parties in neutral locations, where men are not in control. The typical party room in fraternity houses includes a place to dance but not to sit and talk. The music often is loud, making it difficult, if not impossible, to carry on conversations; however, there were more conversations at the low-risk parties, where there also was more respect shown toward women. Although the number of brothers who had steady girlfriends in the low-risk houses as compared to those in the high-risk houses may explain the differences, we found that commercial bars also provided a context for interaction between men and women. At the bars, students sat and talked and conversations between men and women flowed freely, resulting in deep discussion and fewer hook-ups.

Alcohol consumption was a major focus of social events here and intensified attitudes and orientations of a rape culture. Although pressure to drink was evident at all fraternity parties and at both bars, drinking dominated high-risk fraternity parties, at which nonalcoholic beverages usually were not available and people chugged beers and became visibly drunk. A rape culture is strengthened by rules that permit alcohol only at fraternity parties. Under this system, men control the parties and dominate the men as well as the women who attend. As college administrators crack down on fraternities and alcohol on campus, however, the same behaviors and norms may transfer to other places such as parties in apartments or private homes where administrators have much less control. At commercial bars, interaction and socialization with others were as important as drinking, with the exception of the nights when the bar frequented by under-class students became crowded. Although one solution is to offer nonalcoholic social activities, such events receive little support on this campus. Either these alternative events lacked the prestige of the fraternity parties or the alcohol was seen as necessary to unwind, or both.

In many ways, the fraternities on this campus determined the settings in which men and women interacted. As others before us have found, pressures for conformity to the norms and values exist at both high-risk and low-risk houses (Kalof and Cargill 1991; Martin and Hummer 1989; Sanday 1990). The desire to be accepted is not unique to this campus or the Greek system (Holland and Eisenhart 1990; Horowitz 1988; Moffat 1989). The degree of conformity required by Greeks may be greater than that required in most social groups, with considerable pressure to adopt and maintain the image of their houses. The fraternity system intensifies the "groupthink syndrome" (Janis 1972) by solidifying the identity of the in-group and creating an us/them atmosphere. Within the fraternity culture, brothers are highly regarded and women are viewed as outsiders. For men in high-risk fraternities, women threat-

ened their brotherhood; therefore, brothers discouraged relationships and harassed those who treated women as equals or with respect. The pressure to be one of the guys and hang out with the guys strengthens a rape culture on college campus by demeaning women and encouraging the segregation of men and women.

Students on this campus were aware of the contexts in which they operated and the choices available to them. They recognized that, in their interactions, they created differences between men and women that are not natural, essential, or biological (West and Zimmerman 1987). Not all men and women accepted the demeaning treatment of women, but they continued to participate in behaviors that supported aspects of a rape culture. Many women participated in the hook-up scene even after they had been humiliated and hurt because they had few other means of initiating contact with men on campus. Men and women alike played out this scene, recognizing its injustices in many cases but being unable to change the course of their behaviors.

Although this research provides some clues to gender relations on college campuses, it raises many questions. Why do men and women participate in activities that support a rape culture when they see its injustices? What would happen if alcohol were not controlled by groups of men who admit that they disrespect women when they get together? What can be done to give men and women on college campuses more opportunities to interact responsibly and get to know each other better? These questions should be studied on other campuses with a focus on the social settings in which the incidence of rape and the attitudes that support a rape culture exist. Fraternities are social contexts that may or may not foster a rape culture.

Our findings indicate that a rape culture exists in some fraternities, especially those we identified as high-risk houses. College administrators are responding to this situation by providing counseling and educational programs that increase awareness of date rape including campaigns such as "No means no." These strategies are important in changing attitudes, values, and behaviors; however, changing individuals is not enough. The structure of campus life and the impact of that structure on gender relations on campus are highly determinative. To eliminate campus rape culture, student leaders and administrators must examine the situations in which women and men meet and restructure these settings to provide opportunities for respectful interaction. Change may not require abolishing fraternities; rather, it may require promoting settings that facilitate positive gender relations.

References

Barthel, D. 1988. *Putting on Appearances: Gender and Advertising.* Philadelphia: Temple University Press.

Boeringer, S. B., C. L. Shehan, and R. L. Akers. 1991. "Social Contexts and Social Learning in Sexual Coercion and Aggression: Assessing the Contribution of Fraternity Membership." *Family Relations* 40: 58–64.

Brownmiller, S. 1975. *Against Our Will: Men, Women and Rape.* New York: Simon & Schuster.

Buchwald, E., P. R. Fletcher, and M. Roth (eds.). 1993. *Transforming a Rape Culture.* Minneapolis, MN: Milkweed Editions.

Burke, P., J. E. Stets, and M. A. Pirog-Good. 1989. "Gender Identity, Self-Esteem, Physical Abuse and Sexual Abuse in Dating Relationships." In M. A. Pirog-Good and J. E. Stets (eds.), *Violence in Dating Relationships: Emerging Social Issues.* New York: Praeger.

Gwartney-Gibbs, P., and J. Stockard. 1989. "Courtship Aggression and Mixed-Sex Peer Groups." In M. A. Pirog-Good and J. E. Stets (eds.), *Violence in Dating Relationships: Emerging Social Issues.* New York: Praeger.

Herman, D. 1984. "The rape culture." In J. Freeman (ed.), *Women: A Feminist Perspective.* Mountain View, CA: Mayfield.

Holland, D. C., and M. A. Eisenhart. 1990. *Educated in Romance: Women, Achievement, and College Culture.* Chicago: University of Chicago Press.

Horowitz, H. L. 1988. *Campus Life; Undergraduate Cultures from the End of the 18th Century to the Present.* Chicago: University of Chicago Press.

Hunter, F. 1953. *Community Power Structure.* Chapel Hill: University of North Carolina Press.

Jenkins, M. J., and F. H. Dambrot. 1987. "The Attribution of Date Rape: Observer's Attitudes and Sexual Experiences and the Dating Situation." *Journal of Applied Social Psychology* 17: 875–895.

Janis, I. L. 1972. *Victims of Groupthink.* Boston: Houghton Mifflin.

Kalof, L., and T. Cargill. 1991. "Fraternity and Sorority Membership and Gender Dominance Attitudes." *Sex Roles* 25: 417–423.

Kimmel, M. S. 1993. "Clarence, William, Iron Mike, Tailhook, Senator Packwood, Spur Posse, Magic . . . and Us." In E. Buchwald, P. R. Fletcher, and M. Roth (eds.), *Transforming a Rape Culture.* Minneapolis, MN: Milkweed Editions.

Koss, M. P., T. E. Dinero, C. A. Seibel, and S. L. Cox. 1988. "Stranger and Acquaintance Rape: Are There Differences in the Victim's Experience?" *Psychology of Women Quarterly* 12: 1–24

Koss, M. P., C. A. Gidycz, and N. Wisniewski. 1985. "The Scope of Rape: Incidence and Prevalence of Sexual Aggression and Victimization in a National Sample of Higher Education Students." *Journal of Consulting and Clinical Psychology* 55: 162–170.

LaPlante, M. N., N. McCormick, and G. G. Brannigan. 1980. "Living the Sexual Script: College Students' Views of Influence in Sexual Encounters." *Journal of Sex Research* 16: 338–355.

Lisak, D., and S. Roth. 1988. "Motivational Factors in Nonincarcerated Sexually Aggressive Men." *Journal of Personality and Social Psychology* 55: 795–802.

Malamuth, N. 1986. "Predictors of Naturalistic Sexual Aggression." *Journal of Personality and Social Psychology* 50: 953–962.

Martin, P. Y., and R. Hummer. 1989. "Fraternities and Rape on Campus." *Gender and Society* 3: 457–473.

Miller, B., and J. C. Marshall. 1987. "Coercive Sex on the University Campus." *Journal of College Student Personnel* 28: 38–47.

Moffat, M. 1989. *Coming of Age in New Jersey: College Life in American Culture.* New Brunswick, NJ: Rutgers University Press.

Muehlenhard, C. L., and M. A. Linton. 1987. "Date Rape and Sexual Aggression in Dating Situations: Incidence and Risk Factors." *Journal of Counseling Psychology.* 34: 186–196.

O'Sullivan, C. 1993. "Fraternities and the Rape Culture." In E. Buchwald, P. R. Fletcher, and M. Roth (eds.), *Transforming a Rape Culture.* Minneapolis, MN: Milkweed Editions.

Peterson, S. A., and B. Franzese. 1987. "Correlates of College Men's Sexual Abuse of Women." *Journal of College Student Personnel* 28: 223–228.

Sanday, P. R. 1990. *Fraternity Gang Rape: Sex, Brotherhood, and Privilege on Campus.* New York: New York University Press.

West, C., and D. Zimmerman. 1987. "Doing Gender." *Gender and Society.* 1: 125–151.

Questions

1. In your judgment, what sorts of questions would allow a researcher to obtain reliable and valid information about people's (men's and women's) attitudes toward acquaintance rape?

2. What are the elements of a rape culture?

3. On the campus that Boswell and Spade studied, students distinguished between different types of relationships: "hooking up," "seeing each other," and committed. (And men and women defined hooking up differently.) Are similar distinctions made on the campuses with which you are familiar?

4. When Boswell and Spade asked men whether they treated the women on campus with respect, the most common response was "on an individual basis, yes, but when you have a group of men together, no." In your judgment, what might account for the difference?

5. Boswell and Spade conclude that "some settings are more likely places for rape than are others." How do the types of settings that are more likely places for rape differ from those that are less likely places for rape? Explain.

6. Most researchers focus their analysis on the negative impact of rape cultures on women. What are the possible negative consequences of a rape culture on men?

7. Imagine that you've been asked to write a booklet for young college women entitled "How to Be Safe from Rape on This Campus." What would you include in the booklet?

·28·

A Massacre in Montreal

Robin Morgan

In 1990, President Bush signed into law the Hate Crimes Statistics Act. The act required the federal government to gather statistics on the rates of "crimes that manifest evidence of prejudice based on race, religion, sexual orientation, or ethnicity." While the legal concept of hate crime is very modern, the acts that come under its definition are not. In the United States, the prototypical hate crimes were the lynchings of African Americans in the late nineteenth and early twentieth centuries.

Hate crimes are related to the study of deviance in a paradoxical way. On the one hand, the perpetrators of hate crimes are treated (at least by the legal system) as deviant and given negative sanctions. On the other hand, the perpetrators are themselves attempting to give out negative sanctions. The victims of hate crimes are those whom society has, at one time, regarded as deviant, stigmatized, or at best, devalued—people whose race, religion, sexual orientation, or ethnicity does not fall in the dominant majority. To the layperson, hate crimes may appear to be random events. Sociologically speaking, however, they are not quite random. Historically, the rates of what we now call hate crimes have varied according to the amount of legal and social progress devalued individuals have made. Hate crimes might then be defined sociologically as harsh but informal (that is, not legal) sanctions meted out to members of socially devalued groups that are making progress in acquiring legal and social rights. In this reading and the one that follows, two kinds of hate crimes are described. The important thing to notice is the degree to which these acts are "impersonal"—the perpetrator does not know the victims, and indeed, the personality and character of the victim is of little import to the perpetrator. What counts is the group to which the victim belongs.

Although in the technical legal sense, crimes against women do not constitute hate crimes, as you will see in this article, such crimes may fit the sociological definition of hate crimes. The article, "Massacre in Montreal" was written originally as an Op-Ed piece for *The New York Times*. The editor rejected the manuscript, claiming it "made too many connections." Look for those "connections."

"It's the women I've come for. You're all fucking feminists. I'm against feminism. That's why I'm here."

Those were his words, spoken in a quiet voice.

They were the last words ever heard by fourteen young women engineering students before they died, shot by a 22-year-old man who also wounded nine other women and four men during his semiautomatic-rifle rampage through the halls of the University of Montreal on December 6, 1989. His final act was to kill himself.

Newspaper and television reports carried the details. They seemed familiar; we read similar versions of the same story so often. He had purchased the rifle legally because he had no criminal or psychiatric record—no record despite numerous complaints by women neighbors and former girlfriends about his bizarre, sometimes threatening behavior. He was addicted to such combat magazines as *Soldier of Fortune,* to pornography, to movies about terrorism. He loved hanging around gun shops, talking with the boys. He was wearing combat fatigues when he went on his gynecidal spree.

The three-page letter found on his body was virulent with misogyny:[1] females were to blame for everything that had gone wrong in his life—for his inability to graduate from college, his loss of various jobs, his failure to gain admittance to graduate school, the breakups of his friendships or romantic relationships with women. The letter also contained an "enemies list" of fifteen prominent Quebec women, presumably potential targets. Many of these women had not characterized themselves as feminists. But then, neither had most of the slaughtered students. That didn't matter. They were women: they were prey. They endangered men: they must be destroyed.

Honorable men find such violent attitudes and acts appalling. The guy in the street phones in to radio talk-back shows. The psychologists and sociologists write articles, initiate studies, give press conferences, issue quotes. And a further violence is wreaked—by precisely such honorable men. It is the violence of denial, evasion, collaboration. Every possible analysis of the massacre is promulgated—except that based on the spoken and written words of the gunman, Marc Lépine, himself.

---

[1]*Misogyny* means "hatred of women." —Ed.

Because Lépine was half Algerian, some of these gentlemen use the occasion to Arab-bash ("They're all so violent, you know"). Because he hadn't graduated college, some cite class resentment as his motive (although it was his own uneven scholastic record that failed him). Because the rifle had been manufactured in the United States, the importation of such products—and of "American violence"—can be deplored (as if Canada had no home-grown misogyny). Because the victims were women training for nontraditional jobs, there are the predictable sighs and pronouncements that "This is what happens when women refuse to stay home and have babies." Because his background included a "broken" home and battery, heads can be shaken over "the demise of the family" amid condemnations of abstract violence. Because he was raised by a woman, his "craziness" must be a reaction to her (when in doubt, blame mothers).

Why is it again left to women to notice a certain pattern evident in the facts of the case, a pattern the honorable men in their rush to self-serving judgment conveniently ignore?

The "broken" home *should* have been broken; it was a violent home, and the violence was not abstract, but specifically paternal. The father, Rachid Gharbi, tyrannized and battered his wife and two children for years—until the wife managed to divorce him and he returned to Algeria. That wife, Monique Lépine, reclaimed her name, raised both children on her own, became a nurse, and worked hard to support her family, even returned to school for a further degree so as to earn a better salary and improve their lot. In the transcript from her divorce hearing, she had testified that Gharbi repeatedly and unashamedly insisted women were not the equals of men, but were born to serve men. The son was seven years old when the father he so feared left; nevertheless he learned his lesson well. His father's attitude overshadowed the different context in which his mother tried to raise him. Because, subtle or blatant, that attitude was and is reinforced by the entire surrounding patriarchal culture.

Feminism. Yawn. Surely this is the "post-feminist" era, isn't it? Isn't the women's movement dead *yet?* How those damned women do yammer on about their marginal, neurotic complaints.

Once more then. With feeling. Because these "marginal" issues are about the majority of the human species, which happens to be female.

In North America, one out of three women will be raped; two-thirds of all women are victims of battering; a woman is raped every three seconds, beaten every fifteen seconds; one out of every four women experiences sexual abuse before age eighteen; nine out of ten endure sexual harassment at their schools or jobs. Two-thirds of the world's illiterates are female; women and children comprise ninety percent of all refugee populations and eighty percent of all poverty populations. One-third of all families on earth are women-headed. Less than a third of all women have access to contraceptive information or devices, and more than half have no trained help during pregnancy and childbirth. Complications from pregnancy, childbirth, and abortion—which kill more than half a million women per year—are the leading cause of death among women of reproductive age. With nonpregnancy-related reproductive tract infections (RTIs) factored in, the death toll rises to more than a million, with another 100 million women maimed each year. Women are one-third of the world's formal labor force, but receive only one-tenth of world income and own less than one percent of world property. Outside the formal labor force—whether as homemaker, prostitute, nun, fuel-gatherer, water-hauler, farmer, or domestic servant—women's work is regarded as unskilled, marginal, transient, or simply "nat-ural," and is invisible in the Gross Domestic Product accounting of virtually all nations.[2] Nowhere does the work of reproduction of the species itself count as "productive activity."

This is violence.

So is the practice of *sati*—the forced "suicide" of a widow on her husband's funeral pyre—still prevalent, though outlawed, in the subcontinent of India. So is female infanticide, still practiced, though illegal, in China. So are the practices of bride sale, child marriage, polygyny, abandonment, genital mutilation, and gratuitous hysterectomies; so is the two-sided coin of forced concealment in *purdah*[3] and forced exposure in pornography. So is the denial of two basic human rights—reproductive freedom and freedom of sexual choice—to women by fundamentalists of all major patriarchal religions.

Feminism. Yawn. But that's why there's still a women's movement, now worldwide, and growing.

The classroom doors of Montreal University's engineering school have glass panels. When Lépine ushered all males out of the room and then shut the door, the men stood in the corridor. *No one ran for help.* After shooting the first women, he had to pause to empty and refill his rifle magazine. The male teacher and male students did not open the door and rush him, though they were many and he was one. None of them made a move. *They watched him through the glass panel.*

This is violence.

Professor Elliot Leyton, a Canadian expert on mass murders, was quoted as saying "This is one of the very few mass-murder cases

---

[2]See Marilyn J. Waring, *If Women Counted: A New Feminist Economics* (New York: Harper & Row/HarperCollins, 1988).

[3]Purdah is from the Hindu word *parda* meaning "screen" or "veil." It refers to the enforced seclusion of women from the public arena that is practiced by some Islamic and Hindu groups. —Ed.

[4]Not to split hairs but, technically speaking, Jack the Ripper and Ted Bundy were "serial killers"; Richard Speck (who killed eight student nurses in 1968) was a mass murderer. —Ed.

I know of in which women were specifically targeted." The brain reels. Jack the Ripper? Richard Speck? Theodore Bundy?[4]

This is violence.

Canadian feminists tried to point out the obscenity of such erasure, such collaboration-by-analysis. Day after day, they mobilized, massing with pink armbands outside the Montreal cathedral at the victims' funeral, marching on the universities. Night after night, they consoled each other the way women do, by talking and weeping. They telephoned their sisters south of the border, and we phoned them, in shock at the capacity of most men to externalize the Marc Lépines as "other," to deny the commonality of masculinist aggression, to refuse acknowledgment of the banality of sexism, the pervasiveness of woman-hatred, the continuum of violence that creates a normality of terrorism in most women's daily lives.

As women do, we try to make sense of it through understanding, through "womanly compassion." A young woman lying in the hospital with her face half shot away murmurs that she'd like to forgive him, go forward, encourage other women to do the same. An older woman mourning her murdered daughter comments sadly that it does no good to hate, that Lépine was "a poor sick boy." Another bereaved mother says "I can't help but think of his mother. She must be suffering so." This is the human spirit reaching across grief to embrace commonality, not disavow it.

At such moments, every woman, whether she calls herself a feminist or not, shudders with fear and rage. At such moments, every woman

secretly wonders why men hate women so. At such moments, every woman desperately reminds herself that men of conscience do exist, that there are men who actively reject the connection between violence and manhood.

But the honorable men make that difficult. The Québec premier, M. Robert Bourassa, refused women's petitions to close the legislature and universities on the day of the funerals. Such a day of official mourning was only called for, he claimed, "when someone important to the State had died."

Why, this is violence, nor are we out of it.

IN MEMORIAM
_____

Geneviève Bergeron, *age 21*

Hélène Colgan, *age 23*

Nathalie Croteau, *age 23*

Barbara Daigneault, *age 22*

Anne-Marie Edward, *age 21*

Maud Haviernick, *age 29*

Barbara Maria Kleuznick, *age 31*

Maryse Leclair, *age 23*

Maryse Leganière, *age 25*

Anne-Marie Lemay, *age 22*

Sonia Pelletier, *age 28*

Michèle Richard, *age 21*

Annie St-Arneault, *age 23*

Annette Turcotte, *age 21*

Questions

1. Consider the concept of misogyny. Several commentators have pointed out that there is no equivalent word in English for the related concept, hatred of men. Why might this be so?

2. Morgan suggests that for women, there is a "continuum of violence that creates a normality of terrorism in most women's daily lives." What does she mean by this?

3. a. *For women:* Think about the ways in which you "do" daily life. Are there places where you do not go alone, for example, because it's not safe for a woman? What difference would it make if you were a man?

   b. *For men:* Think about the ways in which you "do" daily life. What difference would it make to you if you were a woman?

4. Look back to the sociological definition of hate crimes. Which groups of people in society, in your judgment, are vulnerable to hate crimes?

·29·

Anti-Immigrant Violence

Southern Poverty Law Center

The following article is excerpted from a report by the Southern Poverty Law Center. Founded by attorney Morris Dees, the Center's original mission was to help protect the right of poor people caught up in the criminal justice system. Today, the Center is most famous for its "Klanwatch" program, which tracks the activities of hate groups throughout the nation.

Hostility toward immigrants and efforts by white supremacists to exploit fears about immigration are at their highest levels in 70 years, causing a rash of violent bias crimes against anyone who is perceived as "foreign."

"The brutal violence and hysteria surrounding the immigration issue are almost identical to the 1920s when the Ku Klux Klan became its most formidable," says Klanwatch Director Danny Welch.[1]

"Anti-immigrant violence is an enormous problem that is causing widespread and complex societal problems, and there is not enough attention given to the matter," says hate crime expert Jack McDevitt, associate director of the Center for Applied Research at Northeastern University.

Typical examples include:

- A 19-year-old Vietnamese American pre-med student in Coral Springs, Fla., was beaten to death in August 1992 by a mob of white youths who called him "chink" and "Vietcong."

- Two Hispanic day laborers were shot in a drive-by attack in Vista, Calif., in 1992.

- A Hispanic man in Alpine, Calif., was beaten with baseball bats in October 1992 by six white men at a camp for homeless migrant workers. The assailants later reportedly bragged about "kicking Mexican ass."

- A Hispanic immigrant activist in Davis, Calif., was assaulted twice in April 1993 by white men who wrote "wetback" on her body.

- A 21-year-old Cambodian immigrant in Fall River, Mass., died in August 1993 after being kicked in the head and taunted with racial slurs by a dozen white men.

- An Indian immigrant in New York City was beaten and burned with a cigarette by

---

[1]The Klan was first organized in 1866 by former Confederate soldiers who opposed Reconstruction and wished to maintain white supremacy in the South. Led by Confederate war hero Nathan B. Forrest (1821–1877), members of these *kuklos* (circles) wore white sheets and pillowcases and rode throughout the countryside terrorizing blacks. Within a few years, these circles had spread throughout the South and had organized themselves into the Invisible Empire of the South. Although many white southerners likely sympathized with the Klan, they were appalled by its activities (lynchings and whippings). The original Klan was officially disbanded in 1869, but Forrest and his followers managed to keep blacks from exercising their newly acquired rights to vote and otherwise participate in the public arena.

In 1915, riding a wave of nativist (pro-American) sentiment, the second Klan embraced a larger vision: anti-Catholic, anti-Semitic, anti-African American, and anti-immigrant. By the 1920s, this Klan had spread to the northern and midwestern states. The activities of Klan members contributed to the defeat in 1928 of presidential candidate Alfred E. Smith, a Catholic.

three teenagers who reportedly told him they did not like Indians.

Despite its prevalence, there are no precise statistics available on the number of anti-immigrant hate crimes. The incidents are usually attributed by police to prejudice based on ethnicity so the problem becomes obscured by other types of hate crime.

McDevitt says the raging anti-immigrant sentiment and violence are partially the fault of political rhetoric that blames newcomers for the nation's economic problems.

"The rhetoric sends a message to the hater that no one will care if they go out and bash those people," he said.

Some political candidates claim that problems such as budget deficits, unemployment, higher taxes, rising crime and overwhelmed public facilities such as schools and hospitals could be solved by enacting stricter immigration laws. Other officials blame immigrants for overcrowded and deteriorating roadways, saying the numbers of new vehicles have overburdened their areas.

Polls show a majority of Americans agree with politicians who contend that the country can no longer afford to welcome impoverished immigrants.

Sixty percent of the participants in recent major media surveys were opposed to continuing current immigration policy that in the next decade is expected to attract an unprecedented number of newcomers — most of them Hispanic, Asian and black.

Klanwatch's Welch says that intelligent debate about immigration is necessary, but the issue should not be exploited by politicians to get votes.

"Demagoguery can easily lead to scapegoating and violence," Welch says.[2]

Recognizing that economic problems make white Americans more sympathetic to their message, many hate group leaders are exploiting anti-immigrant fears to attract mainstream followers.

At their public rallies and through their literature, telephone recordings and radio and television programs, hate leaders spread fear that immigrants are overrunning and ruining the country.

White Aryan Resistance (WAR) leader Tom Metzger of Fallbrook, Calif., publishes cartoons about "dirty Mexicans" and the "Asian Invasion," along with scathing editorials that accuse Jews of plotting to establish an international government by bankrupting the country with a flood of immigrants.

Thomas Robb, national director of the Knights of the Ku Klux Klan, urges sending U.S. troops to the Mexican border to repel illegal immigrants.

Young white supremacists — the group most likely to act out violently on prejudices — are particularly susceptible to the anti-immigrant message of hate group leaders, Klanwatch's Welch says.

Hate crimes against immigrants have been linked to white supremacist rhetoric.

A group of Skinheads organized by an agent of WAR's Metzger beat an Ethiopian immigrant to death with a baseball bat in Portland, Ore., in 1990.

A Sacramento teenager who in 1993 firebombed the home of an Asian American city official and several agencies that work with immigrants told authorities that he read white supremacist literature and listened to hate group telephone recordings.

The white supremacist group American Spring, of Orange County, Calif., is organized

---

[2]The concept of scapegoat comes to us from the Old Testament. As told in Leviticus (16:10), on the day of Atonement, the sins of the Jewish people were heaped upon the head of a goat who was then "let go . . . into the wilderness." The term *scapegoat* thus literally means "escaping goat." Today, the concept is used to refer to people who, though they may be completely innocent of any offense, are singled out, blamed, and punished for the misfortunes of others.

solely on the anti-immigration issue. The group stages annual protests in San Ysidro against illegal immigration and calls for a military closure of the border. At American Spring's June 1992 protest, a supporter was arrested after he drove a truck through a mostly Hispanic crowd of counterprotesters.

Anti-immigrant sentiment and violence are most pervasive among whites, but the problem crosses all racial and social lines.

Economic fears and resentments inflamed by political rhetoric are turning ethnic minorities against each other. A prime example occurred during the recent Los Angeles riots when businesses owned by Asian Americans were targeted, despite the fact that Asian Americans had no role in the Rodney King case.

Some native-born Hispanics, Asians and blacks also object to immigrants of their own races.

"They want to pull up the ladder," Northeastern's McDevitt says. "They fear that if too many people come up it behind them, they will lose."

Klanwatch's Welch says the growing number of immigrants and a slow economy pit ethnic groups against each other.

"The anti-Semitic and racist rhetoric of people like Louis Farrakhan of the Nation of Islam just adds fuel to the fire," Welch says.

Attitudes toward immigrants today are frighteningly similar to those of the mid-1920s when the United States passed restrictive laws to halt massive immigration from southern Europe. Klan violence against Catholics, Jews and blacks was rampant during that era, McDevitt notes.

During the 1920s, the Klan grew to its greatest strength with 5 million members, including politicians and other influential government officials who helped get the restrictive immigration legislation passed. The Klan spread from the south for the first time during this period amid widespread fears that millions of European immigrants would take jobs away from native white Americans.

Improved economic conditions and the civil rights movement in the 1960s led to a rebirth of tolerance toward newcomers and a wave of immigration through the passage of a relaxed immigration law.

The hospitality was short-lived, and renewed anti-immigrant sentiment in the 1970s saw the Klan patrolling the U.S. and Mexican borders and organizing attacks on Vietnamese immigrants to drive them away from the Texas shrimping industry.

The Immigration and Naturalization Service (INS) reports that 8.9 million newcomers have arrived in the last decade, mostly from Latin America, Asia and the Caribbean. Another 3 million have entered the United States illegally.

Illegal immigrants are the scapegoats in the immigration policy controversy. The flashpoint is California, where it is estimated that 200,000 illegal immigrants, representing 9 percent of the total population, live in San Diego County alone.

Critics of current immigration policy claim that there are more illegal immigrants living in California than there are legal residents in 18 other states.

Legal immigrants have also flocked to California. More than a third of all legal immigrants, mostly Hispanic and Asian, have settled there. Within a decade whites will probably be a minority in California.

Anti-immigration hysteria fueled by politicians' rhetoric has created a crisis on the border, says Roberto Martinez, of the American Friends Service Committee of San Diego which monitors the violence. Brutal acts against illegal immigrants and other Hispanics by area residents and INS border patrol guards are widespread and frequent, he says.

"It is an explosive situation," Martinez says. "We attribute the violence directly to all of the talk against immigrants—it encourages hate crimes."

A new report by the group details 55 incidents of alleged brutality and other misconduct by INS border guards in 1993 alone, including the death of a Mexican who was chased by border patrol guards and several serious injuries. Ten of the complainants were U.S. citizens, 27 were legal residents or visitors and 18 were undocumented, according to the report.

INS officials say they investigate all complaints and fire guards or take other disciplinary action when there is evidence of physical or verbal abuse. Officials also contend that the complaints are minor in view of the number of people the border patrol apprehends — as many as 1,400 in one night in the San Diego sector alone, they add.

Law Enforcement Support Needed

Among the most troubling aspects of anti-immigration sentiment are the reports of brutality by authorities and the indifference of some law enforcement officers to the plight of immigrants targeted by hate crime, Klanwatch's Welch says.

"Law enforcement officers have a sworn obligation to put their personal feelings aside and protect all people," Welch says. "Immigrants are often terrified and afraid to report the crimes."

Because every area of the nation is becoming more diverse as a result of escalating immigration, all law enforcement agencies should conduct training courses to make officers more sensitive to people of other cultures, Welch says.

Boston is one of many cities that have taken comprehensive steps to meet the challenge of rapidly diversifying ethnic populations.

Deputy Supt. Bill Johnston of the Boston Police Department says city officials recognize the enormity of anti-immigrant violence.

As an example, although Vietnamese make up only 1 percent of the population in Boston, they represent 15 percent of the victims in reported hate crimes in the city, Johnston says. Anti-immigration sentiment is suspected to be the primary motivation in hate crimes against Vietnamese, he says.

To help protect immigrants, Boston is reaching out to immigrant populations through the school system. Police officers regularly visit schools to establish relationships with immigrant children and help their families.

The Boston Police Department has also conducted training courses to teach officers about different cultures, hired interpreters, taught officers simple foreign language skills and published field guides to help officers interact with immigrants.

Police should establish liaisons with the immigrant communities, network with cultural and advocacy groups and publicize their willingness to protect the victims of anti-immigrant violence, says hate crime expert Brian Levin, a Newport Beach, Calif., attorney and former policeman. Information about immigrant communities is available through universities, national cultural advocacy groups, U.S. government publications and census reports.

Even if new laws are passed to restrict immigration, the nation will continue to become more diverse as the large number of immigrants already here relocate from ports of entry such as California, Florida and Texas, Klanwatch's Welch says. Today, at least 19 million foreign-born people live in the United States, more than in any other country.

"It is essential that community and government leaders and law enforcement authorities speak out against anti-immigrant violence to counteract the dangerous messages of white supremacists and some politicians," Welch says. "People need to recognize that hatred and violence are wrong, and they must resist the impulse to make scapegoats of other people."

Questions

1. What does the Southern Poverty Law Center see as the relationship between economic conditions and anti-immigrant violence?

2. Many hate crimes are carried out by relatively young people who have yet to try to earn a stake in the economic system. What do you think might motivate their participation in hate crimes?

·30·
The Land of Opportunity

James Loewen

Many of us who teach sociology in U.S. colleges are frequently puzzled and even stunned by students' reactions to the subject of social inequality. If we blithely explain the extent and consequences of social inequality in the United States, we find our students regarding us as if we are sadly misinformed or (less charitably) have simply gone mad: "What do you mean America is not the land of equal opportunity?" Sometimes students' responses are downright hostile.

Still, if there is one thing sociologists know, it is that there is a great deal of inequality in the United States. The question is: Why does this fact come as such a big surprise to students? Perhaps James Loewen has the answer. He says that students graduate from high school as "terrible sociologists." As you will read, he puts part of the blame for this situation on the content of those social studies and history texts to which students were subjected in elementary, middle, and high school. Loewen is confident that he is right. He explains:

> For several years I have been lugging around twelve [history] textbooks, taking them seriously as works of history and ideology, studying what they say and don't say, and trying to figure out why. I chose the twelve as representing the range of textbooks available for history courses. . . . These twelve textbooks have been my window into the world of what high school students carry home, read, memorize, and forget. In addition, I have spent many hours observing high school history classes in Mississippi, Vermont, and the Washington, DC, metropolitan area, and more hours interviewing high school history teachers.

High school students have eyes, ears, and television sets (all too many have their own TV sets), so they know a lot about relative privilege in America. They measure their family's social position against that of other families, and their community's position against other communities. Middle-class students, especially, know little about how the American class structure works, however, and nothing at all about how it has changed over time. These students do not leave high school merely ignorant of the workings of the class structure; they come out as terrible sociologists. "Why are people poor?" I have asked first-year college students. Or, if their own class position is one of relative privilege, "Why is your family well off?" The answers I've received, to characterize them charitably, are half-formed and naive. The students blame the poor for not being successful. They have no understanding of the ways that opportunity is not equal in America and no notion that social structure pushes people around, influencing the ideas they hold and the lives they fashion.

High school history textbooks can take some of the credit for this state of affairs. Some textbooks cover certain high points of labor history, such as the 1894 Pullman strike near

266

Chicago that President Cleveland broke with federal troops,[1] or the 1911 Triangle Shirtwaist fire that killed 146 women in New York City,[2] but the most recent event mentioned in most books is the Taft-Hartley Act of fifty years ago.[3] No book mentions the Hormel meatpackers' strike in the mid-1980s or the air traffic controllers' strike broken by President Reagan. Nor do textbooks describe any continuing issues facing labor, such as the growth of multinational corporations and their exporting of jobs overseas. With such omissions, textbooks authors can construe labor history as something that happened long ago, like slavery, and that, like slavery, was corrected long ago. It logically follows that unions appear anachronistic. The idea that they might be necessary in order for workers to have a voice in the workplace goes unstated.

Textbooks' treatments of events in labor history are never anchored in any analysis of social class. This amounts to delivering the footnotes instead of the lecture! Six of the dozen high school American history textbooks I examined contain no index listing at all for "social class," "social stratification," "class structure," "income distribution," "inequality," or any conceivably related topic. Not one book lists "upper class," "working class," or "lower class." Two of the textbooks list "middle class," but only to assure students that America is a middle-class country. "Except for slaves, most of the colonists were members of the 'middling ranks,'" says *Land of Promise,* and nails home the point that we are a middle-class country by asking students to "Describe three 'middle-class' values that united free Americans of all classes." Several of the textbooks note the explosion of middle-class suburbs after World War II. Talking about the middle class is hardly equivalent to discussing social stratification, however; in fact, as Gregory Mantsios (1988) has pointed out, "such references appear to be acceptable precisely because they mute class differences."

Stressing how middle-class we all are is particularly problematic today, because the proportion of households earning between 75 percent and 125 percent of the median income has fallen steadily since 1967. The Reagan-Bush administrations accelerated this shrinkage of the middle class, and most families who left its ranks fell rather than rose. This is the kind of historical trend one would think history books would take as appropriate subject matter, but only four of the twelve books in my sample provide any analysis of social stratification in the United States. Even these fragmentary analyses are set mostly in colonial America. *Land of Promise* lives up to its reassuring title by heading its discussion of social class "Social Mobility." "One great difference between colonial and European society was that the colonists had more social mobility," echoes *The American Tradition.* "In contrast with contemporary Europe, eighteenth-century America was a shining land of equality and opportunity—with the notorious exception of slavery," chimes in *The American Pageant.* Although *The Challenge of Freedom* identifies three social classes—upper, middle, and lower—among whites in colonial society,

---

[1]The trouble started when George M. Pullman, owner of the Pullman Palace Car Company, refused even to discuss his employees' grievances (for example, deep wage cuts) with them. The workers' cause was taken up by the American Railway Union, which started a boycott against all Pullman train cars. Because Pullman cars were used on nearly every train running, the boycott brought the entire U.S. rail system to a standstill. President Cleveland called in federal troops to break the strike (Cleveland justified his intervention by claiming that the boycott was interfering with the U.S. mail). —Ed.

[2]The fire broke out on Saturday, March 25. Smoke was first seen on the eighth floor of the building where some 500 people—mostly female—were working. Escape was nearly impossible because the owners of the factory had locked the doors in order to keep their employees at work. Many women and girls jumped to their deaths from the windows of the building rather than face death in fire. —Ed.

[3]The Taft-Hartley Act of 1947 placed serious restrictions on union activities, including the requirement that union leaders swear under oath that they weren't communists. —Ed.

compared to Europe "there was greater *social mobility.*"

Never mind that the most violent class conflicts in American history—Bacon's Rebellion and Shays's Rebellion[4]—took place in and just after colonial times. Textbooks still say that colonial society was relatively classless and marked by upward mobility. And things have gotten rosier since. "By 1815," *The Challenge of Freedom* assures us, two classes had withered away and "America was a country of middle class people and of middle class goals." This book returns repeatedly, at intervals of every fifty years or so, to the theme of how open opportunity is in America. "In the years after 1945, *social mobility*—movement from one social class to another—became more widespread in America," *Challenge* concludes. "This meant that people had a better chance to move upward in society." The stress on upward mobility is striking. There is almost nothing in any of these textbooks about class inequalities or barriers of any kind to social mobility. "What conditions made it possible for poor white immigrants to become richer in the colonies?" *Land of Promise* asks. "What conditions made/make it difficult?" goes unasked. Textbook authors thus present an America in which, as preachers were fond of saying in the nineteenth century, men start from "humble origins" and attain "the most elevated positions."

Social class is probably the single most important variable in society. From womb to tomb, it correlates with almost all other social characteristics of people that we can measure. Affluent expectant mothers are more likely to get prenatal care, receive current medical advice, and enjoy general health, fitness, and nu-

trition. Many poor and working-class mothers-to-be first contact the medical profession in the last month, sometimes the last hours, of their pregnancies. Rich babies come out healthier and weighing more than poor babies. The infants go home to very different situations. Poor babies are more likely to have high levels of poisonous lead in their environments and their bodies. Rich babies get more time and verbal interaction with their parents and higher quality day care when not with their parents. When they enter kindergarten, and through the twelve years that follow, rich children benefit from suburban schools that spend two to three times as much money per student as schools in inner cities or impoverished rural areas. Poor children are taught in classes that are often 50 percent larger than the classes of affluent children. Differences such as these help account for the higher school-dropout rate among poor children.

Even when poor children are fortunate enough to attend the same school as rich children, they encounter teachers who expect only children of affluent families to know the right answers. Social science research shows that teachers are often surprised and even distressed when poor children excel. Teachers and counselors believe they can predict who is "college material." Since many working-class children give off the wrong signals, even in first grade, they end up in the "general education" track in high school. "If you are the child of low-income parents, the chances are good that you will receive limited and often careless attention from adults in your high school," in the words of Theodore Sizer's best-selling study of American high schools, *Horace's Compromise.* "If you are the child of upper-middle-income parents, the chances are good that you will receive substantial and careful attention" (quoted in Karp 1985, 73). Researcher Reba Page (1987) has provided vivid accounts of how high school American history courses use rote learning to turn off lower-class students.

---

[4]Bacon's Rebellion (1676) involved a bloody dispute between settlers and colonial authorities. The settlers' complaints included the fact that the authorities were not providing protection against hostile Native Americans. Shays's Rebellion (1786–1787) resulted from the refusal of Massachusetts legislators to assist debt-ridden farmers who were facing foreclosures. —Ed.

Thus schools have put into practice Woodrow Wilson's recommendation: "We want one class of persons to have a liberal education, and we want another class of persons, a very much larger class of necessity in every society, to forgo the privilege of a liberal education[5] and fit themselves to perform specific difficult manual tasks" (quoted in Lapham 1991).

As if this unequal home and school life were not enough, rich teenagers then enroll in the Princeton Review or other coaching sessions for the Scholastic Aptitude Test. Even without coaching, affluent children are advantaged because their background is similar to that of the test-makers, so they are comfortable with the vocabulary and subtle subcultural assumptions of the test. To no one's surprise, social class correlates strongly with SAT scores.

All these are among the reasons why social class predicts the rate of college attendance and the type of college chosen more effectively than does any other factor, including intellectual ability, however measured. After college, most affluent children get white-collar jobs, most working-class children get blue-collar jobs, and the class differences continue. As adults, rich people are more likely to have hired an attorney and to be a member of formal organizations that increase their civic power. Poor people are more likely to watch TV. Because affluent families can save some money while poor families must spend what they make, wealth differences are ten times larger than income differences. Therefore most poor and working-class families cannot accumulate the down payment required to buy a house, which in turn shuts them out from our most important tax shelter, the writeoff of home mortgage interest. Working-class parents cannot afford to live in elite subdivisions or hire high-quality day care, so the process of educational inequal-

ity replicates itself in the next generation. Finally, affluent Americans also have longer life expectancies than lower- and working-class people, the largest single cause of which is better access to health care. Echoing the results of Helen Keller's study of blindness, research has determined that poor health is not distributed randomly about the social structure but is concentrated in the lower class. Social Security then becomes a huge transfer system, using monies contributed by all Americans to pay benefits disproportionately to longer-lived affluent Americans.

Ultimately, social class determines how people think about social class. When asked if poverty in America is the fault of the poor or the fault of the system, 57 percent of business leaders blamed the poor; just 9 percent blamed the system. Labor leaders showed sharply reversed choices: only 15 percent said the poor were at fault while 56 percent blamed the system. (Some replied "don't know" or chose a middle position.) The largest single difference between our two main political parties lies in how their members think about social class: 55 percent of Republicans blamed the poor for their poverty, while only 13 percent blamed the system for it; 68 percent of Democrats, on the other hand, blamed the system, while only 5 percent blamed the poor (Verba and Orren 1985, 72–75).

Few of these statements are news, I know, which is why I have not documented most of them, but the majority of high school students do not know or understand these ideas. Moreover, the processes have changed over time, for the class structure in America today is not the same as it was in 1890, let alone in colonial America. Yet in *Land of Promise*, for example, social class goes unmentioned after 1670.

Many teachers compound the problem by avoiding talking about social class. Recent interviews with teachers "revealed that they had a much broader knowledge of the economy, both academically and experientially, than they

---

[5]"Liberal education," by definition, is education suited for the free (or liberated) citizen. The contrasting form of education is not "conservative education," but "vocational training."

admitted in class." Teachers "expressed fear that students might find out about the injustices and inadequacies of their economic and political institutions" (McNeil 1983, 116). . . .

Historically, social class is intertwined with all kinds of events and processes in our past. Our governing system was established by rich men, following theories that emphasized government as a bulwark of the propertied class. Although rich himself, James Madison worried about social inequality and wrote *The Federalist* #10 to explain how the proposed government would not succumb to the influence of the affluent. Madison did not fully succeed, according to Edward Pessen, who examined the social-class backgrounds of all American presidents through Reagan. Pessen found that more than 40 percent hailed from the upper class, mostly from the upper fringes of that elite group, and another 15 percent originated in families located between the upper and upper-middle classes. More than 25 percent came from a solid upper-middle-class background, leaving just six presidents, or 15 percent, to come from the middle and lower-middle classes and just one, Andrew Johnson, representing any part of the lower class. For good reason, Pessen (1984) titled his book *The Log Cabin Myth*. While it was sad when the great ship *Titanic* went down, as the old song refrain goes, it was saddest for the lower classes: among women, only 4 of 143 first-class passengers were lost, while 15 of 93 second-class passengers drowned, along with 81 of 179 third-class women and girls. The crew ordered third-class passengers to remain below deck, holding some of them there at gunpoint (Hollingshead and Redlich 1958). More recently, social class played a major role in determining who fought in the Vietnam War: sons of the affluent won educational and medical deferments through most of the conflict (Baskir and Strauss 1986). Textbooks and teachers ignore all this.

Teachers may avoid social class out of a laudable desire not to embarrass their charges. If so, their concern is misguided. When my students from nonaffluent backgrounds learn about the class system, they find the experience liberating. Once they see the social processes that have helped keep their families poor, they can let go of their negative self-image about being poor. If to understand is to pardon, for working-class children to understand how stratification works is to pardon *themselves* and their families. Knowledge of the social-class system also reduces the tendency of Americans from other social classes to blame the victim for being poor. Pedagogically, stratification provides a gripping learning experience. Students are fascinated to discover how the upper class wields disproportionate power relating to everything from energy bills in Congress to zoning decisions in small towns.

Consider a white ninth-grade student taking American history in a predominantly middle-class town in Vermont. Her father tapes Sheet rock, earning an income that in slow construction seasons leaves the family quite poor. Her mother helps out by driving a school bus part-time, in addition to taking care of her two younger siblings. The girl lives with her family in a small house, a winterized former summer cabin, while most of her classmates live in large suburban homes. How is this girl to understand her poverty? Since history textbooks present the American past as 390 years of progress and portray our society as a land of opportunity in which folks get what they deserve and deserve what they get, the failures of working-class Americans to transcend their class origin inevitably get laid at their own doorsteps.

Within the white working-class community the girl will probably find few resources— teachers, church parishioners, family members—who can tell her of heroes or struggles among people of her background, for, except in pockets of continuing class conflict, the working class usually forgets its own history. More than any other group, white working-class students believe that they deserve their low status. A subculture of shame results. This negative self-image is foremost among what Richard Sennett and Jonathan Cobb have called "the hidden injuries of class" (1972). Several years ago, two students of mine provided a demonstration: they drove around Burlington, Vermont, in a big, nearly new, shiny black American car (probably a Lexus would be more appropriate today) and then in a battered ten-year-old subcompact. In each vehicle, when they reached a stoplight and it turned green, they waited until they were honked at before driving on. Motorists averaged less than seven seconds to honk at them in the subcompact, but in the luxury car the students enjoyed 13.2 seconds before anyone honked. Besides providing a good reason to buy a luxury car, this experiment shows how Americans unconsciously grant respect to the educated and successful. Since motorists of all social stations honked at the subcompact more readily, working-class drivers were in a sense disrespecting themselves while deferring to their betters. The biting quip "If you're so smart, why aren't you rich?" conveys the injury done to the self-image of the poor when the idea that America is a meritocracy goes unchallenged in school.

Part of the problem is that American history textbooks describe American education itself as meritocratic. A huge body of research confirms that education is dominated by the class structure and operates to replicate that structure in the next generation. Meanwhile, history textbooks blithely tell of such federal largesse to education as the Elementary and Secondary Education Act, passed under Pres. Lyndon Johnson. Not one textbook offers any data on or analysis of inequality within educational institutions. None mentions how school

districts in low-income areas labor under financial constraints so shocking that Jonathan Kozol (1991) calls them "savage inequalities." No textbook ever suggests that students might research the history of their own school and the population it serves. The only two textbooks that relate education to the class system at all see it as a remedy! Schooling "was a key to upward mobility in postwar America," in the words of *The Challenge of Freedom*.

The tendency of teachers and textbooks to avoid social class as if it were a dirty little secret only reinforces the reluctance of working-class families to talk about it. Paul Cowan has told of interviewing the children of Italian immigrant workers involved in the famous 1912 Lawrence, Massachusetts, mill strike. He spoke with the daughter of one of the Lawrence workers who testified at a Washington congressional hearing investigating the strike. The worker, Camella Teoli, then thirteen years old, had been scalped by a cotton-twisting machine just before the strike and had been hospitalized for several months. Her testimony "became front-page news all over America." But Teoli's daughter, interviewed in 1976 after her mother's death, could not help Cowan. Her mother had told her nothing of the incident, nothing of her trip to Washington, nothing about her impact on America's conscience — even though almost every day, the daughter "had combed her mother's hair into a bun that disguised the bald spot" (Gutman 1987, 386–390). A professional of working-class origin told me a similar story about being ashamed of her uncle "for being a steelworker." A certain defensiveness is built into working-class culture; even its successful acts of working-class resistance, like the Lawrence strike, necessarily presuppose lower status and income, hence connote a certain inferiority. If the larger community is so good, as textbooks tell us it is, then celebrating or even passing on the memory of conflict with it seems somehow disloyal.

Textbooks do present immigrant history. Around the turn of the century immigrants dominated the American urban working class, even in cities as distant from seacoasts as Des Moines and Louisville. When more than 70 percent of the white population was native stock, less than 10 percent of the urban working class was (Gutman 1987, 386–390). But when textbooks tell the immigrant story, they emphasize Joseph Pulitzer, Andrew Carnegie, and their ilk—immigrants who made supergood. Several textbooks apply the phrases *rags to riches* or *land of opportunity* to the immigrant experience. Such legendary successes were achieved, to be sure, but they were the exceptions, not the rule. Ninety-five percent of the executives and financiers in America around the turn of the century came from upper-class or upper-middle-class backgrounds. Fewer than 3 percent started as poor immigrants or farm children. Throughout the nineteenth century, just 2 percent of American industrialists came from working-class origins (Miller 1962, 326–328). By concentrating on the inspiring exceptions, textbooks present immigrant history as another heartening confirmation of America as the land of unparalleled opportunity.

Again and again, textbooks emphasize how America has differed from Europe in having less class stratification and more economic and social mobility. This is another aspect of the archetype of American exceptionalism: our society has been uniquely fair. It would never occur to historians in, say, France or Australia, to claim that their society was exceptionally equalitarian. Does this treatment of the United States prepare students for reality? It certainly does not accurately describe our country today. Social scientists have on many occasions compared the degree of economic equality in the United States with that in other industrial nations. Depending on the measure used, the United States has ranked sixth of six, seventh of seven, ninth of twelve, or fourteenth of fourteen (Verba and Orren 1985, 10). In the United

States the richest fifth of the population earns eleven times as much income as the poorest fifth, one of the highest ratios in the industrialized world; in Great Britain the ratio is seven to one, in Japan just four to one (Mantsios 1988, 59). In Japan the average chief executive officer in an automobile-manufacturing firm makes 20 times as much as the average worker in an automobile assembly plant; in the United States he (and it is not she) makes 192 times as much (Harper's 1990, 19). The Jeffersonian conceit of a nation of independent farmers and merchants is also long gone: only one working American in thirteen is self-employed, compared to one in eight in Western Europe (Harper's 1993, 19). Thus not only do we have far fewer independent entrepreneurs compared to two hundred years ago, we have fewer compared to Europe today.

Since textbooks claim that colonial America was radically less stratified than Europe, they should tell their readers when inequality set in. It surely was not a recent development. By 1910 the top 1 percent of the United States population received more than a third of all personal income, while the bottom fifth got less than one-eighth (Tyack and Hansot 1981). This level of inequality was on a par with that in Germany or Great Britain (Williamson and Lindert 1980). If textbooks acknowledged inequality, then they could describe the changes in our class structure over time, which would introduce their students to fascinating historical debate.

For example, some historians argue that wealth in colonial society was more equally distributed than it is today and that economic inequality increased during the presidency of Andrew Jackson—a period known, ironically, as the age of the common man. Others believe that the flowering of the large corporation in the late nineteenth century made the class structure more rigid. Walter Dean Burnham, has argued that the Republican presidential victory in 1896 (McKinley over Bryan) brought about a sweeping political realignment that changed "a fairly democratic regime into a rather broadly based oligarchy,"[6] so by the 1920s business controlled public policy (1965, 23–25). Clearly the gap between rich and poor, like the distance between blacks and whites, was greater at the end of the Progressive Era in 1920 than at its beginning around 1890 (Schwartz 1991, 94). The story is not all one of increasing stratification, for between the depression and the end of World War II income and wealth in America gradually became more equal. Distributions of income then remained reasonably constant until President Reagan took office in 1981, when inequality began to grow. Still other scholars think that little change has occurred since the Revolution. Lee Soltow (1989), for example, finds "surprising inequality of wealth and income" in America in 1798. At least for Boston, Stephan Thernstrom (1973) concludes that inequalities in life chances owing to social class show an eerie continuity. All this is part of American history. But it is not part of American history as taught in high school.

To social scientists, the level of inequality is a portentous thing to know about a society. When we rank countries by this variable, we find Scandinavian nations at the top, the most equal, and agricultural societies like Colombia and India near the bottom. The policies of the Reagan and Bush administrations, which openly favored the rich, abetted a trend already in motion, causing inequality to increase measurably between 1981 and 1992. For the United States to move perceptibly toward Colombia in social inequality is a development of no small import (Danziger and Gottschalf 1993; Kohn 1990; Macrobert 1984). Surely high school students would be interested to learn that in 1950 physicians made two and a half times what unionized industrial workers made but now make six

times as much. Surely they need to understand that top managers of clothing firms, who used to earn fifty times what their American employees made, now make 1,500 times what their Malaysian workers earn. Surely it is wrong for our history textbooks and teachers to withhold the historical information that might prompt and inform discussion of these trends.

Why might they commit such a blunder? First and foremost, publisher censorship of textbook authors. "You always run the risk, if you talk about social class, of being labeled Marxist," the editor for social studies and history at one of the biggest publishing houses told me. This editor communicates the taboo, formally or subtly, to every writer she works with, and she implied that most other editors do too.

Publisher pressure derives in part from textbook adoption boards and committees in states and school districts. These are subject in turn to pressure from organized groups and individuals who appear before them. Perhaps the most robust such lobby is Educational Research Analysts, led by Mel Gabler of Texas. Gabler's stable of right-wing critics regards even alleging that a textbook contains some class analysis as a devastating criticism. As one writer has put it, "Formulating issues in terms of class is unacceptable, perhaps even un-American" (Mantsios 1988). Fear of not winning adoption in Texas is a prime source of publisher angst, and might help explain why *Life and Liberty* limits its social-class analysis to colonial times in *England!* By contrast, "the colonies were places of great opportunity," even back then. Some Texans cannot easily be placated, however. Deborah L. Brezina, a Gabler ally, complained to the Texas textbook board that *Life and Liberty* describes America "as an unjust society," unfair to lower economic groups, and therefore should not be approved. Such pressure is hardly new. Harold Rugg's *Introduction to Problems of American Culture* and his popular history textbook, written during the depression, included some class

---

[6]*Oligarchy* means "rule by a few" — as opposed to *aristocracy*, which means, technically, "rule by the best few." — Ed.

analysis. In the early 1940s, according to Frances FitzGerald, the National Association of Manufacturers attacked Rugg's books, partly for this feature, and "brought to an end" social and economic analysis in American history textbooks (1979).

More often the influence of the upper class is less direct. The most potent rationale for class privilege in American history has been Social Darwinism,[7] an archetype that still has great power in American culture. The notion that people rise and fall in a survival of the fittest may not conform to the data on intergenerational mobility in the United States, but that has hardly caused the archetype to fade away from American education, particularly from American history classes (Tyack and Hansot 1981). Facts that do not fit with the archetype, such as the entire literature of social stratification, simply get left out. . . .

But isn't it nice simply to believe that America is equal? Maybe the "land of opportunity" archetype is an empowering myth—maybe believing in it might even help make it come true. For if students *think* the sky is the limit, they may reach for the sky, while if they don't, they won't.

The analogy of gender points to the problem with this line of thought. How could high school girls understand their place in American history if their textbooks told them that, from colonial America to the present, women have had equal opportunity for upward mobility and political participation? How could they then explain why no woman has been president? Girls would have to infer, perhaps unconsciously, that it has been their own gender's fault, a conclusion that is hardly empowering.

Textbooks do tell how women were denied the right to vote in many states until 1920 and faced other barriers to upward mobility. Textbooks also tell of barriers confronting racial minorities. The final question *Land of Promise* asks students following its "Social Mobility" section is "What social barriers prevented blacks, Indians, and women from competing on an equal basis with white male colonists?" After its passage extolling upward mobility, *The Challenge of Freedom* notes, "Not all people, however, enjoyed equal rights or an equal chance to improve their way of life," and goes on to address the issues of sexism and racism. But neither here nor anywhere else do *Promise* or *Challenge* (or most other textbooks) hint that opportunity might not be equal today for white Americans of the lower and working classes. Perhaps as a result, even business leaders and Republicans, the respondents statistically most likely to engage in what sociologists call "blaming the victim," blame the social system rather than African Americans for black poverty and blame the system rather than women for the latter's unequal achievement in the workplace. In sum, affluent Americans, like their textbooks, are willing to credit racial discrimination as the cause of poverty among blacks and Indians and sex discrimination as the cause of women's inequality but don't see class discrimination as the cause of poverty in general (Verba and Orren 1985, 72–75).

More than math or science, more even than American literature, courses in American history hold the promise of telling high school students how they and their parents, their communities, and their society came to be as they are. One way things are is unequal by social class. Although poor and working-class children usually cannot identify the cause of their alienation, history often turns them off because it justifies rather than explains the present. When these students react by dropping out, intellectually if not physically, their poor school performance helps convince them as well as their peers in the faster tracks that the system is meritocratic and that they themselves lack merit. In the end, the absence of social-class analysis in American history courses

---

[7]For a discussion of this concept, see chapter 1 in *The Practical Skeptic*. —Ed.

amounts to one more way that education in America is rigged against the working class.

References

Baskir, L., and W. Strauss. 1986. *Chance and Circumstance*. New York: Random House.

Bowles, S., and H. Gintis. 1976. *Schooling in Capitalist America*. New York: Basic Books.

Brezina, D. L. 1993. "Critique of *Life and Liberty*," distributed by Mel Gabler's Educational Research Analysts.

Burnham, W. D. 1965. "The Changing Shape of the American Political University." *American Political Science Review* 59: 23–25.

Danziger, S., and P. Gottschalf. 1993. *Uneven Tides*. New York: Sage.

FitzGerald, F. 1979. *America Revised*. New York: Vintage Books.

Gutman, H. 1987. *Power and Culture*. New York: Pantheon Books.

Harper's. 1990. "Index" (citing data from the United Automobile Workers; Chrysler Corp; "Notice of Annual Meeting of Stockholders"). April 1.

Harper's. 1993. "Index" (citing the Organization for Economic Cooperation and Development). January 19.

Hollingshead, A., and F. C. Redlich. 1958. *Social Class and Mental Illness*. New York: Wiley.

Karp, Walter. 1985. "Why Johnny Can't Think." *Harper's*, June, p. 73.

Kohn, A. 1990. *You Know What They Say. . . .* New York: HarperCollins.

Kozol, J. 1991. *Savage Inequalities*. New York: Crown.

Lapham, Lewis. 1991. "Notebook." *Harper's*, July, p. 10.

Macrobert, A. 1984. "The Unfairness of It All." *Vermont Vanguard Press*, September 30, pp. 12–13.

Mantsios, Gregory. 1988. "Class in America: Myths and Realities." In Paula S. Rothenberg (ed.), *Racism and Sexism: An Integrated Study*. New York: St. Martin's Press.

McNeil, Linda. 1983. "Teaching and Classroom Control." In M. W. Apple and L. Weis (eds.), *Ideology and Practice in Schooling*. Philadelphia: Temple University Press.

Miller, W. 1962. "American Historians and the Business Elite." In W. Miller (ed.), *Men in Business*. New York: Harper & Row.

Page, Reba. 1987. *The Lower-track Students' View of Curriculum*. Washington, DC: American Education Research Association.

Pessen, E. 1984. *The Log Cabin Myth*. New Haven, CT: Yale University Press.

Schwartz, B. 1991. "The Reconstruction of Abraham Lincoln," in D. Middleton and D. Edwards (eds.), *Collective Remembering*. London: Sage.

Sennett, R., and J. Cobb, 1972. *The Hidden Injuries of Class*. New York: Knopf.

Soltow, L. 1989. *Distribution of Wealth and Income in the United States in 1798*. Pittsburgh: University of Pittsburgh Press.

Thernstrom, S. 1973. *The Other Bostonians*. Cambridge, MA: Harvard University Press.

Tyack, D., and E. Hansot. 1981. "Conflict and Consensus in American Public Education." *Daedalus* 110: 11–12.

Verba, S., and G. Orren. 1985. *Equality in America*. Cambridge, MA: Harvard University Press.

Williamson and Lindert. 1980. *American Inequality: A Macroeconomic History*. New York: Academic Press.

Questions

1. Loewen asserts that high school students graduate as "terrible sociologists." To what extent do you agree or disagree with this assessment? Why?

2. Assuming that Loewen is correct about the "mythical" quality of the information given in high school history textbooks, what might be the function of these myths in American society? What might be the dysfunctions?

·31·

Some Principles of Stratification

A Critical Analysis

Melvin M. Tumin

I recall that as a college sophomore taking sociology, one of our reading assignments was "Some Principles of Stratification," by Kingsley Davis and Wilbert Moore. Their argument (simply put) was that people who had higher social class and status positions did so because they deserve it owing to the fact that higher-status occupations were (1) more important to society and (2) more difficult to fulfill. It wasn't an easy article to read, but I became enthralled with it; I found Davis and Moore's account of social stratification to be utterly compelling. Suddenly, everything (about stratification, anyway) made sense to me.

My next moment of epiphany led to a great deal of intellectual development. It happened when I came across the following paper by Melvin Tumin. As Tumin makes clear, the Davis and Moore thesis contains some serious errors in logic. As I reflect back on this now, I suppose my response to Davis and Moore proves that I was one of those "terrible sociologists" to whom Loewen referred in reading 30.

The fact of social inequality in human society is marked by it ubiquity and its antiquity. Every known society, past and present, distributes its scarce and demanded goods and services unequally. And there are attached to the positions which command unequal amounts of such goods and services certain highly morally-toned evaluations of their importance for the society.

The ubiquity and the antiquity of such inequality has given rise to the assumption that there must be something both inevitable and positively functional about social arrangements.

Clearly, the truth or falsity of such an assumption is a strategic question for any general theory of social organization. It is therefore most curious that the basic premises and implications of the assumption have only been most casually explored by American sociologists.

The most systematic treatment is to be found in the well-known article by Kingsley Davis and Wilbert Moore, entitled "Some Principles of Stratification." More than twelve years have passed since its publication, and though it is one of the very few treatments of stratification on a high level of generalization, it is difficult to locate a single systematic analysis of its reasoning. It will be the principal concern of this paper to present the beginnings of such an analysis.

The central argument advanced by Davis and Moore can be stated in a number of sequential propositions, as follows:

1. Certain positions in any society are functionally more important than others, and require special skills for their performance.

2. Only a limited number of individuals in any society have the talents which can be trained into the skills appropriate to these positions.

3. The conversion of talents into skills involves a training period during which sacrifices of one kind or another are made by those undergoing the training.

4. In order to induce the talented persons to undergo these sacrifices and acquire the training, their future positions must carry an inducement value in the form of differential, i.e., privileged and disproportionate access to the scarce and desired rewards which the society has to offer.

5. These scarce and desired goods consist of the rights and perquisites attached to, or built into, the positions, and can be classified into those things which contribute to (a) sustenance and comfort, (b) humor and diversion, (c) self-respect and ego expansion.

6. This differential access to the basic rewards of the society has as a consequence the differentiation of the prestige and esteem which various strata acquire. This may be said, along with the rights and perquisites, to constitute institutionalized social inequality, i.e., stratification.

7. Therefore, social inequality among different strata in the amounts of scarce and desired goods, and the amounts of prestige and esteem which they receive, is both positively functional and inevitable in any society.

Let us take these propositions and examine them *seriatim*.[1]

1. *Certain positions in any society are more functionally important than others and require special skills for their performance.*

The key term here is "functionally important." The functionalist theory of social organization is by no means clear and explicit about this term. The minimum common referent is to something known as the "survival value" of a

social structure. This concept immediately involves a number of perplexing questions, Among these are: (a) the issue of minimum vs. maximum survival, and the possible empirical referents which can be given to those terms; (b) whether such a proposition is a useless tautology since any *status quo* at any given moment is nothing more and nothing less than everything present in the *status quo*. In these terms, all acts and structures must be judged positively functional in that they constitute essential portions of the *status quo*; (c) what kind of calculus of functionality exists which will enable us, at this point in our development, to add and subtract long and short range consequences, with their mixed qualities, and arrive at some summative judgment regarding the rating an act or structure should receive on a scale of greater or lesser functionality? At best, we tend to make primarily intuitive judgments. Often enough, these judgments involve the use of value-laden criteria, or, at least, criteria which are chosen in preference to others not for any sociologically systematic reasons but by reason of certain implicit value preferences.

Thus, to judge that the engineers in a factory are functionally more important to the factory than the unskilled workmen involves a notion regarding the dispensability of the unskilled workmen, or their replaceability, relative to that of the engineers. But this is not a process of choice with infinite time dimensions. For at some point along the line one must face the problem of adequate motivation for *all* workers at all levels of skill in the factory. In the long run, *some* labor force of unskilled workmen is as important and as indispensable to the factory as *some* labor force of engineers. Often enough, the labor force situation is such that this fact is brought home sharply to the entrepreneur in the short run rather than in the long run.

Moreover, the judgment as to the relative indispensability and replaceability of a particular segment of skills in the population involves a

---

[1] *Seriatim* is Latin for "in series." —Ed.

prior judgment about the bargaining-power of that segment. But this power is itself a culturally shaped *consequence* of the existing system of rating, rather than something inevitable in the nature of social organization. At least the contrary of this has never been demonstrated, but only assumed.

A generalized theory of social stratification must recognize that the prevailing system of inducements and rewards is only one of many variants in the whole range of possible systems of motivation which, at least theoretically, are capable of working in human society. It is quite conceivable, of course, that a system of norms could be institutionalized in which the idea of threatened withdrawal of services, except under the most extreme circumstances, would be considered as absolute moral anathema. In such a case, the whole notion of relative functionality, as advanced by Davis and Moore, would have to be radically revised.

2. *Only a limited number of individuals in any society have the talents which can be trained into the skills appropriate to these positions (i.e., the more functionally important positions).*

The truth of this proposition depends at least in part on the truth of proposition 1 above. It is, therefore, subject to all the limitations indicated above. But for the moment, let us assume the validity of the first proposition and concentrate on the question of the rarity of appropriate talent.

If all that is meant is that in every society there is a *range* of talent, and that some members of any society are by nature more talented than others, no sensible contradiction can be offered, but a question must be raised here regarding the amount of sound knowledge present in any society concerning the presence of talent in the population.

For, in every society there is some demonstrable ignorance regarding the amount of talent present in the population. *And the more rigidly stratified a society is, the less chance does that society have of discovering any new facts about the talents of its members.* Smoothly working and stable systems of stratification, wherever found, tend to build-in obstacles to the further exploration of the range of available talent. This is especially true in those societies where the opportunity to discover talent in any one generation varies with the differential resources of the parent generation. Where, for instance, access to education depends upon the wealth of one's parents, and where wealth is differentially distributed, large segments of the population are likely to be deprived of the chance even to *discover* what are their talents.

Whether or not differential rewards and opportunities are functional in any one generation, it is clear that if those differentials are allowed to be socially inherited by the next generation, then, the stratification system is specifically dysfunctional for the discovery of talents in the next generation. In this fashion, systems of social stratification tend to limit the chances available to maximize the efficiency of discovery, recruitment and training of "functionally important talent."

Additionally, the unequal distribution of rewards in one generation tends to result in the unequal distribution of motivation in the succeeding generation. Since motivation to succeed is clearly an important element in the entire process of education, the unequal distribution of motivation tends to set limits on the possible extensions of the educational system, and hence, upon the efficient recruitment and training of the widest body of skills available in the population.[2]

Lastly, in this context, it may be asserted that there is some noticeable tendency for elites

---

[2]In the United States, for instance, we are only now becoming aware of the amount of productivity we, as a society, lose by allocating inferior opportunities and rewards, and hence, inferior motivation, to our Negro population. The actual amount of loss is difficult to specify precisely. Some rough estimate can be made, however, on the assumption that there is present in the Negro population about the same range of talent that is found in the White population.

to restrict further access to their privileged positions, once they have sufficient power to enforce such restrictions. This is especially true in a culture where it is possible for an elite to contrive a high demand and a proportionately higher reward for its work by restricting the numbers of the elite available to do the work. The recruitment and training of doctors in modern United States is at least partly a case in point.

Here, then, are three ways, among others which could be cited, in which stratification systems, once operative, tend to reduce the survival value of a society by limiting the search, recruitment and training of functionally important personnel far more sharply than the facts of available talent would appear to justify. It is only when there is genuinely equal access to recruitment and training for all potentially talented persons that differential rewards can conceivably be justified as functional. And stratification systems are apparently *inherently antagonistic* to the development of such full equality of opportunity.

3. *The conversion of talents into skills involves a training period during which sacrifices of one kind or another are made by those undergoing the training.*

Davis and Moore introduce here a concept, "sacrifice" which comes closer than any of the rest of their vocabulary of analysis to being a direct reflection of the rationalizations, offered by the more fortunate members of a society, of the rightness of their occupancy of privileged positions. It is the least critically thought-out concept in the repertoire, and can also be shown to be least supported by the actual facts.

In our present society, for example, what are the sacrifices which talented persons undergo in the training period? The possibly serious losses involve the surrender of earning power and the cost of the training. The latter is generally borne by the parents of the talented youth undergoing training, and not by the trainees themselves. But this cost tends to be paid out

of income which the parents were able to earn generally by virtue of *their* privileged positions in the hierarchy of stratification. That is to say, the parents' ability to pay for the training of their children is part of the differential *reward* they, the parents, received for their privileged positions in the society. And to charge this sum up against sacrifices made by the youth is falsely to perpetuate a bill or a debt already paid by the society to the parents.

So far as the sacrifice of earning power by the trainees themselves is concerned, the loss may be measured relative to what they might have earned had they gone into the labor market instead of into advanced training for the "important" skills. There are several ways to judge this. One way is to take all the average earnings of age peers who did go into the labor market for a period equal to the average length of the training period. The total income, so calculated, roughly equals an amount which the elite can, on the average, earn back in the first decade of professional work, over and above the earnings of his age peers who are not trained. Ten years is probably the maximum amount needed to equalize the differential. There remains, on the average, twenty years of work during each of which the skilled person then goes on to earn far more than his unskilled age peers. And, what is often forgotten, there is then still another ten or fifteen year period during which the skilled person continues to work and earn when his unskilled age peer is either totally or partially out of the labor market by virtue of the attrition of his strength and capabilities.

One might say that the first ten years of differential pay is perhaps justified, in order to regain for the trained person what he lost during his training period. But it is difficult to imagine what would justify continuing such differential rewards beyond that period.

Another and probably sounder way to measure how much is lost during the training period is to compare the per capita income available to the trainee with the per capita income of the age peer on the untrained labor market during the so-called sacrificial period. If one takes into account the earlier marriage of untrained persons, and the earlier acquisition of family dependents, it is highly dubious that the per capita income of the wage worker is significantly larger than that of the trainee. Even assuming, for the moment, that there is a difference, the amount is by no means sufficient to justify a lifetime of continuing differentials.

What tends to be completely overlooked, in addition, are the psychic and spiritual rewards which are available to the elite trainees by comparison with their age peers in the labor force. There is, first, the much higher prestige enjoyed by the college student and the professional-school student as compared with persons in shops and offices. There is, second, the extremely highly valued privilege of having greater opportunity for self-development. There is, third, all the psychic gain involved in being allowed to delay the assumption of adult responsibilities such as earning a living and supporting a family. There is, fourth, the access to leisure and freedom of a kind not likely to be experienced by the persons already at work.

If these are never taken into account as rewards of the training period it is not because they are not concretely present, but because the emphasis in American concepts of reward is almost exclusively placed on the material returns of positions. The emphases on enjoyment, entertainment, ego enhancement, prestige and esteem are introduced only when the differentials in these which accrue to the skilled positions need to be justified. If these other rewards were taken into account, it would be much more difficult to demonstrate that the training period, as presently operative, is really sacrificial. Indeed, it might turn out to be the case that even at this point in their careers, the elite trainees were being differentially rewarded relative to their age peers in the labor force.

All of the foregoing concerns the quality of the training period under our present system of motivation and rewards. Whatever may turn out to be the factual case about the present system—and the factual case is moot—the more important theoretical question concerns the assumption that the training period under *any* system must be sacrificial.

There seem to be no good theoretical grounds for insisting on this assumption. For, while under any system certain costs will be involved in training persons for skilled positions, these costs could easily be assumed by the society-at-large. Under these circumstances, there would be no need to compensate anyone in terms of differential rewards once the skilled positions were staffed. In short, there would be no need or justification for stratifying social positions on *these* grounds.

4. *In order to induce the talented persons to undergo these sacrifices and acquire the training, their future positions must carry an inducement value in the form of differential, i.e., privileged and disproportionate access to the scarce and desired rewards which the society has to offer.*

Let us assume, for the purposes of the discussion, that the training period is sacrificial and the talent is rare in every conceivable human society. There is still the basic problem as to whether the allocation of differential rewards in scarce and desired goods and services is the only or the most efficient way of recruiting the appropriate talent to these positions.

For there are a number of alternative motivational schemes whose efficiency and adequacy ought at least to be considered in this context. What can be said, for instance, on behalf of the motivation which De Man called "joy in work," Veblen termed "instinct for workmanship" and which we latterly have come to identify as "intrinsic work satisfaction"? Or, to what extent could the motivation of "social duty" be institutionalized in such a fashion that self interest and social interest come closely to coincide? Or, how much prospective confidence can be placed in the possibilities of institutionalizing "social service" as a widespread motivation for seeking one's appropriate position and fulfilling it conscientiously?

Are not these types of motivations, we may ask, likely to prove most appropriate for precisely the "most functionally important positions"? Especially in a mass industrial society, where the vast majority of positions become standardized and routinized, it is the skilled jobs which are likely to retain most of the quality of "intrinsic job satisfaction" and be most readily identifiable as socially serviceable. Is it indeed impossible then to build these motivations into the socialization pattern to which we expose our talented youth?

To deny that such motivations could be institutionalized would be to overclaim our present knowledge. In part, also, such a claim would seem to derive from an assumption that what has not been institutionalized yet in human affairs is incapable of institutionalization. Admittedly, historical experience affords us evidence we cannot afford to ignore. But such evidence cannot legitimately be used to deny absolutely the possibility of heretofore untried alternatives. Social innovation is as important a feature of human societies as social stability.

On the basis of these observations, it seems that Davis and Moore have stated the case much too strongly when they insist that a "functionally important position" which requires skills that are scarce, "must command great prestige, high salary, ample leisure, and the like," if the appropriate talents are to be attracted to the position. Here, clearly, the authors are postulating the unavoidability of very specific types of rewards and, by implication, denying the possibility of others.

5. *These scarce and desired goods consist of rights and perquisites attached to, or built into, the positions and can be classified into those things which contribute to (a) sustenance and comfort; (b) humor and diversion; (c) self-respect and ego expansion.*

6. *This differential access to the basic rewards of the society has as a consequence the differentiation of the prestige and esteem which various strata acquire. This may be said, along with the rights and perquisites, to constitute institutionalized social inequality, i.e., stratification.*

With the classification of the rewards offered by Davis and Moore there need be little argument. Some question must be raised, however, as to whether any reward system, built into a general stratification system, must allocate equal amounts of all three types of reward in order to function effectively, or whether one type of reward may be emphasized to the virtual neglect of others. This raises the further question regarding which type of emphasis is likely to prove most effective as a differential inducer. Nothing in the known facts about human motivation impels us to favor one type of reward over the other, or to insist that all three types of reward must be built into the positions in comparable amounts if the position is to have an inducement value.

It is well known, of course, that societies differ considerably in the kinds of rewards they emphasize in their efforts to maintain a reasonable balance between responsibility and reward. There are, for instance, numerous societies in which the conspicuous display of differential economic advantage is considered extremely bad taste. In short, our present knowledge commends to us the possibility of considerable plasticity in the way in which different types of rewards can be structured into a functioning society. This is to say, it cannot yet be demonstrated that it is *unavoidable* that differential prestige and esteem shall accrue to positions which command differential rewards in power and property.

What does seem to be unavoidable is that differential prestige shall be given to those in any society who conform to the normative order as against those who deviate from that order in a way judged immoral and detrimental. On the assumption that the continuity of a society depends on the continuity and stability of its normative order, some such distinction between conformists and deviants seems inescapable.

It also seems to be unavoidable that in any society, no matter how literate its tradition, the older, wiser and more experienced individuals who are charged with the enculturation and socialization of the young must have more power than the young, on the assumption that the task of effective socialization demands such differential power.

But this differentiation in prestige between the conformist and the deviant is by no means the same distinction as that between strata of individuals each of which operates *within* the normative order, and is composed of adults. The *latter* distinction, in the form of differentiated rewards and prestige between social strata is what Davis and Moore, and most sociologists, consider the structure of a stratification system. The *former* distinctions have nothing necessarily to do with the workings of such a system nor with the efficiency of motivation and recruitment of functionally important personnel.

Nor does the differentiation of power between young and old necessarily create differentially valued strata. For no society rates its young as less morally worthy than its older persons, no matter how much differential power the older ones may temporarily enjoy.

7. *Therefore, social inequality among different strata in the amounts of scarce and desired goods, and the amounts of prestige and esteem which they receive, is both positively functional and inevitable in any society.*

If the objections which have heretofore been raised are taken as reasonable, then it may be stated that the only items which any society *must* distribute unequally are the power and property necessary for the performance of different tasks. If such differential power and property are viewed by all as commensurate with the differential responsibilities, and if they are culturally defined as *resources* and not as rewards, then, no differentials in prestige and esteem need follow.

Historically, the evidence seems to be that every time power and property are distributed unequally, no matter what the cultural definition, prestige and esteem differentiations have tended to result as well. Historically, however, no systematic effort has ever been made, under propitious circumstances, to develop the tradition that each man is as socially worthy as all other men so long as he performs his appropriate tasks conscientiously. While such a tradition seems utterly utopian, no known facts in psychological or social science have yet demonstrated its impossibility or its dysfunctionality for the continuity of a society. The achievement of a full institutionalization of such a tradition seems far too remote to contemplate. Some successive approximations at such a tradition, however, are not out of the range of prospective social innovation.

What, then, of the "positive functionality" of social stratification? Are there other, negative, functions of institutionalized social inequality which can be identified, if only tentatively? Some such dysfunctions of stratification have already been suggested in the body of this paper. Along with others they may now be stated, in the form of provisional assertions, as follows:

1. Social stratification systems function to limit the possibility of discovery of the full range of talent available in a society. This results from the fact of unequal access to appropriate motivation, channels of recruitment and centers of training.

2. In foreshortening the range of available talent, social stratification systems function to set limits upon the possibility of expanding the productive resources of the society, at least relative to what might be the case under conditions of greater equality of opportunity.

3. Social stratification systems function to provide the elite with the political power necessary to procure acceptance and dominance of an ideology which rationalizes the *status quo*, whatever it may be, as "logical," "natural" and "morally right." In this manner, social stratification systems function as essentially conservative influences in the societies in which they are found.

4. Social stratification systems function to distribute favorable self-images unequally throughout a population. To the extent that such favorable self-images are requisite to the development of the creative potential inherent in men, to that extent stratification systems function to limit the development of this creative potential.

5. To the extent that inequalities in social rewards cannot be made fully acceptable to the less privileged in a society, social stratification systems function to encourage hostility, suspicion and distrust among the various segments of a society and thus to limit the possibilities of extensive social integration.

6. To the extent that the sense of significant membership in a society depends on one's place on the prestige ladder of the society, social stratification systems function to distribute unequally the sense of significant membership in the population.

7. To the extent that loyalty to a society depends on a sense of significant membership in the society, social stratification systems function to distribute loyalty unequally in the population.

8. To the extent that participation and apathy depend upon the sense of significant membership in the society, social stratification systems function to distribute the motivation to participate unequally in a population. . . .

Reference

Davis, Kingsley, and Wilbert Moore, 1945. "Some Principles of Stratification." *American Sociological Review* 10: 242–249.

Questions

1. In your own words, how would you summarize Davis and Moore's theory of stratification? How about Tumin's response to Davis and Moore's theory?

2. How would Davis and Moore account for the fact that physicians earn more than, say, truck drivers? Explain.

3. How would Davis and Moore account for the fact that male physicians earn more than, say, female physicians? Explain.

4. Why does Tumin argue that "the more rigidly stratified a society is, the less chance does that society have of discovering any new facts about the talents of its members"? Do you agree or disagree with Tumin on this point? Explain.

· 32 ·

The Uses of Poverty

The Poor Pay All

Herbert J. Gans

If inequality and poverty are so bad, why do they endure? Herbert Gans explains in this classic article that poverty does have its uses. The question is, Who benefits from poverty, and how? *Caution:* while this article isn't hard to read, if you don't read it all the way through, you are likely to miss the author's central point entirely!

Some twenty years ago Robert K. Merton applied the notion of functional analysis to explain the continuing though maligned existence of the urban political machine: if it continued to exist, perhaps it fulfilled latent—unintended or unrecognized—positive functions.[1] Clearly it did. Merton pointed out how the political machine provided central authority to get things done when a decentralized local government could not act, humanized the services of the impersonal bureaucracy for fearful citizens, offered concrete help (rather than abstract law or justice) to the poor, and otherwise performed services needed or demanded by many people but considered unconventional or even illegal by formal public agencies (1949, 71).

Today, poverty is more maligned than the political machine ever was; yet it, too, is a persistent social phenomenon. Consequently, there may be some merit in applying functional analysis to poverty, in asking whether it also has positive functions that explain its persistence.

Merton defined functions as "those observed consequences [of a phenomenon] which make for the adaptation or adjustment of a given [social] system." I shall use a slightly different definition; instead of identifying functions for an entire social system, I shall identify them for the interest groups, socioeconomic classes, and other population aggregates with shared values that "inhabit" a social system. I suspect that in a modern heterogeneous society, few phenomena are functional or dysfunctional for the society as a whole, and that most result in benefits to some groups and costs to others. Nor are any phenomena indispensable; in most instances, one can suggest what Merton calls "functional alternatives" or equivalents for them, i.e., other social patterns or policies that achieve the same positive functions but avoid the dysfunctions.[2]

Associating poverty with positive functions seems at first glance to be unimaginable. Of course, the slumlord and the loan shark are commonly known to profit from the existence

---

[1] Recall that Merton's conception of functions (and dysfunctions) was discussed in chapter 3 of *The Practical Skeptic*. — Ed.

[2] I shall henceforth abbreviate positive functions as functions and negative functions as dysfunctions. I shall also describe functions and dysfunctions, in the planner's terminology, as benefits and costs.

of poverty, but they are viewed as evil men, so their activities are classified among the dysfunctions of poverty. However, what is less often recognized, at least by the conventional wisdom, is that poverty also makes possible the existence or expansion of respectable professions and occupations, for example, penology, criminology, social work, and public health. More recently, the poor have provided jobs for professional and para-professional "poverty warriors," and for journalists and social scientists, this author included, who have supplied the information demanded by the revival of public interest in poverty.

Clearly, then, poverty and the poor may well satisfy a number of positive functions for many nonpoor groups in the American society. I shall describe thirteen such functions—economic, social, and political—that seem to me most significant.

The Functions of Poverty

First, the existence of poverty ensures that society's "dirty work" will be done. Every society has such work: physically dirty or dangerous, temporary, dead-end and underpaid, undignified and menial jobs. Society can fill these jobs by paying higher wages than for "clean" work, or it can force people who have no other choice to do the dirty work—and at low wages. In America, poverty functions to provide a low-wage labor pool that is willing—or, rather, unable to be *un*willing—to perform dirty work at low cost. Indeed, this function of the poor is so important that in some Southern states, welfare payments have been cut off during the summer months when the poor are needed to work in the fields. Moreover, much of the debate about the Negative Income Tax and the Family Assistance Plan has concerned their impact on the work incentive, by which is actually meant the incentive of the poor to do the needed dirty work if the wages therefrom are

no larger than the income grant. Many economic activities that involve dirty work depend on the poor for their existence: restaurants, hospitals, parts of the garment industry, and "truck farming," among others, could not persist in their present form without the poor.

Second, because the poor are required to work at low wages, they subsidize a variety of economic activities that benefit the affluent. For example, domestics subsidize the upper middle and upper classes, making life easier for their employers and freeing affluent women for a variety of professional, cultural, civic, and partying activities. Similarly, because the poor pay a higher proportion of their income in property and sales taxes, among others, they subsidize many state and local governmental services that benefit more affluent groups. In addition, the poor support innovation in medical practice as patients in teaching and research hospitals and as guinea pigs in medical experiments.

Third, poverty creates jobs for a number of occupations and professions that serve or "service" the poor, or protect the rest of society from them. As already noted, penology would be minuscule without the poor, as would the police. Other activities and groups that flourish because of the existence of poverty are the numbers game, the sale of heroin and cheap wines and liquors, pentecostal ministers, faith healers, prostitutes, pawn shops, and the peacetime army, which recruits its enlisted men mainly from among the poor.

Fourth, the poor buy goods others do not want and thus prolong the economic usefulness of such goods—day-old bread, fruit and vegetables that would otherwise have to be thrown out, secondhand clothes, and deteriorating automobiles and buildings. They also provide incomes for doctors, lawyers, teachers, and others who are too old, poorly trained, or incompetent to attract more affluent clients.

In addition to economic functions, the poor perform a number of social functions.

Fifth, the poor can be identified and punished as alleged or real deviants in order to uphold the legitimacy of conventional norms. To justify the desirability of hard work, thrift, honesty, and monogamy, for example, the defenders of these norms must be able to find people who can be accused of being lazy, spendthrift, dishonest, and promiscuous. Although there is some evidence that the poor are about as moral and law-abiding as anyone else, they are more likely than middle-class transgressors to be caught and punished when they participate in deviant acts. Moreover, they lack the political and cultural power to correct the stereotypes that other people hold of them and thus continue to be thought of as lazy, spendthrift, etc., by those who need living proof that moral deviance does not pay.

Sixth, and conversely, the poor offer vicarious participation to the rest of the population in the uninhibited sexual, alcoholic, and narcotic behavior in which they are alleged to participate and which, being freed from the constraints of affluence, they are often thought to enjoy more than the middle classes. Thus many people, some social scientists included, believe that the poor not only are more given to uninhibited behavior (which may be true, although it is often motivated by despair more than by lack of inhibition) but derive more pleasure from it than affluent people (which research by Lee Rainwater, Walter Miller, and others shows to be patently untrue). However, whether the poor actually have more sex and enjoy it more is irrelevant; so long as middle-class people believe this to be true, they can participate in it vicariously when instances are reported in factual or fictional form.

Seventh, the poor also serve a direct cultural function when culture created by or for them is adopted by the more affluent. The rich often collect artifacts from extinct folk cultures of poor people; and almost all Americans listen to the blues, Negro spirituals, and country music, which originated among the Southern poor. Recently they have enjoyed the rock styles that were born, like the Beatles, in the slums; and in the last year, poetry written by ghetto children has become popular in literary circles. The poor also serve as culture heroes, particularly, of course, to the left; but the hobo, the cowboy, the hipster, and the mythical prostitute with a heart of gold have performed this function for a variety of groups.

Eighth, poverty helps to guarantee the status of those who are not poor. In every hierarchical society someone has to be at the bottom; but in American society, in which social mobility is an important goal for many and people need to know where they stand, the poor function as a reliable and relatively permanent measuring rod for status comparisons. This is particularly true for the working class, whose politics is influenced by the need to maintain status distinctions between themselves and the poor, much as the aristocracy must find ways of distinguishing itself from the *nouveaux riches.*[3]

Ninth, the poor also aid the upward mobility of groups just above them in the class hierarchy. Thus a goodly number of Americans have entered the middle class through the profits earned from the provision of goods and services in the slums, including illegal or non-respectable ones that upper-class and upper-middle-class businessmen shun because of their low prestige. As a result, members of almost every immigrant group have financed their upward mobility by providing slum housing, entertainment, gambling, narcotics, etc., to later arrivals — most recently to Blacks and Puerto Ricans.

Tenth, the poor help to keep the aristocracy busy, thus justifying its continued existence. "Society" uses the poor as clients of settlement

---

[3]*Nouveaux riches* is French for "newly rich" (plural). It is a pejorative (negative) label, having to do with the perception on the part of the established upper class that the newly rich are uncouth social climbers. — Ed.

houses and beneficiaries of charity affairs; indeed, the aristocracy must have the poor to demonstrate its superiority over other elites who devote themselves to earning money.

Eleventh, the poor, being powerless, can be made to absorb the costs of change and growth in American society. During the nineteenth century, they did the backbreaking work that built the cities; today, they are pushed out of their neighborhoods to make room for "progress." Urban renewal projects to hold middle-class taxpayers in the city and expressways to enable suburbanites to commute downtown have typically been located in poor neighborhoods, since no other group will allow itself to be displaced. For the same reason, universities, hospitals, and civic centers also expand into land occupied by the poor. The major costs of the industrialization of agriculture have been borne by the poor, who are pushed off the land without recompense; and they have paid a large share of the human cost of the growth of American power overseas, for they have provided many of the foot soldiers for Vietnam and other wars.

Twelfth, the poor facilitate and stabilize the American political process. Because they vote and participate in politics less than other groups, the political system is often free to ignore them. Moreover, since they can rarely support Republicans, they often provide the Democrats with a captive constituency that has no other place to go. As a result, the Democrats can count on their votes, and be more responsive to voters—for example, the white working class—who might otherwise switch to the Republicans.

Thirteen, the role of the poor in upholding conventional norms (see the *fifth* point, above) also has a significant political function. An economy based on the ideology of laissez faire requires a deprived population that is allegedly unwilling to work or that can be considered inferior because it must accept charity or welfare in order to survive. Not only does

the alleged moral deviancy of the poor reduce the moral pressure on the present political economy to eliminate poverty but socialist alternatives can be made to look quite unattractive if those who will benefit most from them can be described as lazy, spendthrift, dishonest, and promiscuous.

The Alternatives

I have described thirteen of the more important functions poverty and the poor satisfy in American society, enough to support the functionalist thesis that poverty, like any other social phenomenon, survives in part because it is useful to society or some of its parts. This analysis is not intended to suggest that because it is often functional, poverty *should* exist, or that it *must* exist. For one thing, poverty has many more dysfunctions than functions; for another, it is possible to suggest functional alternatives.

For example, society's dirty work could be done without poverty, either by automation or by paying "dirty workers" decent wages. Nor is it necessary for the poor to subsidize the many activities they support through their low-wage jobs. This would, however, drive up the costs of these activities, which would result in higher prices to their customers and clients. Similarly, many of the professionals who flourish because of the poor could be given other roles. Social workers could provide counseling to the affluent, as they prefer to do anyway; and the police could devote themselves to traffic and organized crime. Other roles would have to be found for badly trained or incompetent professionals now relegated to serving the poor, and someone else would have to pay their salaries. Fewer penologists would be employable, however. And pentecostal religion could probably not survive without the poor—nor would parts of the second- and third-hand-goods market. And in many cities, "used" housing that no

288 HERBERT J. GANS

one else wants would then have to be torn down at public expense.

Alternatives for the cultural functions of the poor could be found more easily and cheaply. Indeed, entertainers, hippies, and adolescents are already serving as the deviants needed to uphold traditional morality and as devotees of orgies to "staff" the fantasies of vicarious participation.

The status functions of the poor are another matter. In a hierarchical society, some people must be defined as inferior to everyone else with respect to a variety of attributes, but they need not be poor in the absolute sense. One could conceive of a society in which the "lower class," though last in the pecking order, received 75 percent of the median income, rather than 15–40 percent, as is now the case. Needless to say, this would require considerable income redistribution.

The contribution the poor make to the upward mobility of the groups that provide them with goods and services could also be maintained without the poor's having such low incomes. However, it is true that if the poor were more affluent, they would have access to enough capital to take over the provider role, thus competing with, and perhaps rejecting, the "outsiders." (Indeed, owing in part to antipoverty programs, this is already happening in a number of ghettos, where white storeowners are being replaced by Blacks.) Similarly, if the poor were more affluent, they would make less willing clients for upper-class philanthropy, although some would still use settlement houses to achieve upward mobility, as they do now. Thus "Society" could continue to run its philanthropic activities.

The political functions of the poor would be more difficult to replace. With increased affluence the poor would probably obtain more political power and be more active politically. With higher incomes and more political power, the poor would be likely to resist paying the costs of growth and change. Of course, it is possible to imagine urban renewal and highway projects that properly reimbursed the displaced people, but such projects would then become considerably more expensive, and many might never be built. This, in turn, would reduce the comfort and convenience of those who now benefit from urban renewal and expressways. Finally, hippies could serve also as more deviants to justify the existing political economy—as they already do. Presumably, however, if poverty were eliminated, there would be fewer attacks on that economy.

In sum, then, many of the functions served by the poor could be replaced if poverty were eliminated, but almost always at higher costs to others, particularly more affluent others. Consequently, a functional analysis must conclude that poverty persists not only because it fulfills a number of positive functions but also because many of the functional alternatives to poverty would be quite dysfunctional for the affluent members of society. A functional analysis thus ultimately arrives at much the same conclusion as radical sociology, except that radical thinkers treat as manifest what I describe as latent: that social phenomena that are functional for affluent or powerful groups and dysfunctional for poor or powerless ones persist; that when the elimination of such phenomena through functional alternatives would generate dysfunctions for the affluent or powerful, they will continue to persist; and that phenomena like poverty can be eliminated only when they become dysfunctional for the affluent or powerful, or when the powerless can obtain enough power to change society.

Reference

Merton, Robert F. 1949. "Manifest and Latent Functions." In Merton, *Social Theory and Social Structure*. Glencoe, IL: Free Press.

Questions

1. Why does Gans choose to use a *modified* form of Merton's concept of function?

2. What are functional alternatives to poverty?

3. Briefly list the thirteen functions that, according to Gans, poverty fulfills in our society. Where does each function fall in the larger categories of functions to which Gans alludes in his article: economic, social, cultural, political, and status?

4. As far as Gans is concerned which are larger—the functions of poverty or its dysfunctions? Why?

· 33 ·

The Job Ghetto

Katherine Newman and Chauncy Lennon

One of my students expressed the conventional "wisdom" this way: "If people want to bad enough, they can get a job and make something of themselves. It might not be a great job, but at least it's a job. No one has to be poor in this society." In the following article, Katherine Newman and Chauncy Lennon challenge such widely held assumptions about the availability of employment in our society.

To fix the welfare mess, conservatives say, we should stop making life on the dole so comfortable, cut benefits, and force overindulged welfare moms to go out and find honest jobs. Unskilled foreigners can find work, so why can't AFDC[1] recipients? With unemployment rates down, these expectations sound reasonable, particularly to middle-class Americans with stagnating incomes. The premise that jobs are available for those willing to take them is a great comfort to politicians with budget axes in hand and to conservative commentators calling on them to slash benefits. After all, they can claim they're not really casting poor women and children into the streets; they're just upholding the American work ethic.

But can just any warm body find a job? For the past two years, we have studied the low-wage labor market in Harlem, focusing on minimum-wage jobs in the fast-food industry, which are typical of the employment opportunities many reformers have in mind for welfare recipients. After all, these jobs presumably demand little skill, education, or prior work experience — or so the public believes.

The fast-food industry is growing more rapidly than almost any other service business and now employs more than 2.3 million workers. One in 15 Americans working today found their first job at McDonald's — not including Burger King and the rest. As a gateway to employment, fast-food establishments are gaining on the armed forces, which have long functioned as a national job-training factory. No wonder the average citizen believes these jobs are wide open! Yet, in inner cities, the picture looks different. With manufacturing gone, fast-food jobs have become the object of fierce competition.

Downward Pressures

Between 1992 and 1994, we tracked the work histories of 200 people working in fast-food restaurants in central Harlem, where according to official data about 18 percent of the population are unemployed and about 40 percent live below the poverty line. These numbers are typical of the communities where many long-term recipients of public assistance will have to look for work if their benefits are cut off. Some 29 percent of the households in Harlem receive public assistance.

---

[1]Aid to Families with Dependent Children, a form of welfare. — Ed.

Although the 200 workers in our study receive only the minimum wage, they are actually the victors in an intense competition to find work in a community with relatively few jobs to offer. At the restaurants where they work, the ratio of applicants to hires is approximately 14 to 1. Among those people who applied but were rejected for fast-food work in early 1993, 73 percent had not found work of any kind a year later, despite considerable effort. Even the youngest job-hunters in our study (16- to 18-year-olds) had applied for four or five positions before they came looking for these fast-food jobs. The oldest applicants (over 25) had applied for an average of seven or eight jobs.

The oversupply of job-seekers causes a creeping credentialism in the ghetto's low-wage service industries. Older workers in their twenties, who are more often high school graduates, now dominate jobs once taken by school dropouts or other young people first starting out. Long-term welfare recipients will have a tough time beating out their competition even for these low-wage jobs. They will be joining an inner-city labor market that is already saturated with better educated and more experienced workers who are preferred by employers.

Winners and Losers

We tracked nearly 100 people who applied for these minimum-wage jobs but were turned down, and compared them to the fortunate ones who got jobs. The comparison is instructive. Even in Harlem, African Americans are at a disadvantage in hiring compared to Latinos and others. Employers, including black employers, favor applicants who are not African American. Blacks are not shut out of the low-wage labor market; indeed, they represent about 70 percent of the new hires in these jobs. But they are rejected at a much higher rate than applicants from other ethnic groups with the same educational qualifications.

Employers also seem to favor job applicants who commute from more distant neighborhoods. The rejection rate for local applicants is higher than the rate for similarly educated individuals who live farther away. This pattern holds even for people of the same race, sex, and age. Other studies in the warehouse and dockyard industries report the same results. These findings suggest that residents of poor neighborhoods such as central Harlem are at a distinct disadvantage in finding minimum-wage jobs near home.

Mothers of young children face particular problems if they can't find jobs close to home. The costs and logistical complexities of commuting (and paying for longer child care hours to accommodate it) are a big burden.

In searching for jobs, "who you know" makes a big difference. Friends and family members who already have jobs help people get work even in the fast-food industry; those isolated from such networks are less likely to get hired. Personal contacts have long been recognized as crucial for getting higher-skilled employment. This research suggests that contacts are important at the bottom of the job ladder, too.

Native-born applicants are at a disadvantage compared to legal immigrants in securing entry-level work. In fact, even though central Harlem residents are nearly all African American, recent immigrants have a higher probability of being hired for Harlem's fast-food jobs than anyone else. Interviews with employers suggest that they believe immigrants are easier to manage in part because they come from countries where $4.25 an hour represents a king's ransom. Whether or not employers are right about the tractability of immigrants, such attitudes make it harder for the native-born to obtain low-wage jobs.

The people who succeed in getting these minimum-wage jobs are not new to the labor market. More than half of the new hires over the age of 18 found their first jobs when they were younger than 15 years of age. Even the people rejected for the minimum-wage positions had some prior job experience. Half of them also began working before they were 15 years old. Welfare recipients with no prior job experience, or no recent job experience, are going to be at a disadvantage in the competition.

"They Expect Too Much"

One explanation often advanced for low employment in poor communities is that the poor have unrealistic expectations. In this view, they are reluctant to seek (or take) jobs that fall below a "reservation wage," which is supposedly far above the minimum. We asked job-seekers who were refused these entry-level jobs what they were hoping for and what wages they would accept. Their desires were modest: $4.59 per hour on average, which is quite close to the minimum wage. The younger the job-seeker, the lower was the expectation.

These job-seekers were willing to accept even more modest wages. On average the lowest they would take was $4.17 per hour, which is less than the minimum level legally permitted for adult workers. It is striking that many applicants previously had higher salaries; the average wage for the best job they had ever held was $6.79 per hour. Many of central Harlem's job-hunters are suffering from downward mobility, falling into the minimum-wage market even though they have done better in the past.

Comparing job-seekers to jobholders shows the intensity of employment competition in the inner city, but it doesn't tell us how welfare recipients will fare. What assets do welfare recipients bring to the competition compared to other job-hunters? The news is grim.

Nationally, one-third of the long-term welfare recipients have received high school diplomas. Recently hired fast-food workers in central Harlem have completed high school at a higher rate—54 percent. Almost 40 percent of welfare recipients have not held jobs in the year preceding their enrollment in welfare. Yet even the central Harlem applicants rejected for fast-food jobs have had more job experience. They have held an average of more than three jobs before applying for these positions.

In short, it is simply not the case that anyone who wants a low-wage job can get one. As is true for almost any glutted labor market, there is a queue of applicants, and employers can be fairly choosy. When conservatives point to the success of immigrants as proof that jobs are available for welfare moms, they are ignoring the realities of the inner city. Ethnic minorities of all kinds are already locked into a fierce struggle for scarce opportunities at the bottom.

When they go looking for jobs, welfare recipients go to the back of a long line. Policymakers should neither fool nor comfort themselves with the notion that welfare mothers can simply go out and get jobs. Investment in public employment and tax incentives for private employers will be needed on a massive scale if anything like that rosy scenario is to come about. Even then, the competitive hurdles facing the very poor will be high and many better-qualified people will be out there looking to leap over them.

Questions:

1. According to Newman and Lennon's research, what sorts of factors distinguish jobholders and job-seekers in Harlem?

2. How likely do Newman and Lennon think it is that welfare moms will be able to get off welfare and find jobs in the near future? Explain.

· 34 ·

Confessions of a Nice Negro, or Why I Shaved My Head

Robin D. G. Kelley

No matter how much they distort reality, stereotypes exist and have an impact on people's lives. In this article, Robin Kelley recounts his experiences with what, to him, was a new stereotype.

It happened just the other day—two days into the new year, to be exact. I had dashed into the deserted lobby of an Ann Arbor movie theater, pulling the door behind me to escape the freezing winter winds Michigan residents have come to know so well. Behind the counter knelt a young white teenager filling the popcorn bin with bags of that awful pre-popped stuff. Hardly the enthusiastic employee; from a distance it looked like she was lost in deep thought. The generous display of body piercing suggested an X-generation flower child—perhaps an anthropology major into acid jazz and environmentalism, I thought. Sporting a black New York Yankees baseball cap and a black-and-beige scarf over my nose and mouth, I must have looked like I had stepped out of a John Singleton film. And because I was already late, I rushed madly toward the ticket counter.

The flower child was startled: "I don't have anything in the cash register," she blurted as she pulled the bag of popcorn in front of her for protection.

"Huh? I just want one ticket for *Little Women*, please—the two-fifteen show. My wife and daughter should already be in there." I slowly gestured to the theater door and gave her one of those innocent childlike glances I used to give my mom when I wanted to sit on her lap.

"Oh, god . . . I'm so sorry. A reflex. Just one ticket? You only missed the first twenty minutes. Enjoy the show."

Enjoy the show? Barely 1995 and here we go again. Another bout with racism in a so-called liberal college town; another racial drama in which I play the prime suspect. And yet I have to confess the situation was pretty funny. Just two hours earlier I couldn't persuade Elleza, my four-year-old daughter, to put her toys away; time-out did nothing, yelling had no effect, and the evil stare made no impact whatsoever. Thoroughly frustrated, I had only one option left: "Okay, I'm gonna tell Mommy!" Of course it worked.

So those five seconds as a media-made black man felt kind of good. I know it's a product of racism. I know that the myth of black male violence has resulted in the deaths of many innocent boys and men of darker hue. I know that the power to scare is not real power. I know all that—after all, I study this stuff for a living! For the moment, though, it felt good. (Besides, the ability to scare with your body can come in handy, especially when you're trying to get a good seat in a theater or avoid long lines.)

I shouldn't admit this, but I take particular pleasure in putting fear into people on the lookout for black male criminality mainly because those moments are so rare for me.

293

Indeed, my *inability* to employ blackmaleness as a weapon is the story of my life. Why I don't possess it, or rather possess so little of it, escapes me. I grew up poor in Harlem and Afrodena (the Negro West Side of Pasadena/Altadena, California). My mom was single during my formative preadolescent years, and for a brief moment she even received a welfare check. A hard life makes a hard nigga, so I've been told.

Never an egghead or a dork, as a teenager I was pretty cool. I did the house-party circuit on Friday and Saturday nights and used to stroll down the block toting the serious Radio Raheem boombox. Why, I even invaded movie theaters in the company of ten or fifteen hooded and high-topped black bodies, colonizing the balconies and occupying two seats per person. Armed with popcorn and Raisinettes as our missiles of choice, we dared any usher to ask us to leave. Those of us who had cars (we called them hoopties or rides back in that day) spent our lunch hours and precious class time hanging out in the school parking lot, running down our Die Hards to pump up Cameo, Funkadelic, Grandmaster Flash from our car stereos. I sported dickies and Levis, picked up that gangsta stroll, and when the shag came in style I was with it—always armed with a silk scarf to ensure that my hair was laid. Granted, I vomited after drinking malt liquor for the first time and my only hit of a joint ended abruptly in an asthma attack. But I was cool.

Sure, I was cool, but nobody feared me. That I'm relatively short with dimples and curly hair, speak softly in a rather medium to high-pitched voice, and have a "girl's name" doesn't help matters. And everyone knows that light skin is less threatening to white people than blue-black or midnight brown. Besides, growing up with a soft-spoken, uncharacteristically passive West Indian mother deep into East Indian religions, a mother who sometimes walked barefoot in the streets of Harlem,

a mother who insisted on proper diction and never, ever, ever used a swear word, screwed me up royally. I could never curse right. My mouth had trouble forming the words—"fuck" always came out as "fock" and "goddamn" always sounded like it's spelled, not "gotdayum," the way my Pasadena homies pronounced it in their Calabama twang. I don't even recall saying the word "bitch" unless I was quoting somebody or some authorless vernacular rhyme. For some unknown reason, that word scared me.

Moms dressed me up in the coolest mod outfits—short pant suits with matching hats, Nehru jackets, those sixties British-looking turtlenecks. Sure, she got some of that stuff from John's Bargain Store or Goodwill, but I always looked "cute." More stylish than roguish. Kinda like W. E. B. Du Bois[1] as a toddler, or those turn-of-the-century photos of middle-class West Indian boys who grow up to become prime ministers or poets. Ghetto ethnographers back in the late sixties and early seventies would not have found me or my family very "authentic," especially if they had discovered that one of my middle names is Gibran, after the Lebanese poet Kahlil Gibran.

Everybody seemed to like me. Teachers liked me, kids liked me; I even fell in with some notorious teenage criminals at Pasadena High School because *they* liked me. I remember one memorable night in the ninth grade when I went down to the Pasadena Boys' Club to take photos of some of my partners on the basketball team. On my way home some big kids, eleventh-graders to be exact, tried to take my camera. The ringleader pulled out a knife and

---

[1]W. E. B. Du Bois (1868–1963) was the first African American to earn a Ph.D. from Harvard University (1895). He taught sociology at several universities, was a strong advocate for racial integration, and in 1909 founded the National Association for the Advancement of Colored People. Ultimately, Du Bois lost faith in the possibility of integration and began to promote segregation. He was dismissed from the NAACP and moved to Ghana, where he lived until his death. —Ed.

gently poked it against my chest. I told them it was my stepfather's camera and if I came home without it he'd kick my ass for a week. Miraculously, this launched a whole conversation about stepfathers and how messed up they are, which must have made them feel sorry for me. Within minutes we were cool; they let me go unmolested and I had made another friend.

In affairs of the heart, however, "being liked" had the opposite effect. I can only recall having had four fights in my entire life, all of which were with girls who supposedly liked me but thoroughly beat my behind. Sadly, my record in the boxing ring of puppy love is still 0–4. By the time I graduated to serious dating, being a nice guy seemed like the root of all my romantic problems. I resisted jealousy, tried to be understanding, brought flowers and balloons, opened doors, wrote poems and songs, and seemed to always be on my knees for one reason or another. If you've ever watched "Love Connection" or read *Cosmopolitan,* you know the rest of the story: I practically never had sex and most of the women I dated left me in the cold for roughnecks. My last girlfriend in high school, the woman I took to my prom, the woman I once thought I'd die for, tried to show me the light: "Why do you always ask me what I want? Why don't you just *tell* me what you want me to do? Why don't you take charge and *be a man?* If you want to be a real man you can't be nice all the time!"

I always thought she was wrong; being nice has nothing to do with being a man. While I still think she's wrong, it's an established fact that our culture links manhood to terror and power, and that black men are frequently imaged as the ultimate in hypermasculinity. But the black man as the prototype of violent hypermasculinity is as much a fiction as the happy Sambo. No matter what critics and stand-up comics might say, I know from experience that not all black men—and here I'm only speaking of well-lighted or daytime situations—generate fear. Who scares and who doesn't has a lot to do with the body in question; it is dependent on factors such as age, skin color, size, clothes, hairstyle, and even the sound of one's voice. The cops who beat Rodney King and the jury who acquitted King's assailants openly admitted that the size, shape, and color of his body automatically made him a threat to the officers' safety.

On the other hand, the threatening black male body can take the most incongruous forms. Some of the hardest brothas on my block in West Pasadena kept their perms in pink rollers and hairnets. It was not unusual to see young black men in public with curlers, tank-top undershirts, sweatpants, black mid-calf dress socks, and Stacey Adams shoes, hanging out on the corner or on the basketball court. And we all knew that these brothas were not to be messed with. (The rest of the world probably knows it by now, too, since black males in curlers are occasionally featured on "Cops" and "America's Most Wanted" as notorious drug dealers or heartless pimps.)

Whatever the source of this ineffable terror, my body simply lacked it. Indeed, the older I got and the more ensconced I became in the world of academia, the less threatening I seemed. Marrying and having a child also reduced the threat factor. By the time I hit my late twenties, my wife, Diedra, and I found ourselves in the awkward position of being everyone's favorite Negroes. I don't know how many times we've attended dinner parties where we were the only African Americans in the room. Occasionally there were others, but we seemed to have a monopoly on the dinner party invitations. This not only happened in Ann Arbor, where there is a small but substantial black population to choose from, but in the Negro mecca of Atlanta, Georgia. Our hosts always felt comfortable asking us "sensitive" questions about race that they would not dare ask other black colleagues and friends: What do African Americans think about Farrakhan?

Ben Chavis? Nelson Mandela? Most of my black students are very conservative and career-oriented—why is that? How can we mend the relations between blacks and Jews? Do you celebrate Kwanzaa? Do you put anything in your hair to make it that way? What are the starting salaries for young black faculty nowadays?

Of course, these sorts of exchanges appear regularly in most black autobiographies. As soon as they're comfortable, it is not uncommon for white people to take the opportunity to find out everything they've always wanted to know about "us" (which also applies to other people of color, I'm sure) but were afraid to ask. That they feel perfectly at ease asking dumb or unanswerable questions is not simply a case of (mis)perceived racelessness. Being a "nice Negro" has a lot to do with gender, and my peculiar form of "left-feminist-funny-guy" masculinity—a little Kevin Hooks, some Bobby McFerrin, a dash of Woody Allen—is regarded as less threatening than that of most other black men.

Not that I mind the soft-sensitive masculine persona—after all, it is the genuine me, a product of my mother's heroic and revolutionary child-rearing style. But there are moments when I wish I could invoke the intimidation factor of blackmaleness on demand. If I only had that look—that Malcolm X/Mike Tyson/Ice Cube/Larry Fishburne/Bigger Thomas/Fruit of Islam look—I could keep the stupid questions at bay, make college administrators tremble, and scare editors into submission. Subconsciously, I decided that I had to do something about my image. Then, as if by magic, my wish was fulfilled.

Actually, it began as an accident involving a pair of electric clippers and sleep deprivation—a bad auto-cut gone awry. With my lowtop fade on the verge of a Sly Stone afro, I was in desperate need of a trim. Diedra didn't have the time to do it, and as it was February (Black History Month), I was on the chitlin'

lecture circuit and couldn't spare forty-five minutes at a barber shop, so I elected to do it myself. Standing in a well-lighted bathroom, armed with two mirrors, I started trimming. Despite a steady hand and what I've always believed was a good eye, my hair turned out lopsided. I kept trimming and trimming to correct my error, but as my flattop sank lower, a yellow patch of scalp began to rise above the surrounding hair, like one of those big granite mounds dotting the grassy knolls of Central Park. A nice yarmulke could have covered it, but that would have been more difficult to explain than a bald spot. So, bearing in mind role models like Michael Jordan, Charles Barkley, Stanley Crouch, and Onyx (then the hip-hop group of the hour), I decided to take it all off.

I didn't think much of it at first, but the new style accomplished what years of evil stares and carefully crafted sartorial statements could not: I began to scare people. The effect was immediate and dramatic. Passing strangers avoided me and smiled less frequently. Those who did smile or make eye contact seemed to be deliberately trying to disarm me—a common strategy taught in campus rape-prevention centers. Scaring people was fun for a while, but I especially enjoyed standing in the line at the supermarket with my bald head, baggy pants, high-top Reeboks, and long black hooded down coat, humming old standards like "Darn That Dream," "A Foggy Day," and "I Could Write a Book." Now *that* brought some stares. I must have been convincing, since I adore those songs and have been humming them ever since I can remember. No simple case of cultural hybridity here, just your average menace to society with a deep appreciation for Gershwin, Rodgers and Hart, Van Heusen, Cole Porter, and Jerome Kern.

Among my colleagues, my bald head became the lead subject of every conversation. "You look older, more mature." "With that new cut you come across as much more serious than usual." "You really look quite rugged and masculine with a bald head." My close friends dispensed with the euphemisms and went straight to the point: "Damn. You look scary!" The most painful comment was that I looked like a "B-Boy wannabe" and was "too old for that shit." I had to remind my friend that I'm an OBB (Original B-Boy), that I was in the eleventh grade in 1979 when the Sugar Hill Gang dropped "Rapper's Delight," and that *his* tired behind was in graduate school at the time. Besides, B-Boy was not the intent.

In the end, however, I got more questions than comments. Was I in crisis? Did I want to talk? What was I trying to say by shaving my head? What was the political point of my actions? Once the novelty passed, I began getting those "speak for the race" questions that irritated the hell out of me when I had hair. Why have *black men* begun to shave their heads in greater numbers? Why have so many black athletes decided to shave their heads? Does this new trend have some kind of phallic meaning? Against my better judgment, I found myself coming up with answers to these questions — call it an academician's reflex. I don't remember exactly what I said, but it usually began with black prizefighter Jack Johnson, America's real life "baaad nigger" of the early twentieth century, whose head was always shaved and greased, and ended with the hip-hop community's embrace of an outlaw status. Whatever it was, it made sense at the time.

The publicity photo for my recent book, *Race Rebels,* clearly generated the most controversy among my colleagues. It diverged dramatically from the photo on my first book, where I look particularly innocent, almost angelic. In that first photo I smiled just enough to make my dimples visible; my eyes gazed away from the camera in sort of a dreamy, contemplative pose; my haircut was nondescript and the natural sunlight had a kind of halo effect. The Izod shirt was the icing on the cake. By

contrast, the photograph for *Race Rebels* (which Diedra set up and shot, by the way) has me looking directly into the camera, arms folded, bald head glistening from baby oil and rear window light, with a grimace that could give Snoop Doggy Dogg a run for his money. The lens made my arms appear much larger than they really are, creating a kind of Popeye effect. Soon after the book came out, I received several e-mail messages about the photo. A particularly memorable one came from a friend and fellow historian in Australia. In the course of explaining to me how he had corrected one of his students who had read an essay of mine and presumed I was a woman, he wrote: "Mind you, the photo in your book should make things clear — the angle and foreshortening of the arms, and the hairstyle make it one of the most masculine author photos I've seen recently????!!!!!!"

My publisher really milked this photo, which actually fit well with the book's title. For the American Studies Association meeting in Nashville, Tennessee, which took place the week the book came out, my publisher bought a full-page ad on the back cover of an ASA handout, with my mug staring dead at you. Everywhere I turned — in hotel elevators, hallways, lobbies, meeting rooms — I saw myself, and it was not exactly a pretty sight. The quality of the reproduction (essentially a high-contrast xerox) made me appear harder, meaner, and crazier than the original photograph.

The situation became even stranger since I had decided to abandon the skinhead look and grow my hair back. In fact, by the time of the ASA meeting I was on the road (since abandoned) toward a big Black Power Afro — a retro style that at the time seemed to be making a comeback. Worse still, I had come to participate in a round-table discussion on black hair! My paper, titled "Nap Time: Historicizing the Afro," explored the political implications of competing narratives of the Afro's origins and meaning. Overall, it was a terrific session; the room was packed and the discussion was stimulating. But inevitably the question came up: "Although this isn't directly related to his paper, I'd like to find out from Professor Kelley why he shaved his head. Professor Kelly, given the panel's topic and in light of the current ads floating about with your picture on them, can you shed some light on what is attractive to black men about baldness?" The question was posed by a very distinguished and widely read African-American literary scholar. Hardly the naif, he knew the answers as well as I did, but wanted to generate a public discussion. And he succeeded. For ten minutes the audience ran the gamut of issues revolving around race, gender, sexuality, and the politics of style. Even the issue of bald heads as phallic symbols came up. "It's probably true," I said, "but when I was cutting my hair at three-o'clock in the morning I wasn't thinking 'penis.'" Eventually the discussion drifted from black masculinity to the tremendous workloads of minority scholars, which, in all honesty, was the source of my baldness in the first place. Unlike the golden old days, when doing hair was highly ritualized and completely integrated into daily life, we're so busy mentoring and publishing and speaking and fighting that we have very little time to attend to our heads.

Beyond the session itself, that ad continued to haunt me during the entire conference. Every ten minutes, or so it seemed, someone came up to me and offered unsolicited commentary on the photo. One person slyly suggested that in order to make the picture complete I should have posed with an Uzi. When I approached a very good friend of mine, a historian who is partly my Jewish mother and partly my confidante and *always* looking out for my best interests, the first words out of her mouth were, "Robin, I hate that picture! It's the worst picture of you I've ever seen. It doesn't do you justice. Why did you let them use it?"

"It's not that bad," I replied. "Diedra likes it—she took the picture. You just don't like my bald head."

"No, that's not it. I like the bald look on some men, and you have a very nice head. The problem is the photo and the fact that I know what kind of person you are. None of your gentleness and lovability comes out in that picture. Now, don't get a swelled head when I say this, but you have a delightful face and expression that makes people feel good, even when you're talking about serious stuff. The way you smile, there's something unbelievably safe about you."

It was a painful compliment. And yet I knew deep down that she was telling the truth. I've always been unbelievably safe, not just because of my look but because of my actions. Not that I consciously try to put people at ease, to erase conflict and difference, to remain silent on sensitive issues. I can't quite put a finger on it. Perhaps it's my mother's politeness drills? Perhaps it's a manifestation of my continuing bout with shyness? Maybe it has something to do with the sense of joy I get from stimulating conversations? Or maybe it's linked to the fact that my mom refused to raise me in a manner boys are accustomed to? Most likely it is a product of cultural capital[2]—the fact that I *can* speak the language, (re)cite the texts, exhibit the manners and mannerisms that are inherent to bourgeois academic culture. My colleagues identify with me because I can talk intelligently about their scholarship on their terms, which invariably has the effect of creating an illusion of brilliance. As Frantz Fanon said in *Black Skin, White*

---

[2]The concept of cultural capital has gained currency through the work of Marxist sociologist Pierre Bourdieu, who uses the term to refer to specific skills and competencies (for example, the ability to use language and other social skills) that middle- and upper-class parents are able to pass on to their children. Ownership of cultural as well as economic capital provides advantages to members of the middle and upper classes and increases the probability of their success. —Ed.

Masks, the mere fact that he was an articulate *black* man who read a lot rendered him a stunning specimen of erudition in the eyes of his fellow intellectuals in Paris.

Whatever the source of my ineffable lovability, I've learned that it's not entirely a bad thing. In fact, if the rest of the world could look a little deeper, beyond the hardcore exterior—the wide bodies, the carefully constructed grimaces, the performance of terror—they would find many, many brothas much nicer and smarter than myself. The problem lies in a racist culture, a highly gendered racist culture, that is so deeply enmeshed in the fabric of daily life that it's practically invisible. The very existence of the "nice Negro," like the model-minority myth pinned on Asian Americans, renders the war on those "other," hardcore niggas justifiable and even palatable. In a little-known essay on the public image of world champion boxer Joe Louis, the radical Trinidadian writer C. L. R. James put it best: "This attempt to hold up Louis as a model Negro has strong overtones of condescension and race prejudice. It implies: 'See! When a Negro knows how to conduct himself, he gets on very well and we all love him.' From there the next step is: 'If only all Negros behaved like Joe, the race problem would be solved'" (1946).

Of course we all know this is a bunch of fiction. Behaving "like Joe" was merely a code for deference and patience, which is all the more remarkable given his vocation. Unlike his predecessor Jack Johnson—the bald-headed prize fighter who transgressed racial boundaries by sleeping with and even marrying white women, who refused to apologize for his "outrageous" behavior, who boasted of his prowess in every facet of life (he even wrapped gauze around his penis to make it appear bigger under his boxing shorts)—Joe Louis was America's hero. As James put it, he was a credit to his race, "I mean the human race." (Re)presented as a humble Alabama boy, God-fearing and devoid of hatred, Louis was constructed in the press as a raceless man whose masculinity was put to good, patriotic use. To many of his white fans, he was a man in the ring and a boy—a good boy—outside of it. To many black folks, he was a hero because he had the license to kick white men's butts and yet maintain the admiration and respect of a nation. Thus, despite similarities in race, class, and vocation, and their common iconization, Louis and Johnson exhibited public behavior that reflected radically different masculinities.

Here, then, is a lesson we cannot ignore. There is some truth in the implication that race (or gender) conflict is partly linked to behavior and how certain behavior is perceived. If our society, for example, could dispense with rigid, archaic notions of appropriate masculine and feminine behavior, perhaps we might create a world that nurtures, encourages, and even rewards nice guys. If violence were not so central to American culture—to the way manhood is defined, to the way in which the state keeps African-American men in check, to the way men interact with women, to the way oppressed peoples interact with one another—perhaps we might see the withering away of white fears of black men. Perhaps young black men wouldn't feel the need to adopt hardened, threatening postures merely to survive in a Doggy-Dogg world. Not that black men ought to become colored equivalents of Alan Alda. Rather, black men ought to be whomever or whatever they want to be, without unwarranted criticism or societal pressures to conform to a particular definition of manhood. They could finally dress down without suspicion, talk loudly without surveillance, and love each other without sanction. Fortunately, such a transformation would also mean the long-awaited death of the "nice Negro."

Not in my lifetime. Any fool can look around and see that the situation for race and gender relations in general, and for black males in particular, has taken a turn for the worse—and relief is nowhere in sight. In the meantime, I will make the most of my "nice Negro" status. When it's all said and done, there is nothing romantic or interesting about playing Bigger Thomas. Maybe I can't persuade a well-dressed white couple to give up their box seats, but at least they'll listen to me. For now. . . .

Reference

James, C. L. R. 1946. "Joe Louis and Jack Johnson." *Labor Action*, July 1.

Questions

1. Have you ever been a victim of stereotyping—for example, based on your gender, race, ethnicity, sexual orientation, or social class? If you have, how did it make you feel?

2. Early in the article Kelley refers to the "media-made black man." What did he mean by this?

3. Does a shaved head have a different meaning for a black man than for a white man? In other words, would people find a white man with a shaved head to be scary? Why or why not?

4. Kelley says that "any fool can look around and see that the situation for race and gender relations in general, and for black males in particular, has taken a turn for the worse—and relief is nowhere in sight." To what extent do you agree with this assessment?

·35·

The Model Minority Myth
Asian Americans Confront Growing Backlash

Yin Ling Leung

In this article, Yin Ling Leung reveals something of a social paradox: Members of some groups in our society are singled out for discriminatory treatment because they are judged by the dominant group to be "inferior," while others are singled out for discrimination because they are judged "superior." Note that here, the terms "Asians" and "Asian Americans" refer to a wide range of peoples, including Cambodians, Chinese, Filipinos, Hmong, Japanese, Koreans, Laotians, Thais and Vietnamese.

The once predominant media caricatures of Asians such as the effeminate Charlie Chan, the evil Fu Manchu, the exotic dragon-lady Suzy Wong or the docile, submissive Mrs. Livingston are giving way to a more subtle but equally damaging image. The emerging picture of Asians as hard-working, highly-educated, family-oriented, and financially successful— in short, a "model minority"—appears benign at first, even beneficial. However, Asians are experiencing a growing backlash against their "model minority" status. The pervasive perception that Asian Americans are "making it," even surpassing whites despite their minority status, is resulting in discriminatory college admittance practices and a rise in anti-Asian sentiment.

What is now being coined the "model minority myth" began to take root in the late 1960s, after increasing numbers of Asian immigrants came to the U.S. under the Immigration Act of 1965.[1] A 1966 *U.S. News and World Report*

article, entitled "Success Story of One Minority Group in the U.S.," portrayed Asian Americans as hardworking and uncomplaining, and implied that discrimination is not an obstacle for Asian Americans. A rash of similar articles followed, each attempting to reveal the "formula" responsible for Asian American success and prosperity.

The increased numbers of Southeast Asian refugees (the Hmong, Vietnamese, Laotian, and Kampuchean/Cambodians) and the increased immigration from Taiwan, Korea and Hong Kong have made Asians the second-fastest-growing minority population in the U.S. With this increase in numbers, the media has increased its focus on the "success stories" of Asian Americans as a whole. Articles in popular magazines such as *Newsweek, U.S. News and World Report* and others, with titles like "Asian-Americans: A 'Model Minority,'" "The Drive to Excel," "A Formula for Success," "The Promise of America," and "The Triumph of Asian Americans," perpetuate a distorted image of universal Asian-American success. One article in *Fortune* magazine portrayed

---

[1] Center for Third World Reporting. 1987. *Minority Trendsletter,* Winter, pp. 5–7.

Asians as a super competitive force, or "super minority," outperforming even the majority white population.

Myth Versus Reality

A closer examination of the facts, however, reveals holes in both the "model minority" and "super minority" myths. For example, 1980 census figures place the mean family income for Asian American families in the U.S. at $26,456—nearly $3,000 higher than white families. These figures dramatically change, however, if adjusted for the number of workers per family. Because Asians tend to have more workers per family, the total income of a family reflects less per individual. In addition, over 64 percent of Asian Americans live in urban areas of San Francisco, Los Angeles, New York and Honolulu, where the incomes and cost of living are correspondingly higher.

The model minority myth also masks the complexity of Asians in America and the different realities they face. In fact, Asian Americans come from sharply distinct backgrounds which determine their life in the U.S. Many of the "successful" Asian immigrants touted by the media as exemplifying the model minority phenomenon come from families that have been in the states for many generations or from aristocratic, elite, educated, economically-advantaged backgrounds in their home countries. For example, the early Vietnamese refugee boat people were from wealthier and more educated communities than the more recent refugees from Vietnam. In addition, immigrants from China, Japan, and Korea tend to come from relatively more privileged backgrounds.

The more recent immigrants from Southeast Asia, like the Hmong, Laotian, Kampuchean/Cambodian, and the Vietnamese refugees arriving after 1976, do not mirror the image of instant success that the media perpetuates.

These hundreds of thousands of Southeast Asian refugees suffer not only from language difficulties, but also from deep-seated emotional and psychological disorders, resulting from the trauma they experienced in the war-torn countries of Southeast Asia. Asian refugees also face limited work opportunities, substandard wages and lack of health benefits and unhealthy working conditions.

Another facet to [the] model minority myth is the belief that all Asians excel academically. There is no disputing that Asian Americans are "overrepresented" in the nation's colleges and universities. Asians make up approximately 3.7 million or 1.6 percent of the total U.S. population, but comprise 8 to 18 percent of enrollment in the nation's top colleges and universities. At the University of California at Berkeley, Asian students make up a quarter of the student population.

The media links Asian "success" in education with their strong familial bonds. This is, to some extent, an accurate portrayal. Many Asian cultures believe that social mobility is directly tied to education and therefore spend a disproportionate amount of family income on education, as compared to white families. Because it is a considerable sacrifice for most immigrant families to send their children to college, Asian students are often urged by their parents to pursue "safer" professions, such as medicine, engineering and other fields where the economic payback is proportionate to the number of years (and dollars) invested in education.

Even in these "safe" professions, however, Asians are discovering that quiet achievement and good job performance may not amount to promotions. A *Newsweek* article recently pointed to a phenomenon of Asian middle-management professionals, especially in corporate business fields, who "top-out," reaching a plateau beyond which their employers will not promote them.

Backlash: Asians Face Discrimination

Repercussions of the model minority myth on Asian Americans could be described as "the many being punished by the success of a few." Asians of all classes and generations are experiencing a rise in anti-Asian sentiment. This anti-Asian sentiment is expressed both through subtle, systematic discrimination, particularly in higher education, and through racially-motivated violence.

Because of the disproportionate numbers of Asian Americans in the nation's universities, some colleges are denying Asians affirmative action consideration. At Princeton University, for example, where Asians make up approximately 8.5 percent of the entering class, admissions officials no longer consider Asian Americans as a minority group, despite federal regulations which define them as a protected subgroup.

Other prestigious colleges and universities are systematically excluding qualified Asians through the application of heavily subjective criteria. At the University of California at Berkeley, for example, despite a 14 percent rise in applications between 1983 to 1985, the number of Asian Americans admitted to UCB dropped 20 percent in 1984.

The Asian American Task Force on UC Admissions, which conducted a seven-month study, found that the university had temporarily used a minimum SAT verbal score to disqualify applicants. While Asian Americans excel on the math sections of the SAT, their national average on the verbal portion of the test was under 400. The Task Force also found that UCB now relies more heavily on subjective criteria for freshmen admissions. For the fall of 1987, grades and test scores will determine only 40 percent of admittees, while 30 percent will be chosen by subjective factors which tend to operate against Asians.

According to Henry Der, executive director of Chinese for Affirmative Action: "Qualified Asian students are being excluded from the Berkeley campus in substantial numbers. It is apparent that UC policy changes are conscious attempts to limit the growth of Asian students, to the benefit of qualified white students."

Discriminatory practices at UC Berkeley point to a nationwide trend. At Harvard University, where Asians make up 10.9 percent of the first-year class, admitted Asian students had scores substantially higher than white students who were admitted. At Brown University, a study conducted by Asian-American students found that Asian-American admittance rates in the early 1980s had been consistently lower than the all-college admittance rate.

There is increasing evidence that these and other select schools are designing "hidden quotas" to exclude otherwise qualified Asian applicants. For example, a recent survey of Asian-American applicants at Stanford demonstrated that popular images of Asians as narrowly-focused math and science students influenced how admissions officers judged Asians for entrance to college campuses. Just as "regional diversity" was used as a mechanism to keep Jews, who tended to be concentrated in metropolitan areas like New York and Los Angeles, out of elite institutions prior to World War II, "extra-curricular and leadership" criteria are functioning in a similar manner for certain Asians. The Stanford study found that although Asian Americans participated in nearly the same proportion as whites in high school sports, in equal numbers in music and in greater numbers in social, ethnic and community organi-zations, "intentional or unintentional" biases have made many applicants the victims of racial stereotypes.

Black conservative Thomas Sowell and other neoconservatives applaud the divorce of Asians from their minority status. Sowell believes that this will cause schools to be just as rigorous in selecting Asian students as they are at selecting majority white students. In this way, he continues, students will not be mismatched with their schools, a problem he attributes to quota requirements.

Anti-Asian Sentiment Rising

The model minority myth, coupled with the rising economic prowess of Pacific Rim Asian countries and the corresponding economic downturn in the U.S., has given rise to an increase in anti-Asian violence. In 1981, the Japanese American Citizens League recorded seven cases in which anti-Asian sentiment was expressed verbally, legislatively or physically; in 1982 they recorded four; in 1983, 20; in 1984, 30; in 1985, 48.

One explanation for this rise in anti-Asian violence is that Asians are being used as scapegoats[2] for the nation's economic problems. Both business and labor have waged explicitly anti-Asian media campaigns portraying Japanese competition as an explanation for the ills of American industry.

The case of Vincent Chin dramatically demonstrates the potential impact of such campaigns. Chin, a 27-year-old Chinese-American resident of Detroit, was bludgeoned to death by two white unemployed auto workers. The two men, who were merely fined and put on probation, mistook him for Japanese. They saw Chin as a representative of the Japanese automobile imports business, which they blamed for the loss of their jobs. Violence against Asian refugees and immigrants who compete for scarce resources in low-income communities has also dramatically increased.

The Asian Community Responds

Asian Americans are contradicting the very stereotype of the hard-working, uncomplaining

minority by protesting the discriminatory practices in the nation's colleges and in the job market. For example, the Chinese American Legal Defense Fund, a Michigan-based organization, has filed suit against UC Berkeley and several other elite institutions, including Stanford, Princeton, Yale, and MIT. They charge that campuses have imposed "secret quotas" on Asians because of their growing enrollments. In another case, Yat-Pang Au, valedictorian of San Jose's Gunderson High School, with "top test scores and an impressive array of extracurricular activities," is threatening a civil rights suit against UC Berkeley for denying his entrance to the competitive College of Engineering.

At least one school has responded to this pressure by re-examining its admittance policies. A recent study of Asian student admission at Stanford, Brown, Harvard, and Princeton by John H. Bunzel and Jeffrey K. D. Au, both from Stanford, found that Stanford was the only university to buck the trend of declining Asian admissions. The 1986 entering class of Asian Americans increased from 119 last year to 245 this year. Asians at Stanford make up 15.6 percent of the class, still lower than the UC Berkeley, where 26.5 percent of this year's entering class are Asian Americans.

Mobilizations against anti-Asian violence have also begun on the national and the community level. The Japanese American Citizens League, the Violence Against Asians Taskforce, Chinese for Affirmative Action, and other Asian groups have monitored incidents of anti-Asian violence and pressured the U.S. Commission on Civil Rights and other government bodies to confront and investigate the problem. Projects such as the Coalition to Break the Silence and the Community Violence Prevention Project, both in Oakland, CA, are fighting to raise community consciousness on the issue through community forums and legislative testimony. The Coalition to Break the Silence has also developed ties with other organizations doing similar work in Los Angeles, New York, and Boston.

[2]The concept of "scapegoat" was explained in reading 29, "Anti-Immigrant Violence," fn. 2.

Questions

1. What does Leung mean by "backlash"? Can you think of any other examples of this phenomenon?

2. Some people who oppose affirmative action and quotas for blacks and Hispanics are nonetheless in favor of setting limits on how many Asian Americans should be admitted to colleges and universities. What could explain this apparent contradiction?

3. For individual Asian Americans, what difficulties might be caused by being stereotyped as a "model minority"?

·36·

Tales out of Medical School

Adriane Fugh-Berman, M.D.

Recall that the Sadkers (reading 19) observed that girls and boys may sit in the same classrooms, read the same books, and have the same teachers, but they often do not get the same education. In this walk down memory lane, Adriane Fugh-Berman suggests that medical school is similarly bifurcated by gender.

With the growth of the women's health movement and the influx of women into medical schools, there has been abundant talk of a new enlightenment among physicians. Last summer, many Americans were shocked when Frances Conley, a neurosurgeon on the faculty of Stanford University's medical school, resigned her position, citing "pervasive sexism." Conley's is a particularly elite and male-dominated subspecialty, but her story is not an isolated one. I graduated from the Georgetown University School of Medicine in 1988, and while medical training is a sexist process anywhere, Georgetown built disrespect for women into its curriculum.

A Jesuit school, most recently in the news as the alma mater of William Kennedy Smith, Georgetown has an overwhelmingly white, male and conservative faculty. At a time when women made up one-third of all medical students in the United States, and as many as one-half at some schools, my class was 73 percent male and more than 90 percent white.

The prevailing attitude toward women was demonstrated on the first day of classes by my anatomy instructor, who remarked that our elderly cadaver "must have been a Playboy bunny" before instructing us to cut off her large breasts and toss them into the thirty-gallon trash can marked "cadaver waste." Barely hours into our training, we were already being taught that there was nothing to be learned from examining breasts. Given the fact that one out of nine American women will develop breast cancer in her lifetime, to treat breasts as extraneous tissue seemed an appalling waste of an educational opportunity, as well as a not-so-subtle message about the relative importance of body parts. How many of my classmates now in practice, I wonder, regularly examine the breasts of their female patients?

My classmates learned their lesson of disrespect well. Later in the year one carved a tick-tack-toe on a female cadaver and challenged others to play. Another gave a languorous sigh after dissecting female genitalia, as if he had just had sex. "Guess I should have a cigarette now," he said.

Ghoulish humor is often regarded as a means by which med students overcome fear and anxiety. But it serves a darker purpose as well: Depersonalizing our cadaver was good preparation for depersonalizing our patients later. Further on in my training an ophthalmologist would yell at me when I hesitated to place a small instrument meant to measure eye pressure on a fellow student's cornea because I was afraid it would hurt. "You have to learn to treat patients as lab animals," he snarled at me.

On the first day of an emergency medicine rotation in our senior year, students were asked who had had experience in placing a central line (an intravenous line placed into a major vein under the clavicle or in the neck). Most of the male students raised their hands. None of the women did. For me, it was graphic proof of inequity in teaching; the men had had the procedure taught to them, but the women had not. Teaching rounds were often, for women, a spectator sport. One friend told me how she craned her neck to watch a physician teach a minor surgical procedure to a male student; when they were done the physician handed her his dirty gloves to discard. I have seen a male attending physician demonstrate an exam on a patient and then wade through several female medical students to drag forth a male in order to teach it to him. This sort of discrimination was common and quite unconscious: The women just didn't register as medical students to some of the doctors. Female students, for their part, tended (like male ones) to gloss over issues that might divert attention, energy or focus from the all-important goal of getting through their training. "Oh, they're just of the old school," a female classmate remarked to me, as if being ignored by our teachers was really rather charming, like having one's hand kissed.

A woman resident was giving a radiology presentation and I felt mesmerized. Why did I feel so connected and involved? It suddenly occurred to me that the female physician was regularly meeting my eyes; most of the male residents and attendings made eye contact with only the men.

"Why are women's brains smaller than men's?" asked a surgeon of a group of male medical students in the doctors' lounge (I was in the room as well, but was apparently invisible). "Because they're missing logic!" Guffaws all around.

Such instances of casual sexism are hardly unique to Georgetown, or indeed to medical schools. But at Georgetown female students also had to contend with outright discrimination of a sort most Americans probably think no longer exists in education. There was one course women were not allowed to take. The elective in sexually transmitted diseases required an interview with the head of the urology department, who was teaching the course. Those applicants with the appropriate genitalia competed for invitations to join the course (a computer was supposed to assign us electives, which we had ranked in order of preference, but that process had been circumvented for this course). Three women who requested an interview were told that the predominantly gay male clinic where the elective was held did not allow women to work there. This was news to the clinic's executive director, who stated that women were employed in all capacities.

The women who wanted to take the course repeatedly tried to meet with the urologist, but he did not return our phone calls. (I had not applied for the course, but became involved as an advocate for the women who wanted to take it.) We figured out his schedule, waylaid him in the hall and insisted that a meeting be set up.

At this meeting, clinic representatives disclosed that a survey had been circulated years before to the clientele in order to ascertain whether women workers would be accepted; 95 percent of the clients voted to welcome women. They were also asked whether it was acceptable to have medical students working at the clinic; more than 90 percent approved. We were then told that these results could not be construed to indicate that clients did not mind women medical students; the clients would naturally have assumed that "medical student" meant "male medical student." Even if that were true, we asked, if 90 percent of clients did not mind medical students and 95 percent did not mind women, couldn't a reasonable person assume that female medical students would be acceptable? No, we were informed. Another study would have to be done.

We raised formal objections to the school. Meanwhile, however, the entire elective process had been postponed by the dispute, and the blame for the delay and confusion was placed on us. The hardest part of the struggle, indeed, was dealing with the indifference of most of our classmates—out of 206, maybe a dozen actively supported us—and with the intense anger of the ten men who had been promised places in the course.

"Just because you can't take this course," one of the men said to me, "why do you want to ruin it for the rest of us?" It seemed incredible to me that I had to argue that women should be allowed to take the same courses as men. The second or third time someone asked me the same question, I suggested that if women were not allowed to participate in the same curriculum as men, then in the interest of fairness we should get a 50 percent break on our $22,500 annual tuition. My colleague thought that highly unreasonable.

Eventually someone in administration realized that not only were we going to sue the school for discrimination but that we had an open-and-shut case. The elective in sexually transmitted diseases was canceled, and from its ashes arose a new course, taught by the same man, titled "Introduction to Urology." Two women were admitted. When the urologist invited students to take turns working with him in his office, he scheduled the two female students for the same day—one on which only women patients were to be seen (a nifty feat in a urology practice).

The same professor who so valiantly tried to prevent women from learning anything unseemly about sexually transmitted diseases was also in charge of the required course in human sexuality (or, as I liked to call it, he-man sexuality). Only two of the eleven lectures focused on women; of the two lectures on ho-

mosexuality, neither mentioned lesbians. The psychiatrist who co-taught the class treated us to one lecture that amounted to an apology for rape: Aggression, even hostility, is normal in sexual relations between a man and a woman he said, and inhibition of aggression in men can lead to impotence.

We were taught that women do not need orgasms for a satisfactory sex life, although men, of course, do; and that inability to reach orgasm is only a problem for women with "unrealistic expectations." I had heard that particular lecture before in the backseat of a car during high school. The urologist told us of couples who came to him for sex counseling because the woman was not having orgasms; he would reassure them that this is normal and the couple would be relieved. (I would gamble that the female half of the couple was anything but relieved.) We learned that oral sex is primarily a homosexual practice, and that sexual dysfunction in women is often caused by "working." In the women-as-idiots department, we learned that when impotent men are implanted with permanently rigid penile prostheses, four out of five wives can't tell that their husbands have had the surgery.

When dealing with sexually transmitted diseases in which both partners must be treated, we were advised to vary our notification strategy according to marital status. If the patient is a single man, the doctor should write the diagnosis down on a prescription for his partner to bring to her doctor. If the patient is a married man, however, the doctor should contact the wife's gynecologist and arrange to have her treated without knowledge of what she is being treated for. How to notify the male partner of a female patient, married or single, was never revealed.

To be fair, women were not the only subjects of outmoded concepts of sexuality. We also received anachronistic information about men.

Premature ejaculation, defined as fewer than ten thrusts(!), was to be treated by having the man think about something unpleasant, or by having the woman painfully squeeze, prick or pinch the penis. Aversive therapies such as these have long been discredited.

Misinformation about sexuality and women's health peppered almost every course (I can't recall any egregious wrongs in biochemistry). Although vasectomy and abortion are among the safest of all surgical procedures, in our lectures vasectomy was presented as fraught with long-term complications and abortion was never mentioned without the words "peritonitis" and "death" in the same sentence. These distortions represented Georgetown's Catholic bent at its worst. (We were not allowed to perform, or even watch, abortion procedures in our affiliated hospitals.) On a lighter note, one obstetrician assisting us in the anatomy lab told us that women shouldn't lift heavy weights because their pelvic organs will fall out between their legs.

In our second year, several women in our class started a women's group, which held potlucks and offered presentations and performances: A former midwife talked about her profession, a student demonstrated belly dancing, another discussed dance therapy and one sang selections from *A Chorus Line*. This heavy radical feminist activity created great hostility among our male classmates. Announcements of our meetings were defaced and women in the group began receiving threatening calls at home from someone who claimed to be watching the listener and who would then accurately describe what she was wearing. One woman received obscene notes in her school mailbox, including one that contained a rape

threat. I received insulting cards in typed envelopes at my home address; my mother received similar cards at hers.

We took the matter to the dean of student affairs, who told us it was "probably a dental student" and suggested we buy loud whistles to blow into the phone when we received unwanted calls. We demanded that the school attempt to find the perpetrator and expel him. We were told that the school would not expel the student but that counseling would be advised.

The women's group spread the word that we were collecting our own information on possible suspects and that any information on bizarre, aggressive, antisocial or misogynous behavior among the male medical students should be reported to our designated representative. She was inundated with a list of classmates who fit the bill. Finally, angered at the school's indifference, we solicited the help of a prominent woman faculty member. Although she shamed the dean into installing a hidden camera across from the school mailboxes to monitor unusual behavior, no one was ever apprehended.

Georgetown University School of Medicine churns out about 200 physicians a year. Some become good doctors despite their training, but many will pass on the misinformation and demeaning attitudes handed down to them. It is a shame that Georgetown chooses to perpetuate stereotypes and reinforce prejudices rather than help students acquire the up-to-date information and sensitivity that are vital in dealing with AIDS, breast cancer, teen pregnancy and other contemporary epidemics. Female medical students go through an ordeal, but at least it ends with graduation. It is the patients who ultimately suffer the effects of sexist medical education.

Questions

1. According to Fugh-Berman's account, the gender ratio was usually skewed at Georgetown's medical school. In your judgment, would there be less sexism if the ratio of men and women was more equal? Why or why not?

2. Recall the concept of hate crimes from readings 28 and 29. To what extent might it be said that the women medical students were victims of hate crimes? What would be the motive behind these attacks?

Credits

ELIJAH ANDERSON, "The Code of the Streets." *The Atlantic Monthly*, May 1994. Copyright © 1994. Reprinted with the permission of W. W. Norton & Company, Inc.

A. AYRES BOSWELL and JOAN Z. SPADE, "Fraternities and Collegiate Rape Culture: Why Are Some Fraternities More Dangerous Places for Women?" *Gender & Society*, Vol. 10 (2), April 1996, pp. 133–147, copyright © 1996 by Sage Publications, Inc. Reprinted by Permission of Sage Publications, Inc.

CAROL J. S. BRUESS and JUDY C. PEARSON, "Gendered Patterns in Family Communication." In Julia T. Wood, ed., *Gendered Relationships*. Copyright © 1996 Mayfield Publishing Company. Reprinted by permission of the publisher.

THEODORE CAPLOW, "Rule Enforcement Without Visible Means: Christmas Gift Giving in Middletown." *American Journal of Sociology*, 89, pp. 1310–1317, 1320–1323. Reprinted by permission of the publisher, The University of Chicago Press.

WILLIAM J. CHAMBLISS, "The Saints and the Roughnecks." Reprinted by permission of Transaction Publishers. *Society*, November/December 1972. Copyright © 1972 by Transaction Publishers; all rights reserved.

STEPHANIE COONTZ, "How History and Sociology Can Help Today's Families." Excerpt from Chapter 1 from *The Way We Really Are*, by Stephanie Coontz. Copyright © 1997 by Basic Books, a division of HarperCollins Publishers, Inc. Reprinted by permission of Basic Books, a subsidiary of Perseus Books Group, LLC.

SIMON DAVIS, "Men as Success Objects and Women as Sex Objects: A Study of Personal Advertisements." *Sex Roles*, Vol. 23, Nos. 1/2. Reprinted by permission of Plenum Publishing Corporation.

ÉMILE DURKHEIM, "The Normality of Crime." Reprinted with the permission of *The Free Press*, a Division of Simon & Schuster, from *The Rules of Sociological Method*, by Émile Durkheim, translated by Sarah A. Solovay and John H. Mueller. Edited by George E. G. Catlin. Copyright © 1938 by George E. G. Catlin. Copyright renewed 1966 by Sarah A. Solovay, John H. Mueller, George E. G. Catlin.

GWYNNE DYER, "Anybody's Son Will Do." From *War*, by Gwynne Dyer. Copyright © 1985 by Media Resources. Reprinted by permission of Crown Publishers, Inc.

GISELA ERNST, "País de Mis Sueños: Reflections on Ethnic Labels, Dichotomies, and Ritual Interactions." From Philip R. DeVita and James D. Armstrong, *Distant Mirrors: America as a Foreign Culture*. Copyright © 1998 Gisela Ernst-Slavit. Reprinted by permission of Dr. Gisela Ernst-Slavit.

ADRIANE FUGH-BERMAN, M.D., "Tales out of Medical School." Reprinted with permission from the January 20, 1992 issue of *The Nation* magazine.

HERBERT J. GANS, "The Uses of Poverty: The Poor Pay All." *Social Policy*, July/August 1971, pp. 20–24. Reprinted by permission of Social Policy Corporation,

New York, New York 10036. Copyright © 1971 by Social Policy Corporation.

ERVING GOFFMAN, "The Presentation of Self in Everyday Life." From *The Presentation of Self in Everyday Life,* by Erving Goffman. Copyright © 1959 by Erving Goffman. Used by permission of Doubleday, a division of Bantam Doubleday Dell Publishing Group, Inc.

EDWARD T. HALL, "Hidden Culture." From *Beyond Culture,* by Edward T. Hall. Copyright © 1976, 1981 by Edward T. Hall. Used by permission of Doubleday, a division of Bantam Doubleday Dell Publishing Group, Inc.

RANDY HODSON, "The Active Worker: Compliance and Autonomy at the Workplace." *Journal of Contemporary Ethnography,* Vol. 20, 1991, pp. 47–78. Copyright © 1991 by Sage Publications, Inc. Reprinted by Permission of Sage Publications, Inc.

ROBIN D. G. KELLEY, "Confessions of a Nice Negro, or Why I Shaved My Head." From Don Belton, ed., *Speak My Name: Black Men on Masculinity and the American Dream,* pp. 12–22. Copyright © 1995 Robin D. G. Kelley. Reprinted by permission of Robin D. G. Kelley.

CLYDE KLUCKHOHN, "Queer Customs," from *Mirror for Man,* pp. 17–20, 24–27, 30–33. Copyright © 1949 George E. Taylor. Reprinted by permission of George E. Taylor.

YIN LING LEUNG, "The Model Minority Myth: Asian Americans Confront Growing Backlash." *Minority Trendsletter,* Winter 1987, pp. 5–7. Reprinted by permission of the Center for Third World Organizing.

JAMES LOEWEN, "The Land of Opportunity." Reprinted with the permission of Simon & Schuster from *Lies My Teacher Told Me,* by James Loewen. Copyright © 1995 by James W. Loewen.

PHILIP MEYER, "If Hitler Asked You to Electrocute a Stranger, Would You? Probably." *Esquire,* 1970 February, pp. 128, 130, 132. By permission of *Esquire* magazine. Copyright © 1970 Hearst Communications, Inc. Also, *Esquire* is a trademark of Hearst Magazines Property, Inc. All rights reserved.

C. WRIGHT MILLS, "The Promise." From *The Sociological Imagination,* by C. Wright Mills. Copyright ©

1959 by Oxford University Press, Inc. Renewed 1987 by Yaraslava Mills. Used by permission of Oxford University Press, Inc.

HORACE MINER, "Body Ritual Among the Nacirema." Reproduced by permission of the American Anthropological Association and the Estate of Horace Miner, from *American Anthropologist* 58:3, June 1956. Not for further reproduction.

JOHN MIROWSKY and CATHERINE ROSS, "The Social Causes of Psychological Distress." Reprinted with permission from Mirowsky, John and Ross, Catherine E. *Social Causes of Psychological Distress.* (New York: Aldine de Gruyter). Copyright © 1989 by Aldine de Gruyter.

ROBIN MORGAN, "A Massacre in Montreal." From *The Word of a Woman: Feminist Dispatches,* Second Edition, by Robin Morgan. Copyright © 1994, 1993, 1992 by Robin Morgan. By permission of Edite Kroll Literary Agency Inc.

KATHERINE NEWMAN and CHAUNCY LENNON, "The Job Ghetto." Reprinted with permission from *The American Prospect* 22 Summer 1995. Copyright © 1995 The American Prospect, P. O. Box 383080, Cambridge, MA 02138. All rights reserved.

GRETA FOFF PAULE, "'Getting' and 'Making' a Tip." From *Dishing It Out: Power and Resistance Among Waitresses in a New Jersey Restaurant,* 1991, pp. 23–47. Copyright © 1991 by Temple University. Reprinted by permission of Temple University Press.

D. L. ROSENHAN, "On Being Sane in Insane Places." *Science,* Vol. 179, 1973, pp. 250–254, 257. Copyright © 1973 American Association for the Advancement of Science. Used with permission.

MYRA SADKER and DAVID SADKER, "Hidden Lessons." Reprinted with the permission of Scribner, a Division of Simon & Schuster, from *Failing at Fairness,* by Myra Sadker and David Sadker. Copyright © 1994 by Myra Sadker and David Sadker.

THOMAS J. SCHMID and RICHARD S. JONES, "Suspended Identity: Identity Transformation in a Maximum Security Prison." *Symbolic Interaction,* 14 (4), 1991, pp. 415–428. Reprinted by permission of Jai Press Inc.

SOUTHERN POVERTY LAW CENTER, "Anti-Immigrant Violence Rages Nationwide." *Intelligence Report,* Au-